DESIGN for ARID REGIONS

DESIGN for ARID REGIONS

Gideon S. Golany, Editor

VNR VAN NOSTRAND REINHOLD COMPANY
NEW YORK CINCINNATI TORONTO LONDON MELBOURNE

Manufactured in the United States of America

Published by Van Nostrand Reinhold Company Inc.
135 West 50th Street, New York, 10020

Van Nostrand Reinhold Publishing
1410 Birchmount Road
Scarborough, Ontario M1P 2E7, Canada

Van Nostrand Reinhold
480 Latrobe Street
Melbourne, Victoria 3000, Australia

Van Nostrand Reinhold Company Limited
Molly Millars Lane
Wokingham, Berkshire, England

15 14 13 12 11 10 9 8 7 6 5 4 3 2 1

Library of Congress Cataloging in Publication Data

Main entry under title:

Design for arid regions.

  Includes bibliographies and index.
  1. Arid regions.   2. Architecture and climate—Arid
regions.   3. City planning—Arid regions.   I. Golany,
Gideon.
GB612.D43 1982   333.73   82-8428
ISBN 0-442-22924-0   AACR2

Dedicated to my dear ones
Ilan
Avital
Enat
Daleet, and
Sharon Klein

Contributors

CYRUS BAVAR is Associate Professor of Architecture at the University of Tehran and a Member of the National Council of Architects of Iran. He has been the Head of the Department of City and Regional Planning and of Architecture and consultant to the Ministries of Justice and of Housing and Town Planning in formulation of construction bylaws. Dr. Bavar received his Ph.D. in Architecture and Town Planning from the University of Florence and his B. Arch. from Tehran University. In addition to his academic work, Dr. Bavar has been responsible for the master plans of Shiraz and of the industrial town of Kurosh and has cooperated in a design of the master plan of Yazd. He also has worked on special projects of the National Iranian Oil Company.

TERENCE BRERETON BREALEY is Principal Research Scientist in the Division of Building Research of the Commonwealth Scientific and Industrial Research Organization, Australia. He is leader of the Division's Remote Communities Environment Unit, and his research since 1964 into human habitat in arid lands and the humid tropics has resulted in many publications. He is an architect, a Fellow of the Royal Australian Institute of Architects, a Member of the Royal Institute of British Architects, and he holds the degree of M.Arch. (environmental systems) from the Virginia Polytechnic Institute and State University and is a Ph.D. candidate in Architecture at the University of Melbourne.

GARRET ECKBO is a partner in EckboKay, a firm of landscape architects whose major work has included the University of New Mexico; The Tucson, (Arizona) Community Center; Union Bank Square in Los Angeles; the Public Use Plan and Program for Shelby Farms, Memphis, Tennessee; Baylands Master Plan and Byxbee Landfill Park Plan, Palo Alto, California; Vintage Park downtown development, Foster City, California; and Maiden Lane, San Francisco. On a design scholarship, Mr. Eckbo received his Master in Landscape Architecture from Harvard. As part of the Farm Security Administration, he has done site planning and landscape design for numerous projects in several states. Mr. Eckbo has served as Professor and Chairman of the Department of Landscape Architecture at the University of California at Berkeley and as a visiting professor at universities in Japan and Australia. Five of his six books have been translated into Japanese.

EARL FINKLER is a private planning and economic consultant from Tucson, Arizona, currently working on energy, economic and land-use plans for the oil-impacted North Slope Borough of Alaska, as well as for rural communities in Arizona. Prior to his current assignment, he was Principal Planner for the City of Tucson. Mr. Finkler describes himself as a "professional hybrid," for he has combined training and experience in planning, urban affairs, and journalism. He holds degrees in these areas from Marquette University and the University of Wisconsin. He is the author of *Urban Nongrowth: City Planning for People*, published in 1976.

GIDEON GOLANY is Professor of Urban and Regional Planning in the Department of Architecture at The Pennsylvania State University and former chairman of its graduate program. He received his B.A. (1956), M.A. (1962), and Ph.D. (1966) from the Hebrew University, Jerusalem; he also received an M.Sc. (1965) from Technion-Israel Institute of Technology and a Dip. C.P. from The Institute of Social Studies, The Hague, The Netherlands. Dr. Golany has taught at the Technion, the Virginia Polytechnic Institute and State University, and Cornell University and has served as a consultant and planner. He is listed in the *Dictionary of International Biography, Men of Achievement, International Who's Who in Community Service, Who's Who in America, Who's Who in the East, Community Leaders and Noteworthy Americans,* and *Notable Americans.* A widely published author, Dr. Golany has written numerous monographs, articles, and papers. He has also written or edited fourteen books including *Housing in Arid Lands: Design and Planning, Earth-Sheltered Habitat* (in press), *Arid Zone Settlement Planning: The Israeli Experience* (1979), *International Urban Growth Policies: New-Town Contributions* (1978), *Urban Planning for Arid Zones: The American Experience* (1978), *New-Town Planning: Principles and Practice* (1976), *Innovations for Future Cities* (1976), and *Strategy for New Community Development in the United States* (1975).

WILLIAM K. HARTMANN is Senior Scientist at the Planetary Science Institute, Science Applications, Inc., Tucson. After receiving his M.S. and Ph.D. degrees from the University of Arizona, he served there as assistant professor. He was recipient of the Ninninger Meteorite Award in 1965 and has been a frequent NASA consultant. In conjunction with his research and subsequent publications in planetary science, Dr. Hartmann has studied long-range causes and effects of air pollution in an urban arid-zone city, Tucson. He has authored two astronomy textbooks as well as other books and papers.

RODNEY C. JENSEN is Reader in Economics and coordinator of the graduate program in Regional Science at the University of Queensland, Australia, where he received his Ph.D. He also has received a Master of Agricultural Economics from the University of New England in Australia. Prior to his present position, Dr. Jensen served as senior lecturer at Lincoln College of the University of Canterbury, New Zealand. He has been awarded grants and fellowships by the governments of both the Federal Republic of Germany and France. Dr. Jensen has also served as a consultant for government agencies and private firms and has published extensively in the areas of agricultural economics, project evaluation and resource development, and regional and urban economies.

ERIC B. KRAUS is Professor of Atmospheric Science and Physical Oceanography at the University of Miami. He is also Director of the Cooperative Institute for Marine and Atmospheric Studies which is sponsored jointly by the University and the United States National Oceanic and Atmospheric Administration. He has studied in Bergen, Norway, and in Prague where he received his doctorate. Before coming to Miami in 1967 he held appointments with the University of Sydney and the Snowy Mountains Hydro-Electric Authority in Australia, with the Woods Hole (Massachusetts) Oceanographic Institute, and with Yale University. He has led technical assistance missions on behalf of NATO and various UN agencies. Currently he is a trustee of the University Corporation for Atmospheric Research, and Associate Editor of the Journal of Physical Oceanography and a member of several national and international advisory committees. He has written two books and many scientific papers on climate and air-sea interactions.

JOHN L. KRIKEN is currently Associate Partner and Director of Urban Design and Planning for the firm of Skidmore, Owings & Merrill in San Francisco. He received his M. Arch. in Urban Design from Harvard Graduate School of Design and his B.A. in Architecture from The University of California at Berkeley. He has taught at Rice University, Houston, Texas; Washington University, St. Louis; and at the University of California, Berkeley. He was the chief designer for Hemisfair, a Category II Worlds Fair in San Antonio, Texas. As project designer for master plans in ten cities in several countries that include the U.S., Iran, Saudi Arabia and Taiwan, he has received numerous awards for design and planning excellence. His publications include *Developing Urban Design Mechanisms* (1974) and "City Design" in *The Practice of Local Government Planning*, for the forthcoming ICMA publication.

PETER WESLEY NEWTON is Senior Research Scientist in the Division of Building Research of the Commonwealth Scientific and Industrial Research Organization, Australia. He is a member of the division's Remote Communities Environment Unit and has done extensive research on community environment and residential mobility in both urban and remote locations. He has published widely on the theoretical and practical aspects of this work. He received his B.A. and M.A. degrees in Geography from the University Newcastle, Australia, and his Ph.D. from the University of Canterbury, New Zealand. In 1979 he was awarded a CSIRO Postdoctoral fellowship for overseas study and undertook to spend most of this year as a visiting professor in the Faculty of Environmental Studies, University of Waterloo, Canada.

TANER OC is Lecturer in Planning and Planning Theory at the Institute of Planning Studies of the University of Nottingham, England. He received his B.Arch. and M.C.P. at the Middle East Technical University, M.A. in Social Sciences at the University of Chicago where he was a research assistant at the Center for Urban Studies, and his Ph.D. at the University of Pennsylvania. Dr. Oc also has served as Lecturer in Planning at The Queens University of Belfast, Northern Ireland, and at the Middle East Technical University, Ankara, Turkey, and recently he was visiting professor at the George Washington University, Washington, D.C. His publications include "Assimilation of Displaced Rural Migrants in Istanbul and Samsun and the Role of Mass Media in this Process" (1974), "Public Participation in Planning: The British Experience" (1978), and "Advocacy Planning in the 1980's: Response to our emerging crisis" (1981). He recently completed a Department of Environment (UK) sponsored research entitled "Motivations, Aspirations and Perceptions of Environmental Stress in the Inner City." Currently, he is studying planning and ethnic minorities in the UK and USA.

MAHMOOD TAVASSOLI is Assistant Professor of Urban Planning on the Faculty of Fine Arts at the University of Tehran, Iran, where he received a

M.Arch. in 1973. In 1978, he received a Dip. Planning from the University of Edinburgh; he received an M.A. in Urban Design from the University of Manchester in 1979. His publications include "Gonbade Ghabousse." (an example of the use of conical domes in Persian architecture) (1972) and *Architecture in the Hot Arid Zone of Iran* (1975). He was a member of the planning committee for the historic city of Yazd and chief organizer of the city's detailed plan, 1973–76.

METE TURAN is an assistant professor at the Middle East Technical University, Ankara, Turkey. Dr. Turan studied civil engineering at Robert College, Istanbul, and Worcester Polytechnic Institute, Massachusetts, and architecture at Columbia University, New York. He taught at Harvard University Graduate School of Design and the University of North Carolina at Charlotte in the U.S., and currently teaches man-environment relations and environmental design at Middle East Technical University.

WYNN R. WALKER is Associate Professor of Agricultural and Chemical Engineering at Colorado State University where he received his Ph.D. and has previously served as field engineer, research assistant, and research associate. He has presented many papers in the areas of irrigation and desalination to professional societies and published numerous technical articles through the Environmental Protection Agency and in professional journals.

RICHARD WIDDOWS is an instructor at the University of Missouri at Columbia. His earlier positions include Lecturer in Economics at the University of Queensland, Australia, and Lecturer in Economics at North-East London Polytechnic University. His interest in population movement is shown in his two recent publications, *Patterns of Population Movement in Queensland, 1969–71* (with R. J. Christiansen and J. Ellis) (1974) and *Economic Reasons for Population Movement in Queensland, 1961–71* (1976).

MICHAEL D. YOUNG is Socio-Economist in the Division of Land Resources Management of the Commonwealth Scientific and Industrial Research Organization, Deniliquin, Australia, where he is involved in research on the Australian rangelands, supplying information to arid-zone administrators in Australia. He accepted this position after working for the Society of International Missionaries. There he developed rehabilitation programs including vegetable introduction and irrigation.

Preface

Contemporary technological development and the dynamics of growth have led us to ignore consideration of climate in the design of our houses and cities. In the nonarid regions of the globe, urban conglomeration has been taking over good agricultural land irreversibly; with this has come a loss of good food production areas, increasing environmental deterioration, and resource depletion.

Since the end of World War II, there also has been increasing growth in countries which fall partly or fully within the arid or semiarid regions: the Middle East and North Africa; Australia and the southwestern United States; and some countries bordering on the southern fringes of the Sahara Desert—to mention only the largest areas. Especially recently, this growth has been fast and steady; in most cases, it was difficult for these countries to cope with it. Such growth was not only in population; but more particularly, it was in urbanized areas.

More than any other of the many types of climate, the stressed or extreme climate is complicated to deal with; it is harsh, subject to diurnal amplitudes in temperature, and generally uncomfortable for humans. Much of the design introduced recently in those regions is simply an importation with little or no adjustment to the local unique conditions. Moreover, professionals have tended to ignore traditional historical or ancient native achievements in house and city design for a variety of unjustified reasons: lack of understanding or appreciation, absence of local research and study, inability to adjust ancient experience to our modern norms, and the convenience of importing theories and practice from the technologically developed society.

Recently, however, and largely because of the world energy crises, many planners, urban designers and architects have begun to express interest in design with climatic consideration. There is a concurrent realization that new areas for urban and rural development and for sophisticated agriculture exist in arid regions—if proper design is introduced. Indeed, arid region development necessitates broad knowledge, sophisticated technology (especially for agriculture), national and regional efforts, clear goals, persistence, public and private enterprise, and, above all, a pioneering attitude. In the United States, design for climate may appear to be a matter of choice or preference; in Egypt, Israel, or Saudi Arabia, it is more recognizable as a matter of having no alternative but to design for climate. Whatever the case may be, the present system existing in arid regions cannot support future development or adequately meet the needs of the residents.

Another important fact is that arid regions have a highly sensitive ecosystem. The scarcity of water and the extremes in temperature have brought all flora and fauna to the threshold of destruction. Under such circumstances, an equilibrium has come into existence. Thus, any planning and design for the arid regions must allow for these conditions if this balance of the ecosystem is to continue to exist.

I do not wish to give the impression that there has not been a good deal of research and practice with consideration of the arid region's climate. However, nearly all this research work has focused on soil, climate, hydrology, agriculture, flora and fauna, and on the native populations. There has been little research on housing design and virtually none on arid-zone city design. This volume, then, tries to fill this gap in the literature in the belief that we should further the education of urban designers, architects, planners, and decision makers who must plan for and build in the arid environment.

This volume is a combined effort of 16 specialists who are theoreticians and practitioners in the arid region; they have diverse cultural and professional backgrounds. We bring together the experience of Turkey, Iran, Australia, and the United States of America. All the chapters introduced here have been designed and written especially for this book. They reflect life experiences, observations, and research by their authors.

My deep appreciation should be expressed to the many persons who have helped me down the long road of preparing this book. I am especially thankful to my editorial assistants, Dr. Ted Scheckels and Mrs. Deborah Jean Kuritz, both former graduate students in the Department of English at The Pennsylvania State University. Nancy Lord Daniels, my editorial assistant, has worked closely with me in the preparation of this volume as well.

Most supportive was my colleague, Professor Raniero Corbelletti, Head of the Department of Architecture, who has followed the preparation of this volume closely. He deserves my deep thanks and gratitude.

In the belief that it will help improve the design for the arid environment, I present this volume.

Gideon S. Golany

Department of Architecture
The Pennsylvania State University
University Park, PA

Contents

1
Urban Form Design for Arid Regions*

Gideon S. Golany

There has been a recent upsurge in interest in the arid and semiarid regions of the world. Population growth, urban expansion, the need for more food and for alternative energies, and the "discovery" of desertification, all have led to a search for new regions in which settlements may be placed. At last, we are realizing that arid lands are an old/new frontier with the potential of providing a setting where most of these issues can be met—if we pursue innovative planning and design.

During the past two decades, this author has become increasingly aware of burgeoning and large-scale development in the arid regions of the southwestern USA, Australia, India, Pakistan, the Saudi Arabian peninsula, Israel, Egypt, the Fertile Crescent, and in North Africa. It is our belief that the tendency for development within arid regions will accelerate even more in the near future. Whatever the motivations for this development are, the result will be settlements, both rural-agricultural and urban. Governments and developers will find, however, that designing an arid-zone settlement presents a unique challenge requiring innovative approaches. Further, such design is a relatively new field necessitating a great deal of theory and practice—much of which has yet to be formulated.

There have been many factors influencing the designer of the urban configurations. However, designers occasionally have emphasized some of those factors while ignoring the others, thus never achieving a balance and a synthesis among them. Here we are referring to the requisite consideration of all of the following: climatic elements (wind, temperature fluctuation, humidity, and the like), topographical and other physical entities, land-use patterns, social concerns, economic considerations, traffic flow patterns, and last but not least, aesthetic values.

In arid zones, however, we must recognize that some of those factors must receive more attention than others. In this chapter, we will be primarily but not solely concerned with the unique impact of the arid region on urban design requirements so that we may offer guidelines for the optimal design form which will respond to such a stressed climate. We also would like to apply—and indeed feel we must apply—energy saving principles to any proposed urban form. We define stressed climate as that type which has a very low or very high temperature in the daytime and a great differentiation in temperature between day and night. Such a climate may

---

*The analysis and design solutions introduced here are the result of the author's having lived in and personally and extensively researched the arid region.

1

be found in arid regions of North Africa and the Middle East or in the northern continental inland, especially in the plateau regions and close to the polar zone.

Nearly one third of the earth's surface lies in an arid zone. Contrary to common opinion, arid zones can be very warm or very cold and are defined as areas which have dry climate with little or no precipitation, very low humidity, and an annual rate of evaporation that exceeds the annual average precipitation with a resulting constant high deficit in humidity throughout the year; thus, not even dry farming is possible. The sparse annual precipitation in arid zones is further characterized by being turbulent, brief, torrential, and sporadic. The nature of the precipitation causes an increase in runoff, erosion and flooding, conditions that must be considered by the planner when selecting a site and the configuration for a settlement. Other elements which effect planning for arid zones are wind, dust, radiation, lack of soil cover, and finally the isolation which has a psychological impact.

Contemporary Realities

Contemporarily, much of the urban design for arid zones does not address the particular challenges of the stressed climate. Most of the arid-zone urban patterns throughout the world, especially the modern ones, are products of imported concepts from nonarid regions (especially from Europe and North America) which tend to ignore the native historical lessons in design, building materials, housing patterns, and energy-saving considerations; the result often is urban dispersion/sprawl. Modern large-scale development theory and practice have already reached a peak in the Western world and have demonstrated the many advantages of the urban grid pattern, curvilinear configuration of the neighborhood, and cluster form of housing. Those advantages have proved their suitability in many cases for answering some social, economic, and transportation needs. However, our concern here is the degree of suitability of any configuration in the stressed climate *without* considering the degree of success or failure it may enjoy in the nonarid region. It should be clear now that the usual Western patterns are not suitable for a stressed climate; a new and more suitable pattern must be found, and we shall examine the native historical achievement, local climatic conditions, and the modern norms and standards for acceptable housing to develop innovative answers to the problem.

The existing urban pattern in arid zones is also characterized by low density and lengthy road networks and infrastructure, all of which increase investment for construction, expenses for maintenance, taxes, and, most important, energy consumption (Fig. 1-1).

Ancient Experience

Most of the early urban civilizations of the world emerged in the arid or semiarid zones, primarily in the Fertile Crescent of the Middle East and in the Nile region. Early urban centers evolved throughout history; the natives learned to understand the nature of the climatic stress imposed by

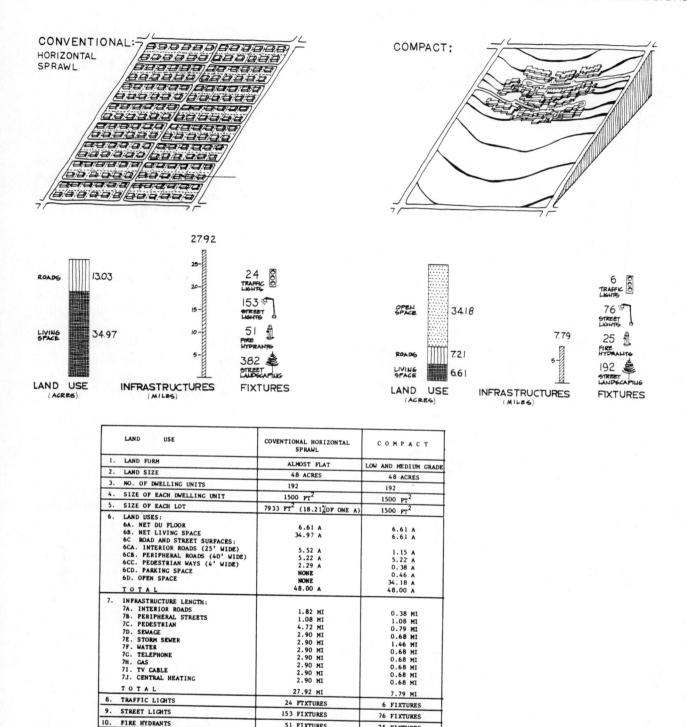

Fig. 1-1. Comparative design for 48 acres with conventional horizontal sprawl or with an equal number of housing units set in compact form on a slope. Note the great differentiation in infrastructure and road networks lengths, open space, and other land uses. The economic and social costs are vastly different; so, too, is the energy consumption.

the region, they dealt with limitation of resources, and they were concerned about conservation of the environmental characteristics. Later, when these ancient civilizations began to plan their cities, they continued to follow and improve those basic precepts. This early urban planning experience emphasized site selection considerations, use of slope placement, adoption of the compact urban form, and development of a special street and alley pattern—all of which had already evolved in meeting the needs of living in a stressed climate. We should make it clear that we see such urban development as a synthesis of a variety of contributing forces which emerged over the years. We are not denying the significance of forces such as defense needs, social cohesiveness, necessity of saving land for agriculture, and optimality of size. It is impossible to isolate definitely the impact of one factor or another on the nature of this early development and planning; however, it has become apparent to this author that climatic consideration stands in the forefront. Climate, at least as a social and economic factor, is omnipresent and cannot be ignored.

If we thoughtfully consider this ancient experience in urban configuration and study the limitations and potentialities of the arid region, we should be convinced that a sophisticated planning process and innovative design solutions are needed. The approach should be comprehensive, based on native experience, technologically advanced, and adjusted to the local ecosystem—the macro- and microregion—without disturbing its balance. Or, to put it another way, the given physical characteristics which are unique to the site must influence our approach: the soil, landforms, resources and, lastly, the vastness of the space.

Soil and Landforms Influencing Design

Arid-zone climatic constraints to a large extent determine the nature of the soil cover and the landform. The dryness, intense radiation, and diurnal temperature fluctuation also result in an absence of vegetation and strong air movement. Recall, too, that limited rain—turbulent and of short duration—causes intense erosion and the transporting of large quantities of soil to the lowland. Thus, there is a continual and long-term process of change in the arid regions.

The most common soil types in arid lands are:

1. Playa
2. Gravel
3. Sand dunes
4. Loess

Location of the first two, playa and gravel, is primarily the result of erosion and deflation. However, the long-term effects of temperature fluctuation also influence the formation of gravel by decomposition of rocks and an increase in the quantity of particles. Eolian dynamics affect sand dunes and the loess as, again, does the diurnal temperature fluctuation.

Playa is a unique type of soil often found in special landforms: closed depressions, lowland, and poorly drained flat and dry basins subject to flooding after rain. Consequently, playa has a surface of fine sand, silts and clay. Typically, it also is salty and does not support vegetation. Playa may cover but a few square meters or may spread over hundreds of square kilometers. The water table is usually close to the surface of playa, and even in arid zones lakes are common to playa regions; such lakes usually are salty because of the intense evaporative process. Since water, even a very little moisture, drastically changes the volume of playa, it does not offer proper support for construction. Likewise, the corrosive salt content adversely affects foundations. Elastic materials may accumulate in playa; and in conjunction with sink holes and depressions, they can make vehicular movement dangerous. Yet, playa may contain important mineral resources.

Sand dunes and loess soil are greatly affected by the eolian process. While the alluvial process is chemical as well as mechanical and produces its own special landforms, the eolian process is mechanical only. Wind freely abrades and erodes rock/soil formations because of the lack of vegetation and makes new landforms, particularly in the stressed climate of the arid zone. Wind can carry particles away from their place of origin at low or great heights as well. The dynamics of transportation and the final landform greatly depend on the size of the particles, wind velocity and force, original structure of the soil/rock, degree of dryness, and on air temperature.

Sand covers one quarter to one third of the world's deserts and is in layers of particles resting on bedrock. Sand dunes may take on various forms such as narrow, smooth, and linear along the coasts of seas, lakes, or rivers; and they are U-shaped, drifting/moving (barchan), transverse, or longitudinal. They also may originate in glacial plains, floodplains, or lake beds. Dunes actually are good for construction, and they offer a good foundation for structures, if they are stable. Unstable dunes must be controlled in the urban setting because sand abrades the buildings and may cover structures and vegetation. Sewage systems and septic tanks perform well in sand, but trenching may be difficult and require lining. Naturally, sand is easy to remove.

The loess soil of the desert is deposited by wind and consists of silt and clay. Loess can cover a large area and may originate at a great distance from its place of deposit. Loess is relatively soft (especially below the thin crust), porous and light colored; it drains poorly horizontally and well vertically; it is subject to easy erosion and is good for agriculture; it presents a gently rolling topography unless intensively eroded to become rugged; and loess is suitable for urban development although it expands and contracts with changes in humidity and/or temperature.

The landforms most common to arid zone are:

1. Piedmont (pediment and alluvial plain)
2. Mesa
3. Alluvial fan
4. Floodplain
5. Coastal plain

Piedmont, a very distinctive landform of arid land and constituting a large portion of it, is the area sloping down from the mountain to the plain below. The upper section, primarily gentle slopes or cliffs, is called the pediment. The lower part which forms an alluvial plain extending from the foot of the mountain to its termination in a playa basin is a coalescence of alluvial fans sometimes called the *bajada*. The pediment allows a wide view of the surrounding environs, facilitates ventilation, usually has a lower temperature than the plain below, and may have some water sources. All these qualities positively support locating a settlement on the pediment. The alluvial plain, on the other hand, is composed of eroded materials which cover the bedrock, and it has a lower gradient than the piedmont; it encompasses large tracts of land, has reasonably good drainage, and can accommodate the development of settlements and transportation.

The mesa is usually made up of alternating hard and soft layers of limestone deposits which are eroded or broken at the edges to form circumferential cliffs. This landform stands out because of its distinctive appearance and isolation in an eroded region; its size and relative elevation varies. Since the mesa is inaccessible, it is easy to defend and would attract settlements when the elevation is such that the humidity is increased. There is an attractive view of the vast landscape from a mesa.

Materials eroded downslope deposit themselves in the alluvial fan shape. This can happen, for example, when a mountain stream exits at the foot of the mountain. Alluvial soils along with gravel make up the deposits. If the stream course fluctuates or if there is a heavy storm, large quantities of materials can be transported downstream so that there is a further expansion of the fan downward. In addition, if there is groundwater present or if the fan area is subject to flooding, it also will expand. The alluvial fan can be a hazardous area for settlement construction and for transportation arteries unless careful plans are made for proper drainage and suitable construction materials. However, good construction materials for building structures and roads elsewhere are usually found in alluvial deposits: fine sand, gravel, silt, mud, boulders, etc.

A floodplain results from stream or river deposits; it has good soil and often is wide and quite flat, although it may be terraced. Such a plain has a high water table after flooding, and parts of it can support agriculture. In arid regions it is important to go back many years to determine areas which may have been flooded at some time. The planner also should anticipate the maximum flooding possible on a given floodplain so that bridges for crossing dry stream beds are sufficiently elevated and long enough to avoid flooding hazards. It may not be wise to build on the floodplain itself, but it will contain useful building materials: rock, sand, and clay, for example.

The coastal plain actually is a sea shelf which has emerged from the sea. "Young" coastal plains are smooth and slope gently toward the sea, while "older" ones are rugged because of the intense drainage. Their proximity to the sea brings the benefits of moisture in the form of fog, dew, and sea breezes and of good beaches. The water table of a coastal plain may be subject to salty water intrusion if overtaxed. Coastal plains are rich in materials for constructing settlements. The soil, however, can only support small structures unless special design principles are observed.

In conclusion, the distinctive soils and landforms of arid regions affect the design of the arid-zone city at nearly all levels: site selection, urban morphology, building materials, and housing design (see Table 1-1).

TABLE 1-1. Summary of Soil and Landforms in Arid Regions and Their Impact on Urban Design.

TYPE	SOIL	FORM	IMPACTS ON SETTLEMENT
Playa	• Product of erosion or deflation • Fine sand, silt and clay • Highly salty • No vegetation	• Closed depression and lowland of small or large size • Poorly drained. It can form highly salty lake • Elastic materials subject to volume change	• Does not support construction • Intensive corrosion • Dangerous for vehicle movement • Has mineral resources
Gravel	• Decomposition of rocks	• Spread along slopes, lowland or plains	• Available building material • Supports good construction
Sand Dunes	• Formed by eolian process with easy transportation • One-third of the world's deserts • Made of fine particles	• Linear along water body coast • U-shape • Barchan • Transverse or longitudinal	• Abrade buildings or cover them • Good for construction & for foundations • Require control • Good for sewage systems • Difficult for trenching
Loess	• Formed by eolian process of far origin • Consists of silt and clay • Relatively soft below thin crust • Porous and light colored • Drains poorly horizontally & well vertically • Good for agriculture	• Gently rolling topographically • Rugged when intensively eroded	• Suitable for urban development • Changes volume with humidity & temperature
Piedmont	• Gravel at the cliffs and alluvial at the plain	• Area sloping down from the mountain to the plain • Includes upper cliffs (piedmont) • Gravel at the low parts	• Wide view to the surroundings • Lower temperature than plain below • Supports settlement construction • Available as building material • Good for transportation
Mesa	• Alternating hard and soft layers of limestone	• Table form with circumferential cliffs and plain at top	• Good for defense • Good ventilation • Higher humidity and lower temperature than its surroundings • Distinctive appearance • Has attractive view
Floodplain	• River deposit • Sand, clay or rocks	• Flat and wide along dry rivers	• Subject to flood • May be good for agriculture • Requires lengthy and elevated bridges
Coastal Plain	• May have fine sand, silt or rocks	• Emerged sea shelf • Young ones are smooth and slope gently toward the sea • Older ones are rugged	• Good beaches • Rich in material for construction • May have salty water table

Goals of Urban Form Design

If our arid-zone city is to be a pleasant place for its citizens to live and work, and if it is to be truly responsive to the world crisis in energy resources, we must carefully consider all aspects of its development. Therefore, our first order of business must be to determine and set the goals we wish to reach in this development. In particular, these goals will reflect the need to respond to the problems created by climatic stress. We must seek to: reduce strong, harmful, and dusty winds; reduce (or possibly eliminate) direct sun radiation; provide plenty of shadowed public and private spaces where necessary; establish social proximity without sacrificing personal privacy; create a pleasing outdoor environment within the stressed climate; plan proximate land uses in neighborhoods so that there is easy pedestrian access to them all. Of course, while we are accomplishing all of the above goals, we shall be emphasizing energy conservation principles throughout.

Ultimately then, the urban form we choose will meet the challenge of the stressed climate of the arid zone by:

1. Minimizing or eliminating the discomfort and stressful conditions at the microclimatic level of the house and street while carefully planning the macrolevel of the entire urban configuration so that it is responsive, too.
2. Maximizing the use of passive energy systems and minimizing the use of active energy to provide for the needs of all socioeconomic groups and to conserve energy resources.
3. Creating a pleasing urban environment which will stimulate and provide a good quality of life for the inhabitants.
4. Integrating in the different scales and levels of the design the unique native environmental, ecological, and cultural elements by use of local building materials, landscaping with native plants to minimize water consumption, and local design styles. The latter may provide a bonus for the planner: a historical heritage of design which meets the problems of climatic stress.
5. Easing the psychological feeling of isolation common to dwellers in such vast areas.

Basic Urban Form Design Principles

First of all, we should recognize that the intrusion of the urban form itself and the form it takes in a region of a given climatic character will influence the microclimate of the site and, to a certain extent, the immediate macroclimate of the region. For example, we will need to find a new balance of heat gain and heat loss in the new settlement. A heat island typically found above a city and the diurnal fluctuation of human activity will contribute to changes in the balance. Heat gain and loss within the city result from the city's overall form and configuration, street patterns and orientation, building material and its color (indeed, the color of the total city), morphology of the city, overall exposure of the city to radiation (sloping or flat location; north or south orientation), and density of vegetation. However, we can state that in the hot/dry climate, the urban form can moderate the climate within the city through increasing heat loss during the day but encouraging heat gain at night—especially in the residential sections.

Because of the complexities of the climate factors and the landforms, it is worth mentioning that any solutions we find to these problems will bring with them a new set of problems which also must be solved. Therefore, our overall plan has to be a compromise, solving climatic problems but avoiding other disruptions.

To meet our previously defined ultimate goal of choosing a suitable configuration for the arid region, we now are ready to draw up a set of principles to follow which will enable us to achieve that goal. Our basic premise will be to synthesize historical, local, native experience within an urban form which meets our modern norms and standards. Let us then consider the following elements which will contribute to the success of our urban form:

1. Regional clustering of settlements
2. Proximity of land uses
3. Urban configuration
4. The city network
5. Compactness
6. Open space design
7. Agro-urban setting

REGIONAL CLUSTERING OF SETTLEMENTS

In contrast to nonarid regions, there are but few factors in addition to normal, standard procedures which should influence the design of the regional distribution pattern of settlements in the arid region. The region-specific factors which do apply in the arid region are:

- Vastness of space which determines the length of utilities, infrastructure, and transportation routes. The latter especially increases energy consumption for transportation, for delivery (goods, water, etc.), or exportation (goods, sewage, garbage).
- Psychological feeling of isolation, a dominant element in the arid-zone settlement, particularly in the early days of the development. This feeling stems from: the inhabitants' surrounding environment of vast space without eye contact with another settlement; the settlement's being relatively small in a large setting; the limitation of having few facilities within the settlement; the lengthy network of supply; the lack of frequent visits with outside friends; and sometimes, the limited variety of associates within the settlement itself.

To ease the above-mentioned limitations, we suggest that the settlement be established in a special grouping pattern rather than as a single isolated settlement.

Regional clustering is defined as the conglomeration of the urban, agro-urban, rural agricultural, regional growth center, and resources (mining, for example) settlements in close proximity to each other in a clustered regional form. This arrangement creates a cohesive unit as far as employment, social services, education, land transporation, and economics are concerned. Regional clustering enriches such settlements both individually and as a group; supports social cohesiveness; provides more of the basic daily needs close by; increases the variety of employment opportunities; improves health services; makes settlement management more efficient and economic; increases social and economic choices; and makes the settlement more attractive to newcomers and encourages them to stay. Above all, regional clustering offers more self-sufficiency and shorter utility lines and transportation networks.

Regional clustering of settlements mandates comprehensive planning of physical, social, and economic aspects of the development and demands efficient coordination of regional management and governance. Our most basic policy recommendation is to proceed on a regional scale, for planning and design in the arid region cannot be truly viable without comprehensive regional planning and development.

PROXIMITY OF LAND USES

The concept of land uses proximity is related directly to the concept of compactness (to be discussed later); both are desirable ways of achieving the same goal. Land uses are to be integrated and yet separated in the same urban fabric. We propose an integrated land-use pattern for the residential area where shopping, offices, clean manufacturing, educational and cultural activities, social services, and restaurants will intermingle with residential land uses. These integrated land uses support proximity, climatic comfort, social interaction, and convenience; they conserve land and intensify its use by all age groups; and finally, they reduce the inhabitants' dependence on transportation. We would plan separate placement of disruptive land uses: major transportation routes and facilities, industrial parks, major shopping centers, etc.

For instance, the principal transportation network should be circumferential to the residential land uses. As such it will act as a buffer zone between the residential zones and nonresidential areas. Our aim in suggesting this land-use proximity is to minimize the proximity. This seeming contradiction in implementation brings positive social as well as economic results in addition to local satisfaction of the needs of the arid-zone city's inhabitants.

Any large vacant tract or zone of land within the arid city is a source for generating heated air during the day or cold air at night. Such space also may generate dust if it is left without any treatment or coverage by vegetation or paving; open space may support air dynamics, wind movement, and albedo. Finally, our arid city should have ample land uses for entertainment and recreation integrated within the residential areas to minimize the feeling of isolation.

URBAN CONFIGURATION

The city is an immense artificial and man-made project which penetrates its environment. Also, it is under a constant process of changes in its vertical and horizontal form, and its configuration has an effect on its internal climate as well. A variety of factors contribute to the city's configuration:

1. *City morphology.* That is, the horizontal skyline and its vertical cross section; the relative heights of the buildings in relation to each other; open or undeveloped spaces within the city and their relation to the adjacent structures.
2. *City network.* Streets, roads, and alleys, all of which form tunnels of air movement and heat exchange.
3. *Orientation* of the city to the solar radiation cycle and to wind direction.
4. The *positioning* of the land uses in relation to each other.

There are some other factors resulting from human activities within the city which affect the climate within the city. Cooking, heating, car operation, industrial activities, and the radiation from the human bodies all influence heat gain. Here, we are primarily concerned with the design aspect of the city within the arid climate, but we also must anticipate the impact of these human activities. It is a well-known fact, for example, that the city has pockets of climate which differ from the climate in other sections of the city. Therefore, we must know the effect of human activities on the reciprocal relationship between the city's configuration and the stressed climate. How they alter the degree of heat gain and heat loss within various sections of the city therefore will influence the degree of human comfort.

The city's configuration can support pollution, ventilation, wind velocity, inversion, and thermal load as well as influence the condition of vegetation and determine the solar radiation within the city. Close or dense configuration in a built-up area loses temperature very slowly toward evening and gains it slowly in the morning, too. Moreover, the addition of trees within the arid urban space improves ambient air temperature because vegetation absorbs radiation and converts it to chemical energy through the photosynthetic process.

Uniform city morphology allows greater absorption of radiation through the roofs because they are not shadowed by higher buildings. Tall buildings scattered within the city will divert winds and can create turbulence. Air above the city has freer movement than within the city itself. A high-rise building standing alone among a number of lower buildings can cause diversion of air downward and can promote ventilation of the adjacent streets.

The cooling process within the central part of the city moves more slowly than in other sections because of the density of the structures and because of increased human and motor vehicle activities. The heated air created in the central part of the city will be rising and will cause air to move in from the peripheral streets. Large asphalt covered open space generates an uprise of heated air and causes air turbulence.

The city's orientation with respect to solar radiation (especially when there is slope placement) determines the degree of heat gain and heat loss and light. The amplitude between day and night temperatures is greater in the arid-zone city than in the nonarid city. This temperature change affects air movement. The above conflicting conditions make it difficult to set a universal rule for "good" urban configuration, suggesting thereby that a compromise may become necessary in order to reach a decision which brings the best possible results.

THE CITY NETWORK

Road and alley networks within a city are channels for air movement and heat exchange and play a significant role in establishing the city climate. Streets in parallel design will support air movement or dusty winds when surfaces are not paved. Such a wind can cause an accumulation of garbage, effect heat exchange, and bring cool wind at night and hot winds during the day. Straight, long alleys and wide open spaces produce similar results.

A grid pattern of streets, usually designed east-west and north-south, causes shadowing on one side of the street only and leaves the other radiated all day; or it will cause shadow or heat in each half of a day. It seems to us that northeast to southwest and southeast to northwest directions for the grid will establish interchange of shadows and radiation along the city's networks.

Fig. 1-2. Winding belowground alley covered by balconies on a steep slope in the hot/dry climate. Such a design configuration will keep the alley shadowed and cool throughout the day.

Narrow and winding streets produce minimal heat exchange, and therefore they are normally shadowed and cooled in the daytime and are warm at night. (Fig. 1-2) They also reduce the effect of stormy or dusty winds. Narrow streets may retain humidity within their spaces; they then will decrease ambient temperature throughout the day.

The primary arteries of the city network should be circumferential to any land use especially in residential areas. A hierarchical system for movement within the city (pedestrian paths within a neighborhood with vehicular traffic largely limited to the periphery) limits and diverts unnecessary traffic (Fig. 1-3). The lack of an expanse of large trees in the arid city increases the noise pollution and is another reason for diversion of traffic. Although pedestrian movement is not intense in the arid city, it will be desirable to design pedestrian paths protected from the stressed climate by shadowing and to note the sun cycle and wind direction (Fig. 1-4).

In conclusion:

1. The city's network should be designed in relation with the daily and seasonal sun cycles.

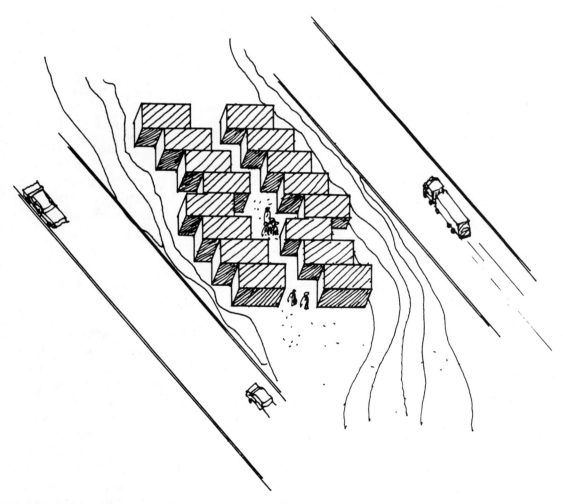

Fig. 1-3. Nonconventional design for compact houses in conjunction with a pedestrian alley which is separated from vehicular traffic and provides a shaded, safe, and quiet pedestrian environment.

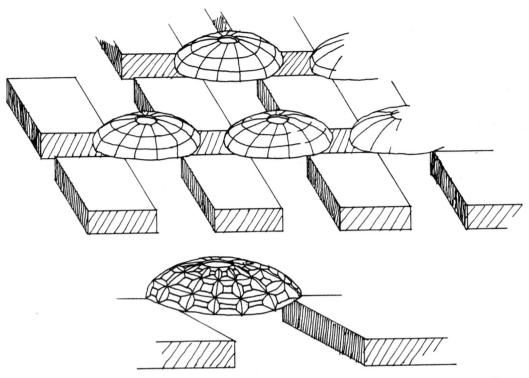

Fig. 1-4. Basic concept of shading with man-made lightweight coverage along an alley or at the crossings. This design still allows for plenty of light, and the alternating light and shadow aesthetically enriches the view along the alley.

2. Alleys should be shadowed and cool throughout the day. This is achieved by considering their orientation and direction, by plantings and by adjusting the building heights to support these goals.
3. Narrow alleys will keep their space cool in the day and warm at night.

COMPACTNESS

Compact cities were developed throughout history for a variety of reasons: social cohesiveness, defense, the saving of agricultural land, economic efficiency, or coping with harsh climate. The latter, however, was a dominant motive in the arid-zone city. Our definition of compactness refers to a city form that is concentrated and firmly unified in its buildings, with consolidated land uses in a close, tight relationship with each other and within themselves, too. This concept is in sharp contrast with the contemporary sprawl and the diffused cities, such as those of the United States, which are spread over large land areas. A compact city can be large nonetheless, formed of multiples of compact units interrelated with each other (Fig. 1-5). More than any other pattern, the compact city has the promising potentiality to ease the effects of a stressed climate.

Compactness does not necessarily mean a higher density of population per house unit or the loss of some privacy, but rather it can introduce the same or lower density per house unit if it is properly and innovatively designed. Further, it can retain and improve privacy and raise the overall

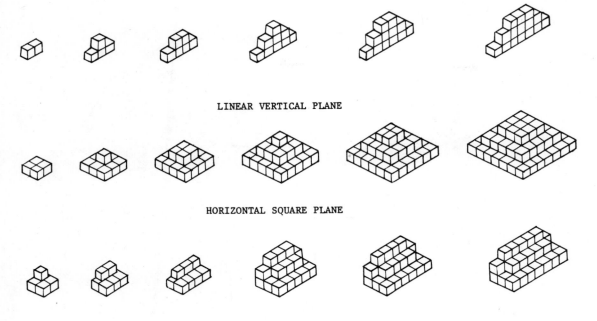

LINEAR VERTICAL PLANE

HORIZONTAL SQUARE PLANE

HORIZONTAL LINEAR SOLID

Fig. 1-5. Basic forms of compact design concept. Suitable for use on flat land or on slopes; terraced to enable use of adjacent space by all units.

urban environmental quality if designed with climatic stress considerations in mind. Another approach to compactness is the development of domed clustered houses. This pattern offers good ventilation, shadowing, proximity, open space for recreation, and much privacy to the units (Figs. 1-6 and 1-7).

Although social and defense needs have been of primary concern in the past, the necessity for human adaptation to the stressed climate now is emphasized by the development of the compact urban form in arid zones. Yet, we should note that the design of ancient cities, while so ordered for other reasons, did provide a more moderate climate than the surrounding environs outside the city. The compact form broke the strong, hot day or cold night winds, reduced the abrasive effect of dusty storms, built in cool air and shadow and therefore encouraged movement, reduced direct radiation and evaporation, minimized heat gain during the day and heat loss at night.

To foster physical unity in the compact city, the designer might well develop the concept of a chain of social and daily service cells (Fig. 1-8). Each of these cells is to be of a reasonable size, large enough for human comfort and the satisfaction of immediate human needs. Each cell forms a compact physical as well as service unit; all the urban cells relate to a central compact service unit. The compact form of all parts contributes greatly to the reduction of the length of the utilities network and consequently reduces maintenance cost and energy consumption.

Finally, since homogeneous groups are more tolerant of density than are heterogeneous groups, the planner may need to develop a plan to attract people of like minds to nearby cells. Although the compact city will not be denser than the normal one in terms of living space per person, here

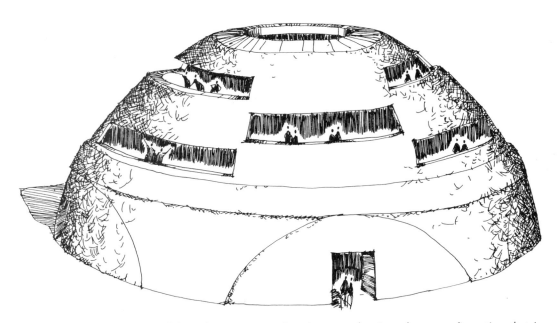

Fig. 1-6. Conceptual form for a compact housing complex in a dome configuration that is suitable for stressed hot/dry or cold/dry climates.

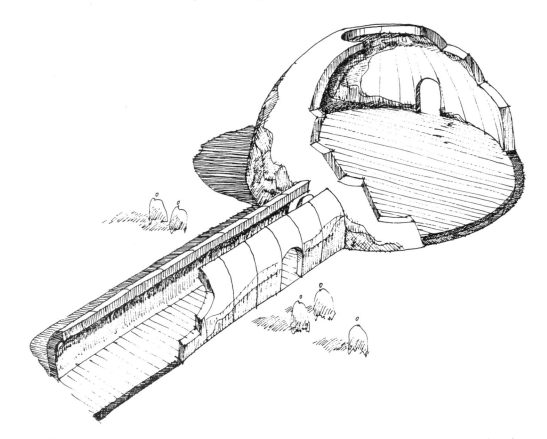

FIG. 1-7. Compact dome design for housing complex which may connect with other similar units. This setting is most suitable for the stressed very cold/dry or very cold/humid climates of central Canada, or central continental high plateaus, or northern regions.

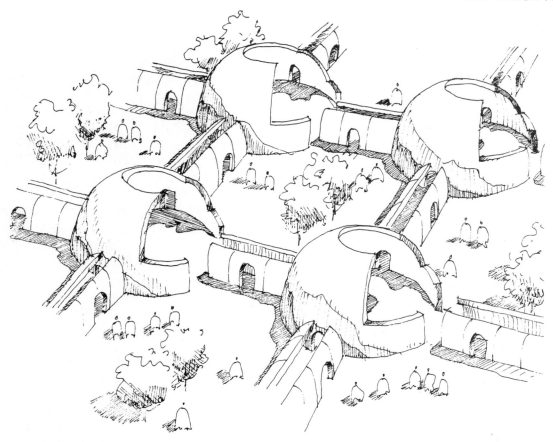

Fig. 1-8. City made up of compact dome design housing and envisioned as interconnected chains of domed cells.

the residents will be compensated by enjoying ample open space within the city itself and at its outskirts. The compact city is one of the most effective settlement design forms to have been introduced, and it offers the following positive features:

1. *Climate*. The compact city responds effectively to problems posed by the climatically stressed (very hot or very cold and dry) regions, intense radiation or intense cold, diurnal and seasonal fluctuation in temperature, strong hot or cold wind, and dusty storms. To a certain extent, the compactness helps retain humidity.
2. *Energy Consumption*. The compact city minimizes heat gain and heat loss and therefore consumes less energy for cooling or heating. It also can climatically moderate outdoor environment with relatively narrow street design, adequate orientation of the streets, self-shadowing configuration, and reduction of vehicle transportation within the residential area.
3. *Infrastructure Reduction*. The compact city allows a very noticeable shortening of all the infrastructure network and transportation system and therefore reduces energy consumption and the cost for planning, development and construction, and especially for maintenance and

management. The final result is a reduction of the load on the taxpayer.

4. *Accessibility*. There is quick and easy access to facilities within the compact neighborhood which facilitates daily services to the residences for education, employment, recreation, shopping, social, and other services. Planned access—some pedestrian and some vehicular, depending on the distance involved—to the larger service centers or the central city is essential.

5. *Land Savings*. The proposed compact design form increases the intensity of land use and therefore saves land for other uses. In addition, we envision the location of the compact city on the slope (which often has not been used) to save the lowland for nonurban development. Location on a slope introduces new dimensions to the city: wide eye contact to the environs, attractive view to the adjacent lowland, good ventilation and fresh air, plenty of light, possibility for plenty of sunshine, much privacy, and good environmental quality (free of pollution and having abated noise).

6. *Social Cohesiveness*. The close and proximate living will intensify social interaction among different age groups, especially among children and elderly persons. For these two groups, proximity is an essential element in their daily social life. We can expect that social life will be pleasant for all social groups of the compact community. More than any other urban form, the compact urban form fosters social interaction.

7. *Saving the Environment*. Developing a compact city destroys less of the environs than does conventional city development. Especially in arid zones, this may be an essential element because of the delicacy of the ecosystem which already is at the threshold of destruction.

Although compact, our city still needs to expand vertically and horizontally. Figures 1-9, 1-10, and 1-11 show innovative possibilities for vertical development. However, expansion should mean a balanced mixture between vertical and horizontal development throughout the city and not in any one section of it. Vertical expansion, in our opinion, should be a combination of both above- and belowground construction. The aboveground level preferably should not exceed three floors, so as to minimize the need for an elevator and keep energy consumption under control, and also in order not to increase population density in the outdoor space. The belowground space can integrate nearly all types of land uses, especially when the city location is on the slope.[1] In addition to its other advantages, slope location enables nearly unlimited sideward expansion, particularly for certain types of land uses: industry, storage, shopping, parking, public gathering, and residential space.

OPEN SPACE DESIGN

Open space design in the arid zone can have more impact on and is more essential to the human comfort than in nonarid zones. The consideration of the location of open space, its pattern of distribution within the city, its size, and its positioning in relation with the adjacent land uses is vital, not necessarily from the functional aspect but rather from the standpoint of the

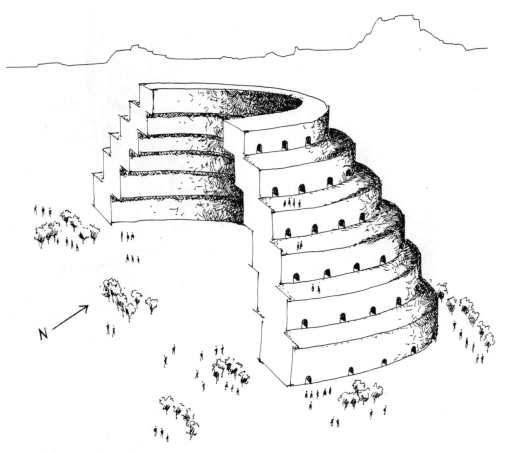

Fig. 1-9. Conceptual scheme suitable for hot/dry climates: compact terraced structure facing north and shadowed to the south; exposed to sunshine part of the day, yet adequately lighted throughout. Most windows facing south will be shadowed by the level above.

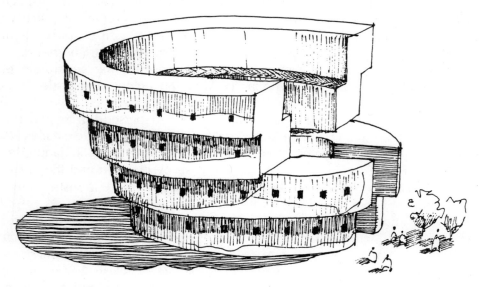

Fig. 1-10. Another form for a compact terraced housing complex in the hot/dry climate with a narrow semicircular base enlarged upward to shadow the lower floors.

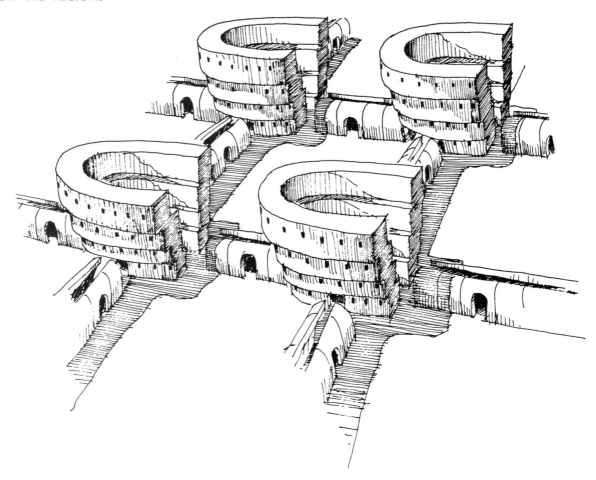

Fig. 1-11. Compact terraced housing complexes envisioned as interconnected cells which may form a neightborhood or an entire city.

microclimate which it can generate. To begin with, no passive open space should exist within the arid city; those areas left in reserve for potential future expansion should be designed and treated as active spaces until their eventual primary use. Such open spaces should at least be paved in order to prevent supporting strong cold or hot winds, the generation of local turbulence, heated air at noon and dust movement, and to decrease albedo.

Active open spaces should be small-sized and dispersed throughout the city rather than being concentrated as one or a few large spaces. A dispersion pattern facilitates proximity to and access from all land uses (especially from residential areas), supports use by children and the elderly, has positive impact on the ambient temperature, establishes large amounts of shadow, and reduces the stress of the arid climate.

In the arid city, water resources are scarce and expensive; therefore, the design of active open space should not follow the conventional Western approach. The design should focus on native plants which require little or no water or which can tolerate brackish water (when available). Grass, for example, is not suitable here; any nonplanted parts should be paved. If we disperse small active spaces within the residential area and throughout the city, this will add aesthetic and comfort appeal to the residents. Dispersion is undeniably necessary in the residential area of the compact form we have suggested. The open space can be a focus for or the nucleus of a group of houses, a section along a pedestrian path, or a landmark to identify a shift from one land use to another.

In short, open space in the arid city should be designed with the following policies in mind:

- Minimizing of open space, especially the passive ones;
- City fractioning and dispersing of open space to avoid generation of cold or hot wind;
- Covering of any open space with vegetation and/or paving to avoid generation of local dust storms;
- Shadowing of open space so that it is cool and to minimize local heat turbulence, avoid reflection and develop useful space. Trees absorb radiation and therefore minimize reflection or albedo.

AGRO-URBAN SETTING

Urban development should be combined with agricultural zones to develop an agro-urban center. It would have to be a unique and sophisticated agriculture using irrigation and greenhouses and combined and integrated within an urban configuration. This new dimension will require a new urban form which in turn will have an impact in moderating the climate of the region. This type of land use also stems from the ancient usage of agrarian land in and near the ancient cities.

The motivation for agro-urban center development can be outlined as follows:

1. To increase self-sufficiency of the urban center and to minimize reliance on the importation of food from the hinterland or other nonarid regions.
2. To reduce the usage of lengthy transportation networks for importing food and therefore reduce energy consumption for transportation and refrigeration; to save time and reduce food prices.
3. To minimize the psychological feeling of isolation within the large arid region; to generate an increase in population and employment possibilities.
4. To naturally increase the relative humidity within the urban environment and consequently moderate its hot/dry climate. Also associated with agriculture are plants and the positive effects of the photosynthesis process.

Conclusion

Arid zones offer largely undeveloped areas for future expansion to satisfy major human needs: for passive energy resources (solar), for agriculture (with special treatment), and for new settlements construction, especially the urban type. In spite of their limitations, arid regions have diverse potentialities for urban as well as for rural development. Science, technology, and an innovative design together with a pioneering spirit are essential for good results. The design must suit the unique and sensitive ecosystem and the great climatic stress.

We may need to readjust our thinking to regard the arid regions as suitable for settlements expansion, but they offer the possibility for agriculture and food production, for urban centers and for new sources of energy. Whatever the motivation for the development of those regions, construction of new urban centers within them is inevitable and necessary. This fact necessitates a new approach to urban forms to respond to the special demands of a stressed climate.

Arid zones were the first to establish urban centers in ancient times in the Fertile Crescent and the Nile of the Middle East or in the Indus Valley in Pakistan. These hydraulic civilizations lasted many millenniums with impressive urban achievements. The study of their urban forms and configurations evolved in response to energy needs and heat gain and heat loss problems. This will help us to rediscover profitable lessons from the past and will guide our fashioning new designs. We must study such aspects as location, orientation, compactness, height, street and alley design, and the overall land-use pattern.

It is important for us to put aside Western urban design when we are developing the arid zone. The native patterns for urban design have evolved through the centuries and suit the unique conditions of the stressed climate. We must research their urban forms and configuration, building materials, colors, plants for landscaping, water usage, and other elements.

Environmentally, the arid zone is a sensitive region where an equilibrium has been established in nature. The character of the stressful climate threatens ecological survival. Flora and fauna as well as physical qualities such as soil and landforms are fragile. This delicate balance should be treated carefully throughout the design process.

Planning, design, and development of urban forms in an arid zone should be comprehensive, innovative, adaptive, and original, yet we must use passive energy and develop under acceptable modern norms.

Notes

1. Gideon Golany, *Earth-Sheltered Habitat: History, Architecture and Urban Design.* (New York: Van Nostrand Reinhold. In press.)

Suggested Readings

1. Adams, R. and M.. Willens, A. and A. *Dry Lands: Man and Plants.* London: The Architectural Press, 1978.
2. Evans, Martin. *Housing, Climate and Comfort.* London: The Architectural Press, 1979.
3. Givoni, Baruch. *Man, Climate and Architecture.* Amsterdam: Elsevier, 1969.
4. Golany, Gideon. *Housing in Arid Lands.* London: The Architectural Press, 1980.
5. ———. *Arid Zone Settlement Planning: The Israeli Experience.* New York: Pergamon Press, 1979.

6. ———. *Urban Planning for Arid Zones*. New York: John Wiley & Sons, 1978.
7. Kenya, Allan. *Design Primer for Hot Climates*. London: The Architectural Press, 1979.
8. Olgyay, Victor. *Design with Climate: Bioclimatic Approach to Architectural Regionalism*. Princeton, N.J.: Princeton University Press, 1963.
9. Saini, Balwant Singh. *Building Environment: An Illustrated Analysis of Problems in Hot Dry Lands*. Sydney, Australia: Angus & Robertson, Publishers, 1973.

2
Catastrophic Droughts

*Eric Bradshaw Kraus**

Drought evokes the image of emaciated bodies huddling apathetically in a parched and dusty land. Yet Bedouins, bushmen, and Australian aborigines have thrived for thousands of years in deserts where water was always a rare and precious commodity. It is obvious that droughts have a different meaning for different groups. Their impact depends on what people have come to expect from their environment.

Given enough time, people can live in almost any natural or social surroundings. The trouble is that environments do not remain the same. They evolve, and the change need not be gradual. More often than not, change will manifest itself in the occurrence of comparatively rare events—not only droughts but also floods or wars or virulent epidemics. The problem for the planner, then, is not only to find the best adaptation to and exploitation of a given set of external parameters, but to make a dynamic response which prevents the inevitable fluctuations in the environmental parameters from being experienced as catastrophes.

This chapter is not concerned with gradual adaptation to an arid environment or with its most efficient exploitation, but with the likelihood and the consequences of catastrophic events. For that purpose, it is necessary to specify the circumstances which turn fluctuations of environmental parameters into disasters. What is meant by catastrophes, in general, and by drought catastrophes, in particular? Any investigation of such events must consider both the characteristics of the environmental strain and the structure of the society or institution upon which they act. Both these factors will be examined briefly below. Their interaction can be seen in some historical cases of drought disasters. A concluding, rather general discussion deals with some of the policies which might reduce an unduly high level of social sensitivity to droughts in the future.

The Threshold of Catastrophe

Evolution can be interpreted as a story of ever increasing mobility and liberation from the dictates of the environment. Man is one of the few creatures—perhaps the only one—who can function within a single lifetime in tropical jungles, on desert sands, and on arctic ice. To this has to be added now the underwater world and the realms of interplanetary space. The freedom to move through such a vast variety of environments was bestowed on us partly by a biological evolution which goes back

*The author's work was supported by the National Science Foundation, Grant Number ATM 76-23687.

beyond the first emergence of warm-blooded animals. Even more, however, it was gained by a technical, cultural, and social evolution which led to the development of artificial life-support systems of continuously growing complexity—from cave households and fur wraps to submarines and space suits. The functioning of all these systems involves intricate interactions between human and environmental factors.

Consider, for example, the survival of an aircraft. It may depend on the turbulence in the environment, but it depends also on the collective expertise of the crew and, beyond that, upon the skill and the integrity of innumerable workmen, designers, engineers, clerks, and others. Disasters can occur if either the environmental turbulence happens to be too violent or if there has been a failure of foresight and responsibility somewhere along the line. These causes do not act independently. Any human shortcoming is likely to be exposed by the environmental strains, and the stress which these exert can be amplified in turn by the human element.

All these factors and relationships are subject to small, unpredictable, more or less random fluctuations. Unfortunate circumstances—depending on the stability of the system—may act together to cause a lasting breakdown of a preexisting equilibrium, in other words, a catastrophe. This certainly happens to the aircraft when it strikes the ground. It also can happen to cities and states, though these generally are not oversensitive to environmental strains. However, if the environmental changes are of overwhelming amplitude or sufficiently abrupt and if they affect social groups which have already become vulnerable for other reasons, then they can have catastrophic effects.

External strains can become particularly severe in some locations. The desert is one of the harshest environments on earth. Its challenge is both spiritual and physical. It may be no accident that all the great monotheistic religions appeared first in an arid environment.

One need only imagine the setting. It is night in the desert. After a blazing day in the windswept emptiness, the dark brings relief to the aching body, parched by heat. Enormous stars hang low over the dustless dry atmosphere. Nothing stirs. The absolute silence is tangible, audible. Here are no whispering trees, no veils of cloud, no grassy meadows for the disporting of gods and goddesses. Here is that voice of stillness in which God spoke to his Prophet Elijah. Here, in the silent world, not soft, not gentle, in this awesome boundlessness of time and space, one man stands alone, touched by Infinity. . . . Such is the challenge of the desert to man's spiritual being. To his biological existence and that of every living thing, it is something else.[1]

The physical challenge of the desert is shared by all its inhabitants. Over countless generations, plants and animals have adapted themselves to a scant and intermittent water supply. Men have complemented this supply with tents and wells and irrigation systems and trade. This has made them more secure in some ways; but as in any development, there was a price to pay. Reduced dependence on the natural environment invariably involves an increased susceptibility to the actions and attitudes of other men. The sheer complexity of an advanced society provides hostages to fortune. A hurricane in Florida today can cause more extensive and more lasting destruction with far greater losses of life than it might have done when the place was known only to a few native Indian hunters. Along the desert margins, the same drought which would have been a passing hardship to a few Bedouins can now cause millions to die from hunger, topple governments, and ultimately, perhaps change the political equilibrium of the world. There is a physical and a social side to any environmental strain.

Rainfall in the Arid Zone

By definition, it is rainfall, or the lack of it, which produces stress in an arid zone. Heat is usually of secondary importance. But when one wants to consider rainfall quantitatively, it is not enough to know the amount which falls on the average over a year. The distribution of precipitation in space and time is equally important, particularly in arid regions.

A shallow farm pond can be filled by a passing shower which may cover only a few acres and which need not last more than an hour or so. Its design and operation will not be affected significantly by slow climatic changes. On the other hand, the design of a large storage reservoir or of an irrigation system has to be based upon the total amount of water which is expected to be available during one or several years over an extensive area. The water level of the reservoir will not be influenced much by short-term local weather vicissitudes, but a long-term increase of the rainfall of a few percent may alter its whole operational economy.

The matter is complicated further because of the peculiar distribution of rainfall values around their average. When one considers maximum daily temperature values, one finds that they are distributed symmetrically with about equally many relatively cold and relatively warm days. By contrast, the distribution of rainfall is skew. There are many days when it does not rain at all, particularly in arid regions. When it does rain, it usually pours. Flash floods can be a risk, therefore, even in the most desiccated desert regions. People who live in these parts usually know about this risk; but catastrophes do occur when a flash flood is unusually large, or when nothing has happened for such a long time that the people have been lulled into a false sense of security.

Floods in arid regions can be expected only at certain times of the year. It only rains in summer along the equatorial margin of the deserts. Along the polar margin, practically all rain falls in the winter. As an example, Fig. 2-1 shows the mean distribution of rainfall in Khartoum, just south, and in Alexandria, just north, of the Sahara. Some kind of natural or artificial water storage in rivers, lakes, or underground reservoirs is essential for people to live permanently in places with such a seasonally variable water supply. Where water is available, irrigation can be used to grow crops the whole year round. However, because the rainfall season is relatively short, it is possible for the annual local supply to be concentrated in a few intense local storms. This sort of distribution may make engineering planning for the provision of drainage just as critical as planning for the storage and allocation of irrigation water.

Outside the central deserts, there are very few places which cannot expect at least some small amount of rain each year. This means that the distribution of annual rainfall is less skew than that of daily or monthly rainfall; it is not symmetric, however. In arid regions, the number of years

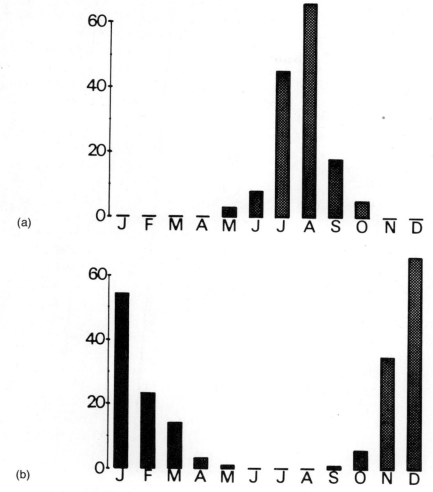

FIG. 2-1. Distribution of mean monthly precipitation in (a) Khartoum, Sudan; (b) Alexandria, Egypt (in millimeters).

with below average rainfall almost invariably exceeds the number of years with above average rainfall. Figure 2-2 plots relative rainfall anomalies in Kano, the principal town of northern Nigeria. Plots of such relative anomalies permit comparison between places that have very different average rainfall amounts. Relative anomalies are deviations of the annual rainfall from the long-term mean, divided by the standard deviation which is a measure of the average variability of the record. If the distribution is symmetric with about an equal number of cases above and below the average, one can expect to find positive anomalies in excess of one standard deviation in about 16 percent of all cases. An anomaly which is larger than two standard deviations would be found in about two cases out of a hundred, and one larger than three times the standard deviation is very rare.

During the period 1911 to 1974, there were 37 years with rainfall below the mean in Kano and 27 summers when it rained more than average. But there were 13 years when the relative anomaly was larger than unity, that is when actual excess rainfall above the mean was larger than one standard deviation. There were only 9 years when rainfall deficits were larger than one standard deviation—this, in spite of the fact that there were more dry years overall. The numbers indicate the skewness of the annual rainfall distribution in Kano. They also show the capricious and variable nature of the precipitation regime in that semiarid region. There is no obvious persistence in the plot of Figure 2-2. Dry and wet years follow each other in an apparently random succession. The longest wet spell was four wet years in a row. Spells of this duration could have arisen quite easily by accident in a record which extends over 64 years.

If one considers conditions over a larger area, things look rather different. Figure 2-3 is based on a composite of all the rainfall records in Africa and Arabia between 10° and 25° north, that is the whole southern flank of the desert region. The columns in the figure represent the averages for all stations of the relative rainfall anomalies shown in Figure 2-2 for Kano. Figure 2-3 suggests that this whole vast area experienced relatively long, wet, or long, dry spells. For example, there were ten relatively wet years in a row between 1927 and 1936 and again between 1950 and 1959. On the other hand, there was not a single wet year between 1967 and 1974. The chance for such long spells to occur by accident is exceedingly small—much smaller than one in a million.[2]

Comparison of the two graphs in Figures 2-2 and 2-3 and of other similar graphs indicates that wet and dry spells in the continental subtropics tend to affect relatively large areas over considerable periods of time. Locally, the dry spells are likely to be interrupted on and off by the odd passing storms, but this does not affect the persistence of a precipitation deficit over a wider area. The persistence of such deficits is evidenced also in the discharge records of streams like the Nile or the Niger which integrate naturally the rainfall over large regions. The story about the seven fat years and the seven lean years in Egypt may well have had a factual basis.

One can focus on still longer time intervals. Historical, archaeological,

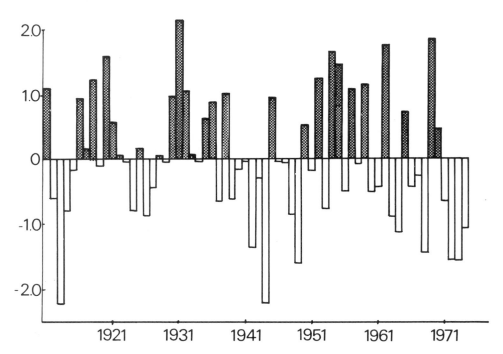

FIG. 2-2. Relative precipitation anomalies (i.e., departures of annual precipitation from average divided by the standard deviation) in Kano, Nigeria.

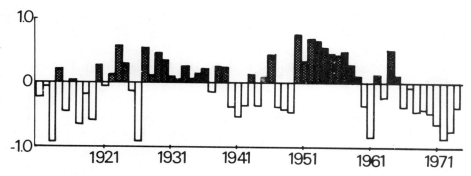

FIG. 2-3. Average (for all stations 10° N–25° N, 30° W–60° E, Africa and Arabia) of relative precipitation anomalies.

and physical studies provide evidence for so-called secular climatic fluctuations which lasted for hundreds or thousands of years. This is still relatively short compared to the time scale of the glacial-interglacial sequence which involves tens of thousands of years. The mean temperature difference between a full ice age and an interglacial stage is also about four times larger than the corresponding difference for any secular fluctuation since then. In marginal areas, however, the amplitude of the secular fluctuations appears to have been sufficient to leave a considerable impact on the development of human affairs.

The implication for planning purposes is fairly obvious. Small villages or towns in arid areas will be exposed to many relatively brief dry spells. If their economy is integrated into a larger region, however, they can safeguard themselves by having water resources which could tide them over a relatively few dry months. The large region as a whole will suffer fewer dry spells, but these tend to be of much longer duration. This makes the establishment of suitable reserves that much more difficult. Climatic fluctuations involving increasing aridity are likely to manifest themselves by more frequent drought spells rather than by the absence of floods or wet years. The effects of secular climatic changes are likely to be felt in one form or another all over the globe.

Lessons of History

Historical and social developments are determined by a combination of many different, uncontrollable variables. It is never possible to explain them categorically as being due to changes in some particular parameters. However, the coincidence, in time, of some notable social and climatic changes is rather striking. While this is no proof, it at least suggests a casual relationship which may have some bearing on future planning. Three cases of apparent climatic causes for social breakdown are discussed briefly below. They deal with the fall of the Old Kingdom of Egypt, the decline of the Pueblo Indians in America, and the results of the recent Sahelian drought in North Africa.

DROUGHT AND THE BREAKDOWN OF THE OLD KINGDOM IN EGYPT

The Old Kingdom of Egypt emerged into recorded history about 3100 B.C. when the country was first unified. If tradition is correct, Menes—the founder of the first dynasty—was a pastoralist conquerer from the south who imposed his authority upon the peasants of the Nile Valley. At that time and during the preceding few thousand years, the Sahara was not quite the extensive desert which it is now. Prairies and even woods covered areas where today there is nothing but sand and stone. Antelopes, buffaloes, and rhinos drank from streams which have long since disappeared; the same water courses provided fish for tribes that have gone the same way. It is uncertain how much irrigation already existed at the time along the Nile, but there is reason to believe that its major development occurred only after Menes' conquests.[3] Though floodplain agriculture was probably the mainstay of Egyptian economy from the very beginning, the surrounding uplands also provided extensive grazing for domestic animals as well as game for food and aristocratic sport. In fact, it could be argued that new social investments like irrigation could not have been brought about as a bootstrap operation without some surplus of capital and labor derived from other sources.

During the Old Kingdom, Egyptian civilization was young and extremely self-confident. New techniques and social institutions provided the basis for an expanding economy. An indigenous script, stone masonry, and new art forms were all developed and perfected within a few hundred years, as were standing armies, some international trade, and a centralized administration. Never before had there been such wealth, such ease, or monuments of such grandeur and magnificence. For the upper classes, at least, life must have been gracious and exciting.

While this was going on, the climate of the world went through one of its secular swings. In Scandinavia and in North America, the elms and the oaks retreated rather precipitously from the northern outposts which they had reached a few thousand years earlier; simultaneously, in North Africa, the desert spread outward once more. As always, it was the odd events which must have been noticed. To people in the affected parts, droughts must have seemed to become more common and, perhaps, more severe. Probably for some time, the environmental changes were masked in Egypt by the excitement of the new developments and by the expansion of irrigation. But the economic expansion could not go on forever, and the demands on the peasants for taxes and labor and produce became progressively greater. Ultimately, it was the agricultural population which had to create all the surplus needed for the construction of the great pyramids and for the semimilitary expeditions which marched to Syria for timber, searched Nubia for gold, and traded for myrrh in Punt. More money was needed not only for a luxurious court with its attendant host of craftsmen and artisans, but also for the provincial nobles and administrators who also began to develop rather expensive tastes.

Something had to give. Suddenly, the social order which had been built up so confidently over the centuries collapsed. Beginning about 2180 B.C., anarchy replaced the previous orderly administration. The immediate cause of this social catastrophe cannot be fully known; however, it seems to have been associated with widespread droughts which affected the whole realm and which were probably a symptom of the general climatic deterioration. In the 22nd century B.C., the expanding desert apparently had reached the headwaters of some of the more important Nile tributaries, causing the effects of the local desiccation in Egypt to be intensified by a calamitous decrease in the life-giving annual floods. Barbara Bell quotes many texts which indicate the severity of the resulting famines.[4] They describe cases of cannibalism, rioting, plundering of storehouses, and crime waves in general. There was internecine warfare between district governors who assumed independence and tried to isolate themselves and their people from the general distress by withholding taxes from the central government.

Drought combined with overtaxation and geographical isolation seems to have been the immediate cause of the Egyptian breakdown. The ensuing dark age lasted some 50 years. By 2130 B.C., authoritative government had been reestablished in southern Egypt. In the following century the whole country was reunified once more, but the effects of the famine and of the social collapse were traumatic and long lasting. The royal household never regained its former unquestioned, monopolistic authority. No pharaoh was ever able again to build pyramids on the scale of a Chefren or a Cheops in the heyday of the Old Kingdom. What is more, the optimism and confidence of the earlier age were not recovered, and the adventurous spirit which had spearheaded the initial development of Egyptian civilization was never recaptured again. From then on, for another 1800 years—in the most enduring of all civilizations—the Egyptians were mostly content to emulate and conserve what had been previously developed.

DEMISE OF THE PUEBLO INDIANS

Never again through history did so much of the world become again quite so favorable for husbandry as it had been at the dawn of civilization before the Egyptian collapse, during the so-called Atlantic Period which lasted from about 6000 to 2400 B.C. Although the desert became a permanent feature afterward and although the northern countries have been somewhat colder ever since, there were other shorter, relatively mild intervals. One of these occurred during the height of the Middle Ages from about 800 to 1250 A.D., when grapes were harvested on English farms and the norsemen pastured their cattle in Greenland. Numerous populous settlements also flourished at that time in the arid areas which later became the deserts of Arizona and of New Mexico. Unlike the ancient Egyptians, the Pueblo Indians left no written records. However, archaeology and a comprehensive study of tree rings which cover more than 15 centuries, provide a good deal of information both about people and climate. The evidence has been discussed and summarized by Ladurie, and I shall quote here from his account.

Crops had been cultivated in the basins of the Little Colorado, the Gila and the Rio Grande Rivers for more than two thousand years before the present. The region had reached an acme of wealth and population density in the twelfth century, when it suddenly started to decline. People left their villages. Vast areas turned into desert. In less than three hundred years, nearly two-thirds of the cultivated area was abandoned. In 1250 A.D., about 230,000 square miles had been farmed; less than 250 years later when Columbus landed in San Salvadore, the farming area had shrunk to some 85,000 square miles. What happened? One factor which stands out is a series of great droughts in the second half of the thirteenth century which affected the whole of the southwestern United States. The tree ring record shows that droughts in the American southwest were never so general and continuous as during the sixty years from 1246 to 1305. Particularly, there was one big continuous drought which lasted from 1276 to 1299.

There must have been the odd drought years before. The Indians who lived in the area had tried to provide against lack of water. They had invented and generally applied irrigation and the terracing of steep valleys. But these flimsy engineering structures were of little use during a calamity like the drought of the thirteenth century which fell like a divine curse upon a population, which probably was already as numerous as could be carried by the land during the best of times. In the wake of the drought came hunger and a reversal of the previous demographic trend.

The rains returned again after 1305 but the climate had apparently become much more variable than it had before. Though there is evidence of disastrous flooding, particularly in the fourteenth century, the wet periods alternated with other dry episodes. This variability must have accelerated the erosion of soil which had already been damaged by irresponsible land clearance, deforestation and the mere establishment of agriculture. With the continuous deterioration of the land, the social decline was never reversed.[5]

One cannot be sure that environmental changes caused the decline of the Pueblo Indians. There is no evidence in America of a social superstructure like that which seems to have overtaxed the capacities of the Egyptian peasants, but there may have been other social or political or medical causes. However, it is certain that a secular climatic fluctuation which was accompanied by severe drought conditions coincided with or preceded the decline. Overpopulation and the concomitant large pressure on the available natural resources probably increased the vulnerability of the population to these conditions, causing them to assume catastrophic proportions.

DROUGHT IN THE SAHEL AND IN AUSTRALIA

The recent African drought may have had more victims than any other known episode of this kind. It certainly had more publicity, but droughts are inevitable in arid lands. On the tropical fringes of the world's deserts, they also tend to be extensive. The dry spell indicated by Figure 2-3 for the years 1968 to 1974 was experienced not only along the southern rim of the Sahara all the way across Africa and from Senegal to Ethiopia, but it also affected the Indian desert margins in Rajastan as well as the semiarid northern parts of Australia. Though this drought has been considered a manifestation of another secular worldwide climatic deterioration by some writers, it was probably no more extensive or severe than other dry spells which afflicted the same countries during the period of World War II and even more so during the first one or two decades of the century. For example, Roche, et al. report that the lowest cumulative five-year discharge of both the Senegal River at Bakel and of the Niger River at Koulikoro was recorded in 1940 to 1944.[6] The water yield of the River Nile at Aswan dropped by nearly 50 percent during the two decades following the year 1895 compared with the preceding 20 years. The latest African drought, which reached its climax in 1972, was therefore something which could be expected statistically to recur at least once every 50 years or so. The question then is why it had such singularly disastrous effects. Why were no similar disasters reported during earlier drought episodes, and why did nothing of the sort occur in Australia where the drought was just as severe?

Part of the difference may be due simply to modern communications. Starving people could not be seen on TV before. However, that is not the whole story. Probably, there was also mass starvation of peasants during earlier droughts in Africa, but the social structure as a whole usually continued to function, maybe because the upper classes—merchants and the tribal nobility—were then better equipped to muddle through reasonably well. By contrast, the only persons able to escape the afflictions of the drought of the 1970s may have been some bureaucrats and military men—the largely alien, new aristocracy.

It is instructive to compare the consequences of droughts in Australia with the simultaneous developments in the Sahel. To start with, it is doubtful that anyone died from hunger in Australia. It is not only that there are fewer people per square mile in the Australian outback and that they are wealthier individually than their Sahelian counterparts; what is more important, perhaps, is an integral infrastructure which allowed them to exchange their wealth in local town stores and supermarkets against imported food and other requirements. If necessary, they usually could get credit and bank overdrafts and later, government drought relief. There were roads and trucks available to take much of the livestock over thousands of miles to the unaffected pastures in the south of the continent or to send them to slaughter houses. All that does not mean that people in the Australian drought areas did not lose money. Some went bankrupt, many suffered financial hardships, but it is unlikely that anybody went seriously hungry.

For some hundreds of years until the turn of the century, there had been a traditional infrastructure in the Sahel which provided an analogous sort of protection, at least for some groups of people. The Tuareg tribal lords who held dominion over a large part of the area and merchants in the towns which dotted the desert edge like ports along a seacoast used to have diversified sources of income and capital. Besides tributes in kind and taxes or rents from the peasant population, they also earned money from trade and from the transportation of goods. They organized caravans which traversed the Sahara between the Niger and the trading posts of southern Algeria, Tunis, and Libya. They traded southward, supplying dates, hides, meat and, particularly, salt to the sedentary black population in the humid monsoonal regions, buying millet or grain from them in turn. Lovejoy and Baier report that nomad traders could purchase a load of millet along the rivers of the southern Sudan, trade it for salt in the Tuareg heartlands of the central Sahara 500 miles to the north, and retrade once more for millet in the south, yielding a gross profit 80 times the value of the original stock.[7] The capital accumulated through these and similar enterprises helped to finance a primitive banking system. Part of it was also invested in grain storage which provided a cushion in periods of droughts and in estates which were often deep in the humid agricultural areas where drought was not much of a problem.

When droughts occurred in the Sahel, the nomad lords tended to move south into the wetter monsoon belt where many of their estates were located. They were accompanied or followed by their retainers and also by many of the servile farmers from the drier regions. Like swarming locusts, they would feed in the humid regions until conditions improved again farther north when they moved back to the open country and the more salubrious desert climate. As the herds expanded again after the droughts, they could support a larger population. The herd owners would then loan some animals to the poorer nomads who had become temporarily sedentary, enticing them in this way to take charge of their other animals and to engage in transportation and trading activities once more.

This traditional dynamic system of expansion and contraction began to malfunction with the imposition of European rule. Colonial penetration northward from the Gulf of Guinea established new trading routes toward the distant south along the river valleys and, particularly, on the new railway from Port Harcourt on the ocean to Kano in the Sahel. This not only undermined the overland trans-Sahara trade but also reduced the dependence of the people living in the savannah on the commercial capital for trading and production, supplied in the past by sheiks and desert merchants. Apart from changing the trade pattern, the European administrators tended to interfere with the former social hierarchy. The new system which they brought with them may have been more just in principle than the old feudal pattern of mild extortion or exploitation; but under the test of hard times it was not noticeably more effective. Other strains arose from an abortive revolt of the Tuaregs against the French during World War I and from the imposition of new national boundaries which interfered with free movement after World War II.

So it came about that the traditional responses did not work anymore when the rains began to fail again in the late 1960s. Drought turned into disaster because there were no indigenous financial resources to meet the emergency and because new political and economic constraints had restricted the access of the desert people to the land and to the agricultural produce of the wetter monsoon regions. The area over which the strain could be distributed was therefore reduced. At the same time, the population density had become much larger than before. Even the well-meaning administrative efforts to provide water by sinking numerous new wells turned out to contribute to the disaster. Great herds congregated around these wells until everything within walking distance of the wellheads was eaten bare. The animals died, and the desert spread into the trampled, overgrazed land.

The drought has now ended in the Sahel, and the land—sometimes at least—is green again. In 1976, it may have carried less animals than it could because it takes time to replenish the herds. However, even after full recovery, there probably will be no return to the old economic pattern in the Sahel. The control of servile villages by desert lords is finished. The Tuaregs are unlikely to regain the favorable trade terms which they once enjoyed. This has affected the replenishment of their herds as it has affected their romantically aristocratic style. It is now a different kind of world in the Sahel. The existing, though intermittent, grazing resources will probably attract other livestock investors from the south; but it is doubtful whether this will make life easier or safer for the local villages and for the seminomadic people along the desert fringe.

Conclusion

What can be done in arid regions to reduce the sensitivity of people in villages, towns, or countries to fluctuations in their available water resources? Can planning help to prevent these fluctuations from becoming catastrophic? There clearly can be no general answer to such questions. A traveler in the desert may plan for emergencies by taking a few jerry cans of water along on his camel or in his jeep. If he is stranded and his supply gives out, he is likely to be dead within a few days. In a city, the solution to his problem would be no more distant than the nearest bar or water tap. Cities live longer than their individual inhabitants. They have access to a larger reservoir of resources. City planning has, obviously, a different time perspective than the planning of one's personal affairs. An organized state or an economically integrated region would be even less sensitive than a city to short-term environmental vicissitudes, despite the fact that these may have a catastrophic character locally. Planning is likely to be required, in this case, on a still longer time scale.

In actual fact, direct human water consumption is rarely a deadly critical factor. The amount of water which people drink is relatively small. During a drought, they may be inconvenienced by having to go farther for their water supply or they may have to pay for its transport; but very few people are likely to die from thirst in the modern world. They may starve, however. Agriculture and industry depend on relatively copious water reserves, and they can be critically affected by fluctuations in the supply.

Pastoralism or agriculture without irrigation is always precarious in arid regions. To persist, communities along the desert fringe had either to be content with very small demands on their environment or they had to diversify their sources of income. Historically, this was done often by trade or war. Neither of these activities makes great demands on water resources; both are often very profitable. Many historical international trade routes depended as much on desert traverses as on ocean passages. The caravaneer, like the sailor, provided the necessary professional expertise. Both had to be backed up by organization and capital resources which offered further opportunities for remunerative investment. As on the sea, trading ventures helped also to develop the means and skills for predatory warfare which often paid even better.

In today's world, the desert has lost much of its former importance as a universal highway for trade. Local military raids are no longer profitable either—if they are feasible at all. Yet, the need for diversification remains. In theory, at least, one can enumerate other possible opportunities. In many arid regions, there are mineral resources which have not yet been fully exploited. Tourism offers other possibilities in a few well-endowed places. Heavy industry usually makes large demands on reliable water resources and is, therefore, rarely suitable. However, if capital, know-how, and markets are available—and these are large if's—there is no reason other industries could not flourish. Electronics, for example, is positively favored by a dry environment.

All of this does not mean that agriculture and pastoralism have no role to play. In fact, the potential contribution of the arid lands to the average food supply of the world is far from negligible. However, this potential is intermittent. The desert fringe is a very unsafe place for the subsistence farmer who tries to eke out a hand-to-mouth living. Nor is it suited for any social experiments in an independent and self-sufficient economy.

For a few hundred years during the height of the Roman Empire, the Nabateans in the Negev desert maintained flourishing farms which used only the scant local rainwater. They were able to do that because they could sell food at presumably exorbitant prices to the caravans which carried precious luxuries from India and Southern Arabia to the Roman market. The profitable sale of provisions to these caravans may have built up sufficient capital reserves to tide the Nabatean farmers over the inevitable dry years when they could wring nothing from their soil. It is unusual, however, for peasants to be in such a happy position. Few can possibly build up the capital reserves which might tide them over a series of dry years. Insurance and backing have to come, therefore, through a larger integrated economic system if the potential of the arid lands is to be exploited in an orderly manner. The experience of the ancient Egyptians and of the Pueblo Indians and of the Sahel farmers all suggests that such an integration cannot be very effective unless it covers more than a single climatic region or zone. In the case of major dry spells or secular fluctuations, it may have to involve the whole of humanity.

Notes

1. Evenari, Michael, Shanan, Leslie, and Tadmor, Naphtali. *The Negev; The Challenge of a Desert.* Cambridge, Mass: Harvard University Press, 1971, pp. 9–10.
2. Kraus, E.B., Subtropical droughts and cross-equatorial energy transports, *Monthly Weather Review,* **105,** 1977, 1009–1018.
3. Wilson, J.A. *The Burden of Egypt.* Chicago: University of Chicago Press, 1951, p. 31.
4. Bell, Barbara. The dark ages in ancient history, *American Journal of Archaeology,* **75,** January 1971, 1–26.
5. Ladurie, Emmanuel LeRoy. *Times of Feast, Times of Famine: A History of Climate Since the Year 1000.* Garden City, N.Y. Doubleday & Company, 1971.
6. Roche, M., Rodier, J. and Sircoulon, J. Aspects meteorologiques et hydrologiques des sécheresse récente en Afrique de l'ouest, In *Proceedings International Union of Geodesy and Geophysics,* 1975.
7. Lovejoy, P.E. and Baier, S. The desert side economy of the Central Sudan, In *The Politics of Natural Disaster,* ed. M.H. Glantz. New York: Praeger, 1975, pp. 145–175.

3
Desalination as a Strategy in Arid-Zone Salinity Management

Wynn R. Walker

The development of desalination technology in the United States has been guided by the basic objective outlined by Congress for the United States Department of the Interior's Office of Water Research and Technology:

> to provide for the development of practicable low-cost means for producing from sea water or from other saline waters (brackish and other mineralized or chemically charged waters) water of a quality suitable for agriculture, industrial, municipal, and other beneficial consumptive uses.

This objective has prompted substantial research and technological development, although application to large-scale systems is only now beginning to occur. The traditional scope of saline water conversion programs has been limited to the reclamation of otherwise unsuitable water for specific needs and the use of product water directly rather than its return to receiving waters in order to improve the resources' overall quality.

With the mounting desire to manage salinity on a large regional or basin-wide scale, the potential for applying desalination within the framework of an overall salinity control strategy should be seriously considered. In fact, the use of such systems to solve critical salinity problems is already being planned as part of the Colorado River International Salinity Control Project of the United States and the Republic of Mexico.

When considering regional salinity control, desalting costs can be expressed in dollars per unit volume of salt extracted in the brine discharge rather than in the conventional costs per unit volume of reclaimed water. In this manner the respective feasibility of desalination and other alternatives for salinity management can be systematically compared when developing strategies. To demonstrate the possible role of desalination technology in the regional planning of arid zones, we can consider the case where salinity of irrigation water is a problem. The possible strategies to solve this problem would include the desalting of water prior to agricultural use, the desalting of water as it returns to a preserve after irrigation, and the reduction of this returning flow through improvements in local irrigation practices.

Desalination Costs

In general, the costs associated with desalting systems may be classified either as those incurred during construction or those incurred annually to operate and maintain the facilities. These costs are subject to inflationary pressures and must, of course, therefore be periodically updated. Once costs are so adjusted, various relationships between costs and system performance can be determined.[1]

CAPITAL COSTS

The capital costs delineated in 1976 by this author are referenced to functions for mid-1971 and updated to prevailing price levels with various reported cost indices.[2] The costs of construction, steam, and site development can be estimated at the present time by employing the *Engineering News Record*'s Construction Cost Index. In July 1971 this index was 952, whereas in January 1981 it had risen to 3372. Consequently, an early 1981 cost estimate would be 3372/952 or 3.54 times the 1971 function. Other capital costs during construction such as interest, the owners' general expenses, and initial and working funds are functions of construction, steam, and site development costs and are therefore updated automatically. Land costs may be estimated at a current basis using existing land prices.

Estimates of capital costs for feedwater and brine treatment facilities require that several other inflationary factors be considered. For example, pipeline costs are adjusted by using the Bureau of Reclamation's Concrete Pipeline Costs Index (CPI)—1.17 for July 1971. Others are similarly adapted by using the bureau's Pumping Plant Cost Index (PPI)—1.26 for July 1971, the bureau's Pumps and Prime Mover Cost Index (PMI)—1.41 for July 1971, and the bureau's Canal and Earthwork Cost Index (EI)—1.27 for July 1971.

The annually adjusted construction costs are then divided according to whether or not the costs represent depreciating capital. Depreciating capital costs are multiplied by a fixed charge factor (FCR) which is the percentage of the total depreciating capital cost that is encompassed by interest, amortization, insurance, and taxes. Nondepreciating capital costs are, on the other hand, multiplied by the prevailing interest rate.

ANNUAL COSTS

Annual costs must also be adjusted for inflation. Labor, materials, and steam generation facility operation and maintenance are updated using the Bureau of Labor Statistics' Labor Cost Index SIC 494-7, which was 3.76 in July 1971. Chemical costs are multiplied by the present-to-1971 ratio of costs for chemicals and allied products, as computed by the Bureau of Labor Statistics (104.4 for 1971). Present fuel and electricity costs are estimated using current prices; replacement costs are expressed as functions of plant capacity and are thus not updated by using cost indices.

EFFECTIVE COSTS

Having described the individual costs associated with desalting systems, it is necessary to express such costs in either dollars per unit volume of product water (if water supply feasibility is at issue) or dollars per unit of salt extracted (if salinity control is at issue, as it is here). These costs are determined in this study by dividing the total annual costs by the annual volume of product water or brine salts.

Depreciating capital costs for the plant itself and the feedwater or brine salt disposal systems are multiplied by the FCR. Nondepreciating costs are then multiplied by the interest rate, added to the annually adjusted depreciating costs, and finally combined with the remaining annual costs; thus, using the eight capital cost categories and six annual cost elements described in 1976 by this author, we find that

$$C_{pw} = \frac{FCR \sum_{i=1}^{6} C'_i + I_r \sum_{i=7}^{8} C'_i + \sum_{i=9}^{14} C'_i}{C_p \times U_f \times 3.65 \times 10^{-4}} \qquad (3\text{-}1)$$

for costs per unit of product water, and

$$C_s = \frac{FCR \sum_{i=1}^{6} C'_i + I_r \sum_{i=7}^{8} C'_i + \sum_{i=9}^{14} C'_i}{C_b \times C_{bo} \times U_f \, 3.65 \times 10^{-4}} \qquad (3\text{-}2)$$

for costs per unit of salt extracted in which,

C_{pw} = unit cost of product water ($/m³)
C_s = unit cost of brine salts ($/metric ton)
C'_i = total annual cost for element i ($/year) (feedwater + plant + brine):
    C'_1 = construction cost
    C'_2 = steam generation
    C'_3 = site development
    C'_4 = interest during construction
    C'_5 = initial costs
    C'_6 = owner's general expense
    C'_7 = land
    C'_8 = working capital
    C'_9 = labor and materials (operational)
    C'_{10} = chemicals
    C'_{11} = fuel
    C'_{12} = electricity
    C'_{13} = steam generation operation and maintenance
    C'_{14} = replacement
C_p = product water volume (m³/day)
C_b = brine volume (m³/day)
C_{bo} = TDS concentration in brine (mg/ℓ)
FCR = fixed charge factor
I_r = interest rate
U_f = use factor (fraction of total time in actual operation)[3]

Evaluating Available Desalination Processes

Saline water conversion processes involve the use of a semipermeable barrier which excludes the flow of either water or salt. The barrier may be a membrane which excludes salt—such as that used in electrodialysis

(ED)—or one that exchanges salt for hydrogen and hydroxide ions which then unite to produce water-ion exchange (IX). The barrier may also be a "phase boundary" which excludes the salts. For example, vaporization of water using multistage flash (MSF), vertical tube evaporation-MSF (VTE-MSF), and vapor compression-VTE-MSF (VC-VTE-MSF) leaves the salts in the remaining solution, as does solidification of water using vacuum freezing-vapor compression processes (VF-VC).[4] The driving potential for all of these processes is either thermal (in distillation and freezing), pressure (in RO), electrical (in ED), or chemical (in IX) energy.

The application of a desalination technology to regional water quality management tends to be a very site-specific problem. As a result, generalizing concerning costs is difficult. Therefore, it might be useful at this point to note the effective cost models' sensitivity to various input parameters relative to an arbitrary "base" so that the relative importance of the different variables can be ascertained. (Table 3-1 presents the base values of some typical input parameters that might be established for an irrigation return flow problem.)

DESALINATION SYSTEM CAPACITY

Desalting costs expressed in terms of dollars per ton of salt removed, or dollars per m³ of product water, exhibit substantial economies of scale. For the "base" condition, the scaled effects relative to product water

TABLE 3-1. Standardized Desalting Model Input Parameters for Variable Sensitivity Analyses.

C_p	$= 1.5 \times 10^4$ m³/day (4mgd)
TDS_i	$= 5000$ mg ℓ
TDS_p	$= 500$/mg ℓ
ENR	$= 1354$
BLS_1	$= 4.93$
BLS_2	$= 181$
CPI	$= 1.88$
PPI	$= 1.98$
PMI	$= 2.13$
EI	$= 1.92$
D_b	$= 1000$ m (3280 feet)
D_f	$= 100$ m (328 feet)
D_{ib}	$= 100$ m (328 feet)
D_{if}	$= 1000$ m (3280 feet)
E	$= 1.07$ (3.5 feet)
E_c	$= \$7.2 \times 10^4$/M Joules ($20/1000 kwh)
FCR	$= 0.0856$
F_r	$= \$1.2 \times 10^3$/M Joules ($1.14/MBTU)
I_r	$= 7\%$
L_p	$= \$4,942$/ha ($2000/acre)
T	$= 15.6°C$ (60°F)
U_f	$= 0.90$
Na	$= 1260$ mg/ℓ
Mg	$= 123$ mg/ℓ
Ca	$= 393$ mg/ℓ
K	$= 8$ mg/ℓ
HCO_3	$= 106$ mg/ℓ
Cl	$= 2035$ mg/ℓ
SO_4	$= 1075$ mg/ℓ
NO_3	$= 0$ mg/ℓ

capacity for each process are illustrated in Fig. 3-1.[5] In nearly every process, the unit costs at 950 m³/day are two to four times the cost at 121,000 m³/day. The VTE-MSF, VC-VTE-MSF, and RO costs at the lower values are 3.5 to 3.6 times those at the upper capacities, indicating a much greater importance of this scale for them than for MSF (2.80), VF-VC (2.78), or ED (2.13). (Of these specific processes, electrodialysis is most significantly affected by input parameters and therefore should be evaluated more closely.) This scaled factor (capacity) for desalination technologies will generally make small installations for salinity control prohibitive, since other measures for reducing salinity will certainly be cheaper. However, as the scope of implementation increases and the marginal costs of desalting thereby decrease, these technologies may become highly competitive with the various other alternatives. Consequently, a major parameter in a salinity control analysis should be the level of implementation.

FEEDWATER SALINITY

When evaluating desalting costs, the feedwater salinity is also an important parameter. The distillation and freezing methods are not substantially limited by input salinity, since the same measures are necessary to desalt

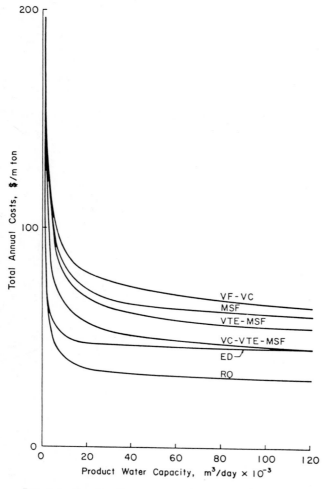

FIG. 3-1. Desalination costs as functions of capacity.

1000 mg feedwater as for 10,000 mg. Consequently, the higher the feedwater salinity, the lower the unit cost for these processes. Reverse osmosis and electrodialysis, on the other hand, use membranes to remove salt and therefore are directly affected by feedwater salinity. Calculations made at the "base" condition with various levels of salinity are plotted in Figure 3-2. It is assumed that individual ionic species do not create limiting conditions.

Using all the methods (except electrodialysis), the costs at 2000 mg/λ would be double those at 5000 mg/λ and five times those at 13,000 mg/λ. However, the ratio between the rate of desalination and the cost ratio diminishes toward increasing salinity values. The electrodialysis process is significantly less affected by feedwater salinity, mainly because of its modular construction and the direct proportion between power consumption and salinity.

Operation and Maintenance. Unlike the fairly predictable construction cost items, operation and maintenance costs are subject to year-to-year inflationary pressure which cannot always be effectively predicted. At the "base" condition, the operation and maintenance costs were typically somewhat more than 50 percent of the total annual costs, as shown in Table 3-2.

It is interesting to note the effect of interest rates on the relative impor-

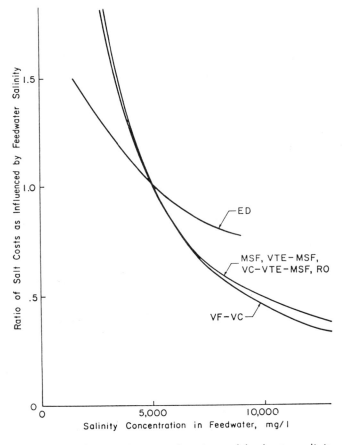

FIG. 3-2. Desalination costs as functions of feedwater salinity.

TABLE 3-2. Operation and
Maintenance (O & M) Costs of
Different Desalination Processes.

PROCESS	PERCENTAGE OF TOTAL ANNUAL COST ATTRIBUTABLE TO O & M
MSF	60%
VTE-MSF	57%
VC-VTE-MSF	46%
ED	58%
RO	56%
VF-VC	56%

tance of operation and maintenance costs. For example, if the interest rate were increased from 7 percent (the base) to 10.5 percent, O & M costs decline from more than 50 percent to 39 percent (about 11 percent in most cases). This 50 percent increase in interest rates interestingly increases unit costs by a low of 21.5 percent for MSF processes compared to 28.6 percent for VC-VTE-MSF systems. In each case studied, the changes in feedwater salinity due to changed capacity did not affect these percentages, except for electrodialysis. In the case of ED, operation and maintenance percentages ranged from 58 percent to 66 percent as the capacity increased from the base figure to 121,000 m³/day.

Specific items among the operating expenses are also of interest in water quality management planning. For instance, electrical and fuel costs accounted for the percentages of total annual costs outlined in Table 3-3. This data illustrates the importance of electrical costs for membrane and freezing processes and fuel costs for distillation methods of desalination. Rate increases for both electricity and fuel, we should note, produce proportional increases in annual costs. For example, in a MSF system, if electricity rates increase 50 percent, annual costs will increase 4.9 percent.

LAND

Because land area for desalting systems is a nondepreciating capital cost and can therefore be amortized indefinitely, land costs for the base condition ($5,000/ha) account for only 1 to 8 percent of total annual costs as shown in Table 3-4.

TABLE 3-3. Electrical and Fuel Costs of Different Desalination Processes.

PROCESS	COST OF ELECTRICAL POWER	COST OF FUEL
MSF	9.8%	32.0%
VTE-MSF	5.4%	33.4%
VC-VTE-MSF	2.1%	24.0%
ED	27.5%	0 %
RO	20.4%	0 %
VF-VC	32.8%	0 %

TABLE 3-4. Land Costs of
Different Desalination Processes.

PROCESS	LAND COSTS AS A FRACTION OF TOTAL ANNUAL COSTS
MSF	3.8%
VTE-MSF	3.9%
VC-VTE-MSF	4.8%
ED	5.8%
RO	7.7%
VF-VC	0.7%

FEEDWATER AND BRINE TREATMENT FACILITIES

Of the factors which must be considered when evaluating desalting feasibility, the feedwater and brine disposal facilities may be the most site-specific variables. The costs were computed using feedwater wells 100 m deep and 1000 m from the plant, and brine injection wells 1000 m deep and 100 m from the plant. Table 3-5 presents the results. Differences in the values recorded there reflect different volumes of feedwater and brine and different overall costs. Thus, the choice of a feedwater or brine disposal system is very important in evaluating alternative processes. Feedwater wells, for example, may account for approximately 15 percent of the costs of feedwater and brine disposal systems. Another choice, evaporation ponds, would cost about 70 percent more than brine injection wells for each alternative except VF-VC, in which case they would cost approximately 7 percent less. Thus, the selection of such facilities should be considered carefully for each potential location.

Salinity Control by Improving Irrigation Systems

Improved management and structural rehabilitation are often regarded as the most feasible treatments for an irrigation system to improve the quality of return flow. Indirect approaches such as limiting irrigation diversions, establishing effluent standards and land-use regulations, and developing economic incentives might also be considered, although they appear more

TABLE 3-5. Cost Attributable to
Feedwater and Brine Disposal
Facilities of Different Desalination
Processes.

PROCESS	PERCENTAGE OF TOTAL ANNUAL COSTS ATTRIBUTABLE TO FEEDWATER AND BRINE DISPOSAL FACILITIES
MSF	21%
VTE-MSF	21%
VC-VTE-MSF	25%
ED	30%
RO	40%
VF-VC	12%

difficult to implement. Whenever salt removal is the objective, however, whatever the method used, measures should affect the segments of the irrigation system which contribute to the magnitude of local groundwater flow. This may be accomplished by reducing seepage from the various elements of the conveyance system and minimizing deep percolation due to overirrigation. Return flow quality may also be improved by relief and interceptor drainage which collect subsurface flows before a chemical equilibrium is reached with the ambient soil or aquifer materials. The respective feasibility of individual measures must, however, depend on the evaluation of cost-effectiveness functions for controlling each alternative input to the groundwater region where salt pickup is assumed to occur based on the analysis of soil and aquifer chemical behavior. Thus, the relationship between groundwater flow and salt accumulation can be determined in such a manner that control costs can be related to possible reductions in salt pickup.

The mathematics of these cost-effectiveness functions are too involved for this brief presentation. Since canal and ditch lining is among the more popular salinity control measures and demonstrates the pertinent concepts, the following discussion will be limited to this alternative.

The contribution to local or regional salinity problems of irrigation water conveyance networks may be the result of a number of factors. First, unlined channels allow seepage into underlying soils and aquifers where naturally occurring salts might then be dissolved and transported into receiving waters. Second, the structure and management of a system may support large areas of open water or phreatophytes which, through evaporation and transpiration, concentrate salinity in return flows. Finally, the operation of the system may preclude efficient water use by the individual irrigator, especially if deliveries are not made in accordance with crop needs. The costs of remedying these problems are generally incurred by those responsible for the lining and rehabilitation of the waterway. However, if improved management is necessary, some costs associated with educational programs and legal or administrative adjustments may also be incurred.

To test the feasibility of conveyance system improvements relative to other salinity control measures, the mathematical model developed in the following paragraphs will deal with one principal channel improvement—lining with concrete, one which is generally applicable in terms of both technology and cost.

Seepage from conveyance networks may be reduced or eliminated by lining the perimeter with an impervious material such as concrete, plastic, asphalt, or compacted earth. Concrete is, however, probably the most commonly employed lining material because of the combined advantages of its low cost, easy application, availability, minimal maintenance, and low permeability. The costs of concrete linings (either slip-form or gunite) will vary with local economic and topographic conditions, channel geometry and size, and requirements for water management, safety, and environmental safeguards. It is therefore important to prepare cost estimates on a case-by-case basis, although for planning purposes it is useful to have more generalized information, such as is provided by the model presented here.

A review of concrete lining costs by this author in 1976 indicated that such costs could be reasonably well estimated as a function of the wetted perimeter and updated to future conditions by using an appropriate cost index.[6] A simpler methodology based on design discharge can also be used and will provide us with a starting point.

Data presented by the United States Department of the Interior in 1963 and 1975 and by Evans, et al., in 1981 were related in the following formula:

$$U_c = k_1 Q^{k_2} \tag{3-3}$$

where,

U_c = unit lining cost ($/m)
Q = design discharge (m³/sec)
k_1, k_2 = regression coefficients[7]

After adjusting the data using the Bureau of Reclamation canal and earthwork cost index to a base time of 1980, the k_1 and k_2 values were 99.34 and 0.56 respectively. It should be noted, however, that, even in the same locale, these unit costs vary substantially. Equation 3-3, therefore, is intended only as a general estimating formula. The unit costs in equation 3-3 include only the earthwork, relocation, and lining costs; they do not include costs for fencing, diversionary structures, safety structures, etc. The latter costs are also highly variable depending upon the many site-specific conditions. An examination of such costs as given by the United States Department of the Interior showed a 1980 range from $25/m to $98/m with an average of $61.60/m.[8] Consequently, the construction cost may be written in 1980 dollars as:

$$C_c = 99.34Q^{0.56} + 61.60 \tag{3-4}$$

In addition to the construction costs, one must also consider service facilities, engineering fees, the cost of investigations, and other administrative expenses. The Bureau of Reclamation uses a factor of about 35 percent for these costs. Thus, equation 3-4 can be written for total capital cost as follows:

$$C_c = 134.11Q^{0.56} + 83.16 \tag{3-5}$$

where,

C_c = 1980 value of concrete canal linings in $/m.

In order to calculate the total costs for a given length of canal, ditch, or lateral, equation 3-5 must be calculated over the applicable length. Because water is continually being withdrawn from a conveyance channel, both wetted perimeter and discharge decline along the length of the channel. The distribution of these parameters may thus be estimated in a number of ways if specific measurements are not available. For instance, a linear decline can be assumed or the decrease can be formulated in terms of acreage distributions. Assuming a linear decrease, the wetted perimeter at a specific location would be

$$WP = WP_m(1 - bL/L_t) \qquad (3\text{-}6)$$

in which,

WP_m = the wetted perimeter at the channel inlet (m)
L = length from inlet to specified point (m)
L_t = total length of channel (m)
b = empirical constant representing the fraction of maximum wetted perimeter remaining at end of the channel.

And for the design discharge:

$$Q = Q_m(1 - bL/L_t) \qquad (3\text{-}7)$$

where,

$$Q_m = \text{inlet channel capacity } (m^3/sec).$$

Combining equations 3-5 and 3-7, we get

$$C_c = 134.11 \times Q_m{}^{0.56} (1 - bL/L_t)^{0.56} + 83.16 \qquad (3\text{-}8)$$

Then, the total capital costs for lining L meters of channel ($\bar{C}_c$) are determined by integrating equation 8 as it varies from 0 to L meters:

$$\bar{C}_c = 134.11 \times Q_m{}^{0.56} \frac{L_t}{1.56b} [1 - (1 - bL/L_t)^{1.56}] + 83.16 \times L \quad (3\text{-}9)$$

Equation 3-9 assumes that lining proceeds in the downstream direction; however, the choice of either upstream or downstream lining direction would depend on their relative cost-effectiveness. To make this choice, it is first necessary to define the salinity control effectiveness resulting from a particular lining project. The change in salt loading due to lining may be written as follows:

$$\Delta S_1 = \Delta S_c\, V_s \left[\frac{Q_g - Q_p}{Q_g} \right] 10^{-6} \qquad (3\text{-}10)$$

where,

ΔS_1 = reduction in salt loading due to the linings (metric tons/m annually).
ΔS_c = difference between the equilibrium salinity concentration in the return flows and the salt concentrations in the seepage water (mg/λ).
Q_g = total groundwater addition $(m^3/year)$
Q_p = phreatophyte use of groundwater $(m^3/year)$
V_s = total volume of seepage $(m^3/m/year)$, as

$$V_s = N_d \cdot \Delta SR \cdot WP' \qquad (3\text{-}11)$$

in which,

N_d = number of days per year seepage occurs

WP' = wetted perimeter of original channel m

ΔSR = change in seepage rate affected by lining $(m^3/m^2/day)$

It should be pointed out that ΔSR might also be written as a length-distributed parameter in this model, if measurements or other data are available.

Substitution of equations 3-6 and 3-11 into equation 10 leads to an expression than can be integrated over the length of the lining to determine the total salinity control. This expression for downstream lining would be

$$S_c = K_2 L \left(\frac{1 - bL}{2L_t} \right) \qquad (3\text{-}12)$$

in which,

$$K_2 = \Delta S_c \, N_d \, \Delta SR \left[\frac{Q_g - Q_p}{Q_g} \right] WP'_m \, 10^{-6} \qquad (3\text{-}13)$$

The question of lining direction can be addressed by approximating the marginal costs at both ends and then comparing the results. First, let K_1 and K_3 be defined respectively as follows:

$$K_1 = 134.11 \cdot Q_m^{0.56} \qquad (3\text{-}14)$$

$$K_3 = 61.60 \qquad (3\text{-}15)$$

Then the marginal cost estimate could be estimated by dividing equation 3-9 by equation 3-8:

$$MC = \frac{K_1 \, (1 - bL/L_t)^{0.56} + K_3}{K_2 \, (1 - bL/L_t)} \qquad (3\text{-}16)$$

in which,

MC = marginal lining cost estimate (\$/ton)

Thus, at the inlet where $L = O$, the marginal cost estimate (MC) would be

$$MC_i = \frac{K_1 + K_3}{K_2} \qquad (3\text{-}17)$$

whereas, at the end where $L = L_t$, the marginal cost estimate (MC_u) would be

$$MC_u = \frac{K_1 \, (1 - b)^{0.56} + K_3}{K_2 \, (1 - b)} \qquad (3\text{-}18)$$

Subtracting equation 18 from 17 and simplifying would give us

$$MC_i - MC_u = \frac{K_1}{K_2}\left(1 - \frac{1}{(1-b)^{0.44}}\right) + \frac{K_3}{K_2}\left(1 - \frac{1}{(1-b)}\right) \qquad (3\text{-}19)$$

Under the assumptions of this model, equation 3-19 will always be negative, leading us to conclude that lining should always proceed downstream. Consequently, the cost-effectiveness functions for concrete lining is determined from equations 3-12 and 3-9, by solving for the independent variable L in equation 3-12 and substituting the resulting expression into equation 3-9. The resulting cost-effectiveness function is

$$\bar{C}_c = K_1'\left[1 - \left(1 - bxf(S_c)/L_t\right)^{1.56}\right] + 83.16 \times f(S_c) \qquad (3\text{-}20)$$

in which,

$$K_1' = \frac{K_1 L_t}{1.56b} \qquad (3\text{-}21)$$

$$f(S_c) = \frac{L_t}{b} - \left[\left(\frac{L_t}{b}\right)^2 - \frac{2L_t}{K_2 b} \times S_c\right] \qquad (3\text{-}22)$$

Comparative Evaluation of Irrigation Control and Desalination

The preceding paragraphs demonstrate the complexity of determining optimal irrigation return flow quality controls. These problems of complexity can be significantly alleviated by "staging" the calculations.[9] This procedure can take several forms, but its additive format is the easiest to understand. In this format, from the array of irrigation control alternatives, the optimum is determined as a function of control level. The optimum is similarly determined for the desalting alternatives. And then, the two cost-effectiveness functions are combined to produce the optimal overall strategy. To demonstrate these concepts, desalting will be compared to canal lining for the conditions in the Grand Valley of western Colorado.

There are fourteen major canal and ditch systems in the Grand Valley, ranging in length from 74 km for the Government Highline Canal (17 m³/sec capacity) to 4 km for the Mesa County Ditch (1 m³/sec capacity). The pertinent parameters for each canal, along with the contribution of seepage to salt loading, were found by using equation 3-20. The resulting functions were then minimized using the Jacobian Differential Algorithm developed by this author and G. V. Skogerboe in 1973 for a range of possible salinity reductions desired from a canal lining program.[10] The results are presented in Figures 3-3 and 3-4. Figure 3-3 shows total capital constructions costs as a function of the realized annual salt load reduction. The upper curve is the minimum cost associated with each value on the x-axis. Underneath the upper curve are the separate costs attributed to the various valley canals. For example, if the contribution of canal seepage to the salt loading problem was to be reduced by 87,500 tons annually through lining, the capital construction cost would be approximately $27 million, with $13.5 million for the Government Highline Canal, $8.7

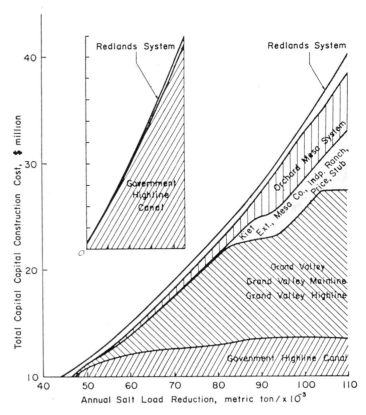

FIG. 3-3. Optimal canal lining costs as functions of annual salt reduction for the Grand Valley of western Colorado.

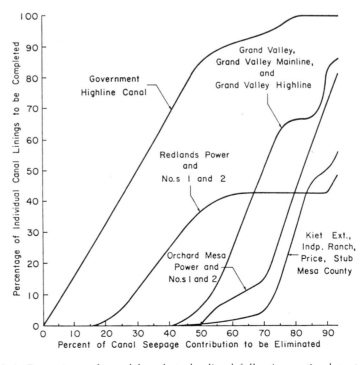

FIG. 3-4. Percentage of canal length to be lined following optimal cost policy.

million for the Grand Valley system, $2.2 million for the small ditches (e.g., Price, Stub, etc.), $1.6 million for the Orchard Mesa System, and the remainder for the Redlands system. Figure 3-4 illustrates how much of the respective canal systems would be lined under this optimal cost policy.

The results obtained when canal lining policies are optimized is interesting, for they demonstrate the need to initiate linings on more than one

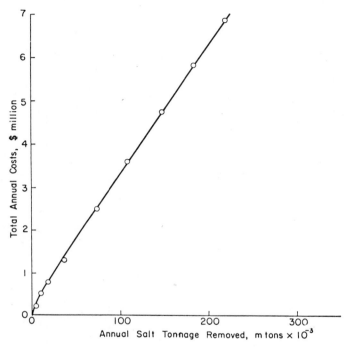

FIG. 3-5. Desalination costs as functions of annual salt removed for the Grand Valley of western Colorado.

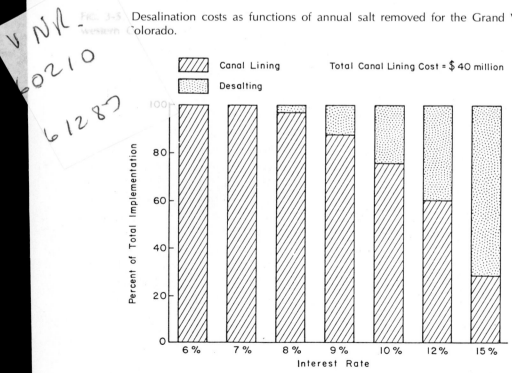

FIG. 3-6. Optimal implementation of canal lining and desalting processes for the Grand Valley of western Colorado at various interest rates and a total cost of $40 million.

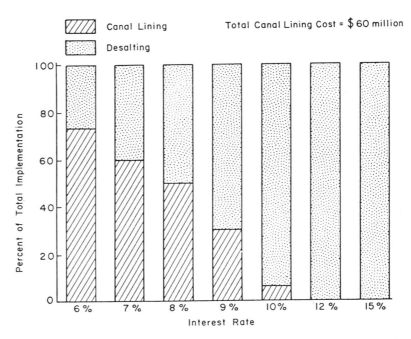

FIG. 3-7. Optimal implementation of canal lining and desalting processes for the Grand Valley of western Colorado at various interest rates and a total cost of $60 million.

segment of the conveyance system when full-scale implementation begins. The savings, if implementation occurs following an optimal cost strategy, amount to approximately 30 percent in this case.[11]

The evaluation of desalting involves, first, determining the most effective process and, second, the best feedwater-brine facilities. In the Grand Valley, reverse osmosis is clearly the most advantageous.

A summary of desalting costs as a function of salt removed is given in Figure 3-5. It might be noted here that, whereas irrigation control costs (at least for canal and ditch linings) exhibit increasing marginal costs with scale, the reverse is true for desalting technologies. Consequently, early improvements (or ones of a small scale) favor irrigation system improvements while larger operations demand desalination. Thus, rather than selecting one method, the above evaluations argue for combining technologies. Thus, if we were to advocate canal lining and desalting by reverse osmosis for the Grand Valley, we would combine Figs. 3-3 and 3-5 in an optimal manner. This optimal canal lining-desalting strategy for the Grand Valley is given in Figure 3-6 for seven values of interest, since, during the analysis, the parameter having the largest single influence on the respective feasibilities was the interest rate. Interest rates, of course, are not the only important factor. For example, Figure 3-7 was prepared using canal lining costs 50 percent higher than computed above. It is obvious that desalting would be employed more in this case. The reverse, however, would be true if our desalting cost estimates proved to be conservative.

Conclusion

Salinity management is generally one of the major water quality problems in the arid zones. Urban as well as agricultural effluents contribute to the high salinity concentration which already exists. Consequently, long before full use of water resources in a region occurs, salinity becomes a constraint on development. As one alternative for managing salinity, desalination is competitive with many measures traditionally considered. The results presented in this chapter illustrate the need to fully evaluate the various alternatives during the planning process in order to determine the most cost-effective policy.

The applications of desalination to arid-zone salinity management will increase in relative feasibility in those conditions where wastes and return flows have high salinity concentrations and where large-scale treatment is necessary. Desalting has the further advantage of being comparatively free of institutional constraints such as those encountered during modification of historical water use practices. Costs of desalting systems are very high in relation to many alternative salinity control measures, but future technological developments will undoubtedly diminish desalting costs whereas more traditional approaches may not be similarly benefited.

Notes

1. A detailed analysis of desalination costs was presented by this writer at the International Conference on Managing Saline Water for Irrigation, held in August 1976 at Texas Tech University in Lubbock. The paper was entitled ''Integrating Desalination and Agricultural Salinity Control Technologies'' and was based on W. L. Prehn, et al., *Desalting Cost Calculating Procedures,* Research and Development Progress Report no. 555 (Washington, D.C.: Office of Saline Water, United States Department of the Interior, 1970) and *Desalting Handbook for Planners* (Denver, Col.: Bureau of Reclamation and Office of Saline Water, United States Department of the Interior, 1972).
2. Walker, ''Integrating Desalination and Agricultural Salinity Control Technologies.''
3. Ibid.
4. On VF-VC, see R. F. Probstein, ''Desalination,'' *American Scientist,* **61,** no. 3 (May–June, 1973), 280–293.
5. Ion exchange has not been included here because of a high amount of total dissolved solids in the feedwater.
6. Walker, ''Integrating Desalination and Agricultural Salinity Control Technologies.''
7. See *Linings for Irrigation Canals* (Denver, Col.: Bureau of Reclamation, United States Department of the Interior, 1963), and Evans et al., *Irrigation Field Days Report* (Fort Collins: Agricultural Engineering Department, Colorado State University, 1976).
8. R. G. Evans, W. R. Walker, and G. V. Skogerboe, *Optimizing Salinity Control Strategies for the Upper Colorado River Basin,* Report No. AER 80-81RGE=WRW-GVS1 (Fort Collins: Department of Agricultural and Chemical Engineering, Colorado State University, January 1981).
9. G. L. Westeson, ''Salinity Control for Western Colorado.'' Unpublished Ph.D. dissertation, Agricultural Engineering Department, Colorado State University, Fort Collins, Colorado, June, 1975.
10. *Linings for Irrigation Canals.*
11. *Desalting Handbook for Planners.*

Suggested Readings

Bureau of Reclamation and Office of Saline Water. *Desalting Handbook for Planners.* Denver, Col.: United States Department of the Interior, 1972.

Prehn, W. L., et al. *Desalting Cost Calculating Procedures.* Research and Development Progress Report no. 555. Washington, D.C.: Office of Saline Water, United States Department of the Interior, 1970.

Probstein, R. F. Desalination. *American Scientist,* **61,** no. 3 (May–June, 1973), 280–293.

Symbol of unbaked clay (mud) at Chale'-Ghare'. Smoothed and polished through centuries, it still resists the hazards of the climate. Similar systems are found all along the desert fringe. Source: all photographs not otherwise credited are from the author's personal collection.

4
Urban Form as Physical Expression of the Social Structure in the Arid Zones of Iran

Cyrus Bavar

If you take one of the few roads that connect the towns and villages of the hot and dry parts of central Iran, within a few days you will get an overall picture of the life and the architecture of these fascinating regions. Here and there, you will come across communities flourishing in the desert; there will be conglomerates of clay and brick interwoven in the red and gold terrain. Everywhere there is the same material, the same old-looking worn-out appearance; the harmony with nature gives you the sensation of watching the same features from different angles (see Figure 4-1). In most cases, in the vicinity you can see the purple mountains that ensure the main source of water for the settlement (see Figure 4-2).

The architectural pattern is fluid and plastic; sharp angles are rare, for the long years of harsh conditions have made them soft and round. Although the settlements differ in size and scale—from less than 500 to 50,000 inhabitants and more—and sometimes they are hundreds of kilometers apart, the similarity shows the skillful touch of the same sculptor in all of them (see Figures 4-3 to 4-7).

A second glance discloses another aspect of the physical appearance of these communities: the introduction and the use of new methods of construction. Occasionally, one comes across buildings completely different from the dominant texture. Here, steel, glass, and jack-arch roofing—typical features of modern construction—can be found. These, chosen at random, look completely alien to the integrated environment.

Such structures are evidence of a more dramatic transformation during recent decades. The rapid economic development of Iran stimulated drastic changes in all directions. As a result, Iran has become a melange—a mixture of incongruous elements affecting every aspect of life.*

Background

Until recently, Iran was an agricultural country. People, despite their enduring centuries of difficult conditions, managed to grow enough food for

---

*Since this chapter was written great political changes have occurred in Iran. But this, at least for the time being, will not have much impact on the architecture in arid regions of Iran.

FIG. 4-1. Zavareh, Iran: General view.

FIG. 4-2. View of a small (population 5000) village, Aghda, Iran, with mud-brick houses and other characteristic elements. From the personal collection of Simon Ayvasian. Used with permission.

their limited population. But with the beginning of industrialization, this equilibrium was totally disturbed. Since then, the dislocation of the rural population has been immense. Fields are being abandoned, and each year fewer people show interest in working the soil. Now more than half of our food has to be imported, and the greenery around the Kavir towns is becoming less distinct. Also, the chaotic transformation of urban features stands out. The natural and geographical conditions or human factors that once were the basic elements in adopting form or material in the architecture of a community have been ignored. No matter if the particular region

FIG. 4-3. General view of suburban Natanz near Kashan, Iran.

FIG. 4-4. Rastagh, a small village near Isfahan, Iran.

is old or new, arid or humid, hot or cold, historical, industrial, or agricultural, the same material and the same forms often have been used in cosmopolitan and rural areas for all types of new buildings.

Generally, clay has been the material most frequently used in the construction of Iranian towns, though brick and wood also have been used (see Figure 4-24). Stone, except for important buildings, has been used as ornament. However, some towns like Yazd produce the best kind of marble in Iran.

Despite the introduction of modern technology, climatic and geographical conditions have not lost their impact on the architectural characteristics in the arid zones. Due to many factors, these communities, especially

FIG. 4-5. Nain (near Isfahan). General view.

FIG. 4-6. General view of Zavareh showing plasticity of forms and variety of vault-roofing.

the smaller ones, more than any other region in Iran have conserved their long-lived architectural character in harmony with nature and the private and social lives of the inhabitants. The overall homogeneity and integrity of external appearance, as well as the size and scale of houses are still preserved, and many architectural details such as internal courtyards and thick walls of clay and brick are still in use. Narrow streets, wind-towers, and *qanats* (underground canals) are there as they were hundreds of years ago.

FIG. 4-7. General view of Zavareh showing a north-south main street.

Except for the two strips in the northern and western sections of the country, Iran consists mostly of dry land and arid mountains—the dominating condition that has ruled the social structure and the physical form of more than 30,000 communities. Vast states such as Khuzistan, Kirman, Baluchistan, and much of Khorasan and Fars are considered arid according to international standards; in the center there is a desert that occupies about one fourth of the whole country. However, we will limit our study by focusing on a zone that is among the most arid regions of the world. In most of its parts, the yearly rainfall is less than 100 mm; relative humidity seldom exceeds 20 percent.

LAND AND NATURAL CONDITIONS

Viewed from the air, Iran is primarily an arid plateau with a succession of lofty and arid mountain ranges extending across the country. Here and there are areas of intense cultivation dotted around the towns. Along the shores of the Caspian Sea is a narrow strip of vivid green which stands in marked contrast to the aridity of the plateau. In the southern section, the land drops down to the waters of the Persian Gulf and the Gulf of Oman.

Iran's plateau lies about 600 m above sea level and is the remnant of an old sea; on the southeastern border is the swampy area of Sistan with an extreme temperature range and minimal annual rainfall. As Beny describes it: this plateau "encircled by five countries, . . . form[s] a vital bridge, first, within its borders between two of the most richly endowed bodies of water—the Caspian Sea and the Persian Gulf—and, second, a friendly bridge culturally, spiritually and politically, between the East and the West."[1]

Four ranges of mountains—the Zagros, extending from the northwest to the southeast; the Alburus, running parallel to the southern shores of the Caspian; the Khorasan, extending into the eastern region; and the Mokran, rising in the southeastern area—have tightly surrounded the triangle of the Iranian plateau. In the middle of the plateau, there is a lowland which is considered the most arid, lifeless desert of the world.[2] This region extends from the eastern and southern parts of Tehran, up toward Kirman, and east to the Afghanistan border and is divided into two parts: the Dasht-i-Kavir in the north and the Dasht-i-Lut in the south. The former consists of mud and salt plains where no plant grows and no animal lives. In some cavities where there is less salt, life is possible. On the other hand, Kavir-i-Lut is totally lifeless, and very few explorers have had the courage to cross it. It is said that "the great deserts of central Asia like Gobi, compared to this region, are considered fertile lands . . ."; but around the same Kavir where the riverbeds of the ancient times are situated, land is fertile and fit for agriculture. Also since there is an immense temperature difference between the summer and winter, wherever water can be provided there will be a good crop.[3]

Yet water has always been a vital problem in Iran and artificial irrigation has been common even in prehistoric times. During the reign of the Achaemenidae, *qanats* came into existence. Today, using the same system, residents in many cases carry water at a depth of nearly 100 m over distances of 30 to 40 km. In this way, they can provide water for the desert fringe towns (see Figure 4-8).

Of course, topography and climatic conditions have made adaptation very difficult. As a whole, Iran is considered a subtropical country, but natural factors such as mountains, lakes, and altitude have caused variation in different parts of the territory; cold, warm, hot, humid, dry, and extra dry are constant climatic conditions. Rainfall is directly related to the presence of mountains; but from the northwest to the southeast, this relationship becomes less apparent. Temperature fluctuation on the plateau is enormous; during the day, it gets up to 25°C. The same increase is true of the relative humidity. It differs from place to place and is lowest in the center of Iran. In the Kavir fringe region, the relative humidity fluctuates enormously during the year and even throughout the day. For example, in Yazd, the temperature fluctuates between more than 38°C in summer and −2°C in the winter. Humidity reaches a maximum of 67 percent in December and a low of 5 percent in August. Average rainfall is about 88 mm per year.[4] Because this is a dry land, the sky is serene and cloudless, and the sunshine is bright. The low humidity means a quick loss of heat, so nights are cold.

Winds, whether generated in the Kavir or coming from other parts, are dry and hot. They usually bring sand and dust and damage crops, gardens, and livestock. They cover roads, damage towns, fill rivers, and continually change the features of the land. To further complicate matters, the topography and poor road conditions limit communication and therefore assistance from one community to another.

All of the capitals of Persia, from the time of the Medes in the seventh

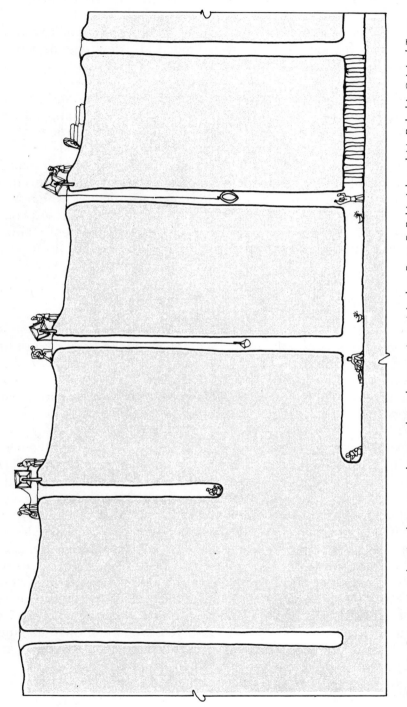

FIG. 4-8. Cross section showing how an underground canal system (*qanat*) is dug. From F. Rahimieh and M. Robubi, *Original Town and House in Iran* (Tehran: Student Society of University of Tehran, n.d.).

century B.C., have been situated along the two principal roads of the desert fringe; on the commercial and military road from the east to the west, there are Hamadan, Qazvin, Rayy, Damghan, and finally Tehran; on the road from the north to the south, there are Isfahan, Pasargade, Estakhr, and Persepolis. Religious centers like Qom and Meshed are also situated along the same roads.

Since almost all of the towns on the Kavir fringe are confined between desert and rocky mountains, mobility is limited to a few regions. Except for the route that connects Tehran, Isfahan, and Shiraz, there are usually rough, dusty, gravel roads. Access to many small towns is by way of beaten earth paths originally used by animals and now traversed by automobiles. Except for a few towns like Yazd and Kerman equipped with modern means of communication—such as a railway, an airport, etc.— many regions still lack adequate means of transportation.

Clearly, from prehistoric times to the present, life on the Iranian plateau has been constantly at the mercy of its climate and topography. Nevertheless, the Iranians have continued to build, creating structures which have reflected many aspects of their economic and social lives. These people have succeeded in adjusting to and improving their environment. Though progress is evident, the process has been arduous and not always rewarding.

HISTORICAL SETTING

The history of the Kavir fringe communities situated around the great desert of central Iran goes back to the age known as the beginning of the Epoch Arid. At this time, the mountain-dwelling hunters followed their animals and moved from their caves to vegetated areas near riverbeds. There they built mud-brick houses, cultivated food, wove fabrics, and made pottery. From this time, there was progressive and continuous development of this civilization.

As a result of centuries of building and rebuilding, these settlements multiplied and gradually became important centers that connected the East and the West for thousands of years. The oldest settlement known in the plateau is Sialk (near Kashan), established about 5000 B.C. Excavations reveal architectural forms and remnants of these people's pottery and utensils that are very similar to what we find in small villages today. Objects like seashells indicate that Sialk has long had trading relations with the settlers of the Persian Gulf. Basically, there were three successive periods of civilization in Sialk. The existence of early civilization has been proved in Rayy, Qom, Saveh, and Damghan. The chain of settlements on the Kavir fringe kept expanding; by the time of the Achaemenidae (c. 500 B.C.), Isfahan (Aspadana), Kashan, and Yazd were well-established communities, and Veramin, Kerman, and Robat-i-safid during the reign of Sasanians (640 to 222 B.C.) were important centers. In time, Natanz, Ardestan, Nain, Bafgh, Bam, and other smaller settlements eventually came into existence.

The progress in these towns was slow but steady. The unfavorable natural conditions, such as being scattered across hundreds of kilometers of rough land and having the traveling caravans as the only means of communication, considerably slowed down the progress of civilization.

However, the same geographical situations helped them become for many centuries one of the main reference points for transactions between the different cultures of the East and the West. They absorbed these cultures and developed them. The Arab invasion (A.D. 642) provided an early opportunity. In spite of Islam's ban of various kinds of art, it encouraged new ideas and concepts that enriched architecture all over Iran.[5] Throughout the reigns of the caliphates, Samanids, and Seljuks, civilization kept on flourishing. Finally, in the early 13th century Rayy and Kashan's art reached a climax.

During the Mongol invasion of Persia (A.D. 1220), "the finest cities of Persia were obliterated, their inhabitants slaughtered in ghastly heaps, [and] only abandoned ruins . . ." remained.[6] But the urban culture of the Persians overcame the nomadic habits of the Mongols. Towns were rebuilt; and by the time of the Safavid Dynasty (1499 to 1736), they reached the height of their prosperity. Architecture by this time was refined and mature, everywhere encrusted with dazzling tiles.

Patronage has always played a vital role in Persian art. After the Safavids were overthrown by Mahmood Afghan in 1730, there was a short period of military strength and prosperity under the reign of Nader-Shah-Afshar (1736 to 1748) and Karim-Khan-i-Zand that came to an end with the conquest of Qajar tribes from northern Iran. During the reign of Qajarieh (1779 to 1925) and because of continuous wars, the incompetence of Qajar kings, their religious fanaticism, and the newly-born problem of Western countries trying to exploit the natural resources, the state of the country's economy suffered a constant decline. As a result, the patronage of art became limited to support of painting and literature. With few exceptions, the art of construction was left to a group of mediocre masons. Unlike the master builders of the Safavid period who perfected the systems of the past and invented brilliant new ways of building and decorating buildings, these people were only copying from the past— making bad copies that lacked the precision of form and construction and harmony in color of the originals.

With the development of better means of transportation, the construction of new roads, and the flourishing of important towns in other areas, most of the towns of the Kavir fringe began to seem less important. These disadvantages plus the previously mentioned natural barriers gradually pushed these towns into isolation. With the mid-20th century industrialization of the country, depopulation precipitated the decline.

When we look at social influences, and more specifically religious ones, we will see three major religious movements in Iranian history. Each has had an impact on the life, culture, and the social organization of the community. Paganism gave way to Mithraism (worship of the sun-god) with the migration of Aryans. Theism was introduced by the prophet Zoroaster in the form of Dualism—the constant war between God and the devil. This religion basically advocated good deeds, pure thoughts, and unadulterated language (600 B.C.). Zoroastrians worshiped divinity in fire temples. Islam brought monotheism and many other new concepts to Iran.

Each of these religious movements had its impact on the life-style and consequently on the civilization's art and architecture. With the dominance of Mithra, there were hundreds of fire temples. Later there were numerous mosques. Furthermore, though the temples and fire temples were owned and run by priests and magi, the philosophy of Islam, its rituals, and the mosque itself were a part of the everyday life of the people. Many schools of language and theology were attached to the mosques, and Muslim rulers showed great enthusiasm in building schools and universities (madrasseh). It is interesting to see that in spite of the frequent struggles and the trying times, and in spite of inevitable problems resulting from cultural differences, the urban pattern and architecture inspire consistency and harmony and reflect the material and nonmaterial aspects of their life. As Arthur U. Pope says,

> She [Iran] has invented and perfected certain basic forms and techniques which enabled her to develop an architecture marked by imposing scale, simplicity, and expressiveness of mass. . . . No historical shock, however drastic, completely broke the chain. Interruptions there were, yet they always permitted, even provoked, a resumption.[7]

Influence of the Physical Environment

Geographical conditions play an important role in any art that has a long history in one region. Art expresses character; it is born of practical as well as spiritual needs, and its elements are all drawn from experience.[8] The territorial environment sets the stage for all of man's activities, defines his opportunities, conditions him mentally and physically, and supplies both material and motives for his art. While geography has become less important in more complex, cosmopolitan communities, every single element in the desert towns of Iran—with negligible exceptions—indicates the relationship between geography and architecture; high walls to withstand sand storms, wind towers, qanats, interwoven houses, and narrow, winding streets which produce sufficient shade are only a few examples.

Climate has its own role. The air in the desert area of Iran is dry and clear. Rain is a rarity; for several months in a year, the sky is clear, cloudless, and very blue. At night the sky is full of bright, shining stars; it is as if you can stretch out your hand and touch them. It is said that Kerman has the most beautiful sky in the world. The contrast between the architecture of the cold, dark northern areas and that of the hot, dry, and highly illuminated regions is familiar to all, and Persian architecture was forced to various expedients to subdue light often so intense that it seemed incandescent.

Natural resources have power over the arts. In Persia crafts were closely related to the supply of raw materials. Persians could make good carpets, beautiful pottery, and good silk; but they did not advance in the art of porcelain. Carpet weaving flourished where wool, water, and a proper source of dye was available. Kashan and Natanz, to this day, are famous for pottery because essential ingredients are accessible, such as the needed type of clay. Silk weaving was very well-developed in Yazd, Isfahan, and Kashan where the silkworm flourished, and wood carving was found in Caspian regions. Even the radiant colors of miniatures were made possible by the availability of mineral dyes. The lack of kaolin was the reason porcelain did not develop in Iran as it did in China.

Themes and motifs were provided by the environment. In the beginning, the people drew animals, but they later turned to trees and flowers. The flora, so dramatic in the natural setting, inspired in Persians a passionate and mystical flower worship—from the Achaemenid pomegranate, to the Sasanian tree, to the botanically perfect flower of the Safavids. But these people did not just imitate nature; they also created images of dragons, winged monsters, and the like that had no parallel in nature. They also developed and altered the illustration of flowers at later dates. With the Mongol invasion, Chinese miniatures became an important influence and developed to the extent that they became an indispensable part of Persian art. Gradually, the miniaturists began to use traditional Persian motifs—flowers, animals, and geometric design—and adorned their work with Persian calligraphy. By the 15th century, you can find the essence of the whole history of Persian art in one single work. Geometric motifs have always had an important role. They are especially notable in the design of glazed tiles used on the inside and outside of buildings.

When we examine Iran's potential, we can see that it offers the optimal environment for fostering productive energy. Where life is too hard, mere survival absorbs all strength and ability. Where life is too easy, there is a lack of stimulus and equally sterile inertia results. In Iran's history, the people have managed to rise above their daily needs. Because of this, they have used their environment to advantage.

Influence of Culture and Tradition

The art of Iran since early times has played an influential role in the history of the world. Iran's deepest concerns and most significant ideals are incorporated in her art. For instance, the most important factors influencing, motivating, and supporting Persian art, in general, and Persian architecture, in particular, are religion, poetry, mathematics, the natural environment, and political and economic issues. Each of these has some-how been reflected in the three major characteristics of Persian art: continuity, conservatism, and traditionalism.

Arthur U. Pope considers continuity as the major characteristic of Persian art. This characteristic provides a common thread through all changes of fashion. Pope says Persian history witnessed different courses of philosophy, different religions, invasions, and catastrophes; but no matter how great a shock may have been, the course of Iranian art continued: ". . . thus the principle of continuity so substantial and so characteristic, became in itself a historic canon . . ."[9] During centuries of exposure to numerous invasions, these people had developed a kind of defense mechanism in the form of resistance to new ideas and imposed new ways of life; they did adopt concepts, but in their own way. This interrelated traditionalism and conservatism, together with their inborn pride, helped them to conserve their identity throughout history. The Mongol invasion proved the survival power of Persian tradition; although libraries were destroyed, methods of thinking were cherished by a handful of scholars who had escaped the mass murder; great epics, recited by heart, passed from one generation to another. Moreover, geographical features favored conservation of old ways. The local artisan, no matter who was governing, continued as before.

Religion and art, the two fundamental and eternal concerns of humanity, have always been related to each other. In the central plateau of Iran, religion presided at the birth of art and in some form sustained it through its maturity. It has provided motifs, checked art's progress during the early Islamic period, and finally promoted the masterpieces of the Safavid period. Religious ideas not only dominated motifs for small artisans and famous artists who were at the service of kings and influential priests, but also were strong influences on features of towns and consumed economic resources in construction of mosques, temples, monuments, and *madrasseh*. The influence of religious beliefs is likewise clearly reflected in the architecture of houses up to this date.

However, the Arab invasion brought drastic changes. With Islam came a new language and a political and social reorientation. Old habits and traditions were replaced by new doctrines, interests, and values. But as sudden and deep as this interruption was, the invaders had no powerful artistic doctrine and achievement which could take root in this moment of confusion. Persian architects were no longer called to build colossal palaces.

In the beginning, the Islamic philosophy of sacrificing the material life for the coming life after death drew all attention to the erection of mosques; and other local buildings imitated the design of mosques. It took centuries before what we know as Islamic architecture developed. The Arabs appear to have been greatly awed by the glory and sophistication of Persian palaces. As their power grew, the Arabian caliphates began to imitate the Persian court and government systems. During the reign of the Abbassides, important offices such as ministers of the caliphate were occupied by Persians who patriotically promoted science and art. Many learned men of the court were Persians, too. Thus it was Persian civilization that influenced the Islamic world of the time. The Arabic language did affect the Iranian mentality by facilitating the means of their expressing themselves. The iconoclastic tendencies of Islam helped to expel the Hellenistic naturalism of Sasanid times, focusing attention toward the very different world of metaphysics; ''. . . but in depth, the Iranian spirit was scarcely stirred by these inferior aliens.''[10]

Architecture was slow to reflect the new era. The Muslims used the old fire temples, and mosques followed Sasanian models—Ivan and Tagh-i-Kasra—for centuries. It took almost three centuries before Islamic philosophy was clearly reflected in Persian art; by then, it had become an integral part of the whole pattern.

Established religion is almost invariably conservative; the divinely ordained scheme must be protected from human vagaries. In the beginning, it was a vehicle for the expression of broadly religious ideas which would not likely be subject to change. The Sasanian religion involved a long established reverence for ancient ideas. Since the Islamic religion was in itself conservative, it helped intensify the conservatism of the Persians.

When Islam became the official religion and sole repository of law and was incorporated into daily life, it naturally was bound to have a deep influence on the Persian culture. However, national pride and the belief in their own civilization enabled the Persians to exploit this religion. They altered and mastered Islam's teachings; and by the time of the caliphates, in art, architecture, politics, science, and administration, Persian ideals, habits, and thought prevailed.

During the first three centuries of Islam, architecture was the master art, especially in the construction of religious buildings all over the invaded world. It continued to be so for many centuries and was enriched by other contemporary arts. There was, for example, the beautiful calligraphy that adorned the most beautiful masterpieces.[11] The art itself, and particularly some principles of design, definitely reflect the Persians' traditional interest in mathematics. Exactness and practicality are obvious in their well-calculated planning and design as well as in the rationality of the traditional use of urban land.

When we look at the long surviving expressions of culture and tradition, it is important to note that the geographical features favored the retention of the local culture in various parts of the plateau. Here life proceeded much as before, and the common artisans continued to work in the old style which bolstered the conservatism of their art. When we look at the significance of artistic expressions and attitudes on a social level, we will see that the continuity of basic principles in urban forms on the one hand and the changes of character in art and architecture on the other (through many social adjustments) can illuminate the relation between aesthetic culture and political and economic background.

For many centuries within their feudalistic government, patronage was a strong tradition; so the best works of art and architecture belong to the periods when there was a powerful monarch such as Shah Abbass-i-Safavid supporting them. That is why most of the works of art in Iran have been in monumental form and scale and why the popular architecture has continued on its own. But since all classes were dominated by traditionalism, popular customs and beliefs indirectly controlled even the taste of monarchs who reflected these traditions in their achievements.

Urban Characteristics

The desert fringe communities vary in size and importance: there are small villages and well-developed cities. In the small settlements there is usually a cluster of mud houses where man and beast live side by side. A few other elements such as a public bath or a school building may be the dominant features (see Figure 4-9).

The structure of these communities is very simple. Houses are built where there is some source of water. A few cultivated areas surround the whole community. Survival is the main concern. In front of each house—and in many cases for a group of houses—there is a mud oven (*tanour*) where the people bake their bread or cook their food. Occasionally, the oven is inside a room.

Uniting the community there is usually a chief, the patron, *kadkhoda*, or patriarch of the community. He manages the community's everyday life and acts as a judge in the case of quarrels and conflicts. For more serious problems and needs such as hospitalization and higher education, such a community is almost totally dependent on nearby towns.

Each town or old historic village has its unique characteristics. Indeed, each of them has its own identity, and we can follow the influences of ancient civilizations through the gradual changes in architectural design. The relationships among the features of a town indicate a response to the

FIG. 4-9. Zavareh, on the fringe of the desert.

climatic condition and cultural needs. Yazd, Kashan, Zavareh, and Aghda are typical examples. Here city walls, houses, *caravanserais*, water reservoirs, ice reservoirs, *qanats*, gardens, bazaars, and other elements show how these people confronted their geographical barriers, established economic relations, and built safety features (see Figures 4–1 to 4-11).

The desert communities, like most cities of Iran, had a marked focus and circumference. A protective wall marked the outer limits, while the center was composed of either a fortress or an open square—and later a mosque and bazaar. The town which exists within the citadel walls (see Figure 4-10) goes back many centuries, whereas the walled town with an open space as the principal feature appeared much later.[12] The protective wall has surrounded almost every group of buildings. For instance, as Pope explains, even ". . . an orchard will be enclosed by a wall with a tower at each corner; a farm or village will have, in addition, a tower or two flanking chief entrances. . . . *Caravanserais*, when isolated, are especially adequately protected."[13]

The city wall is usually made of sun-dried bricks and is very thick at the base and narrow near the top. A wall for defensive purposes was sometimes encircled by a moat, often very wide and deep. In those instances, the entrance to the city was by a viaduct. The towers along the wall were high and usually circular. These walls and towers, still visible in most towns and villages, are sometimes in use today, but now they function as army bases and barracks. The ancient wall and the citadel of Bam are very good examples of this complex protective element (see Figures 4-12 and 4-13).

FIG. 4.10. Nain. View showing the old citadel.

FIG. 4-11. Nain.

Where a square or *maydan* served as a focus of a city, the principal monuments were the palace or the Friday Mosque, with the government house and the bazaar. The best example of this system is Isfahan.

City planning was also determined by the social structure. The segregation of classes and crafts could be seen in the layout of the quarters and streets. The city was generally divided into quadrants and other subdivisions which were usually occupied by particular classes of people. Today, even though this kind of division has been abandoned, these quarters are

FIG. 4-12. Citadel and protective wall, Bam, Iran. From the personal collection of Farhad Soltani. Used wth permission.

FIG. 4-13. Wall and citadel of the old town of Bam. From the personal collection of Farhad Soltani.

still called by the names of the classes which originally frequented them. For instance, one often finds the Arab quarter or the potters' quarter.

As we can see, the cities' structure was practical and functional. However, gradually the original simple plan of a definitely marked center and circumference, with the two main roadways connecting the chief city gates and cutting the enclosed area into quadrants, was blurred by growth. Houses were built outside, and the city extended beyond its outline— sometimes in the form of an evenly distributed periphery and sometimes as an adjacent settlement. Today's townscapes of old cities of the plateau on the desert fringe do not follow exactly the pattern of the *maydan* or have the citadel as their focus. The main focus today is the complex typically represented by the bazaar and Friday Mosque (see Figure 4-14).

In bigger towns, where the introduction of modern transportation has required different kinds of roads, some wide asphalt roads have been constructed. In most instances, new streets have cut through the existing narrow and winding streets and alleys with no regard for the real nature of the town or its integrated texture (see Figure 4-15). At the crossroads, the municipalities have made circular areas around which new means of entertainment such as movie theaters are situated. There are usually pools

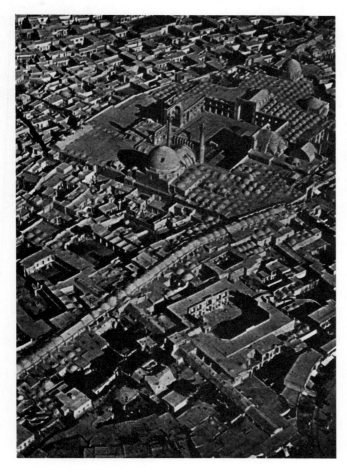

FIG. 4-14. Typical view of a desert community showing the vertebrate column of the bazaar connecting the mosque and *caravanserais* and popular zones. From the personal collection of H. Toofanian.

Fig. 4-15. Yazd, Iran. View showing new roads cutting into the old texture.

and fountains in these areas. But although these complexes of *maydan*, movies, and newly built shops have composed a center of attraction, people still prefer to gather, to do business, and have social intercourse in the bazaar. The cool, adequately lit, cozy, and intimate environment of the bazaar is much preferred, especially by the older members of the society. The *maydan* has seldom had an important role in the life of these people because of its openness, exposing the occupants to the hot sun and making the threat of theft or attack of more concern.

In so far as the landscape is concerned, these communities are somewhat two-dimensional. There is a flat surface on which buildings (at most two stories) are spread horizontally. In this panorama, towers, minarets, and domes wth their shining turquoise tiles against the clay roofs and the sandy background are outstanding. These elements have actually become the vertical reference points, while the bazaar complex—(the mosque, the old attached *caravanserai*, which now functions as a warehouse, the bazaar itself, and a small *maydan* in front of it) is the horizontal reference point (see Figures 4-5 and 4-14).

Today, with the emergence of a piped water system, rapid transportation, electric coolers, refrigerators, etc., many of the architectural elements of the town, such as water reservoirs, ice reservoirs, and *caravanserais*, are losing their function. Many are being demolished, and others are being used for new purposes.

When we look for the reasons these changes originally took place, we see that an increase in security accompanied them. For example, in Qazvin, the original determining feature was the avenue connecting the palace to the principal mosque. This artery became the focus of the business life of the city and gave life to the concept of the bazaar. Afterward, with the flourishing of commerce, the *caravanserais* gained more importance and became the terminus of the main street; and the mosque became a part of the bazaar.[14] In many cities like Qazvin, the commercial route passes by the face of the *caravanserais* and goes through the bazaar, thus forming an artery connecting one side of the town with the other. In this way, the goods can be directly delivered to the merchants. But the great mosque still is the focus of the internal life of the city. Therefore, many streets and lanes connect different parts of the town to the mosque (see Figure 4-14).

There have been other changes in the structure of the city itself. By the 16th century, protective city walls began to lose their function, for they were scarcely needed. Houses, each in its own walled garden, were crowded together making a compact and many-walled mass (see Figures 4-16 and 4-17). Open planning also permitted the creation of bigger and more beautiful gardens.

Let us have a look at Yazd—the characteristic desert fringe town.[15] It was originally enclosed in an unfired brick wall with six towers and one gate. The bazaar was situated by the gate and continued to a *maydan* called Lord. Shops, *hojreh*, were situated along both sides of the passage leading to a *caravanserai*. The central quarter of Yazd, still intact, tells us a lot about pre-Islamic times. Here there is a bastion pattern with perpendicular streets all connected to the Lord square. Almost all major streets run north-south, and the narrow streets together with the height of the walls create enough shade to make hot summer afternoons sufferable (see Figure 4-18). The houses in the community are usually two stories; the basement is used to store food and the ground floor to shelter the animals; the rest of the home is designed for the family. These structures were made of unfired earthen bricks. The wind tower system helps keep the shelter cool and aired.

The structure and patterns can still be seen in most arid-zone towns of Iran. Courtyards and internal gardens are below street level in order to provide more shade (see Figures 4-18 and 4-19). Outside the bastion are cultivated areas that have expanded with the population. Irrigation has always been man-made; water comes from wells and *qanats*. In smaller communities, the first public element to appear was baths near sources of water. These were followed by a coffee shop, a bakery, and the like. It is interesting to note that the mosque was not the first public building to be erected.

These small communities led a collective life; people's duties were

FIG. 4-16. Yazd. Typical urban elements.

FIG. 4-17. Composition of houses in Yazd.

interrelated, and they acted as a part of an extended family. In fact, the family pattern was obvious in all aspects of the social structure, and it gave the communities the integrity that still exists today. The architecture

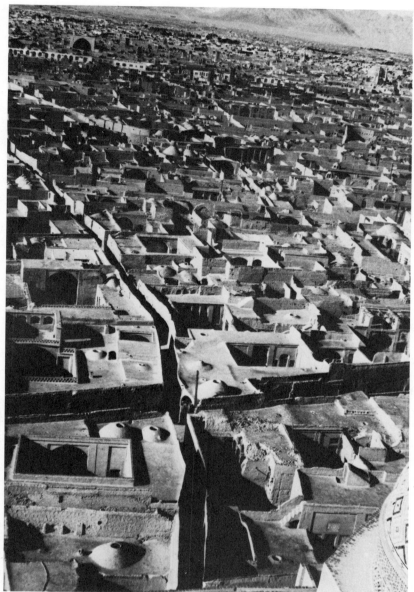

FIG. 4-18. View of the old town of Yazd showing two crossing streets, courtyards, and other elements.

even reflected the collective physical, economical, and cultural needs of these people. Expansion was through organic growth: different construction occurred when it was needed and when the existing means permitted its development.

Within each family unit, patterns of behavior were predictable. Each family used to keep some poultry, a milking cow, or a goat in the house. They were mostly peasants working the land and using their extra time on handicrafts or other indoor activities. With the gradual growth of the societies, new social classes, such as the clergy or merchants, emerged and gave birth to professional classes. The changes were acceptable to the society at large, for their long-lived feudal system of government favored class distinction.

FIG. 4-19. Agha School in Kashan, Iran. Note level of the yard in comparison to the street.

Urban and Architectural Elements

In Persia, artistic crafts have always been closely related to the supply of raw material. In the desert zones the available materials are limited. Limestone, imported wood, and clay are the cheapest and most frequently used. Modern materials such as steel and cement are recent introductions used primarily for the foundations or roofs of some important or commercial buildings. New materials—especially the combination of steel and glass—are being increasingly used; they facilitate construction by making it simple and quick. However, these buildings seldom reflect anything characteristic of arid regions.

FIG. 4-20. Roofing system and plantation ring used in Bam. From the personal collection of Farhad Soltani.

FIG. 4-21. Typical ventilation and lighting system, Kashan.

STONE

The use of stone goes back to prehistoric times because of its availability in most parts of the arid regions. It was usually used when permanence was the primary consideration—in fortresses, great *caravanserais*, bridges, and mosques. Ali-Abad *caravanserai* on the old road between Reyy and Saveh is of stone, for example.

WOOD

Though wood is scarce, it has also been used for many centuries for roofs and porches, as binders to increase the elasticity of brick buildings, and as

FIG. 4-22. Roof ventilation in Nain. From the personal collection of Simon Ayvazian. Used with permission.

beams set horizontally in the walls. The most frequently used wood has almost always been cypress. In the old buildings, the other wooden elements such as doors and windows are usually beautifully worked. They are massive in size and ornamented with carvings or metalwork, and they give a sense of beauty, solidity, and durability. Today, this woodwork is being replaced by metal.

BRICK

The use of unfired brick goes back to 5000 B.C., but from the Sasanid period brick played an important role in construction. In central Persia, brick was introduced during the reign of Qaznavids (c. A.D. 1000) and was more generally used by the time of the Seljuks (c. A.D. 1100).

FIG. 4-23. Typical light and ventilation system, Yazd.

FIG. 4-24. A cistern along the road, Aghda.

It is understandable why this material was so frequently used. Due to the small size of the units, brick has surprising elasticity. It has withstood distortion to a degree that Greek or Roman masonry could not endure. Brick was cheap and permitted experimentation, so there developed various new and important structural forms. Experience with raw and fired bricks helped to develop the fundamental forms. By the time of the Seljuk period, the decorative possibilities of brick also replaced the glazed mural paintings of former times.

Of course, not all types of bricks are equally adaptable to these purposes. Sun-dried bricks have advantages over oven-fired bricks for flexibility and adjustability. An overhead view of a Persian desert town showing thousands of vaults defying all regularity (see Figures 4-20 to 4-23) gives the impression that there is nothing that cannot be done with a vault built of unfired bricks. Both unfired and fired bricks are the most commonly used materials throughout Iran, and they dominate Kavir architecture. Besides being the common materials found in the architecture of the country, they are also the distinguishing features in the arid-zone towns of Iran, and an integral part of these communities; in spite of modernization of urban design, they still function as indispensable components of these towns.

QANAT

In a land where there are many rainless months in a year, water is very important. Centuries ago, inhabitants of the Iranian plateau learned how to combat the scarce supply of water in the city. Their original sources were great cisterns and undependable water supplies—wells and rivers with temporary water. Later, the water was transported through underground

FIG. 4-25. Water reservoir with wind towers, Yazd.

canals (*qanats*) that to this day protect it from evaporation and carry it from the mountain foot to the settlement clean and fresh (see Figure 4-8). This system made possible the continuation of life in the area and even permitted the people to cross the dreadful central desert of Iran.

The *qanat* system was a well-developed application of the underground tunnel plan. It consisted of many wells of different depths that were connected at the bottom through canals. These canals stretched all the way to the mountains or hills where enough water was available throughout the year. Sometimes the distance exceeded 10 km, and the canals were at a depth of close to 100 m. The water so provided was then stored in reservoirs and used for everyday life—for public baths, mosques, gardens, groves, and the cultivated areas surrounding the town. In the confrontation between man and nature in Persia, man has often been victorious. Water transported from icy streams in the mountains also had the effect of moderating the temperature in the areas where it was used.

AB-E-ANBAR

Seasonal rivers and wells were useful, but the only way of satisfactorily providing the water from these sources was through a conduit and storage systems. The conduit might be underground or at the surface of the water, but the reservoir (*ab-e-anbar*) would eliminate evaporation. In central Iran, water storage systems were highly developed. Here roofed tanks kept the river water or rainwater for a long period; there were also reservoirs that could automatically gather rainwater and reserve it. The tank was always situated underground, and a vault at ground level covered it. In order to keep the water fresh and ventilated, wind towers were built around the tank. These specially designed towers carried air down to the surface of the water (see Figures 4-24 to 4-27).

FIG. 4-26. Famous cistern with six wind towers, Yazd.

FIG. 4-27. Water reservoir, Yazd.

FIG. 4-28. View of the old bazaar, Kashan.

Because of their importance, *ab-e-anbars* are situated near crossroads and therefore create a reference point. These reservoirs used to be sized to the scale of the whole town. In some cases, as in Yazd, each house had its own *ab-e-anbar*. Along the desert roads, there used to be water tanks and domed cisterns every two leagues (12 km). These could be seen from a distance (see Figure 4-24).

YAKHCHAL (ICE RESERVOIR)

Still another public amenity designed to alleviate summer discomfort was the storage pit in which the winter ice or snow could be kept through the hot months. Usually such a pit was underground; but today, one often sees a kind of beehive hut built of clay for this purpose. To exploit the winter cold, the clay walls were built high and thick against the sun to

FIG. 4-29. Inside Yazd's bazaar.

produce permanent shade. In the winter, as ice formed behind these walls, it was gathered and stored in these deep pits and protected by a vault or dome. The thick clay layers provided a very efficient insulation that preserved the ice for many months. Even in Tehran, before electric refrigerators became commonly used, one could buy natural ice in summer.

CARAVANSERAI

In modern times, as in the old days, the *caravanserai* can be a combination of a motel, a commercial center, a water station, a protective fort, a station for road services, and a refreshment stand for the traveling man and his animal. It is as old as commerce itself. Basically, a *caravanserai* consists of a square which is surrounded by a protective wall and is guarded by one fortress on each corner. Two more fortresses, often higher and more complicated, flank the entrance gate. The lodgings were originally built around the central square. The space between the wall and the living quarters was arranged for the animals. On both sides of the gate there were staircases leading to a second floor where usually the lodgings for the privileged classes were located. The residential area was always equipped with a well or a water reservoir.

FIG. 4-30. Vault in a bazaar where two *rastehs* cross.

Most *caravanserais* were situated by roads and were found a day's travel apart. Others were near shrines or *madrasseh*, and some were adjacent to the bazaar. The *caravanserai* and the bazaar were the most distinctive and most important features in the town. The *caravanserai* was indispensable in Persia, for food and water supplies were uncertain and there was a danger of nomad raids. It was also a cultural institution of considerable importance. Here people of all classes met, so there was always a constant exchange of ideas and information. Today, the remaining *caravanserais* have acquired different functions: those on the roads are mostly used as army bases; those flanking the bazaar have been turned into embarkment stations, warehouses, and shops; and the Shah-Abbas Grand Hotel in Isfahan was originally a *caravanserai* adjacent to a *madrasseh*.

BAZAAR

The bazaar has always been a very important element in Iranian society. Not only is it the connecting link between two or more of the most important reference points in the town, but it is also the place where the influential merchants and clergy are in continuous contact. The bazaar also has always had a great role in the political events in Iran. In general, it is the center of movement and energy in every town.

Fig. 4-31. Bazaar in Kashan.

The bazaar has a linear architecture; it begins at a *maydan*, but its direction is different in each town. It consists of a complex of galleries with a vaulted roof. Where the galleries (*rastehs*) meet, the intersection forms a much higher vault. On the top of each vault, there is a hole that takes care of light and ventilation for the interior. On the two sides of these galleries, shops (*hojreh*) are situated side by side on a platform about 70 to 100 cm above the central passageway. These shops or *hojrehs* are in the form of pavilions, and their doors are opened exclusively to the inside passage (see Figures 4-28 to 4-32).

Except for the shops, alongside the *rastehs* there are mosques, coffee houses, water fountains, baths, schools, and one or more *caravanserais*. The Friday Mosque usually is also connected to the bazaar. Thus we can see that the linear complex of the bazaar in itself functions as an integrated body as well as a vital artery in the life of the town. It blends in

FIG. 4-32. Illumination and ventilation of typical bazaar.

with the texture of surrounding residential quarters so that the only access to some of them is through the bazaar.

Along the galleries, at different intervals, the continuation of shops is interrupted by an opening that leads to the courtyard of a mosque or to a *caravanserai*. Here there is air and light and a view of the trees and the small pool which gives a sense of freshness to the passerby. When we look at the functional structure of the bazaar, once again we see the traditional class division: each profession—blacksmiths, shoemakers, goldsmiths, and other professional groups—has its own section.

FIG. 4-33. Wind tower and living quarters, second floor of aristocratic house, Sirjan, Iran.

FIG. 4-34. Wind tower, Nain.

However, today in big cities like Tehran, the bazaar is losing its position in the commercial life of the people; it has to compete with office buildings, supermarkets, and department stores. Nevertheless, it has always kept its essential role in the old texture of the town and smaller communities.

WIND TOWER

One of the most conspicuous features in arid-zone cities like Yazd and Kashan where the temperature runs high, is the wind tower (see Figures 4-33 to 4-37). The structure is a solid and usually square shaft, from 8 to 15 m high, with an open colonnade top which carries air down into the underground chamber where the family takes refuge during the hot season. Each house of any consequence is equipped with a tower, while the great houses have several. Wind towers and ventilated reservoirs keep the water fresh. The direction of wind tower openings is invariably toward the prevailing wind.

Houses

The type of house built in the arid zone is a dominating factor·in the town design. It may be big or small, decorated or plain; but the designs,

FIG. 4-35. Alley showing arch and wind tower of a house, Yazd.

FIG. 4-36 Ventilation system, Bam. From the personal collection of Soltani and Heiat.

FIG. 4-37. Famous wind tower which catches wind from all directions, Sirjan.

patterns and even the materials used in a private house are all similar. Together the houses form a homogeneous background that binds all the horizontal and vertical elements in an integrated complex (see Figures 4-38 and 4-39).

FIG. 4-38. View of Zavareh, showing yards and wind towers. From the personal collection of Hamid Toofanian.

The typical unit is a small house with a small courtyard in the center, around which rooms are arranged. Walls and roofs are thick and made of clay or brick; the yard is situated on a lower level so that it is shaded most of the time (see Figure 4-40). It retains the cool night air for a long time during the day and at the same time keeps the private life of the women in the house out of the sight of strangers. The concept of walled houses seen all over Iran today is more emphasized by the religious concept of women's status and function in the social life than by the necessity for protection. The common traditional belief of Muslims has been that women should be kept covered and in the house.

All the rooms open toward the yard; some have small windows that look onto the alley. In this year-round home, the *ivan* (a three-sided room) is an important part of the house. The one facing north is always in the shade and is used during the summer, and the one facing south is used during the winter when the sun is shining (see Figures 4-41 to 4-43). These houses are built together back-to-back and wall-to-wall, forming a conglomerate separated here and there by narrow, winding alleys. These lanes in some parts are covered by a vault or projection on a house. They form a small square (*hashti*), and many doors of the houses open onto the *hashti*. It is said that one of the reasons for covered alleys is to prevent a man on horseback from passing through—i.e., a defense against raiders (see Figure 4-44). In the past, some private houses—especially those of the time of the Seljuks—were distinguished by the glamor and decorations which usually characterized great religious buildings: carved plaster, elaborate brick facing, and turquoise glazed tiles were a few typical features (see Figure 4-45).

Conclusion

The inhabitants of central Iran, the people who have chosen to live on the fringe of one of the most arid deserts of the world, have century after century been building and rebuilding to create the architecture of their arid zones. Highly developed art appeared in Iran with the first civilization; but in contrast to the Greek art, the primary purpose of art was not representation but decoration. In the Iranian art of almost all periods, this passion for decoration was realized with impeccable technical skill and prolific inventiveness. Safavid architecture is a living example.

In the chain of communities of the desert region, life is harsh and the

(A)

(B)

FIG. 4-39. (A) General view of Chale' Ghare'. From the personal collection of Cyrus Bavar; (B) detailed view of Chale' Ghare'. From the personal collection of Iraj Shahrooz. Used with permission.

struggle for survival intense; but the people kept advancing slowly and solidly. Conquerors from the north, south, east, and west kept raiding, plundering, and massacring; but these people continued to create, invent, and construct. Caravans, hoping for a fruitful trade and relying on the facilities these communities promised, kept traveling in all directions from one town to the other. These caravans, besides carrying different kinds of merchandise, also conveyed new devices and inventions, ideas, and phi-

FIG. 4-40. Yard of rich man's house, Kashan. From the personal collection of Hamid Toofanian.

FIG. 4-41. Internal courtyard, Natanz. From the personal collection of Hamid Toofanian.

FIG. 4-42. Citadel of Bam.

losophies. In these regions where the only channels of communication were earth and gravel roads, the caravans were the real link among towns, people and civilizations.

However, the introduction of a new culture, whether by conquerors or by traveling caravans, was very slow and always indirect. The experienced and skeptical people of the desert communities were not easily impressed by novelty; on the contrary, they had developed a strong resistance to change. The conservatism and traditionalism which are known as the outstanding characteristics of these people are clearly reflected in their art and architecture. A view of a desert fringe community of today could have belonged to a community 200, 500, or 1000 years ago.

Nevertheless, these people did absorb the new cultures and used them in the context of their own culture and philosophy. That is why their urban form possesses unparalleled harmony and continuity—despite being affected by thousands of years of exposure to a harsh climate. Moreover, from the time of the Safavids, the religious beliefs and social values have become so influential that the introduction of a new way of life has been very difficult; and even though behavior may have changed on the surface, in essence, the people remain the same. The steel and glass houses and ample straight roads are treated the same way brick houses and winding lanes were. There is the old life inside a new shell—a much more uncomfortable shell than the old ones.

Actually, because of political and economic factors, the slow-moving evolution almost ended around the 18th century. After this period came two centuries of almost complete stagnation that only ended with the

(A)

(B)

FIG. 4-43. Ardakan: (A) all *ivans* and wind towers facing the same direction; (B) opposite view.

recent economic and industrial changes in the country. The tumult caused by the unpreparedness of the people to adapt to the rapid industrialization has, in turn, brought about chaos, especially in the field of architecture which reflects the confusion in the economic and cultural aspects of the society.

Throughout the centuries in Iran, the paternalistic feudal system governing all societies of the desert fringe and religious beliefs have kept women secluded and separate. Perhaps this was the main reason the recent flood of industrial changes left people unguarded. Perhaps this also explains why everything old is disintegrating so fast. In a feudal system, and particularly in towns that used to function as citadels in themselves, the social structure is very simple. Apart from the closely related governing class, there are ordinary people who also live very intimately; everybody knows everything about everybody, and collective problems draw people even closer to one another. This characteristic is mirrored in the composition of their homes.

Fig. 4-44. Lane in Kashan.

When we look at the social structure of this feudal system, we see three classes. Between the upper strata and the majority of the peasant class, there was an intermediate class composed of merchants and craftsmen. The same composition is reflected in the arrangement of the bazaar and *caravanserais* connecting the *args* (the palace or government seat) to the mosques and popular quarters. The *maydan*, as a symbol of activity in the open, has never proved functional in these communities. Important *maydan* are usually adjacent to the bazaar—the best example is a *maydan-i-shah* in Isfahan—that provides a much more desirable atmosphere for business and social talk. Coffee houses, kebab houses, and ice-cream stands inside the bazaar furnish the people with good food and cold and hot beverages. The bazaar protects them from sun, wind, and rain, and gives them freedom of movement. It, unlike the *maydan*, forms an integrated element that provides all the comforts needed.

Today industrial commercialism is having a devastating effect on art, architecture, and the social and intellectual life of the people. Even the Mongol invasion seems insignificant when we look at the changes today. The logical relationship between architecture and geography and the cultural and practical needs of the people has been shattered. That is why, when we talk of the expressiveness of the urban form in the arid zones of

FIG. 4-45. Famous Broojerdi house, Kashan.

Iran, we refer to the time and elements that really belong to that specific environment.

At the present, not only land and building speculation is devastating these areas, but municipalities, with the help of architects and town planners influenced by Western planning methods, have brought disintegration to the whole pattern. I do not deny the advantages that technology and industrial building systems can bring about; but when applying them in these specific environments, one should be careful that enthusiasm does not lead to mistaking the means for the goal. Concepts such as zoning, direct, ample streets, and high-rise buildings have not proved to be an entirely successful solution even in the European countries where they have beem formulated; it is absurd to suppose that they will function here where the basic needs are so different. Methods from the Western world should not be applied directly in a country like Iran. The importance of this conclusion cannot be overemphasized. Just as an approach in the temperate region may be inappropriate in a desert region like Iran, so may the industrial, commercial, so-called modern approach be ill-advised for general application in Iran.

A supermarket or department store will never replace the organic character of the bazaar that makes all kinds of social and human relationships possible. Since the usual dimensions of these communities put services within walking distances, in designing master plans, there is no need to lay out streets through bazaars, cutting them to pieces. Tangential roads together with the improvement of existing streets can provide an efficient network for the movement of man and machine. When brick—the most flexible prefabricated unit—is adequate, cheap, functional, and easy to use, there is no need to shift to expensive sophisticated prefabrications that are not in harmony with existing architecture and require advanced techniques not available among these people. High-rise buildings, as well as steel and glass structures, because of climatic factors such as sand, dust winds that become hotter with altitude, and the lack of shade, are not functional. Traditional elements such as brick walls, internal gardens, semiunderground quarters with natural ventilation through wind towers and *ivan* systems not only provide thermal isolation and protect against sand and dust, but they also help to generate air currents that moderate temperatures. Cylindrical roofings, vaults, and domes diminish the surface exposed to the sun and help to moderate temperature as well.

There are elements that can happily be employed in the architecture of these regions to help bring about gradual modernization without controversy. Even when taller buildings are indispensable, the same concepts can and should be considered. The use of familiar and homogeneous materials together with the consideration of basic concepts in harmony with the climatic, geographical, and social characteristics of these regions will preserve its valuable integrity, no matter what kind of technique is chosen. For ultramodern experiments such as multistory, overlapping buildings using materials such as fiberglas and the like which are discussed frequently nowadays, it is advisable to choose a new territory and not mix them with existing communities.

Notes

1. Rollof Beny, *Persia: Bridge of Turquoise* (Boston, Mass.: New York Graphic Society, 1975), p. 12.
2. R. Ghirsham, *L'Iran des Origine à L'Islam*, tr. Mohammad Mo'in (Paris: Payot, 1961), pp. 2–4,
3. Ibid, p. 5.
4. Mahmood Tavassoli, *Architecture in the Hot Arid Zone* (Tehran: National Library, 1974), pp. 11, 15, 90–92.
5. Arthur Upham Pope and Phillis Ackerman, *A Survey of Persian Art*, 12 vol. (London: Oxford University Press, 1938), I, 3, 9; III, 897, 930.
6. Ibid, I, 91–92.
7. Ibid, I, 5, 14.
8. The distinction between art and architecture is new, so in this discussion, their meaning will be considered synonymous.
9. Pope and Ackerman, I, 10.
10. Ibid, I, 12.
11. See Rollof Beny's *Persia*: *Bridge of Turquoise* for the best views of Iran in magnificent color.
12. Pope and Ackerman, III, 1391
13. Ibid, III, 1245–1252.
14. For more information see Pope and Ackerman, III, 1393.
15. The original town of Yazd, now drowned in Kavir sands, is situated within 36 km of the city.
16. See Pope and Ackerman, III, 912–938.

Suggested Readings

Beny, Rollof. *Persia: Bridge of Turquoise*. Boston, Mass.: New York Graphic Society, 1975.
Ghirsham, R. *L'Iran des Origine à L'Islam*. Tr. Mohammad Mo'in. Paris: Payot, 1961.
Pope, Arthur Upham, and Ackerman, Phillis. *A Survey of Persian Art*. 6 Vols. London: Oxford University Press, 1938.
Tavassoli, Mahmood. *Architecture in the Hot Arid Zone*. Tehran: National Library, 1974.

5
Town Planning and Cultural and Climatic Responsiveness in the Middle East

John Lund Kriken

The best examples of contemporary town planning in the desert regions of the Middle East have combined traditional concepts of settlement with modern techniques of building and climatic adaptation to create communities which are liveable despite the hostile environment. The use of indigenous and traditional building principles recognizes unique cultural needs as well as the pragmatic realities of heat, dust, and lack of water. The heritage of the Middle Eastern settlement is a source of inspiration and continuity in designing a new town which is compatible with the rapid urbanization of the Middle East.

Introduction

The institutional and physical setting for Middle Eastern new towns has a number of common characteristics. Most new towns are a part of national development programs in support of an expanding industrial base including new ports and petrochemical and other oil-related developments. Most opportunities for such growth occur in remote and physically difficult areas. The sites for these projects are typically flat without landscape or physical features of any kind. They often require earth moving just to accomplish simple stormwater runoff. Water, and especially potable water, is scarce. The sites are also prone to regional flooding and require some form of protection. Finally, since many of these sites are located close to seaports and are on unusually flat topography, they have a high water table restricting excavation and foundation design.

The climate is also harsh. Hot temperatures are combined with high wind, sand storms, and low relative humidity. Extreme temperatures may reach 50°C (122°F) during the summer months. The hot, dry climate has an enormous effect on people's life cycle during at least nine months of the year. The cycle is dictated by the sun. The waking day is divided into three parts. Work and school are concentrated in the morning hours from six until one o'clock in the afternoon. Afternoons are devoted to lunch and rest at home, while the evening is a time to shop, visit, or participate in leisure activities.

Taken as a whole, these conditions represent a tremendous obstacle to planning, building, and living in new desert settlements. Yet in every instance, there are clues within the historic patterns of villages and cities that suggest how these problems might be approached.

In planning these new towns, an analysis of the traditional principles of settlement and building forms provides the necessary link between historic settlement patterns and the requirements of a modern new town.[1] The traditional principles integrate the town plan to the indigenous cultural and climatic forces of the region. The building forms describe an array of traditional spatial components and conceptual building blocks whose contemporary equivalents are inherently applicable to a new town. Together these elements provide the basis for an adaptive planning order which can organize the uses and physical character of the community. Based on past experiences in Iran and Saudi Arabia, the subjects of principles, forms, and orders provide a useful overall organization for a discussion of town planning.

Principles

CULTURE

The principle of sense of place can be described by the Persian concept of *makan*. As man attempts to perceive his position in the universe, the relationship between those things that are external (manifest or macrocosmic) and those that are internal or within the individual (hidden or microcosmic) is fundamental to his world view.

Sense of Place. The contrast between that which is hidden and that which is manifest is found at virtually all levels of a spatial hierarchy. It is most evident in the use of walls which differentiate private courts from public space. For example, while the outer walls of the dwelling are shown to everyone passing and while some areas of the dwelling unit are considered suitable for the entertainment of guests, the true nature of family life is only evident far within the dwelling's walls, in the interior garden court, and in the most private areas of the home. In the Middle East, the garden's open space within the dwelling is perceived as place, in contrast to the Western perception of the building as place (see Figure 5-1). In the West, for example, the exterior facades of the dwelling are given architectural treatment. In the East, this attention is concentrated on the facades of the interior courtyard.

Hierarchy. The relationship of macrocosm to microcosm is expressed by the spatial contrasts at all scales, from the regional to the personal. That which is hidden at one level of hierarchy becomes manifest at a lower level. Similarly, that which is manifest at a given level becomes hidden as one ascends to a larger scale. In the broadest sense, the mountains which surround many Mideast cities are regional containers, defining a space for human settlement. At the scale of the city, the perimeter wall traditionally provides a sense of security from the aggression of nature and man, while it defines the city within the vast expanse of open land.

The organization of urban spaces into a hierarchy of manifest and hid-

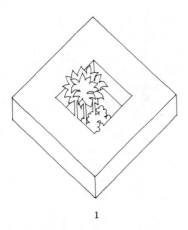
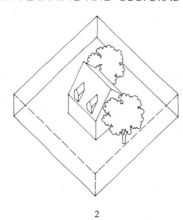

1   2

FIG. 5-1. (1) Garden as space; (2) building as space. Source: All drawings in this chapter are from Skidmore, Owings & Merrill and Mandala Collaborative, *New Town near Bandar Shahpour, Iran* (Tehran, Iran: Ministry of Housing and Town Management, 1974).

den space establishes a unique perception of the city. The city can be viewed as a sequence of spatial elements which change from manifest to hidden as they are viewed from different vantage points. As one proceeds through major public spaces, there are glimpses of previously hidden areas of the city. Finally, at the scale of the dwelling unit, this distinction between spaces is one of outer pedestrian space and private residential courtyards or gardens (see Figure 5-2).

CLIMATE AND DESIGN

The importance of climate in the planning and design of a new town in the desert permeates all consideration of environmental design. To make a town as responsive as possible to climatic conditions, several basic techniques for minimizing the effect of the sun and dust may be used in the planning process. It is also important for planners to guide the architectural design of future buildings in the town. There are three general techniques for promoting the comfort of individuals. They are the use of shadow and breeze and of water elements, and the minimization of the impact of solar radiation. In traditional desert settlements, all three techniques are used.

Shadow. The typical dwelling unit is composed of an outer wall surrounding the building which has an interior atrium and an external garden. The internal and external spaces have different kinds of shadow and provide comfort at different times of day. The interior atrium, a source of light for the rooms that surround it, provides indirect exposure during the hottest hours of the day when the family rests inside. The atrium also acts as a vertical passage and carries a constant flow of warm air upward, while cool air enters to make the adjoining living areas comfortable. During the summer months, the external garden is a comfortable place only in the morning and evening. Then the temperature is low enough to allow activity outside where the trees provide shadow and where lower shrubs can channel cool breezes (see Figure 5-3).

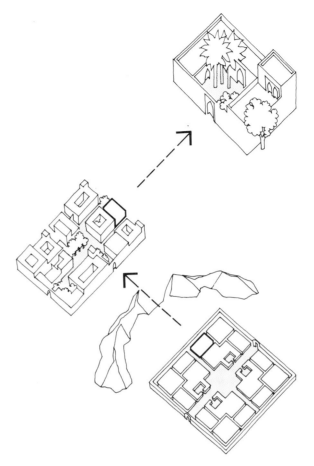

FIG. 5-2 Hierarchy of scale, from city to individual dwelling.

Water. The importance of water as a planning principle stems from its role as the source of life in desert regions. When used for irrigation, it can turn a barren desert into a thriving settlement. The Iranian landscape, for example, is marked by systems of subterranean aqueducts, called *qanat*, which have traditionally fed water to arid areas and which make settlement in the desert possible. Complementing the use of water as a life-giving element is its use as a form-giving element at the scale of the city and as a cooling element at the scale of the dwelling unit. At the city scale, the pragmatic and symbolic value of water significantly orders the form of settlement. Irrigation water for agriculture and urban landscape is traditionally provided by open channels, flowing by gravity. In the city these water elements are located along prominent corridors of pedestrian activity where they serve as visual amenities, adding to the sense of place (see Figure 5-4).

Compactness. The practicality of planning principles also is evidenced in building design. Compactness is the technique of minimizing the amount of building surface exposed to the direct radiation of the sun. Compactness can be specified in many ways, but it is most clearly evidenced by the ratio of exposed building surface to the enclosed living volume. A one-story, single-family dwelling totally detached from its surroundings

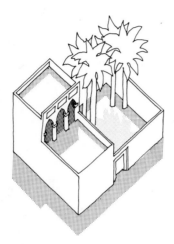

Fig. 5-3. Shadow.

exhibits the greatest amount of exposed wall and roof area to usable floor area. A two-story dwelling can double the usable floor area while less than doubling the amount of exposed building surface. If a number of two-story dwelling units are attached in a row, sheltered areas can be multiplied while adding smaller proportions of additional surface area. As one combines dwelling units into multi-family residential building blocks, the ratio of exposed surface to usable area continues to drop (see Figure 5-5). At the scale of the city, the amount of land area not specifically designated as enclosed private space can be significantly reduced through the principle of compactness. The density of residential areas can reach the level where most external pedestrian spaces are sheltered from direct sunlight.

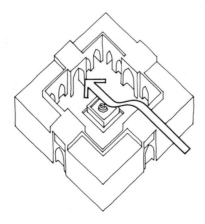

Fig. 5-4. Water as a cooling element.

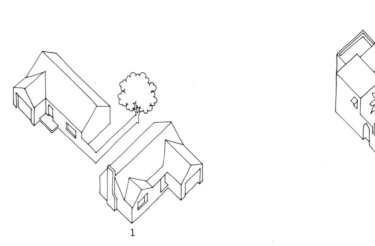

FIG. 5-5. (1) Separate buildings; (2) clustered buildings.

Orientation. Because of the severity of the climate, orientation of all structures must be carefully determined. To minimize the effect of the hot sun, planners should design all buildings so that their major window exposure faces north and south. The north face of a building has no direct sun exposure; while the south face, though exposed to sunlight, can be controlled. In the summer months, the angle of the south sun is quite high at midday so that a porch, overhang, or similar device will provide an effective protecting screen for the occupied spaces inside. In the winter, the lower angle of the southern sun allows the sun to pass through the protective screen to warm the face of the building. The effect of the sun on a building's east and west facades is more difficult to control since the angle of the sun is lower in the morning and afternoon. Exposure to this orientation should be minimized or carefully considered in terms of potential heat gain. Although this concept cannot be applied to all buildings (since various portions of the town will have nonparallel orientation), it is possible to orient a vast majority of the dwelling units to north-south. Where the desired orientation is not feasible, a technique of creating building screens to diffuse the light and heat of the sun can be employed (see Figure 5-6).

In desert regions, buildings are constructed with a minimum of openings so that the amount of direct sunlight entering the structure can be controlled. Windows are small and infrequent, and indirect lighting is prefera-

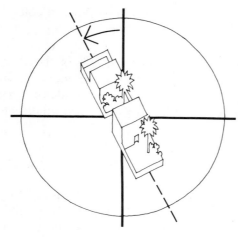

FIG. 5-6. Building orientation.

ble to direct exposure. In the design of buildings in a new town, a technique of providing all structures with a second outer shell of screening elements may be used to reduce the amount of direct light entering buildings and to minimize the direct exposure of living and working areas to the heat and glare of the sun. Screens or porches are placed on facades of those buildings facing toward the sun. Screens may also be used to cover pedestrian spaces (see Figure 5-7).

Forms

GATEWAY

The process of perceiving the hidden and manifest aspects of a given place is accentuated by movement toward it or through it. The changing nature of spaces in the levels of hierarchy has been previously noted, and the importance of such movement is shown by the use of gateways in Persian town plannning and architecture. Archetypically, the gateway stands for the right of passage in either direction between the manifest and

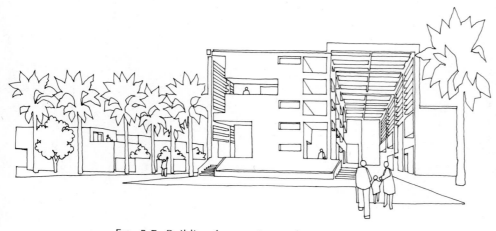

FIG. 5-7. Building fenestration and sun protection.

hidden aspects of life. At the scale of the city, the gateway provides access through the city's wall and serves as an articulation of entry and a means of orienting visitors and residents to the city's major corridors of movement. The gateway is also used at the scale of the district and individual cluster of residences. Neighborhoods, *mahalleh*, in the traditional cities of Iran are very closely defined by the use of walls and gates. This theme of enclosure is repeated, even at the scale of the individual dwelling unit (see Figure 5-8).

PATH

Within the city is the path, a universal term applied to all elements of a pedestrian movement system. Since the urban principles of sense of place, hierarchy, and compactness are combined in the use of this element, it is the most prevalent spatial component in traditional cities. Paths occur at all levels of hierarchy. They are part of a positive spatial network which is formed by the walls of buildings. Paths vary in width and height and are continuously used by residents, for they are designed to be in shadow most hours of the day. Where building walls are not present to provide shadow, linear gardens serve as paths, protecting pedestrians by a canopy of trees.

The archetypal path is the bazaar or *souk*, the shaded linear shopping area of the traditional Eastern city. The bazaar form is most noticeable at the city scale in major shopping areas, but it is repeated at lower levels of hierarchy, such as the local commercial convenience (see Figure 5-9). The bazaar is repeatedly intersected by minor paths running into residential areas. The contrast between hidden and manifest space is heightened at these points where the public area is distinctly separated from the private neighborhood (see Figure 5-10).

PLACE

Symbolic design is also characteristic of the Persian concept of the room. Within the room, a microcosm of the universe is created. The floor represents the earth; the walls extend vertically beyond the limits of the

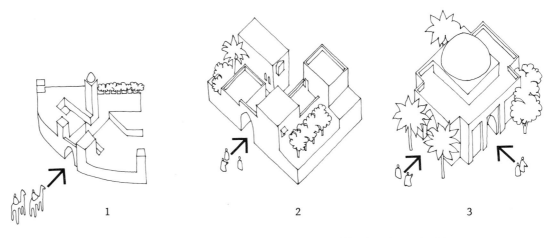

FIG. 5-8. Gateways: (1) town; (2) neighborhood; (3) building.

FIG. 5-9. Path through bazaar.

room, and the roof returns one to the temporal world. In the traditional Persian city, the great room, or *timchah*, depicts this cosmology while serving as a functional component of the multiuse bazaar. Where secondary pathways cross, the intersection is manifested in a great interior room, a nodal space with subsidiary alcoves for the sale of merchandise. A *timchah* will often be devoted to only one type of merchandise and will be related to the support facilities of a particular group of craftsmen (see Figure 5-11).

GARDEN

The garden has a position in Persian cosmology as a symbol of paradise. The most common example of this concept is the oasis sheltered from the oppressive climate. The use of gardens as spatial elements follows these conceptual principles. The classical form of the Persian garden is consis-

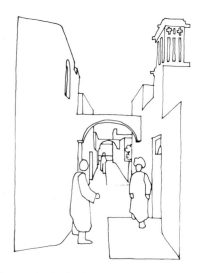

FIG. 5-10. Path through residential areas.

FIG. 5-11. The *timchah*.

tent with that of the macrocosm in the Islamic sense of place, *makan*. The garden is conceived in two ways: that of *bagh* (garden) and *hayat* or *maydan* (courtyard). The former consists of a central pavilion surrounded by an open space surrounded by a perimeter wall. When the configuration of this general form corresponds to a square accentuating the four coordinates, the garden becomes the traditional *Chahar Bagh*, or four gardens. This form can be interpreted as an expression of movement from the outer walls toward the spiritual center of the pavilion and from the central pavilion outward through the paradise of nature (see Figure 5-12A). In contrast to the symbolism of the *Chahar Bagh* with its central pavilion, the traditional open court or garden, *hayat* or *maydan*, is always an inward-oriented space. It is the epitome of a positive space defined only by its container, a perimeter wall (see Figure 5-12B).

The concept of a garden surrounded by a wall (*hayat*) has been used in the gardens of dwelling units and at a larger scale, in garden squares (*maydan*) in public places. The *Chahar Bagh*, a place of linear movement, has developed from the symmetrical form of the square to a rectangular form. The *Chahar Bagh* in Isfahan is an example of this classical form developed into a processional space (see Figure 5-12C).

ORDERS

CONTEXT

An exemplary project is useful to illustrate the application of these traditional principles and forms to the design and planning of a modern new town. A typical project, a new town near Bandar Shahpour, has been under construction in the province of Khuzestan, Iran. Here a flat plain stretches southwest from the Zagros Mountains to the head of the Persian Gulf. Khuzestan is part of a larger hydrological region of five great rivers

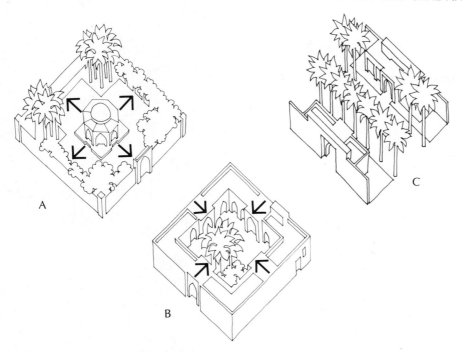

FIG. 5-12. Relationships between building and garden: (A) four gardens (*Chahar Bagh*); (B) courtyard (*hayat*); (C) linear garden.

which converge and flow into the gulf. The Tigris and Euphrates flow southeast from Mesopotamia and modern Iraq; and the Dez, Karheh, and Karun flow south through the province. These rivers have played a fundamental role in the history of this region, and Khuzestan has been one of the principal growth areas of Iran. Rich in oil and located on the Persian Gulf, Khuzestan is a developing area for the oil drilling, refining, and petrochemical industries. It is also a major port (see Figure 5-13).

The projected growth of the area prompted the decision to build a major new town in the vicinity of the Bandar Shahpour port and industrial complex. This 30-year project was designed to provide housing and services to meet the needs of a population of 200,000 people. The Plan and Budget Organization in cooperation with the Governor General of Khuzestan initiated this project by employing consultants to select a site and prepare plans for a new town.

The new town is an integral part of a development plan for Khuzestan. Adapted to regional growth needs, it will serve as a catalyst, giving physical order to the economic, social, and cultural vitality of the region. The provision of urban services, contact with urban life, and access to the modern sector of the Iranian economy for people in the small surrounding settlements are important parts of the plan. Agriculture is another high priority, and the construction of dams for water storage and irrigation is a key to future agricultural development in this area.

The selection of a location for the new town was based on an evaluation of environments within reasonable commuting distance of the port. Since the port of Bandar Shahpour is on an island reclaimed from the gulf, the adjacent area is swampy and devoid of vegetation. The industrial complex also produces high levels of air pollution which will increase as

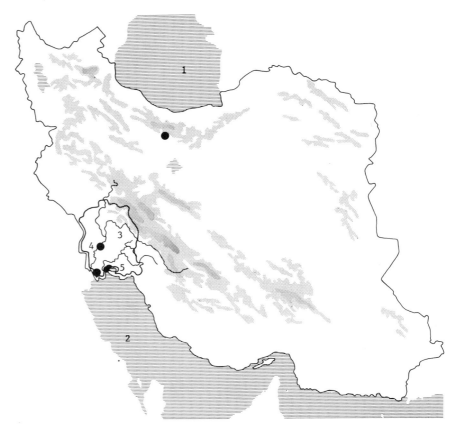

FIG. 5-13. Province of Khuzestan, Iran: (1) Caspian Sea; (2) Persian Gulf; (3) Province of Khuzestan; (4) Ahwaz; (5) Bandar Shahpour.

further development occurs. Thus, lands immediately adjacent to the port were not suitable for a large new town. The site selected is within 28 km of Bandar Shahpour. It has the lowest air pollution potential of all the sites considered because of its separation from the industrial area on the gulf and because of the direction of prevailing winds. The site is along the southern edge of the Jarrahi River, providing a visual amenity for the proposed town, which in turn increases the potential quality of life for its residents. It was determined to be environmentally and economically the most suitable site for the new town.

WATER

Once the site was selected, the community had to determine the best way to use resources. The Jarrahi River watershed above the new town site generates a flood plain covering the general vicinity of Bandar Shahpour. Regular flooding with poor drainage in the winter along with low water levels in the summer have combined to reduce agricultural production in the area. Because of the risk of major flooding, steps had to be taken to insure a safe environment for the town. Also the enormous investment in facilities and infrastructure within the town had to be protected.

Two alternatives were investigated. One required a perimeter earth berm (dike) to surround the town, separating the town from the visual amenity of the river and providing no protection for the larger region. The second and selected alternative proposed a large detention reservoir located upstream of the town and a diversion levee to spill excess flood waters directly into the Persian Gulf (see Figure 5-14). Since the detention reservoir allows a managed flow of water past the new town site, a lake can be created at its northern edge. This lake is shaped to complement the land uses along the edge, and its level will be maintained at an elevation consistent with the safety and visual amenity required. In additin, the controlled level of water in the Jarrahi facilitates the constant irrigation of the agricultural areas within the region.

Water elements in the new town parallel the traditional water uses previously described. Irrigation water for the town's landscape is made visually prominent by using open channels wherever possible. The water of the Jarrahi River is stored in the detention reservoir and flows into a channel along the Chahar Bagh, the town's major boulevard. The Chahar Bagh forms a main ridge gradually dropping in elevation from east to west. Hence, water flows by gravity along the boulevard and then along subsidiary branches paralleling arterial roads. The irrigation system is

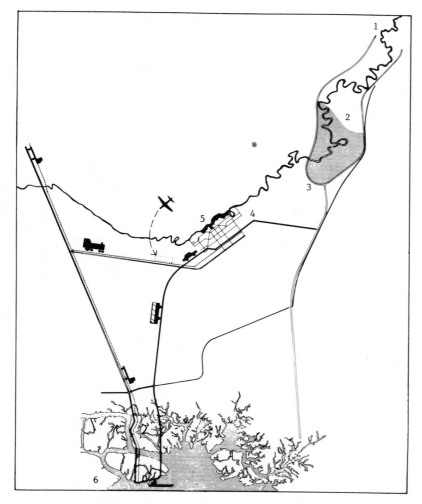

FIG. 5-14. Plan for regional flood control system: (1) Jarrahi River; (2) detention reservoir; (3) spillway; (4) irrigation channels; (5) earth borrow from river for site grading; (6) Bandar Shahpour.

further extended to provide water to the landscape on the edges of the town and to the agricultural zone beyond the town perimeter. The objective of the system is to make the greatest possible use of this precious element (see Figures 5-15 and 5-16).

The irrigation system, along with the roads and utilities, established the orientation of the town's buildings. These systems are organized parallel to the river with an optimum north-south, climate-responsive orientation. Inside the town, water elements in the form of pools, and fountains are placed at important activity areas and at all levels of the spatial hierarchy. The landscape of the town is also punctuated by slender towers, serving both as elements in the water storage system and as points of orientation throughout the town. At the level of the dwelling unit, pools of water are located within public courts of apartment buildings and in the private courtyards and gardens of the single-family dwellings.

SERVICES

Linked to the river's northern edge and to incoming utilities on the south and west, the new town is supported by its order of services. Irrigation is the most traditional order with precedents in all the towns and villages of Iran. The other utility systems and civil engineering requirements link the city to the most contemporary technologies.

One of the more costly investments in new town construction is for site preparation. Due to the very flat topography of the site, a considerable

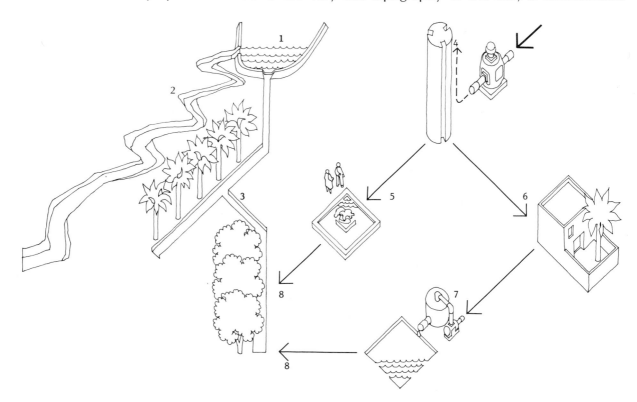

FIG. 5-15. River irrigation and potable water system: (1) retention basin to control flooding; (2) natural river flow; (3) man-made gravity-flow channel for irrigation of public places; (4) gravity storage tanks; (5) irrigation of minor open spaces; (6) domestic use; (7) water treatment; (8) recycling to town irrigation.

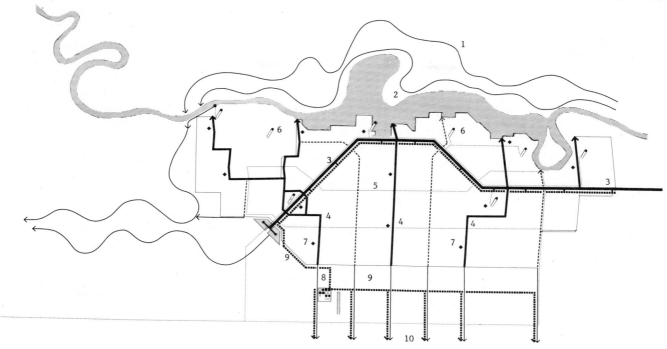

FIG. 5-16. Order of water: (1) irrigation system for regional park; (2) Jarrahi River transformed into lake; (3) irrigation channels through Chahar Bagh; (4) channels from Chahar Bagh through district spine; (5) pressurized irrigation of low-density areas; (6) water tanks in shape of minarets; (7) surface water storage; (8) waste water treatment; (9) recycling to irrigation; (10) agricultural use.

amount of earth fill is required to allow the gravity utility systems to function. Alternatives to gravity such as pumping as well as various gravity slope directions were investigated to establish the least costly solution. Since the natural landform slopes away from the river (due to flood siltation), this direction was ultimately adopted as the primary direction of slope. The site is being prepared wth a main ridge line, and the land is sloped to either side. These sloped sides are further articulated by secondary ridges and valleys (see Figure 5-17). Of course, such planning necessi-

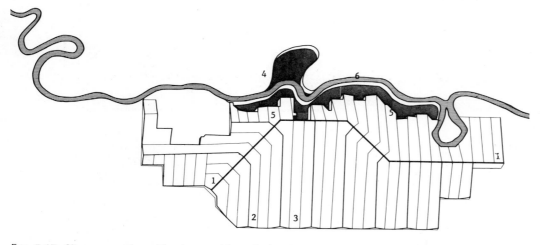

FIG. 5-17. Site preparation: (1) primary ridge (Chahar Bagh); (2) secondary ridge; (3) valley; (4) borrow area for regional park/town; (5) borrow area for town; (6) Jarrahi River.

tates an organized use of land. The major source for earth is between the southern side of the Jarrahi River and the northern edge of the new town. A future lake will replace all of the earth removed and will create an important amenity in the town.

A light industrial zone paralleling the town on its southern edge has been established for the location of utility services. Waste water flows by gravity to a treatment plant in this zone. Purified, it is pumped back into the town-wide irrigation system. Solid waste is also treated in this zone creating compost for future agricultural areas bordering the town.

Though the town is served by a national electric distribution line, the Iranian government wished to pursue a total energy system. In the planned total energy system, power is generated by gas-fired turbines which are located in the light industrial zone. Waste heat from the turbines fires high temperature, high pressure boilers which feed into central utility plants in various parts of the town. There, hot water becomes transformed through absorption chillers into chilled water for air conditioning. Each house and building in the town is equipped to convert chilled water into cool air in the summer and hot water into warm air during the winter months (see Figure 5-18).

MOVEMENT

Movement in the traditional town is generated along the shaded pathway that begins in the bazaar or *souk* and radiates from it like the veins of a leaf. Contemporary modes of movement are more varied and not as easily drawn into an organic form. The objectives of the town's circulation system are three-fold. First, the system should distribute the trip destinations so as to create as balanced a system as possible. In other words, trips

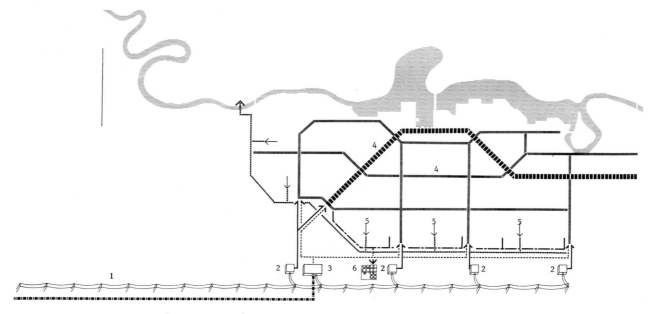

FIG. 5-18. Order of services: (1) utility corridor (potable water, gas, and high tension electricity); (2) electrical substations; (3) electrical generator; (4) major distribution network (underground electricity, water, and hot water); (5) sewage collection system; (6) waste treatment plant.

to the port go in the opposite direction from trips to the town center. This minimizes the number of lanes required in any one direction. Second, the system should channel trips to the port so as to prevent disruption of the residential areas by means of an expressway running parallel to the town's southern edge. The third objective is to create a ceremonial road, the Chahar Bagh, oriented toward transit traffic and linking all the major gathering places in the town (see Figure 5-19). Though there are many cultural conflicts in Middle Eastern countries because of public transit use, it is heavily patronized in large Iranian cities. In the new town, the importance of transit is even greater, due to the necessity for daily commuting to the port and petrochemical plants. Transit within the town is a bus system composed of intercity loops and regional loops. The regional bus system operates with large capacity vehicles on special rights-of-way. These buses make frequent stops in all the town centers before connecting to the regional freeway.

The pedestrian system, the most intimate aspect of the order of movement, is also the most integrated with the residential and service environments of the new town. Pedestrian paths intersect the vehicular and transit networks on the edges of the centers. The centers themselves contain car-free zones which are a mixture of bazaar paths and public gardens. The private automobile is stored adjacent to or beneath its destination in the fabric of the town.

SHADOW NETWORK

When the traditional forms of the path, place, and garden are linked to form a continuous network of enclosed and shaded spaces, an order of shadow throughout an entire city can be created. The shadow network makes it possible to walk from any location to a destination without enduring the direct impact of the sun. The network is formed by a number of different techniques, ranging from totally enclosed spaces, such as the bazaar arcade, to an open area shaded by only a canopy of trees. The

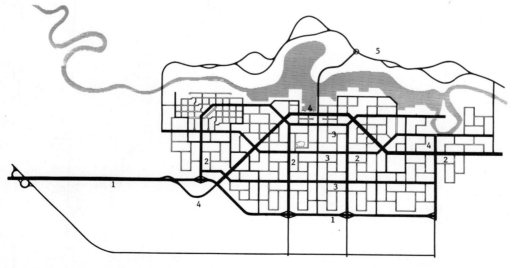

FIG. 5-19. Order of vehicular movement: (1) regional expressway; (2) north-south arterials; (3) east-west arterials; (4) Chahar Bagh; (5) parkway.

quality of shadow, therefore, changes as one moves along the various parts of the system. The most common component of the shadow network is a path, or *kucheh*, with shade created by its narrow width and the high building walls which form its edges (see Figure 5-20).

In the plan of the Bandar Shahpour new town, the order of shadow is created by the use of traditional forms and their contemporary equivalents. A network of residential pathways form the major components of the system. These pathways are created by arrangement of medium density residential buildings oriented to maintain a shadowed linear space during all hours of the day. The pathways are punctuated by nodes in the form of interior rooms. Integrated with lower and higher density residential areas, they also link the town's multiuse centers—places of shadow where movement and gathering are possible despite the high temperatures (see Figure 5-21).

GATHERING

In the Iranian city, activities are traditionally located along a linear network to make them accessible to the greatest number of residents. As expressed in the section on the path as a traditional form, a system of multiuse centers at various levels of the service hierarchy is located along the network. These public spaces devoted to a number of activities and facilities are considered part of the traditional order of gathering places (see Figure 5-22).

In the plan for the new town, there are five basic types of multiuse centers which form the nodes and intersections of the shadow network. At the highest level of hierarchy, the town center serves the entire population of the town. The town center is actually a series of gathering places, each with a specific type of activity. There are zones devoted primarily to civic activities, including places of religious worship, hospitals, cultural facilities, and government buildings. There are also zones devoted primarily to commercial activities, including light industry and wholesale businesses, office buildings, hotels, restaurants, and amusement areas. All these activities are linked together by the shadow network of the retail bazaar.

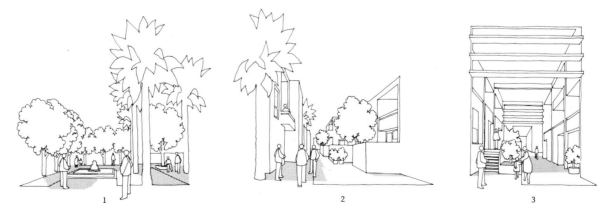

FIG. 5-20. Shadow network: (1) natural tree canopy of the garden providing shadow for leisure activities; (2) narrow pedestrian path shaded by building walls; (3) covered path in bazaar and between walk-up apartments.

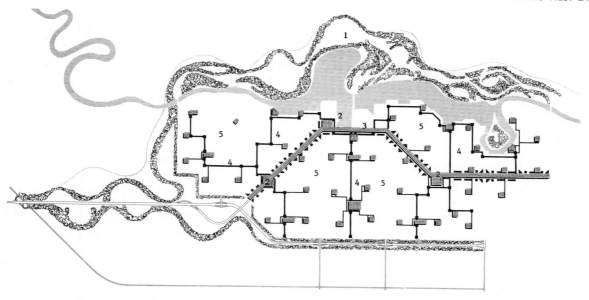

FIG. 5-21. Order of shadow: (1) regional park providing garden shadow; (2) *maydan* or shaded public square; (3) Chahar Bagh; (4) district spine with continuous shadow provided by built form; (5) shadow of trees and narrow pathways in low-density areas.

The second highest level of service hierarchy includes two community centers located along the town's major boulevard, the Chahar Bagh, to the east and west of the town center. Community centers include the same array of activities and facilities as the town center, but serve half the town's population or approximately 75,000 residents. The next level of hierarchy is the district center. The ten district centers are places of gathering including commercial, civic, recreational and educational facilities. Such areas are oriented toward the approximately 15,000 residents within walking distance. The lowest level is the local center which consists of retail stores and a school. The facilities in these centers are arranged as continuations of the residential pathways of the shadow network.

As we have seen, the places of gathering are intended to be locations for the interaction of residents and the integration of diverse activities. They are zoned for multiple uses in order to achieve the maximum daily cycle of activity. In this manner, not only economy but also amenity can be maintained (see Figure 5-23).

RESIDENCE

With the use of buildings and walls to achieve maximum shadow and the distinction of private from public open space, residential areas often look very similar on the surface, regardless of the economic level of their population. The distinction between income levels is more visible within the dwelling unit and its private courtyard. Apartment living, previously a rarity in Iran, is becoming more prevalent as life styles change toward contemporary needs, and as land, building, and infrastructure costs increase.

In the new town, there is a broad variety of residential environments,

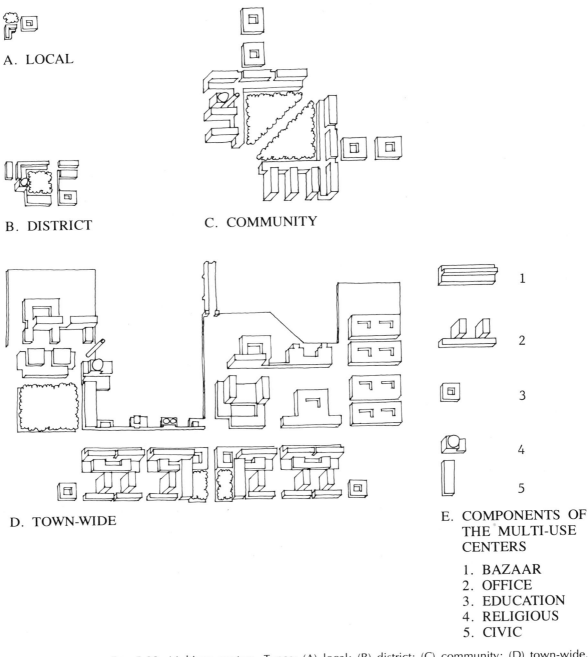

A. LOCAL

B. DISTRICT

C. COMMUNITY

D. TOWN-WIDE

E. COMPONENTS OF
THE MULTI-USE
CENTERS

1. BAZAAR
2. OFFICE
3. EDUCATION
4. RELIGIOUS
5. CIVIC

FIG. 5-22. Multiuse centers. Types: (A) local; (B) district; (C) community; (D) town-wide. Components (E): (1) bazaar; (2) office; (3) education; (4) religious; (5) civic.

designed to appeal to the widest possible range of economic levels and cultural values. The traditional Iranian single-family dwelling, surrounded by a wall and having a private interior court or garden, is located in the lower density areas. Although all income groups are represented in this area, great care has been taken to integrate different income levels and still maintain homogeneous neighborhoods. This area consists of one- and two-story dwellings which have a variety of internal configurations and architectural treatments. Most families with more than four members will live in this area.

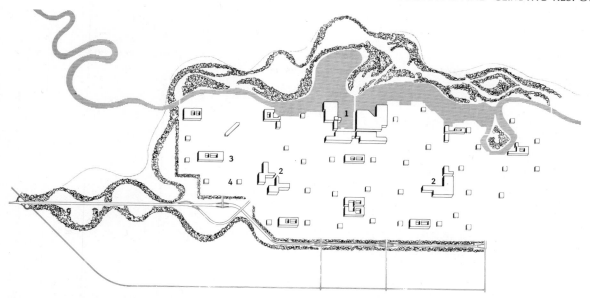

FIG. 5-23. Order of gathering: (1) town center; (2) community center; (3) district center; (4) local center.

The two types of higher density residential environments in the new town are organized as linear spines along transit and pedestrian corridors. The spines offer dwellings for all income groups and all family sizes. The spine along the Chahar Bagh is the highest density spine, including buildings of five and six stories with elevators. Most dwelling units in this area are intended for smaller families with few children. The walk-up apartment spine is comprised of three-story buildings. Because of the greater proportion of children in this spine and its close relationship with the district commercial centers and the single family residential area, it is organized to provide major movement corridors in the pedestrian shadow system. Specifically, these apartment buildings are placed close together and spanned by a roof to provide sun-protected walking and recreation spaces (see Figures 5-24 and 5-25).

Conclusion

In work of this kind, there remain a number of unresolved or partially resolved issues. Most of these questions are related to the dynamics of building a 200,000-person community over an extraordinarily short period of time. For example, the town's population will vary over the course of development. In the first phases, the population will be young, with few children and with a high proportion of expatriates or foreign nationals. In later phases, the population will assume the family size typical of the nation and will be primarily Iranian. Yet there is considerable concern over the potential clash of these mixed cultural values in the early phases of development. The principles discussed earlier provide a means for insuring some level of social and individual privacy which will make the adjustment less difficult.

Regardless of the character of the first phase population, the early

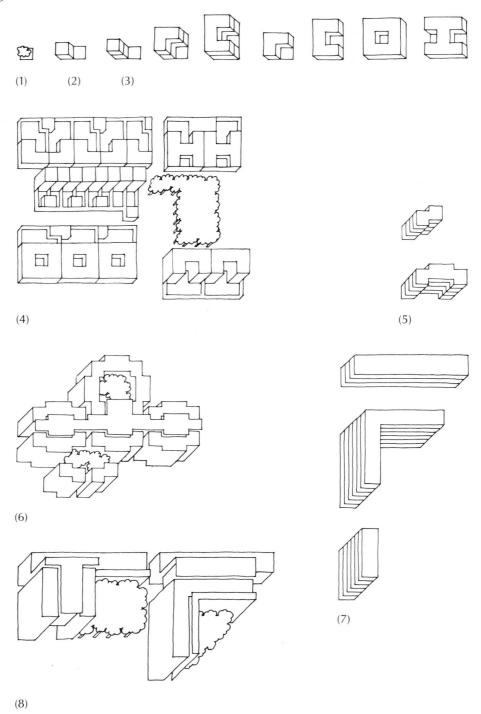

FIG. 5-24. Types of dwellings and residential environments: (1) courtyard; (2) single-story units around courtyard; (3) two-story units around courtyard; (4) single-family cluster; (5) walkup apartment unit; (6) walk-up apartment cluster with covered pedestrian path; (7) apartment unit with elevator; (8) apartment unit (with elevator) cluster.

housing construction must reflect the ultimate projections for a larger family size. Such conditions require several single persons to live together in a one-family house. Again, the traditional principles which require a dwelling to be zoned to ensure privacy make them easily subdividable.

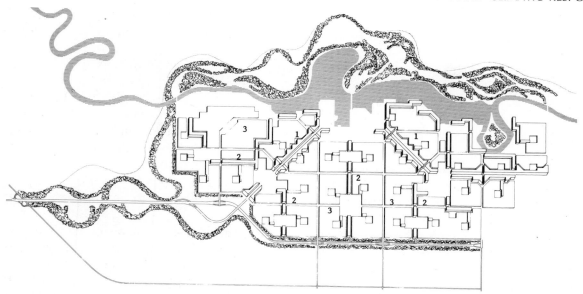

FIG. 5-25. Order of residence: (1) apartments (with elevators) along town spine; (2) walk-up apartment spine; (3) single-family residential area.

The requirement for fast implementation is a major concern in the planning process. Construction worker housing, for example, is a historic problem in remotely located new towns. For at least five years, the construction worker population will exceed the town population. The problem is further complicated because the construction worker population is composed of rural laborers and foreign nationals. At best, this problem should be viewed in a regional context where at least the

FIG. 5-26. Aerial view of town looking south toward the port.

Iranians may be housed in expanded nearby villages as part of a regional housing program. Typically, the foreigners are housed in temporary housing near the site.

The planning and construction of a new town, however complex programmatically, logistically, and otherwise, is comparatively simple compared to establishing its institutional structure and providing manpower for institutional services. Only in our most recent new-town work have these problems been addressed simultaneously with the physical planning process. Because of the skilled labor scarcity in every field, a manpower training program should be an integral part of the overall planning and construction effort. Even with an intensive program of this kind, the majority of skilled labor and professionals will have to be imported during the early years.

Finally, the necessity of providing shelter for so many people over so short a period of time can threaten any plan that is not precisely tuned to system building technology and construction management procedures. These considerations must be incorporated into the planning and design process. The international new-town building experience, especially in desert climates, is an extraordinary challenge which has few professional parallels. The collective problems it represents are considerable. Thankfully, a beginning point can be found within the local historic traditions of village and city building that can serve as an inspiration in an otherwise difficult environment (see Figure 5-26).

Note

1. On traditional Iranian settlements, see Nader Ardalan and Laleh Bakhtiar, *The Sense of Unity* (Chicago: The University of Chicago Press, 1975).

6
City Planning In the Hot, Dry Climate of Iran

Mahmood Tavassoli

A look at the works and writings of foreigners who have discussed Iran's architecture shows that researchers have an archaeological viewpoint. Indeed, they generally do not clarify or deal with an indigenous architectural process; nor do they provide an analysis of spatial form. They need to concentrate more on monumental architecture.

Purely descriptive ways of looking at the architectural problems have made examiners ignore the real factors in the towns and the architecture in Iran. Scientists could recognize the spatial forms and their evolution through history if they studied socioeconomic circumstances, cultural changes, and other factors such as the all important climatic conditions in Iran.

It is also important to consider the sociospatial structure of the towns, a topic ony recently explored.[1] By surveying, analyzing, and examining over ten small and large towns, I have been able to formulate a hypothesis concerning the sociospatial structure of Iranian towns in the hot, arid region. When we look at the dwellings in the hot, arid zones, we also must consider the role and effect of climatic factors on the physical structure of the town and dwellings. The information collected is largely based on observational survey techniques and many interviews with local masons and architects, heads of old families, and elders of the neighborhoods who have considerable knowledge about social life in the spatial forms of the historic towns, cities and courtyard houses.[2] Then again, there is some valuable literature.[3]

Finally, we must consider the modern situation and current problems of historic towns. To do this, we must discuss changes caused by the unexpected increase of industries and motor vehicles and the more recent speculation and uncontrolled development in the historic towns and cities.

Sociospatial Structure of Towns

In the hot, arid regions in ancient times, most of the desert towns were fortresses with the outer defensive walls usually forming a square enclosing them. The circulation pattern inside the city generally paralleled the walls, for most of the intersections were perpendicular. The simplest walled town usually had a single entrance. The main road from this main gate to the geometrical center of the fortress was the main bazaar. The bazaar opened onto the *lard*, the central square, and then continued through to a defensive wall opposite the main gate where a water storage facility or a water source was often located. To one side of the central square, an inner castle or town *narin-ghalleh* was built. These components still exist in a few of the cities such as Yazd, Nain, and Maybod in the central, hot, arid region of Iran.[4]

Pyrnia describes the physical structure of the pre-Islamic Iranian towns, and his explanation is based largely on vast experience and primary examination.[5] With the help of sociohistorical studies that have begun recently in Iran, a more accurate schema of the pre-Islamic Iranian towns can be drawn.

The arrival of Islam marked an important addition to the city: the *Masjid-i-Jami* or Friday Mosque. At this point, the main elements of town planning became the *bazaar*, the *tekieh* (town square or assembly hall), the *hosseinieh* (neighborhood square or private assembly hall or a house), the *madrasseh* (theological seminary), the *ab-e-anbar* (water storage or cistern), and the *hammam* (public bath).

These components have a special socioeconomic and cultural meaning relative to the specific sociospatial locations and interrelationships of these elements within the city. A survey-analysis of different towns shows that these components generally constituted small or big complexes which were grouped rather than dispersed throughout the city. Small complexes generally served a neighborhood, while the main and the biggest complex in the town included the main bazaar and served the whole town, region, or, in special cases, the nation.

The distribution of the complexes within the town was based on neighborhood divisions. Towns and cities were usually divided into different neighborhoods comprised of different social classes, different religious groups, and different handicraft producers. Each neighborhood was an economic component or administrative part of the city. Each area was usually named for the head of that neighborhood, the main local product within the neighborhood, or the leading clergyman. Each neighborhood also has one center, architecturally designed according to the social status of the dwellers. The head of each neighborhood was responsible to the local governor of the city who, in turn, was responsible to the central government.[6]

The main bazaar within the main complex of the city served not only as a market place, but also as an exhibition area. People spent their leisure time either shopping or browsing in the bazaar. In addition to its economic function, the bazaar had a very strong sociopolitical spatial sense. From the social history of Iran, one may understand very well how the sociopolitical events in the bazaar and in the Friday Mosque distinguished them as sociospatial forms.

The main complex of the town and other neighborhood centers within the town had an important spatial relationship maintained through the main thoroughfares. The surveys of the towns and cities within the hot, arid region show that the main communication routes were these main passageways throughout the town and neighborhood centers. Along the line of these passageways or at their intersections, neighborhood centers were located.[7]

When looking at the main structure of the walled city of Yazd (see Figures 6-1 to 6-3), one sees a main passage extending through the heart of the Friday Mosque and the various elements that have grown up around

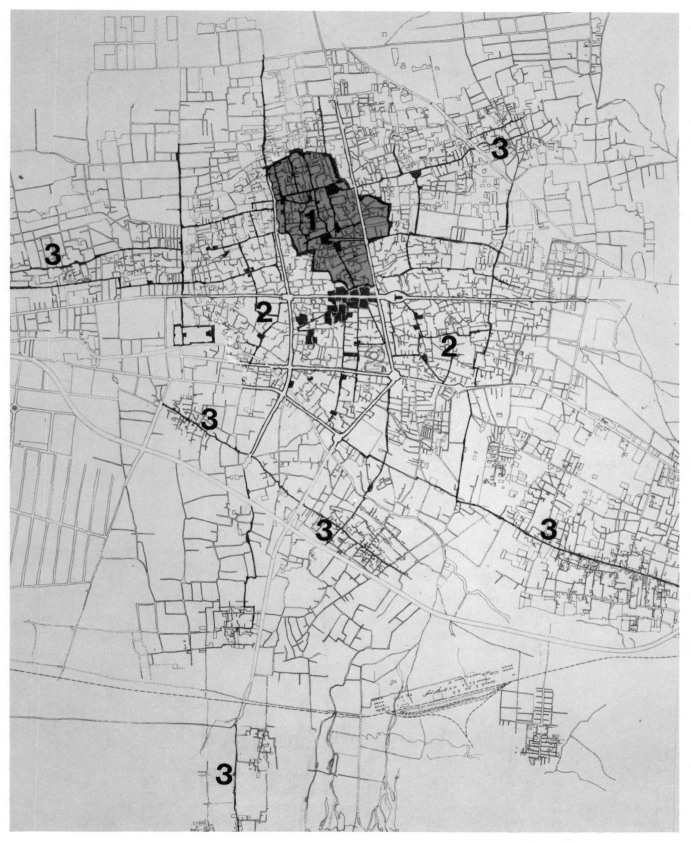

FIG. 6-1 Yazd, Iran: (1) historical section; (2) later expansion; (3) rural areas.

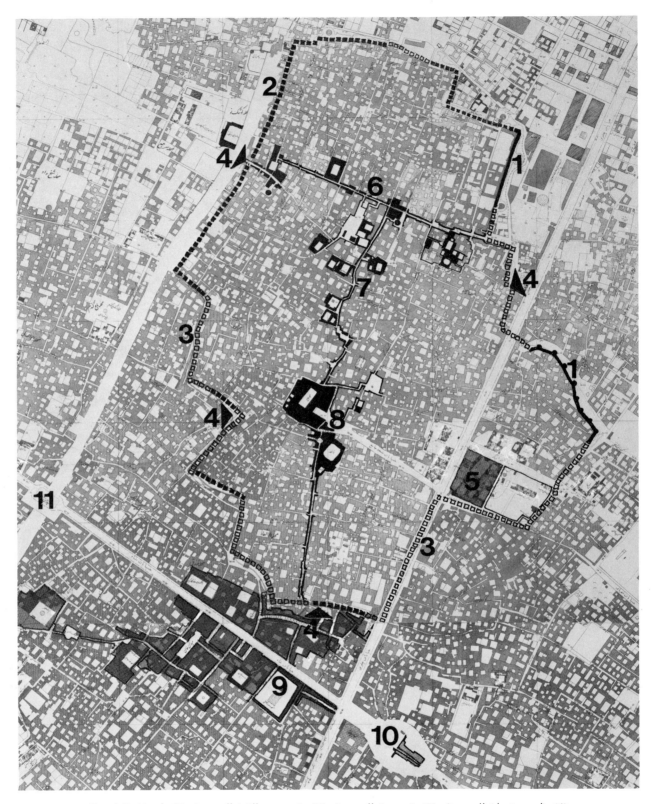

FIG. 6-2. Yazd: (1) city wall (still present); (2) city wall (traces); (3) city wall (destroyed); (4) main city gates; (5) citadel (now government offices); (6) historical street fronted by aristocratic houses, one of the 14th century; (7) another historical street (passing through the Friday Mosque); (8) active city bazaar; (9) a main *tekieh* (religious and social square); (10) and (11) square (destroyed). From Mahmood Tavassoli, *Architecture in the Hot Arid Zone* (Tehran, Iran: Payam, 1975), pp. 22-27.

FIG. 6-3. Yazd city wall.

it. In the formal structure of the town of Nain (see Figure 6-4), the walled city is irregular. One of the main gates opens onto the bazaar in the linear town and extends through the heart of the town. Here the *narrin ghalleh* or the inner castle (pre-Islamic) stands. At the edge of the area containing the bazaar and the *narrin ghalleh* is the Friday Mosque. Elements like the *tekieh* and the *ab-e-anbar* are adjacent. The walled city was divided into approximately seven neighborhoods, and each had its center at the intersection of the main passageways. Different elements in neighborhood centers met the requirements of the inhabitants of the neighborhood. The center, the most flexible element in the neighborhood structure, was a place where religious, retailing, and leisure activities were centered. During the holy days the *tekieh* or the *hosseinieh* and also the symbolic elements within them (the *nakhl*) were decorated according to religious customs (see Figure 6-5). Figure 6-6 shows the location of these elements in Zavareh. Sometimes one or two of these neighborhood center elements or an entire center would be named after a wealthy landowner, an aristrocrat, or a big master in the guild hierarchy who lived in that district.[8]

Investigations show that up to several decades ago there were over 80 quarters in the city of Yazd.[9] In the Middle Ages these quarters or neighborhoods characteristically provided the residences of a variety of social classes. Although some quarters were predominantly upper-class, there usually were a number of poorer inhabitants who worked in the work-

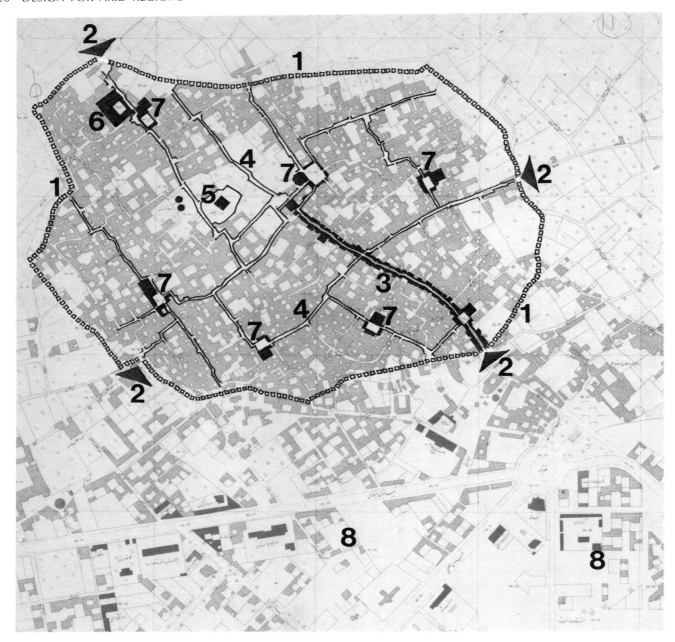

FIG. 6-4. Nain, Iran: (1) town wall; (2) gates; (3) bazaar; (4) passageways; (5) central castle; (6) Friday Mosque; (7) neighborhood center; (8) new expansion.

shops belonging to the nobility and also middle-class residents who had their own means of production including workshops.

In the quarters, it was common for rich dwellings, the neighborhood centers, and often more monumental elements to be placed along the main passageways. As Figure 6-2 shows, one of the two main passage-ways in Yazd displays such planning. It stretches between two of the main gates of the walled city and links several neighborhood centers. Some of the houses of the aristocratic families as well as the central square of the old town (surrounded by a number of historic buildings) are located along this passage. This characteristic arrangement also exists in the town of Nain (see Figure 6-4) and the small town of Zavareh (see Figure 6-6).

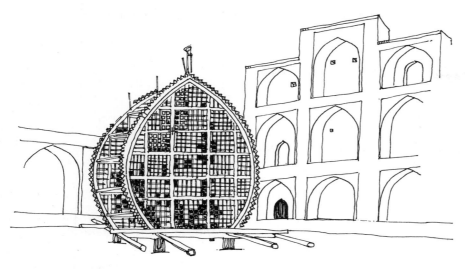

FIG. 6-5. *Nakhl,* an element decorated and shown in the *hosseinieh* during religious ceremonies.

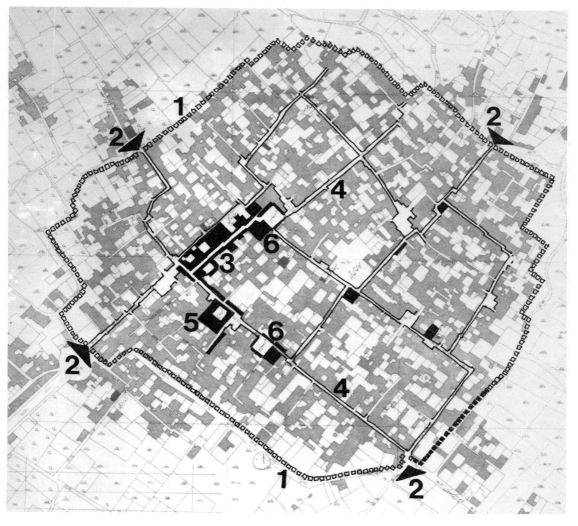

FIG. 6-6. Zavareh, Iran: (1) town wall; (2) position of the gates; (3) bazaar: (4) main passageways; (5) Friday Mosque; (6) two *hosseinieh* (religious squares), large and small.

Influence of Climate on Settlement Structure

Climate, a dominant factor which influences the evolution of an architectural style, is especially important in Iran. Since the effects are easily observable in the smaller villages, an examination of these villages can prove extremely valuable. The particular climatic problems that caused the people of the hot, arid zone to find solutions through the architecture of their settlements are as follows: high radiation and temperature in the summer; diurnal fluctuations of temperature; the seasonal fluctuations from the hot, dry summer to the cold, dry winter; low humidity; limited water supplies; and dusty, sandy winds.

Common climatic characteristics in various regions of the world create common design problems, so it is advantageous to look at various architectural solutions to these problems. In the hot, arid climate of the indigenous settlements of Iran, particularly interesting design solutions are found.

Actually, the overall structure of the town is compressed and compact. Houses are very close together, sometimes becoming so much a part of one another that walls are shared and boundaries between houses become unrecognizable. Numerous narrow or enclosed passageways facilitate the movement between districts, as Figure 6-7 shows. The parapets of houses make the passageways deeper and keep some part of the roofs always in shade. The compactness of the structure prevents the penetration of hot radiation (see Figures 6-8 and 6-9). Walls and roofs are usually thick so that they protect the interiors from external heat. The houses are traditionally built of mud, so they have a low rate of heat absorption and also reflect the sunlight. The practicality, availability, and relatively low cost, as well as the skillfulness and experience of the craftsman in working quickly and efficiently with the material, show why mud has become the primary building material. Mud domes are the most common means of covering spaces. The form of the dome allows winds to cool its surface easily, and it also ensures minimal frequency of intense radiation at any one point (see Figure 6-10). The double dome is an excellent solution to the problem of intense radiation. The space between the inner and the outer dome acts

FIG. 6-7. Yazd's compact structures, narrow streets, deep courtyards and summer areas of its houses with their backs to the afternoon sun.

FIG. 6-8. Narrow street in Yazd behind the Friday Mosque and crossed by the buttresses supporting the high wall under the Mosque's big dome.

FIG. 6-9. Narrow and shaded street crossed by mud buttresses, Kashan, Iran.

FIG. 6-10. Compact combination of mud brick domes, Kashan.

as an insulation layer. Therefore, when there is intense summer solar radiation, the outer dome becomes extremely hot, while the inner dome remains cool. Circulation of air between the two domes from openings reduces the radiation problem.

The structure of the city is open to the favorable winds and closed to unfavorable ones, particularly when the directions of the cool, pleasant or dusty, unpleasant winds are quite distinct. The cool, pleasant winds are drawn into the heart of the city by means of wind towers or *badgir* (see Figures 6-11 to 6-16). Cool night air is retained in the deep basements and deep courtyards. Another way of using the strong prevailing winds of this area involves the windmills which are seen in eastern Iran. The large wall which faces the prevailing winds not only funnels the wind through the mill, but also acts as a windbreak for the villages (see Figures 6-17). This protection is important, for these winds can reach speeds of 120 km/hr.

I have already mentioned the narrow, shaded passageways in Iranian desert towns. The narrowness of these passageways excludes the hot afternoon sun. The walls along the two sides of these narrow streets are usually high and supported by arches because there are outward lateral pressures acting on the walls from the vaulted spaces (i.e., those belonging to the arched roof rooms of the houses). Some sections of the narrow streets are completely enclosed, particularly in and near neighborhood centers.

Yazd is one of the most important cities exhibiting the traits of traditional arid zone adaptation. The general circulation pattern of the oldest part of Yazd consists of a series of perpendicular narrow passages defined by the sections of the old city walls which still exist. This old section of the historic city of Yazd has experienced few changes. The names of the

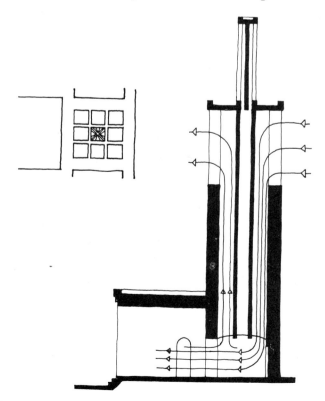

Fig. 6-11. Two-story *badgir* leading to tower, Aghda, Iran.

FIG. 6-12. Two-story *badgir* belonging to aristocratic family, Abarque, Iran.

central square, the gates of the city, the bazaar (see Figure 6-18) and some components of the town or neighborhood centers are, for instance, the same as they were during the fifth century after Islam, and in some cases, even during the pre-Islamic period.

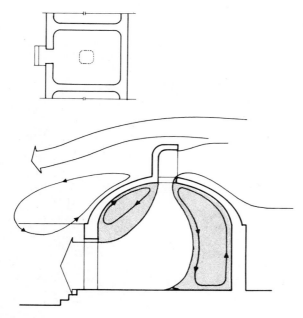

FIG. 6-13. One-sided *badgir* (one for one room) in Mehneh, village in Khorasan Province, Iran.

FIG. 6-14. Boshrouyeh, Iran: one-sided *badgir* open toward favorable winds.

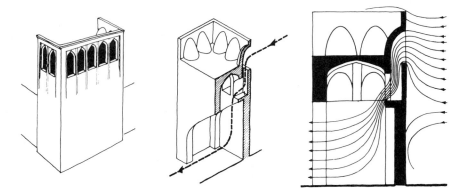

FIG. 6-15. Wind paths through three-sided *badgir*.

FIG. 6-16. Four-sided *badgir*, Sirjan, Iran.

FIG. 6-17. Khorasan and Sistan windmills.

Many other settlements in the hot, arid zones possess the same general qualities. At the level of the traditional, individual house or group of houses, there is great similarity throughout the arid zone. In these regions the streets are narrow, the walls are high, and some of the streets are covered to avoid the heat of the sun and extreme brightness. Thus, a cool and shaded refuge is made (see Figure 6-19).

The spatial structure of a familial complex, usually occupied by aristocrats, or even simple houses, have presented problems for the life style and socioeconomic activities of the traditional Iranian family. Furthermore,

FIG. 6-18. Old Bazaar Shahy and seminary around Friday Mosque, Yazd.

the nature of these structures has presented climatic difficulties. Existing literature gives very little information about the sociohistorical evolution of the Iranian family. However, a survey analysis of the houses shows that the household production space, different guest rooms, and workshop space have been the basic components of the old houses.

The traditional house of the hot, arid zone has a courtyard around which various closed or semiclosed spaces are situated. The two main areas of the house, as Figure 6-20 shows, are the summer and the winter areas. The summer area faces away from the hot afternoon sun (towad the northeast). This orientation in some cities, such as Yazd, by chance has the summer areas facing the *ghibleh* (GH). The *ghibleh* wall faces Mecca, the Muslim holy city.

The main components of the summer area are as follows: *talar*, a semiclosed space that faces the courtyard; *badgir*, a ventilation wind tower; *hozekhane*, a closed or semiclosed space in which usually there is a pool; *panj-dari*, a five-door room, large and proportionate; and *sardab*, a deep basement. These general elements are not necessarily found in any one summer area. The *talar* and *sardab* are generally common in all types of houses. The *badgir*, the symbol of the city in the hot, arid zone, is usually highest in the houses of the richest families. Favorable prevailing winds enter one side of the vents of the wind towers, then are channeled down into the *talar, sardab,* or *hozekhane*. Here the stream of air combines with the water vapor given off to increase humidity and create a pleasanter environment. Because of the difference of pressure between the vents of the *badgir* facing the prevailing wind and the vents facing away from the wind, the air is drawn up from the spaces below and expelled from the tower to rejoin the ambient air stream. In the hot summer afternoons when the external temperatures are high, the inhabitants retire to the *sardab*.

In the courtyard, there are usually small gardens and a pool to aid summer comfort. Shading trees often prevent penetration of excess radia-

FIG. 6-19. Local bazaar, Sirjan.

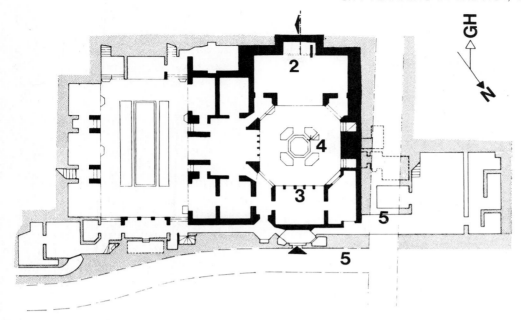

FIG. 6-20. Aristocratic family's housing complex: (1) wind tower; (2) summer area (talar); (3) winter area; (4) courtyard; (5) streets.

tion, and a second deeper courtyard may enable underground water to be brought to the surface. The added depth of these courtyards helps retain the night coolness for longer periods of time.

The winter areas of the houses are usually simple. The main elements of the house, the wind tower and deep basement, are climatically meaningful in the hot, arid zone and are generally located in the summer area. In the winter area, a five-door or three-door room is the main element. This area is opposite the summer quarters and takes advantage of the favorable winter sun.

On the two remaining sides of the courtyard there are various spaces such as storage areas, kitchens, extra rooms, basements, and cellars. In the underground spaces, dwellers keep extra foods and grain in case of drought or food shortage. The whole spatial structure of the house looks inward to a central space, with parapets built well above the roof lines in order to create shade and preserve privacy—all helping residents to adapt to the severe environmental problems.

Conditions and Problems in the City

There are a variety of vernacular villages, towns, and cities in Iran which have gradually evolved throughout the centuries. The pattern of these communities is functional; here rural and urban spatial form responds inexpensively to climatic problems. At the same time, these settlements reflect the cultural behavior and socioeconomic circumstances of their past dwellers.

The urban components such as neighborhood centers and main passageways still indicate the life of the past. However, they are no longer as active as they once were, for the influential socioeconomic relationships and cultural factors of the past are not the same today. There have been many changes in the social life and production methods during the last few decades. For example, traditional household and workshop production in the cities, including textile handicraft, weaving, spinning, carpet-making and so on, have generally moved into factories. Because of the various new means of communication and entertainment, television, cinema, etc., the old social relationships have been weakened. Therefore, within a house and an urban system, the spaces that were set aside for these human activities have lost their function and more or less have become useless.

Towns and cities have largely evolved without a recognition of urban problems. The compact structure of the city has been divided into pieces by many irrelevant wide streets. A lot of main passageways and bazaars have been widened or buildings demolished to form transport avenues. The principal objective here has been to facilitate the penetration of automobiles into the compact structure of the city, and a lot of available urban traditional open spaces (*tekieh*, *maydan*) were changed to traffic squares because of their width and size.

FIG. 6-21. Narrow street, Yazd, where wooden buttresses have replaced the ruined mud ones.

TABLE 6-1. Housing conditions in the city of Yazd (Iran).

Classification areas (S=area)	1 Percentage demolished	2 Percentage derelict	3 Percentage conserved	4 Percentage structurally sound, architectually important	5 Percentage new development with no architectural value
Built-up area within the old city (S=5/6 km²)	6	17	42	8	27
Built-up area within the old walled city. (S=0.7 km²)	9	22	55	3	11

Such new developments in the historical towns do not follow a relevant logic. Accelerated misuse of Western building technology has unfortunately changed the historical, practical urban features. Now the old areas of the towns lack fundamental services, and vehicles cannot penetrate. Modern city services have been concentrated in the new developments. City landowners, especially those possessing urban land, have had a considerable influence on urban speculation. As a function of these considerations, historical areas of cities in Iran are falling into ruin and have become the shelter of the urban poor. This ruin has been accelerated by the gradual increase in the number of vacant houses in these areas.

Table 6-1 and Figure 6-21 which relate to the historic city of Yazd illustrate the difficulties and problems resulting from the poor physical condition of the buildings. As we can see, within the boundary of the walled city, the number of derelict buildings and also demolished buildings is increasing. This is a serious danger for the central urban environment of most of the hot, arid-zone cities (see Figure 6-22). Vacant housing exists to some extent in Table 6-1's classifications two, three, and four.

Demolished areas have created inaccessible holes within the compact structure of the cities. These holes increase as vacant houses fall into disrepair. This city leprosy is gradually rotting the inner areas. The private sector, the main developer, has not been interested in investment to develop these holes. Cost of site clearance, the inaccessibility of the site, the lack of urban services in historic inner areas, the poverty environment, and more recently the constraints on planning (mainly in conservation areas)—all can be considered as the main reasons for the lack of concern of the private sector in investment.

Today, studies show that the conservation cost for a large, old house with a high architectural value is approximately equal to the cost of buying land and building two new houses with average standards or one big house with high standards. This conservation cost does not even include the cost of establishing modern services within the house.

FIG. 6-22. Compact structure featured in some ruined areas in the heart of historical section of Nain.

Conclusion

Such are the problems of decline in and disproportionate expansion around the historic areas of the hot, arid zone in Iran. Development of settlements under the conditions of rapid urbanization appears to be growing increasingly out of control and at odds with the general aims of the previously prepared master plans. This lack of control is especially evident when preparation of master plans and the corroboration of them through governmental authorities has made planning decision processes lengthy.

Despite the existing situation where private developers and their profit motives have the main role in the development process, effective planning can only be achieved through the establishment of a publicly supported agency to deal with the problems of inner cities in the hot, arid zone of Iran. It should draw its members from the qualified university researchers, professional planners, urban designers, architects, private developers, public authorities, and (mainly) local community representatives. This agency should plan on a short-term basis. The decisions, because of the poor condition of the inner areas, should be protected by sanctions and approved by responsible authorities with a minimum delay. There are workers and craftsmen to do this work; all that is necessary is a proper plan.

Notes

1. Valuable research in this field can be found in Ahmad Ashraf, "Historical Specificity of Iranian Cities in Islamic Era," *Journal of the Social Sciences* **1**, no. 4 (June 1974), 7–49.
2. Part three of this chapter is based on chapter two of a book previously published in Persian: Mahmood Tavassoli, *Architecture in the Hot Arid Zone* (Tehran, Iran: Payam, 1975).
3. The most valuable series of articles for the study of Persian architecture are by M. K. Pirnia in the *Iranian Journals of Archaeology and Art* (in Persian).
4. Extracted from an interview with M. K. Pirnia, February 1972. Chapter two of Tavassoli, *Architecture in the Hot Arid Zone*, discusses this interview.
5. Interview with Pirnia.
6. Mahmood Tavassoli, "Socio-historical Studies of Neighborhood Organizations," in *Detailed Plan for the Historic City of Yazd, First Phase*, ed. Mahmood Tavassoli (Tehran, Iran: University of Tehran, 1976), pp. 29–63.
7. Mahmood Tavassoli, "Considerations of Urban Social Spaces," in *Detailed Plan*, pp. 219–251.
8. Tavassoli, "Socio-historical Studies."
9. Ibid.

Selected Readings

Ashraf, Ahmad. Historical specificity of Iranian cities in Islamic era. *Journal of the Social Sciences*, **1**, no. 4 (June 1974), 7–49.

Behnam, J. and Rasekn, S. Morphology of Iranian cities and Housing form in Iran. In *An Introduction to Sociology of Iran*. Kharazmi, Iran, 1969, pp. 441–476.

Khosrovi, Khosrov. Relation between village and city and City and village in Islamic era. In *Rural Sociology of Iran*. Tehran, Iran: University of Tehran, the Faculty of Social Sciences and Cooperative Studies, 1972, pp. 31–47.

Pirnia, Mohammad Karim. Articles dealing with Persian architecture and cities in *Iranian Journals of Archaeology and Art, Iranian Journals of Art and People,* and *Iranian Journals of Art and Architecture*.

Tavassoli, Mahmood. Spatial form of the Persian vernacular architecture. In *Architecture in the Hot Arid Zone*. Tehran, Iran: Payam, 1975, pp. 21–71

Vadiie, Kazem. Housing and housing type in Iran. In *An Introduction to Human Geography of Iran*. Tehran, Iran: University of Tehran, 1970, pp. 153–177.

7
Architectural and Environmental Adaptation in Slope Settlements

Mete H. Turan

Throughout history man has developed tools and other means to free himself from the restricting limitations of his natural environment. Within the parameters of its sociocultural capacity and faculties, each society, through its responses to nature (namely the mesoenvironment or the architecture), provides the means to terrestrial existence as opposed to the more primitive arboreal survival. In this terrestrial existence, the process that takes place is of an ecological nature and therefore involves the conservation and dissipation of energy, the maintenance of a mutual balance between man and his environment, and adaptation.

There is hardly a natural environment in which human life could have been perpetuated had not man adapted to the constantly changing forces of his habitat. Thus, adaptation has provided man with the ability to transcend the limitations of his biological faculties and his natural environment. While lower animals basically adapt through genetic mutation (i.e., biological adaptation), man adjusts through both biological and cultural means. By culture, I mean the integral whole consisting of tools, artifacts, and the organization of social actions, beliefs, attitudes, and ideologies—in short all of those "exosomatic" means employed to maintain life in the natural environment. Cultural adaptation to nature does not necessarily mean that culture is determined by environmental conditions; it would be a great misconception to assume that the physical environmental elements are the only factors which characterize a culture. Whatever man produces is part of both the cultural and the natural environment. Also cultural products become part of the natural environment; they, like man, are also subject to the laws of nature. By acting upon and modifying the natural environment, man produces a natural result; however, for operational reasons and for the sake of clarity, "we proceed with artifice, we call his results artificial and the products he has made and the environment he has modified cultural."[1] Otherwise, the dichotomy of natural vs. artificial, as Stea points out correctly, loses its validity.[2]

Man's Response to Nature

One form of adaptation among man's cultural responses to nature is exploitation, which occurs as man turns available materials to practical usage in order to survive.[3] While bringing about a change in the ecological relationship (man's physical environment, i.e., nature including man), exploitation tends to reduce stress arising from physical environmental forces; man alters his position in this ecological community by securing control over the physical environment. During this process of adaptation, there are inevitable changes or additional strains imposed upon the environment itself. In return, man has to cope with the newly developed physical forces as consequences of his own purposive activities. Once the stability of the ecological structure is forced beyond the limits of resilience, there are reciprocal effects of changing patterns of human activity upon the environment. Thus, man not only adapts to changes brought about by the physical environmental forces but also copes with the alterations in the environment that he himself has produced. As Lukacs remarks, the natural environment is therefore a "social category," for the environment is first affected and eventually shaped by the social environment.[4] Therefore, man must comprehend the coherent elements which unite him to his environment. This is the environmental consciousness that man develops as a result of his direct experience with the concrete conditions of the environment and social relations. Environmental consciousness must be dialectical, for it must be in accordance with the activities and purposes that are generated in a life process.

In Mannheim's words, a "historically evolving consciousness" determined by social conditions affects the individual's behavior in the environment and his interpretation of the environment.[5] This variation occurring within a structural transition with respect to the physical environment has intended and attributed meanings. Intended meanings, wherein the individual experiences the environment as an "intrinsically coherent whole," become attributed meanings within such a transition.[6] When the act of personalization of the environmental elements—objectification—leads to alienation as environmental elements acquire an existence independent of the individual, attributed meanings take the place of intended meanings.[7] Then, in place of environmental consciousness, man develops a narrow perspective manifested in the present-day mode of production. For many years the individual society (both in the capitalist and socialist camps) has thrived on inventing expedient solutions to many problems (least among them the environmental ones) that have traditionally hindered the progress of human welfare. However, now the industrial system has itself become a hindrance, for it has grown into an economically wasteful, ecologically dangerous, and sociopolitically deterrent agent. The mode of production that governs most societies is characterized by the "capability of enormously magnifying human productivity by endowing men with literally superhuman abilities to control the physical and chemical attributes of nature."[8]

The wreckage of the natural environment is partly achieved through compulsive production of generally futile, poorly designed, inefficacious, and increasingly expensive construction materials and methods. Meanwhile, real environmental needs are not met; in turn, there is an arbitrary manipulation of the environment and of men. The notion of domination over nature, despite the highly advanced rationality of science and technology, is firing back at its masters. Such mastery over nature as the statement of philosophical and scientific advancement is not identical with domination of nature as the concrete manifestation of events related to the totality of conflicts in modern societies. The fundamental misconception comes from the fact that the rationally and technologically ideal form cannot be transplanted in its entirety and in an untouched form to cure the ills of society, deeply rooted in social conflicts. As Leiss explains, "No matter how superior the consciousness of a civilization may be in itself this attribute cannot nourish rational human behavior so long as the violent struggle for existence persists."[9]

The environmental conditions we confront today are fundamentally the result of the idea of an external nature outside of man and the vulgar pragmatic conceptions of mastery over nature. Actually, the environmental events since the industrial revolution and the degradation with which we are faced constitute a *reductio ad absurdum* of the present-day use of technology, or more generally of the mode of production to which the two main socioeconomic systems—capitalism and socialism—are committed. The bourgeois ethos of economic development central to capitalism has failed to produce an environmental consciousness; the gradual depleting of natural resources, the disruption of the environment, and the environmental chaos prevailing especially in large urban and industrial centers do not suggest the possibility of much hope for a better prospect in the future: the garnering of wealth is a predominant driving force. Since the means of production are also in the hands of a minority group, it is especially difficult to change its social values and to develop an environmental consciousness in its members.

Such typically capitalistic manipulation and abuse of the land also exist in socialist systems, even though the reasons may be different. Heilbroner, in his look at the bleak human prospect, argues correctly and convincingly that "Both socio-economic systems are committed to a civilization whose most striking aspects is its productive virtuosity."[10] Despite the farsighted warnings of Engels that when abused, "nature takes its revenge on us," the situation in the socialist societies does not look much different or more promising.[11] "Rapacious use of the productive forces of the soil," is Lenin's description of the capitalist large-scale production and competition.[12] But the very same large-scale production deeply rooted in the overriding priority of economics has been the main cause of environmental disruption in most of the socialist states. For example, most of the major Soviet cities are confronted with air pollution, erosion (e.g., as some seacoast lines retreat, some buildings disappear), water pollution, and climatic disruption due to gigantic hydroelectric stations and irrigation reservoirs.[13]

Therefore, modern scientific rationality ruled by pragmatism and instrumentalism is far from bringing alternative solutions to the technological problem of mastery over nature and consequent political domination. Using Marcuse's distinction between the two kinds of mastery over nature, "repressive" and "liberating," we cannot see how we can direct mastery toward liberation without the free development of needs immediately following material satisfaction.[14] As long as civilization and its imperatives of present-day production treat nature as an instrument of destructive productivity, the repressive nature of mastery cannot be overcome; nor can the repression of man (for mastery of nature in its repressive sense also means mastery over man) as a result of passivity imposed on him through technological fetishism, be directed to a liberation. An environmental consciousness, developed through direct experience with the environment and leading to an intended meaning rather than an attributed one, can bring about qualitative instead of only quantitative changes. They will, through liberation, direct the mastery over nature.

Architecture in Environment

Like man and nature, architecture and environment cannot be thought of separately. There is a dialectical interaction that exists between them, and the nature of this interaction is generously displayed in the vernacular examples of architecture. By building in accordance with the environmental forces, man is creating part of the larger environment. Man's initial attempts in architectural activity start as a mere protection from the environmental forces. However, when this is done along with the internal dynamics of nature, there is a merger of the man-built environment (architecture) with the natural environment. In this blending, architecture becomes the environment. The dialogue between man and nature in the vernacular experience reflects a definite stability in the value of the architectural-environmental relations. Actually, through architecture, man attempts to overcome some environmental forces; but through an environmental *praxis* as a result of such a dialogue, his production is transformed back into the environment. Architectural stability established through such a dialogue preserves a valid appearance for a long time, and the artifacts are able to survive the manifold changes in social relations. This characteristic of vernacular architecture can be attributed to several factors at play: they are not the products of certain fashion periods; they are flexible enough to stand alterations that are imposed by changes in the social forces; they exhibit characteristics that require a relative continuity in the totality of the building process—tools, materials, structural systems, construction methods, etc.—as opposed to the discontinuity observed in the building process of societies with market economies; they are the products of man's direct relations and experiences with the environment; hence, they are skillfully responsive to the environmental forces; and they display respect for other people and their environment.[15]

While adhering to no boundaries between the aesthetic and the conceptual dimensions of actual construction, vernacular architecture reveals another characteristic which establishes a close correlation between handicraft and art. Under this link between handicraft and art, the laws determining the evolution of the vernacular definitely differ qualitatively from those of institutionalized architecture. It also takes a long time for a concept to develop into a building element and for it to be refined considerably.[16]

Cultural inheritance also affects the continuity of the building process. This inheritance is categorically different from biological inheritance; it shows, contrary to its biological counterpart, a Lamarckian character. In addition to the continuity required in the building process, vernacular architecture also possesses the succession and inheritance of cultural symbols and accustomed images of past experiences. Neither the cultural symbols nor the images that are inherited are devoid of some material meaning attached to them, for the appearance of a symbol occurs after several lines of development. Malinowski outlines the concurrent integration as "the ability to recognize instrumental objects, the appreciation of their technical efficiency, and their value, that is, their place in the purposive sequence, the formation of social bonds and the appearance of symbolism."[17] Some losses from the original meaning or from their purposive sequence may have occurred, but the symbolic values are still part of the culture since some of "its ideas and feelings" are made concrete through those symbols.[18]

Cultural inheritance can become a problem; for what was once a direct response to natural forces in the dialogue between architecture and environment, a few generations later can become an indirect response and an alienated reaction. There are two reasons for this. On the one hand, what is acquired initially and developed through direct experience with the environment is the outcome of an environmental consciousness, which, in time, may turn into accustomed behavior. On the other hand, the propensity to be concerned only with the formal and mechanical qualities of the response and to imitate what is assumed to be better leads to an alienation between man and the environment. The latter is the direct result of the changing social relations and the forceful imperatives of technology and the alternatives (in most cases poor substitutes to those of the vernacular) brought about by it. At present, the dialectic of environment and architecture is epitomized in the changing socioeconomic relations which establish control over the building process through profit-bringing materials and active design elements which, more than ever, ardently but harmfully exploit the resources of the natural environment. The source of this so-called rationality lies deep down in the irrational social and political (and concurrently environmental) behavior fed by the uncontrolled interactions between man and his environment. The result is misuse, waste, and destruction.

It is not the primacy of economic motives that constitutes the decisive difference between vernacular and institutionalized architecture, but the environmental totality and its quality. The harmonious relationship between architecture and man's environment is what is primarily lacking in the institutionalized building which is conceptually, but erroneously and dangerously, named artificial. There cannot be an artificial environment if the forces of nature and other environmental factors are considered within the design and construction, i.e., within the architectural process. An artificial environment can only exist when active design elements outweigh passive design considerations. In the case of vernacular architecture where the passive design elements are much in accordance with the dynamics of the environmental forces, what starts out as protection against certain forces of the environment turns into an integrated element of the environment. Thus a unity of opposites is achieved by the frugal interaction of architecture and the environment; a quantitative change is turned into a qualitative change. This phenomenon is quite different from that found with institutionalized architecture which has a tendency to cut the umbilical relationship that must exist between architecture and the environment.

Vernacular Approaches

CLIMATIC REALITIES

The approaches to climatic classification vary according to the selected criteria in the climatic system and the purposes which they aim to achieve. Yet there has not been a very detailed global evaluation of climate specifically for architectural purposes. Either some generally accepted classifications, such as W. Köppen's, have been used; or more arbitrary ones, like the Mahoney Tables, have been designed for architectural purposes.[19] Griffith's attempt at a climatic classification, particularly for housing, seems no less elementary than the assumptions or modifications of others.[20] Since an attempt at a new classification is beyond the scope of this study, a listing of the general characteristics of a hot, arid climatic zone will suffice: high air temperatures in the summer; large diurnal temperature fluctuations both in summer and winter; low relative humidity (the highest occurring in the winter months); insignificant rainfall in the summer months (the mean annual rainfall does not exceed 500 mm and in most cases it is less than 400 mm, but in some exceptional cases where the altitude is higher than 1000 m, it can reach up to 700 mm); and high solar radiation (both in summer and winter). (Some of the climatic data for the area investigated in Turkey are presented in the Appendix.)

The area studied in Turkey (see Figure 7-1) is a strip approximately 200 km wide. It extends from the central Anatolian plateau to the southeast toward the Fertile Crescent—the sickle-shaped area starting from northern Israel and Jordan, going through modern-day Syria and Lebanon, and reaching to northern Iraq and southern Turkey. The whole area exhibits more or less similar characteristics except for the small strip indicated on the map. Because of the mountainous region extending from the northeast corner of the Mediterranean Sea directly to the northeast toward Lake Van, a narrow strip approximately 100 km wide shows variation in climatic data, especially in humidity and rainfall.[21] Excluding this mountainous strip, the hot, arid zone has a dry season for about five to six months of each year.

A COMPARATIVE LOOK AT THE PAST

Adverse climatic conditions require a suitable microclimate in and around the houses; landscaping and planning (both at architectural and town scales) demand special attention in order to be economically feasible, socially acceptable, and ecologically frugal. This is especially true in

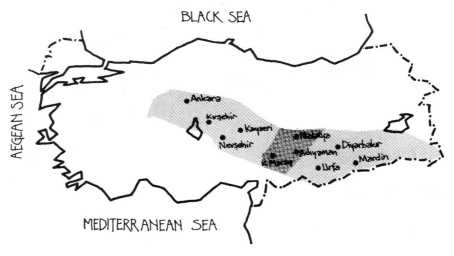

FIG. 7-1. Hot, arid zone, Turkey.

societies having an economy of scarcity.[22] Here the margin for error and ill-use of both the environmental factors and the materials must be very small, and a high level of performance and behavior is expected from the building and the town. For centuries a striking feature of the dwellings and the settlements in the central Anatolian plateau toward the Fertile Crescent has been the use of adobe or stone building materials and stepping terraces on which the settlements are formed. The reconstructed flat-roofed house of the Assyrian merchant colony (Karum) at Kultepe is similar in design and form to the houses still predominant in the area today. Near that area, Akköy (see Figure 7-2) has a southerly facing, gently sloping topography very much in accordance with the Karahoyuk Koyu and built on the ancient ruins of Karahoyuk just north of the main mound at Kultepe (Kanesh).[23]

The tradition of this type of building featuring a generous southern orientation, has been carried on since the Neolithic period (e.g., Catal Huyuk, 6000 B.C.), through the Early Bronze period (e.g., Assyrian Karum, 2000 B.C.) and the Late Bronze period (e.g., Bogazkoy of Hittites, 1500 B.C.), up to the present.[24] Even when there were no multistory buildings, the terracing of the roofs toward the south was achieved by building platforms at different levels in harmony with the sloping topography.[25] This design included a more effective wall surface where heat was stored. It also permitted natural light to enter the different levels of the platforms and cross-ventilation to occur during the hot summer days.

The schematic reconstruction of Catal Huyuk shows many parallels in the overall complexity of its planning and architectural features—more or

Fig. 7-2. Akköy in Göreme Valley (Cappadocia), featuring a primarily southern orientation with an aspect angle of 195°.

less direct adaptive responses to the environmental forces. Buildings rising up the slope of the mound at different levels ease the lighting conditions for individual dwellings and shrines and allow the heat to be stored in the massive sun-dried rectangular mud bricks. Catal Huyuk displays stepping terraces starting from an initial height of one story in the south or the west to three stories respectively in the northern or the eastern sides of the building complex.[26] Although the location of this Neolithic town is outside the boundaries of the hot, arid zone indicated on the map, Catal Huyuk has similar climatic characteristics to the central Anatolian plateau.

This type of architectural response to the particular environmental forces is not, of course, restricted to this part of the world. Man's struggle to set up his community and form his social bonds in similar environmental conditions can be observed in many places.[27] The validity of such solutions for the particular environments are rooted in man's knowledge and direct experience in his environment. Until certain laws of nature are known to man, he is at the mercy of the unknown; but once these laws are learned and understood, man can exploit them to his own advantage. As long as this exploitation is done with the minimum amount of damage to the environment, man's mastery over nature will be a liberating one; otherwise, mastery over nature, as discussed earlier, can be repressive. The problem of this repressive type of mastery was true even among the societies prior to industrialization (the effectiveness range of these solutions was not as wide as today's and not as quick since the mode of production and techniques had not been developed to its present level). The stability achieved in architecture and the environment on the basis of such a dialogue and the appearance of its nature, however, cannot be above history and society.[28]

Among the examples of similar responses to environmental conditions of hot, arid areas in a different location and culture are those of the American Indian of the Southwest. Figure 7-3 gives the predominant settlement types. There were many influencing factors in the shaping of these settlements: houses built by the Hopis show an appreciation for the needs of defense against the aggressive and marauding nomads; the apartment houses built high up on the mesas overlooking their cultivated fields on the valley floor below or the dwellings built and carved in the middle of a sheer wall, without any doubt had deliberately been made to discourage attackers. Multiband villages protected by deserts and plateau escarpments could not have been much of an attraction for the intruders except for the fairly reliable but rather limited supply of water and for the not very frequently existing surplus of food.[29]

However, Knowles has shown in his detailed study of Acoma that the careful layout of the multiband settlements has some other purpose than just security and that the tiered sections of the buildings which step down and expose broad surfaces to the south demonstrate an attempt to establish a meaningful relationship between the buildings' arrangements and the sun. A comparison of seasonal energy profiles shows clearly the advantage of terracing the section toward the south. Furthermore, the no-shadow-casting multiband layout ensures each row constant solar access.[30] Thus we can see that the settlement has a year-round, efficient system for using energy in every home.[31] The energy balance, not over a short period but throughout the year, is set in the most efficient way for a typical unit as well as for the whole settlement. There is also proof of comfort in this Indian environment.

Despite the existence of many houses along the foot of the mesa, their owners prefer to live in their old villages most of the year.[32] Attempts since the late 1880s by the United States government to get the Hopi to come down from their settlements on the mesa tops (e.g., Walpi, Sichomovi, and

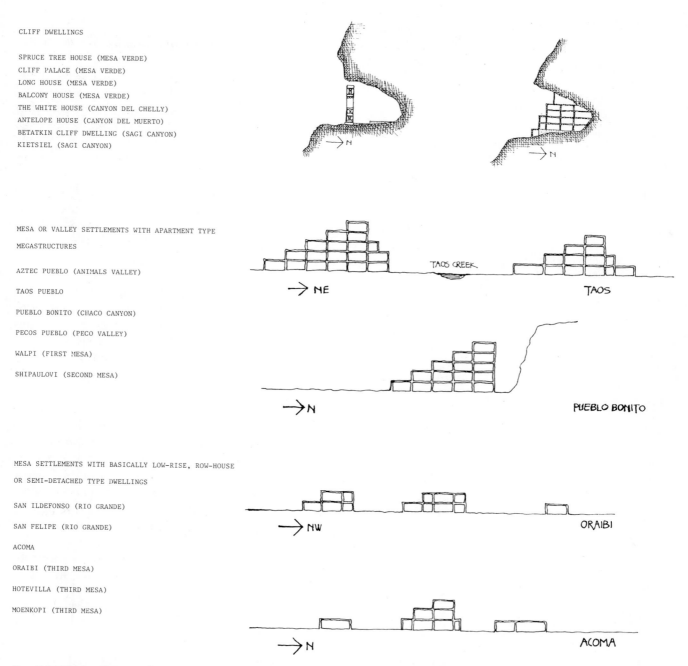

CLIFF DWELLINGS

SPRUCE TREE HOUSE (MESA VERDE)
CLIFF PALACE (MESA VERDE)
LONG HOUSE (MESA VERDE)
BALCONY HOUSE (MESA VERDE)
THE WHITE HOUSE (CANYON DEL CHELLY)
ANTELOPE HOUSE (CANYON DEL MUERTO)
BETATKIN CLIFF DWELLING (SAGI CANYON)
KIETSIEL (SAGI CANYON)

MESA OR VALLEY SETTLEMENTS WITH APARTMENT TYPE
MEGASTRUCTURES

AZTEC PUEBLO (ANIMALS VALLEY)

TAOS PUEBLO

PUEBLO BONITO (CHACO CANYON)

PECOS PUEBLO (PECO VALLEY)

WALPI (FIRST MESA)

SHIPAULOVI (SECOND MESA)

MESA SETTLEMENTS WITH BASICALLY LOW-RISE, ROW-HOUSE
OR SEMI-DETACHED TYPE DWELLINGS

SAN ILDEFONSO (RIO GRANDE)

SAN FELIPE (RIO GRANDE)

ACOMA

ORAIBI (THIRD MESA)

HOTEVILLA (THIRD MESA)

MOENKOPI (THIRD MESA)

FIG. 7-3. Predominant settlement types of the southwestern (U.S.) Indian tribes (No attempt has been made to be exhaustive in the listing of these three major types of dwellings; nor has there been any other criterion used except the prevailing climatic conditions (those of the hot, arid zones) in this rather crude classification that is mainly based on the physical aspects of the settlements.)

Hano) have been unsuccessful. Only the economically desperate families who could find new work opportunities and better public services moved to new settlements (e.g., Kiakochomovi—Lower or New Oraibi). The initial tendency at the start of these new settlements had been to build houses in compact rows—a degenerated and deformed version of the older settlements, the multiband organization of the mesa tops. The lack of organization and planning resulted in haphazard settlements in sharp contrast to that of the mesa settlements.[33]

Studies of other Indian settlements indicate the practicality and superiority of Pueblo construction. This most likely explains why some of the Indian settlements have been continuously occupied for centuries (e.g., in the case of Acoma, the Keresan-speaking Pueblos have occupied their mesa site since prehistoric times).[34] For over a thousand years of occupancy, except for some modifications and minor surface treatments, the form of the Acoma pueblo has not been radically changed.[35] Knowles found superiority in the cliff dwellings and apartment house type megastructures similar to the row house or semidetached type dwellings.[36] In the cliff dwelling, at the Long House pueblo, Knowles found the efficiency of energy received and concurrently stored higher in winter than in summer. Of course, this is not surprising, for the cave offers protection from the high summer altitude of the sun.

At Pueblo Bonito, the way surfaces receive solar energy and transmit the stored energy to interior spaces shows a remarkable performance. In the first place, efficiency of the energy used is higher in winter (when needed the most) than in summer; secondly, highly stable winter efficiency provides the best means for solar energy to be stored and later reradiated during the cold night. On the other hand, during the summer solstice, the energy efficiency profile is lower. Furthermore, it does not show the same stability that the winter profile exhibits; it is higher in the morning when the ambient air temperatures are lower. Hence, there is not only seasonal mitigation, but also a daily mitigation of quite large fluctuations in insolation.

Though some of the cliff dwellings were large enough for only a few extended families (e.g., the Balcony House), some were large complexes, housing about 200 people (e.g., Cliff Palace). On the other hand, megastructures built on the mesa tops or in the valleys are considerably larger in size: in the number of rooms (e.g., Aztec: 500 rooms; Pecos: 660 rooms; Pueblo Bonito: 800 rooms), in height (pueblos like Taos, Bonito are nearly four- to five-stories in certain places). The cliff dwellings were smaller in size out of sheer necessity, for they had to be suitable for the caves or ledges on which they were built. However, regardless of the size, general features of their architecture characterize very clearly the similarities of responses to the utilization of the solar energy.

ENERGY BUDGET OF A SLOPE SETTLEMENT

The evolution of a predominant house type in hot, arid regions was outlined in an earlier study.[37] The performance of individual dwelling units under the given adverse climatic conditions has shown the mitigating effect of the building types under daily fluctuations of insolation. Analysis was made only on the basis of materials used in construction and the form of the buildings. Thermophysical properties of materials used in vernacular solutions use solar energy more advantageously than today's commonly used materials under the same environmental conditions. Consequently, vernacular solutions considerably reduce the extra heat required to raise the indoor temperatures to comfortable levels.

The form of these settlements also shows ecological economy. A common physical characteristic of the settlements in this region is their slope orientation: regardless of the size of villages, towns, or larger cities, a high percentage of settlements are located on the southern (southeastern or southwestern, as well) slopes. Location depends on other environmental factors such as topography, wind patterns, vegetation, and such pedologic forces as soil types, drainage, and erosion. When we examine the distribution of the solar radiation received on slopes with different orientations (see Figure 7-4), we see that the southerly facing slopes make the best use of the insolation. This type of dialogue with the environment can arise only from direct experience.

Unfortunately, these vernacular examples which show adaptability and practicality do not always continue to be followed. The modern-day prodigal attitude toward environmental design shows short-sighted or narrowly defined economic priorities. The frequent misuse of technology, the waste of economic means, and concurrently, the gradual destruction of the environment is minimized if not totally eliminated in examples of vernacular architecture.

Mardin

Centuries long persistence in the use of slope settlements in this or similar regions demonstrates the validity and rationality of such an approach. The history of Mardin—one of the major slope settlements in southeastern Turkey—is a good example of this perseverance (see Figure 7-5). Dating back to the third millennium B.C., Mardin has been a location for some of the agricultural societies of the Fertile Crescent.[38] Its geographic location

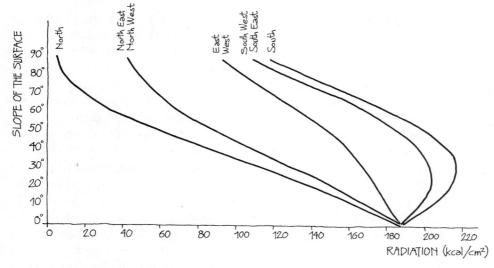

FIG. 7-4. Distribution of radiation on surfaces with different slopes and orientations.

FIG. 7-5. Mardin, Turkey, southern orientation with an aspect angle of 175°.

and its dramatic topography make it very desirable not only in security and defense terms but also from economic and ecological points of view. The hill rises sharply from the plain to the south of it; a milder slope of 20° to 25°, upon which present-day Mardin rests, climbs toward the top of the hill. This is followed by a steeper stretch on top of which are the ruins of the ancient citadel (see the map in Figure 7-6). This hill, known as the bird's or eagle's nest, connects to another plateau in the north.

According to one source, the city of Mardin had developed into a large and an important center of agricultural and economic activities until A.D. 442.[39] However, the Black Death that was killing large numbers of people in the area around that time finally reached Mardin and forced the inhabitants to evacuate the city. A century later the city was entirely reconstructed on the orders of a Roman commander, Ursianos. It took 47 years, 100 architects-engineers, 250 master builders, and countless others to complete the new town of Mardin. Only after the completion of the new city (A.D. 541), did inhabitants start coming back to it; they were even encouraged and assisted by Ursianos to set up small farms on the outskirts

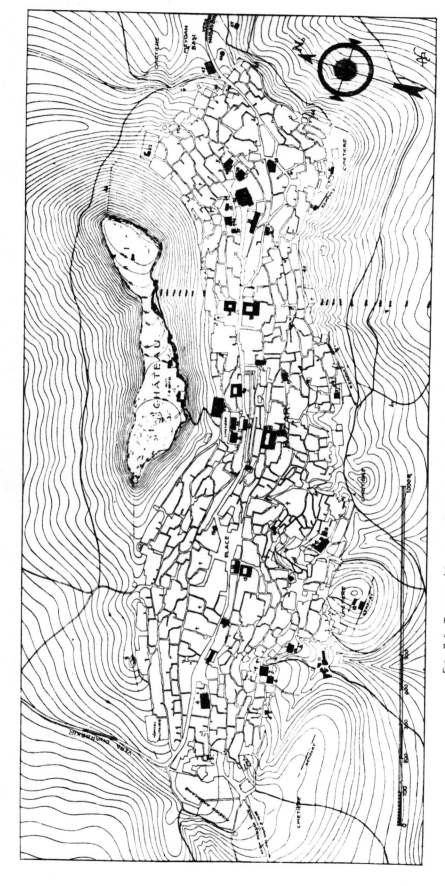

Fig. 7-6. Topographic map of Mardin showing the settled area and the citadel. From A. Gabriel, *Voyages Archeologiques dans la Turquie Orientale* (Paris: E. de Boccard, 1940), p. 8.

153

of the new town. The structural complexity of the present-day settlement makes it very difficult to believe that such complex architectural relations could emerge from a plan. We do not know the complexity of the organization of Ursianos' plan, nor the precise size of the complete city. We do know, however, that the new city was located on the same southerly facing slope. This permitted the individual units and the stepping terraces to have uninterrupted access to the sun.

Resemblances of the present environment to that of the past go beyond orientation and settlement. At the architectural scale, as opposed to the town scale, striking similarities exist among structures of different eras, though they are centuries apart. In its historical evolution, Mardin had also served the Babylonians as one of their important centers, though it was not as important nor as famous as Babylon itself. One of the Seven Wonders of the World, the Hanging Gardens of Babylon—the city famed for its sensual living—became legendary from the days of Nebuchadnezzar (d.562 B.C.). After the death of the last great Assyrian ruler, Assurbani-pal, the leader of Babylonia, Nabopolossar established (625 B.C.) his independence. Thus, what is generally known as the Chaldaean or New Babylonian Empire was founded. Mardin at the time was under Nabopolossar's rule.[40] His son Nebuchadnezzar, the reputed builder of the Hanging Gardens of Babylon, was sent on a mission to Mardin and its surroundings many times.

This immediately brings to mind the question: are there resemblances between the famous Hanging Gardens of Babylon and the settlement pattern of Mardin? The cultural diffusion is inevitable when the conditions, physical and social, are not very far removed from each other. Furthermore, when the social and commercial bonds are very strong, and when the two cities happen to be under the same rule, the speculation of

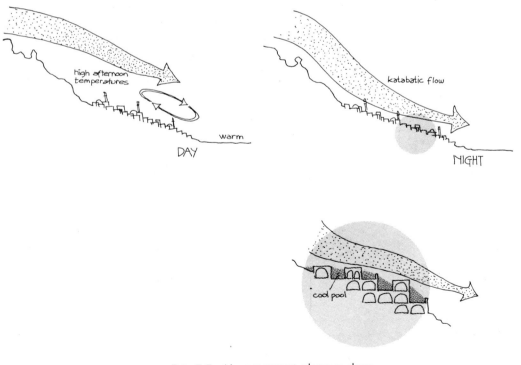

FIG. 7-7. Air movement along a slope.

cultural diffusion in this particular case starts having some foundation to it. Especially when we remember that Mardin was under the rule of this first Babylonian state for close to three centuries, the grounds for speculation become even wider. Therefore, it is not very surprising to find similarities between today's houses at Mardin and reconstructed sections of the gardens of Babylon.[41]

Very dry and hot summers made it imperative to adapt to the natural forces and to work in harmony with the environment. (For data on climate of Mardin, see the Appendix.) Fortunately, the discomfort of high temperatures during the day is partially mitigated by the breezes caused by temperature differences between the plain below the hill and the city itself. The prevailing summer wind is from the north. However, this wind cannot under normal conditions provide comfort for the city; the hill north of the settlement acts as a barrier, creating a protected area right over the city. Nevertheless, the high temperatures right above the city rise and cause an air movement from the plain below and an almost continuous breeze.

At night the situation changes: the cooling city surface gives rise to a difference in the air density along the slope. Due to gravity, the heavier air at the top flows down; as a result, a gentle breeze brushes the city. The downhill flow of cool air, called katabatic flow, also causes cool pools in the lower areas where there is comfortable outdoor sleeping. (See Figure 7-7). Figure 7-8 shows the outdoor sleeping *tahts* [thrones].) The north-

FIG. 7-8. Dwelling exterior in Mardin showing outdoor sleeping *tahts*.

south direction of both day and nighttime breezes also creates relatively comfortable pockets along the north-south oriented pedestrian walkways and steps (see Figure 7-9). The effect of the slope on air movements in the summer provides a definite advantage over settlements located on flat surfaces.

In the winter months, the advantage of the slopes for air movement still prevails. The predominant winds then come from the south and over the plain. Their pattern changes when they hit a building since this creates calmer eddies on the leeward side. This effect reduces the convective dissipation. Also due to the compact planning on all four sides, the buildings either reduce the advective dissipation to insignificant levels or completely eliminate it. The modified surface and the atmosphere in the city considerably alter the energy balance. A good indicator of this is the ratio of energy between the sensible and latent heat transfer, generally known as the Bowen ratio.

In urban areas, the modified hydrological cycle causes the Bowen ratio to be higher than in nonurban areas (e.g., grasslands, forests) because there is the extensive use of the sensible rather than the latent heat transfer. This phenomenon is even more exaggerated where there are slope settlements, for here the absence of large open or green areas rarely results in latent heat transfer. For settlements built on flat plains, the

FIG. 7-9. Typical pedestrian walkway running along north-south axis, Mardin.

Bowen ratio will be smaller because the latent heat transfer will be larger. This is due to an increase of areas subject to evapo-transpiration. The overall effect of this is more energy loss in settlements on flat plains than in those on slopes. The compactness of an environment like Mardin also helps control the typical city energy losses.

The only natural input (gain) in the energy balance is solar radiation. The degree of use of the incoming energy and the success of man in converting this to reduce the environmental stresses depend primarily on three factors: form, orientation, and materials. In Mardin, the cardinal southern slope (the steeper—about 25° to 30°—it is, the more efficient the whole system becomes) allows no shadows to be cast upon the individual units (see Figures 7-10 and 7-11). This slope also has a close interaction with the form of both the units and the whole complex. Knowles' surface-to-volume ratio, which he defines as "susceptibility to the stresses of environmental variation," emphasizes the importance of the overall form; his rather thorough analysis of pueblos reinforces the form's significance.[42]

Other Turkish Slope Settlements

Our observations and studies, particularly of Mardin (see Appendix) and generally of the other slope settlements in hot, arid zones in Turkey (see Figures 7-12, 7-13, 7-14, 7-15), show similarities to the findings about

FIG. 7-10. Relatively new section of Mardin facing southeast.

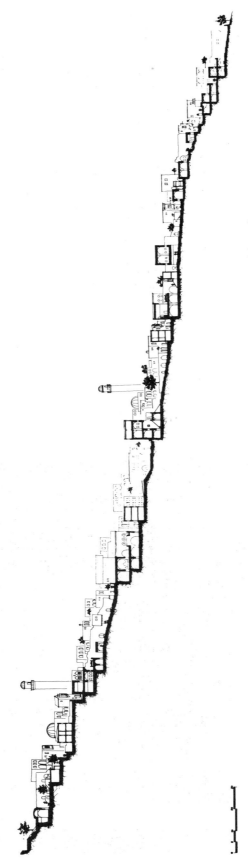

FIG. 7-11. Cross section of Mardin, looking east (This section of the chapter could not have been completed without the encouragement and assistance of Yasemin and Yilmaz Aysan, Vacit Imamoglu, and Salih Memecan who joined me on the trip through the hot, arid region of Turkey in a very warm and dry summer month. Their help in surveying and taking measurements and their criticism are highly appreciated. I am particularly grateful to S. Memecan for the final drawing.)

158

Fɪɢ. 7-12. Narince Köyü, a small village in the Adiyaman area, Turkey.

pueblos. All of these similarities suggest that there is no cultural monopoly in the response to environmental forces; instead, there are direct responses to the environment and a liberating mastery over nature. A close, harmonious bond has been established in these responses. Calculations of the energy-budget (see the Appendix) clearly show the difference between the settlements on a southern slope and those on flat plains in a hot, arid zone. This difference is approximately a 50 percent increase in the heat required to maintain the same indoor temperatures on flat plains under the same environmental conditions. In other words, the amount of energy consumed to heat the buildings on a flat plain needs to be 50 percent more than that needed for a sloped settlement. Furthermore, a flat plain settlement desirous of those results must cover an area twice as large as the slope areas.

When the effect of materials on this area is introduced, we see a gross increase in the heat required to raise the indoor temperatures to comfortable levels.[43] When brick is compared to the massive stone used for construction in Mardin, we also find that a 64 percent increase in energy is needed to maintain the same temperature. As Knowles states,

It is difficult to attribute such particular relationships to chance. . . . [The inhabitants and the builders have been] aware of the relationships between the form

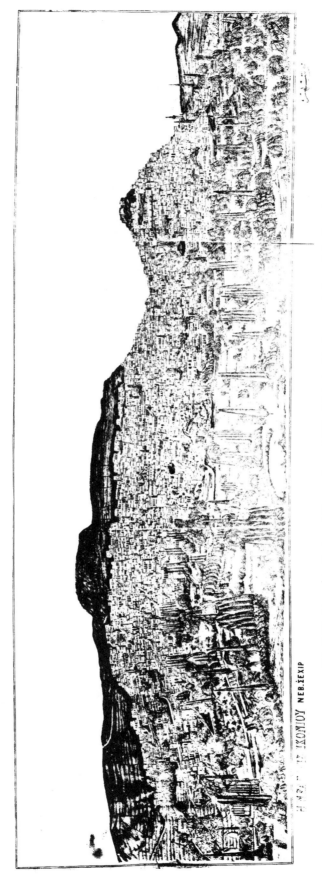

FIG. 7-13. Nevsehir, Turkey. Lithograph ca. 1880. Printed with the permission of Aysil and Yıldırım Yavuz.

FIG. 7-14. Göre, Turkey; southeast orientation with an aspect angle of 125°.

of their constructions and the dynamics of earth and sun; in fact, they must have worked from a fairly distinct mental image. . . .[44]

Conclusion

With an understanding of the environmental forces and the use of them in harmony with the sociocultural demands, man has created habitats that are far superior to today's products of a narrowly defined interpretation of the environment. This type of interpretation is not limited to a particular economic system but applies to the present mode of production as discussed earlier. Therefore, changing Lukacs' word "capitalism" to "the present mode of production," we can state that,

> under [the present mode of production], the scope of art is much more narrowly confined; it can exercise no determining influence upon the production of consumer goods and indeed the question of its own existence is decided

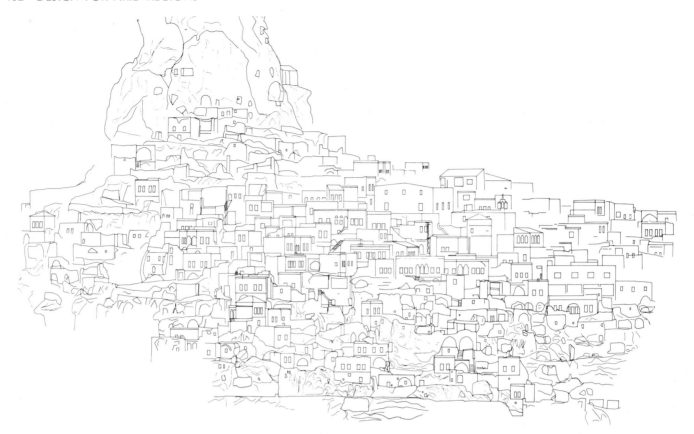

FIG. 7-15. Ortahisar, Turkey (photogrammetric drawing). Printed with the permission of Photogrammetry Center, Department of Restoration, Faculty of Architecture, M.E.T.U.

by purely economic factors and the problems of technical production governed by them. (*As in modern architecture.*)[45]

Yet, some measures must be taken, especially since the household use (heating, lighting, cooking, cooling) of energy is almost as much as industry's consumption—now 35 percent of the total energy consumption.[46] The dialectical nature of the relationship between architecture and environment, in particular, and man and environment, in general, must be understood and reflected in our approaches to the environmental problems before it is too late; for "... if nature is in crisis and shows all the symptoms of a precocious senility, society will be fatally emptied of any drive toward the future."[47]

Notes

1. Richard A. Watson and Patty Jo Watson, *Man and Nature: An Anthropological Essay in Human Ecology* (New York: Harcourt, Brace & World, 1969), p. 21.
2. David Stea, "Landscape Dichotomies: Pat Phrases and Preservation," *Landscape*, **20**, no. 1 (October 1975), 44–48.
3. *Exploitation* and *relocation* have been defined as the two basic forms of adaptation in man's cultural response to nature. See Mete Turan, "Environmental Stress: An Ecological Approach with Special Reference to Housing," unpublished. Ph.D. dissertation, Columbia University, 1974, pp. 101–131; Ralph L. Knowles, *Energy and Form: An*

Ecological Approach to Urban Growth (Cambridge: Massachusetts Institute of Technology Press, 1974). Knowles defines two forms of adaptation to the environment as *transformation* and *relocation*.

4. Georg Lukacs, *History and Class Consciousness*, trans. R. Livingstone (Cambridge: Massachusetts Institute of Technology Press, 1971), pp. 234–239.

5. Karl Mannheim, *Ideology and Utopia*, trans. L. Wirth and E. Shils (New York: Harcourt, Brace & World, 1936), p. 68.

6. Kurt Koffka, *Principles of Gestalt Psychology* (New York: Harcourt, Brace & World, 1935), p. 176.

7. For a more detailed analysis of *alienation* and *environmental stress*, see Turan, *Environmental Stress*, pp. 1–45.

8. Robert L. Heilbroner, "The Human Prospect," *The New York Review of Books*, 24 January 1974, 27.

9. William Leiss, *The Domination of Nature* (New York: George Braziller, 1972), p. 121; See especially pp. 101–123 for a discussion of the mastery over nature when viewed from pragmatic motives devoid of a social context. Despite its "high level of generality and abstraction," Leiss' book sheds a brilliant light on the historical tendencies involved in the conquest of nature by man.

10. Heilbroner, p. 29. According to Heilbroner, the roots of the common problems in the industrialized civilization of both the socioeconomic systems lie in the fact that ". . . industrial civilization achieves its economic success by imposing common values on both its capitalist and socialist variants. There is the value of the self-evident importance of efficiency, with its tendency to subordinate the optimum human scale of things to the optimum technical scale. There is the value of the need to 'tame' the environment, with its consequence of an unthinking pillage of nature. There is the value of the priority of production itself, visible in the care both systems lavish on technical virtuosity and the indifference with which both look upon the aesthetic aspects of life." (p. 27).

11. Frederick Engels, "The Part Played by Labour in the Transition from Ape to Man," from *Dialectics of Nature* in Karl Marx and Frederick Engels, *Selected Works*, 3 vols. (Moscow: Progress Publishers, 1970), **3**:74.

12. Vladimir I. Lenin, "Marxist Views on the Agrarian Question in Europe and in Russia," in *Collected Works*, 45 vols. (Moscow: Progress Publishers, n.d.), **6**: 347. Also quoted in I.P. Gerasimov, et al., eds., *Man, Society and the Environment*, trans. Y. Shirokov (Moscow: Progress Publishers, 1975), p. 24.

13. Marshall I. Goldman, "Environmental Disruption in the Soviet Union," in *Man's Impact on Environment*, ed. Thomas R. Detwyler (New York: McGraw Hill, 1971), pp. 61–75; also in the same source, see Philip P. Micklin, "Soviet Plans to Reverse the Flow of Rivers: The Kama-Vychegda-Pechora Project." pp. 302–318.

14. Herbert Marcuse, *One-Dimensional Man* (Boston: Beacon Press, 1964), pp. 225–246.

15. Aydın Germen, "Yöre Mimarisi," *Mimarlık*, **11**, no. 5 (1974), 5-9; Selahattin Önür and Suha Özkan, "Kalın Duvar Örüntüsü ve Kapadokya'da Mimarlık," *Mimarlık*, 11, no. 5 (1974), 10–15; Amos Rapoport, *House Form and Culture* (Englewood Cliffs, N.J.: Prentice-Hall, 1969), p. 5.

16. Mete Turan, "Vernacular Architecture and Environmental Influences: An Analytical and Comparative Study," *M.E.T.U. Journal of the Faculty of Architecture*, **1**, no. 2 (1975), 227–246.

17. Bronislaw Malinowski, *A Scientific Theory of Culture* (New York: Oxford University Press, 1960) p. 136.

18. Rapoport, *House Form*, p. 47.

19. Victor Olgyay, *Design With Climate* (Princeton, N.J.: Princeton University Press, 1963). Olgyay makes use of Köppen's classification with some modifications; Anatoliy N. Rimsha, on the other hand, accepts with some reservations Alisov's genetic classification. See Rimsha, *Town Planning in Hot Climates* (Moscow: Mir Publishers, 1976), pp. 133–44; see United Nations, Department of Economic and Social Affairs, "Design of Low Cost Housing and Community Facilities," In *Climate and House Design* (New York: United Nations, 1971).

20. John F. Griffith, *Applied Climatology* (London: Oxford University Press, 1966), pp. 96–98.

21. Detailed maps and extended information can be found in various Turkish geography

books. For example, see Sırrı Erinç, *Tatbiki Klimatoloji ve Türkiye'nin İklim Şartları* (Istanbul: Hidrojeoloji Enstitüsü Yayınları, 1957), pp. 101–117, 151–164, 198–209.

22. James M. Fitch, *Architecture and the Esthetics of Plenty* (New York: Columbia University Press, 1961), pp. 14–28, 227–284.

23. Seton Lloyd, *Early Highland Peoples of Anatolia* (London: Thames & Hudson, 1967), p. 45; this should not be confused with the Karahüyük of Konya Plain, dating back to the Early Bronze period (2500 B.C.); Rudolf Naumann, *Eski Anadolu Mimarlığı* trans. B. Madra (Ankara: Türk Tarih Kurumu Yayınları, 1975), p. 237.

24. Naumann, pp. 368–390.

25. Ibid, p. 377 fig. 495.

26. James Mellaart, *Çatal Hüyük: A Neolithic Town in Anatolia* (New York: McGraw-Hill, 1967), p. 62.

27. See, for example Amos Rapoport, "The Pueblo and the Hogan," in *Shelter and Society*, ed. Paul Oliver (London: Barrie & Jenkins, 1969), pp. 66–79; Subhi Hussein Al-Azzawi, "Oriental Houses in Iraq," in *Shelter and Society*, pp. 91–102; David Etherton, "Algerian Oases," in *Shelter in Africa*, ed. Paul Oliver (New York: Praeger Publishers, 1971), pp. 172–189; George F. Carter, *Man and the Land: A Cultural Geography*, (New York: Holt, Rinehart & Winston, 1968), pp. 52–133; Turan, "Vernacular Architecture."

28. Lukacs, pp. 234–235, discussing the relative independence of art and its development according to its inner laws, argues that the stability in the value of art and the semblance of its nature as something above history and society are rooted in the fact that art provides a dialogue between man and nature. To what degree this may be true in the case of pure art is debatable; but in the case of reshaping the environment, the dialogue established between man and nature manifests itself in the material production and the conservation of nature. Although conservation of nature is a form of art and has its own inner laws, the semblance of its nature is still in a social category.

29. Fred Eggan, *Social Organization of the Western Pueblo* (Chicago: The University of Chicago Press, 1973), p. 129.

30. Knowles, *Energy and Form*, pp. 27–34.

31. Ralph Knowles, "Solar Energy, Building and the Law," *Journal of Architectural Education*, **30**, no. 3 (1977), 68–72.

32. Eggan, p. 134.

33. Ibid. (In another study, it was found that the Navajos, despite their strong preference for modern housing, had conflicting feelings about the house form and settlement pattern. Besides the cultural adaptational problems, there were rightfully emphasized complaints about the energy consuming appliances associated with modern housing.) See Peter Z. Snyder, Edward K. Sadalla, and David Stea, "Socio-cultural Modifications and User Needs in Navajo Housing," *Journal of Architectural Research*, **5**, no. 3 (1976), 4–9.

34. Eggan, p. 223.

35. Leslie A. White, *The Acoma Indians*, 47th Annual Report, Bureau of American Ethnology (Washington D.C.: Smithsonian Institution, 1932), pp. 17–192.

36. Knowles, *Energy and Form*, pp. 20–26, 35–43.

37. Turan, "Vernacular Architecture."

38. For a detailed account of Mardin's history, see Hanna Dolapönü, *Tarihte Mardin* (Istanbul: privately published, 1972); Ara Altun, *Mardin'de Türk Devri Mimarisi* (Istanbul, privately published, 1971); Minorsky, "Mardin," *Islam Ansiklopedisi*, (Istanbul: M.E.B. Yayınları, 1956), **7**: 317–322.

39. Dolapönü, p. 30.

40. Ibid, p. 25.

41. George B. Toby, Jr. *A History of Landscape Architecture: The Relationship of People to Environment* (New York: American Elsevier Publishing Company, 1973), p. 32.

42. Knowles, *Energy and Form*, p. 2.

43. Turan, "Vernacular Architecture."

44. Knowles, *Energy and Form*, p. 44.

45. Lukacs, p. 236. Italics added for emphasis.

46. The figure given is for the United States. See S. Fred Singer, "Human Energy Production as a Process in the Biosphere," in A Scientific American Book, *The Biosphere* (San Francisco: W. H. Freeman, 1970), pp. 107–114.

47. Tomas Maldonado, *Design, Nature and Revolution: Toward a Critical Ecology*, trans. M. Domandi (New York: Harper & Row, 1972), p. 75.

Selected Readings

Detwyler, Thomas R., ed. *Man's Impact on Environment*. New York: McGraw-Hill, 1971.

Fitch, James M. *American Building: The Environmental Forces That Shape It*. 2nd ed. Boston: Houghton Mifflin, 1972.

———, *Architecture and the Esthetics of Plenty*. New York: Columbia University Press, 1961.

Gerasimov, I.P., et al., eds. *Man, Society and Environment*. Trans., Y. Shirokov. Moscow: Progress Publishers, 1975.

Knowles, Ralph L. *Energy and Form: An Ecological Approach to Urban Growth*. Cambridge: MIT Press, 1974.

Leiss, William. *The Domination of Nature*. New York: George Braziller, 1972.

Lowry, William P. *Weather and Life*. New York: Academic Press, 1969.

Oliver, John E. *Climate and Man's Environment: An Introduction to Applied Climatology*. New York: John Wiley & Sons, 1973.

Turan, Mete H. Environmental stress: An ecological approach with special reference to housing. Unpublished Ph.D. dissertation, Columbia University, 1974.

Wheeler, Reuben. *Man, Nature and Art*. London: Pergamon Press, 1968.

Appendix

I. Energy-Balance for a Settlement

Comparison of energy-budgets of two types of settlements in hot-arid zones:

    a. Settlement on a south-facing slope of approximately 20°
    b. Settlement on a flat plain.

For a settlement the energy-budget can be summarized as:

$$a_s S_i + \epsilon\sigma\,(T_r^4 - T_u^4) + h_c\,(T_a - T_u) + E + H + (H_h + E_h) + M = O$$

where,

    a_s : short wave absorptivity;
    S_i : short wave energy incident on the system;
    ϵ : emissivity;
    σ : Stephan-Boltzmann constant;
    T_u : effective temperature of the urban "canopy" of the settlement;
    T_r : effective radiative temperature of the sky;
    T_a : temperature of free air just above the canopy;
    h_c : convective transfer coefficient;
    E : latent heat transfer;
    H : sensible heat transfer;
    H_h : sensible heat transfer by advection;
    E_h : latent heat transfer by advection;
    M : energy stored and utilized within the system.

Written descriptively:

(+)	$a_s S_i$	(heat load from the sun)
(−)	$+ \epsilon\sigma\,(T_r^4 - T_u^4) + E + H$	(vertical dissipative flux)
(−)	$+ h_c(T_a - T_u)$	(convective dissipation)
(−)	$+ (H_h + E_h)$	(advective dissipation)
(+)	$+ M$	(stored and utilized)

Calculation for the energy-budget for a settlement:

a. on a south-facing slope	(cal/cm²/min.)		b. on a flat plain	(cal/cm²/min)
$a_s S_i$	.40×1.4	= +.56	.40×1.35	= +.54
$\epsilon\sigma(T_r^4 - T_u^4)$				
	.9×.817×10⁻¹⁰ ×(275⁴−280⁴)	= −.03		= −.03
H		= −.60		= −.65
E		= −.15		= −.20
$h_c(T_a - T_u)$	33.5×10⁻³ ×(273−280)	= −.23	37.5×10⁻³ ×(273−280)	= −.27
(V=3.2 m/sec)			(V=4.2 m/sec)	
$H_h + E_h$		=		= −.05
M		= +.45		= +.66

NOTE: $h_c = (5 \times 10^{-3})V^{1/3}$, when V is in cm/sec; notice the 47 percent increase in the heat necessary to maintain the same indoor temperatures under the same environmental conditions.

Sources: Rudolf Geiger, *The Climate Near the Ground* (Cambridge, Mass.: Harvard University Press, 1966), pp. 5–54, 224–251; William P. Lowry, *Weather and Life* (New York: Academic Press, 1969), pp. 113–151; John E. Oliver, *Climate and Man's Environment* (New York: John Wiley & Sons, 1973), pp. 5–19, 223–248; Turan, "Vernacular Architecture and Environmental Influences: An Analytical and Comparative Study," *M.E.T.U. Journal of the Faculty of Architecture*, **1,** no. 2 (1975), 227–246.

II. Turkish Arid Zone Climatic Data

TABLE 7-1. Mean High/Low Temperatures (°C) For Some Turkish Cities.

	I	II	III	IV	V	VI	VII	VIII	IX	X	XI	XII	ANNUAL
ANKARA	4.1	5.6	18.0	17.4	22.4	26.5	30.1	30.3	25.7	19.9	13.5	6.5	17.7
	−3.5	−3.0	0.0	4.8	9.4	12.3	15.2	15.4	11.2	6.6	2.8	−0.8	5.9
KIRŞEHİR	4.8	6.6	11.0	17.3	22.2	26.2	29.4	29.9	25.6	20.2	13.6	7.3	17.8
	−4.2	−3.1	−0.6	3.9	8.2	11.8	15.0	14.9	10.2	5.1	1.1	−1.8	5.0
NEVŞEHİR	4.3	5.7	9.9	15.5	20.6	24.2	27.7	28.0	23.3	17.9	13.1	7.5	16.5
	−3.0	−3.3	0.4	4.4	8.5	10.9	12.2	12.0	8.6	5.8	4.5	0.2	5.1
KAYSERİ	4.2	6.0	10.8	17.4	22.7	27.0	30.6	30.8	26.3	20.5	13.6	7.0	18.1
	−6.8	−5.3	−1.7	2.6	6.8	9.5	11.4	10.9	6.8	3.1	−0.6	−4.1	2.7
K.MARAŞ	9.2	10.5	15.3	20.8	26.4	32.0	35.3	35.9	32.0	26.6	18.7	10.9	22.8
	1.2	2.4	5.2	9.1	13.4	18.0	20.6	20.4	17.5	12.1	7.1	3.0	10.8
ADIYAMAN	7.7	9.5	14.3	20.4	25.6	32.4	37.0	36.9	32.2	24.6	17.5	10.4	22.4
	1.2	2.2	5.4	9.5	13.7	19.3	23.2	22.9	18.3	13.0	7.9	3.4	11.7
MALATYA	2.6	4.5	10.6	18.0	23.6	29.1	33.3	33.4	28.5	20.9	12.6	5.0	18.5
	−4.0	−2.8	1.6	7.2	11.8	15.8	19.3	19.4	15.0	9.5	4.2	−1.1	8.0
URFA	9.3	11.5	15.7	21.8	28.4	34.3	38.5	38.3	33.7	26.8	19.0	12.0	24.1
	1.4	2.4	4.8	9.3	14.2	19.5	23.5	23.4	19.3	13.6	8.4	3.7	11.9
DİYARBAKIR	6.6	8.9	14.2	20.4	26.5	33.2	38.2	38.2	33.2	25.3	16.7	9.2	22.5
	−2.4	−1.1	2.0	6.8	11.0	16.0	21.6	20.9	15.7	19.6	4.4	−0.2	8.7
MARDİN	5.1	6.5	10.5	16.8	23.4	30.0	34.3	34.2	29.5	21.9	14.4	7.6	19.5
	0.2	1.0	4.0	9.3	14.7	19.9	23.8	24.3	20.4	14.0	8.2	2.9	11.8

Source: *Meteoroloji Bülteni.* Ankara: T.C. Gida Tarim, Hayvancilik Bak. gi. D.M.I. Gn. Md., 1974.

A - 2

TABLE 7-2. Diurnal Maximum Temperature Differences (°C) for Some Turkish Cities.

	I	II	III	IV	V	VI	VII	VIII	IX	X	XI	XII	ANNUAL
ANKARA	17.9	22.8	21.2	24.3	21.6	21.1	22.3	22.6	23.7	23.8	20.2	18.4	24.3
KIRŞEHİR	25.0	24.3	23.3	26.8	24.2	24.8	25.5	25.6	25.8	25.5	23.1	26.7	26.8
NEVŞEHİR	15.9	20.0	17.7	18.3	19.7	22.3	23.4	25.2	23.2	18.6	16.0	9.2	25.2
KAYSERİ	32.8	26.1	29.1	28.6	29.6	29.3	28.8	29.9	30.4	30.6	26.5	25.2	32.8
K.MARAŞ	16.5	16.7	17.5	19.4	26.0	28.0	30.0	29.0	22.4	26.0	21.1	15.0	30.0
ADIYAMAN	13.3	15.7	16.3	22.2	18.6	19.3	20.4	19.8	19.1	17.0	16.2	14.5	22.2
MALATYA	24.5	17.3	18.9	19.7	19.1	22.1	21.6	25.1	23.2	19.8	17.3	19.1	25.1
URFA	19.3	16.7	21.2	22.0	22.8	21.6	22.4	22.7	20.7	21.8	20.4	19.3	22.8
DİYARBAKIR	22.1	21.2	27.1	26.2	28.6	32.0	27.5	31.2	28.6	28.9	25.3	27.0	32.0
MARDİN	15.0	11.9	14.8	17.0	18.0	19.4	17.3	16.5	16.8	17.5	18.5	11.1	19.4

Source: Meteoroloji Bülteni.

TABLE 7-3. Wind Velocity and Direction (M/SEC) in Some Turkish Cities.

	SUMMER				WINTER		
	MEAN	MAX.	DIR.		MEAN	MAX.	DIR.
ANKARA	3.3	3.6	→↙		3.0	3.4	↗
KIRŞEHİR	2.0	2.8	↓		1.3	1.9	↓
NEVŞEHİR	2.0	2.7	↗ ↓		3.5	4.7	↓↖
KAYSERİ	1.8	2.0	↑		1.8	2.3	→↑
K.MARAŞ	4.3	6.2	↙		2.1	2.9	↙
ADIYAMAN	3.5	4.2	↓		3.0	4.4	↙
MALATYA	1.5	1.8	↗↖		1.2	1.9	↑
URFA	3.4	4.4	↘		2.3	2.8	→
DİYARBAKIR	2.8	3.7	↗		2.5	2.9	↘
MARDİN	2.3	2.7	↓		2.7	3.2	↑

Note: All summer maximums occur in July; most of the winter maximums occur in March.
Sources: Celik, Aliye P. *İklimle Dengeli Bina Tasariminda Mahoney Tablolarinin Türkiye'ye Uygulanabilirliği Yönünden Tartisilmasi,* TBTAK Yapi Araştirma Enstitüsü No. a13, Ankara, 1973,. Cölasan, Umran E. *Türkiye Yer Rüzgárlari,* Ankara; T.C. Tarım Bakalığı D.M.İ. Gn.Md., 1967. *Meteoroloji Bülteni.*

A - 3

TABLE 7-4. Mean and Minimum Relative Humidity in Some Turkish Cities.

	I	II	III	IV	V	VI	VII	VIII	IX	X	XI	XII	ANNUAL
ANKARA	78	75	65	57	57	50	42	40	46	56	70	77	60
	19	19	5	6	11	5	3	3	4	9	17	25	3
KIRŞEHİR	78	76	69	61	60	53	47	48	53	62	73	78	63
	10	18	10	8	10	7	7	10	7	9	12	11	7
NEVŞEHİR	71	70	64	57	52	49	43	42	47	56	62	70	57
	27	18	11	7	10	12	10	6	8	13	13	19	6
KAYSERİ	76	75	70	63	61	56	49	48	54	65	73	78	64
	21	17	13	8	10	9	10	6	9	9	16	22	6
K.MARAŞ	72	73	64	57	56	48	49	48	45	52	62	74	58
	21	21	11	10	9	5	6	3	2	4	13	24	2
ADIYAMAN	73	71	62	52	47	29	24	23	30	46	59	73	49
	14	23	7	4	3	1	1	1	3	3	6	7	1
MALATYA	76	73	62	52	47	37	31	20	34	50	69	78	53
	20	17	8	3	8	3	3	2	3	2	11	19	2
URFA	71	67	60	53	43	30	27	28	32	42	58	69	48
	8	1	1	4	1	1	1	1	2	0	2	1	0
DİYARBAKIR	77	73	65	61	55	34	24	24	28	46	67	77	53
	13	7	10	7	6	5	1	2	3	2	3	10	1
MARDİN	76	70	64	57	46	33	30	32	36	47	59	70	52
	7	11	3	6	4	1	2	2	0	3	9	12	0

Source: Meteoroloji Bülteni.

171

8
Migration Problems in Turkey: Arid-Zone Society in Transition

Taner Oc

During the past quarter century, population explosion has been a worldwide concern.[1] At first, advances in medicine and the dissemination of medical services to larger populations helped decrease mortality rates. Because fertility rates remained constant, nations had to accept the responsibility of providing for these additional people. Furthermore, countries of the Third World experienced unprecedented urbanization as a consequence of internal migration.[2]

Turkey, an arid zone, is no exception to this typical pattern. Here the population tripled in the first 50 years of existence, and the net population increase for the decade of 1960 to 1970 averaged close to 3 percent per annum.[3] At the time of the nation's birth, 1923, Istanbul was the only city with a population of more than 100,000; but 50 years later, there were 21 such cities. The most dramatic upsurge of urbanization took place between 1960 and 1970. In this decade alone, the number of cities with a population of 100,000 or more increased from 9 to 20; and the population residing in such cities almost doubled, increasing from 3,417,000 to 6,744,000.[4] This dramatic urbanization, population implosion, is forecast to continue at an increasing rate. Dr. E. Jurkat shows that by 1985 Turkey will have 52 cities with a population of 100,000 or more.[5] As a consequence of population implosion through rural-urban migration, over 40 percent of the population in Istanbul and 60 percent of the population in Ankara (the nation's two largest cities), are migrants born in the rural areas of the country.[6] The rapid urbanization, the changing pattern of migration, and the social and economic pressures of this migration led to various policies within the framework of national development plans.[7] However, though migration is properly placed in the national context, knowledge about urbanization and social transformation is not incorporated into policy making. Therefore, it is necessary to discuss urbanization and social transformation in Istanbul as an example for outlining the policy implications of the process of social transformation.

City as Focal Point of Change

Two facts are particularly useful in the study of social transformation. As George Foster indicates, the first is that cities are focal points of change and the second, that major shifts in the economic basis are central accompaniments to the transformation process.[8] Thus, when we look at the arid-zone city, economic transformation should be incorporated in our studies as part of a complex process of migration and social transformation.[9]

In studies we see that social transformation in developing countries is part of the study of modernization, and modernization is intertwined with industrialization and urbanization. Generally, modernization is defined as "those social changes that generate institutions and organizations like those found in advanced industrial societies."[10] However, successful continuous modernization is dependent on the expansion of various indices of social mobilization within a society. In a transitional society, the most significant and comprehensive type is urbanization, for "the city is a type of mutation in culture that has far-reaching effects on social structure and on social institutions, . . ." and "cities alone have developed the complex of skills and resources which characterize the modern industrial economy."[11] Social transformation is defined by urbanization, which in Reismann's words,

is social change on a vast scale. It [urbanization] means deep and irrevocable changes that alter all sectors of society. . . . The impetus of urbanization upon society is such that society gives way to urban institutions, urban values, and urban demands.[12]

As Hauser asserts, "the city represents not only a new form of economic organization and changed physical environment. It also is a profoundly modified social order affecting man's conduct and thought."[13] Urbanization produces the city as a physical and economic artifact and also produces "urbanism as a way of life."[14] Thus, migration to the cities in developing countries, including those in the arid zone, leads to various mutations of urbanism through social transformation of the migrants.

The migrants, upon their move to the city or its fringes, change from agrarian to nonagrarian productive relationships. These new relationships can relate to urban industries, urban services, or a set of varying degrees of marginal urban employment with varying levels of organization. This change from an agrarian to a nonagrarian economic (productive) relationship induces differentiation and proliferation of relationships. In other words, upon their move to the city migrants find themselves in a new set of productive relationships. The organizational level of these relationships is related to their economic absorption in the city. Thus, social transformation can be defined by new social institutions and relationships emerging as a consequence of the new productive relations and interaction with the new environment, the city.

Urbanization literature asserts the role and importance of the economic absorption of the migrants, which, in turn, helps us to explain the emerging patterns of social transformation.[15] It is the lack of economic absorption which leads to the development of urban kinship patterns and enclaves and to problems of adjustment and social transformation. Absorption of the migrants into the urban economic environment brings about structural change leading to social transformation.[16] This change is a complex process molded by economic, technological, social, cultural, and various other dimensions such as climate; but the economic dimension is most important.

Economic Transformations in Turkey

Knowledge of economic transformations and migration in Turkey is essential for a proper understanding of the process of social transformation in Istanbul.

Various studies show that the main factor contributing to migration in Turkey is economic displacement or exodus from the countryside. The only viable alternative for the economically displaced peasant is moving to the non-agrarian occupations of the city.[17] As Kiray argues,

> it is important to understand the process involved in the origins of the migrants. Only then can one clearly see that there is a structural change in the relative positions of these people in the process of production. The main reason for their coming to the city in the numbers they do is the rapid change in the pre-modern agricultural production system.[18]

So migration is not simply horizontal mobility from one locality to another. It is a process bringing about basic changes in the form and relations of production. Thus, within this framework, social transformation is a process involving changing organizations and relationships in the city.

Until recently, Turkey was dominated by a premodern, arid-zone agrarian economy. During the interwar period after the founding of the republic, certain attempts were made to facilitate economic transformation by improving rail links and introducing state-owned industry to various regions. However, the country remained "a thousand Turkeys" as Frey describes it.[19] Indeed, Turkey was comprised of 40,000 self-supporting, closed subsistence villages with a delicately balanced subsistence economy. To be precise, population growth, land tenure, and production were three balancing factors within the closed system of the village unit. The social order of such a community is defined by an ideal folk society as described by Redfield.[20] A period of rapid economic change came in the late 1940s when the country had begun to feel the pressures of post-World War II transformations in the world. Though very skeptical of foreign aid which had contributed to the decay and downfall of the Ottoman Empire, the Inonu government approved of the Marshall Plan. Later, the changed government in 1950 opened the country further to the demands of international markets, and considerable economic growth followed in Istanbul and some other parts of the country.[21] The construction of a network of highways connected different parts of the country and helped the villages to be integrated into the national and the international economy. This period of change is described by Lerner.[22]

The most important changes in this period were the transformation of the agrarian socioeconomic structure and the increasing rate of population growth. These were the factors responsible for the massive migration to Ankara and Istanbul. More precisely, between 1946 and 1955, the land tenure of the country was changed, and about 500,000 families were eventually displaced because 40,000 tractors were introduced to the arid plains of Anatolia.[23]

This was accompanied with the change to cash crops—a change from a subsistence economy to a market economy. Kiray describes this change:

1. The sharecropping system was changed and the sharecroppers became either agrarian workers or were displaced immediately.
2. The small land owners who could not obtain credit for tractors were displaced, and land was consolidated in the hands of the middle size land owners who were able to buy tractors and increase their productivity and capital.

3. Land not suitable for cultivation, that is grazing land, was cultivated; but crops soon ceased due to rapid erosion of topsoil. Since the land was no longer viable for animal husbandry, more villages were displaced.

4. The closed economy of the subsistence village was opened to the national market economy, and in this process the credit system operated by the small town merchants further impoverished the small land owners and forced them to move.[24]

Thus, both sharecroppers and small landowners, who once produced the wealth of premodern society through the simple technology of plow and ox, now lost their livelihoods with the introduction of improved modern technology. The consequence was migration to the cities causing unprecedented urban implosion. However, one could argue that about one fourth of these migrants could have remained on their farms if proper credit mechanisms had been provided.[25]

Some cities like Istanbul flourished after 1950 as a result of both a changing agroeconomic structure and investments in industry. The emergence of cash cropping and a market economy led to the growth of new centralized functions in cities like Istanbul.[26] This city also had its share of industrial growth reflected by the ecology of the squatter settlements.[27] After 1960, a planned economy was introduced with the dual goals of constant economic growth and reduction of regional disparities. The impact of this transformation in economy is reflected by the sudden change in the flow of migrants to regional centers which was recorded by the 1965 census. This new migration pattern is still continuing; though the major cities, Istanbul and Ankara, get a large number of migrants, the share of the regional centers is increasing. Thus, having outlined the economic transformation of Turkey and the factors displacing the peasants from the arid plains of Anatolia, we can turn to the social transformation of migrants in Istanbul.

SOCIAL TRANSFORMATION IN ISTANBUL

The basis of social transformation is the change from kin-based social organization manifested by agrarian productive relationships to non-kin-based social organization molded by new economic relationships. Migration to Istanbul is a move into a new environment with nonagrarian productive relationships, and the nature and extent of the economic absorption in this arid-zone city define the process of social transformation. Conditioning and experience have made adjustment difficult. Throughout the years, over 60 percent of the migrants coming to Istanbul have been employed as unskilled laborers. Therefore, only about 30 percent of the migrants have now acquired jobs requiring skill, training, and/or education.[28] Yet they do not experience a change to organized urban productive relations. Although most migrants are able to retain face-to-face relationships, they work without schedules and lack specialized skills.

If we look at their rural background, we can see why socialization is problematic. Life in the village offers limited social opportunities. Here inhabitants usually socialize with kin and with neighbors who are also kin. That is, they work and socialize within the same homogeneous community. The change from this pattern to more heterogeneous relationships in Istanbul is necessary. Research shows that migrants who moved to the city in the 1950s and who still have unskilled jobs continue to socialize with kin. However, the percentage of migrants socializing with kin has decreased; and the percentage of migrants socializing with non-kin, workmates, and neighbors has increased considerably for the more recent migrants with skilled occupations.[29]

The kinship relationship, based on sharing and mutual help, is functionally related to the agrarian productive relationship requiring different forms of cooperation. Theoretically, social transformation in the city should strip the family to its bare essentials—the nuclear family of father, mother, and children replacing the extended family. The family as a unit of social life should be emancipated from the burdens of the larger kinship groups characteristic of the village.[30] However, recent studies have shown that kinship ties continue to exist in the urban areas of both industrial and transitional societies. Aldous states that the family is urbanized to the extent that as a group it often takes on the formal character of a voluntary association.[31] Hinderinck and Kiray show that agroeconomic changes have broken up the extended family in Turkish villages. As nuclear families, however, they still retain their old pattern, especially in providing financial aid.[32] As a matter of fact, in spite of the financial aid available through banks, mutual funds, and friends in Istanbul, the majority of the migrants with unskilled and skilled jobs seek financial aid within the kinship network.[33] Furthermore, self-employment encourages the retention of economic organization based upon parental relationships.

Another aspect of the homogeneous village life is kin-based respect and information patterns. Within the closed community, the family transfers accumulated knowledge from one generation to the other, and experienced elders are the sources of information. On the urban scene, the experiences of agrarian life do not provide answers to many issues; therefore, on the whole, migrants have acquired new sources of information in the city and discarded the old, useless patterns. The all-knowing elders are replaced by the educated and non-kin who range from workmates to executives. Accountants, lawyers, and other professionals provide specialized needed information for migrants. This change tends to be a function of time and occupation. The *muhtar* representing the neighborhood offers a variety of legal, civic, and other needed information.[34]

With such opportunities available, there is at least a chance for a better future. In the village community with an agricultural base, people do not demonstrate social or economic mobility because there are no opportunities. In fact, as outlined in the previous section, the majority of the migrants have experienced downward mobility prior to their migration by becoming agrarian workers. On the other hand, in Istanbul, although mobility is defined by their initial employment in the city and the transformations of the urban economy, city life offers more opportunities for social and economic ascension; migrants may become skilled workers and technicians in modern factories.[35]

Still there is downward mobility among the migrants in Istanbul. As a result of the low organizational level of the urban economy, migrants are not properly absorbed by the economy. They also lack job security, for unskilled labor is highly dispensable. Hence, for security, many people within a family must be employed. Since this often involves children, there is little possibility for intergenerational social and economic mobility. Consequently, people find themselves in a poverty trap.[36]

Nevertheless, studies concerning the literacy change and training of the migrants in matched samples indicate that they are willing and able to equip themselves with the necessary skills. The organizational levels of the productive relationships determine the nature of the knowledge and skills of the migrants. However, because of the low organizational level of the urban economy in Istanbul, the demand for skills and training is rather limited. About 60 percent of the migrants with skilled jobs do not receive formal training prior to employment.[37] When they do, this experience is an extension of the feudal pattern of master-apprentice relationships and is an indication of the productive relationships in Istanbul.

We must note that the migrant in Istanbul is no longer a marginal person: migrants are a significant part of the society. However, Kiray and others argue that the new economic environment "in the city is amorphous and this state perpetuates itself for such a long time that squatter housing and petty trade become a style of life for which" they prefer to use the terms pseudourbanization and pseudourbanites.[38] Kiray also says:

> one has to accept that squatters represent the spatial patterning of a very slow process of change of the old basic social structure into a new one, where the agricultural sector is changing faster than non-agricultural production and parallel organizational aspects under marketing competetion.[39]

Migrants who normally find their first rented accommodations in various parts of Istanbul are ambitious to move to the squatter areas and to acquire a house for security reasons.[40] Through economic absorption, the migrants may also receive the benefits of social security coverage with health, unemployment, and retirement benefits. Because they have found security in their new environment, these people have more readily changed to non-kin-based patterns.[41]

Coffeehouses could provide an environment for greater social interaction among citizens in communities, but they still cater only to men. In the village, as Boran explains, these institutions were the first to specialize in entertaining male kinship.[42] In Istanbul, the coffeehouses are also suitable places for business meetings for the self-employed, as news centers, and as job centers for the marginally employed. Also because of religious sex segregation and confined living quarters where living and sleeping areas are not differentiated, strangers are not entertained in the privacy of the home. In examining this pattern, one sees no change in the internal structure of the family.[43] Husband and wife still live in different social worlds and are psychologically independent. Thus, problems of social transformation in Istanbul and cities with similar pressures make the formulation of responsive policies a pressing responsibility.

Policy Implications of Social Transformation

Urban implosion is a fact in Turkey and in other arid-zone countries, and policies should be based on adequate knowledge of the processes of economic and social conditions in the city.

GUIDELINES FOR TURKEY

Based on the knowledge of social transformation outlined above, I suggest several guidelines for future policies in Turkey and other countries faced with similar agroeconomic conditions generating an unprecedented urban implosion:

1. Economic absorption of the migrant induces and facilitates social transformation.
2. Specialization and organization of the urban center, defining the new environment for the migrant, is important for social transformation.
3. To induce change, employment in traditional occupations should be eliminated by higher levels of organization.
4. Migrants will acquire skills and literacy if their occupations and environment necessitate such developments.
5. Migrants changing from the secure, extended family-kin-based relationships have a basic need for security in the city.
6. The poverty trap can be broken only by making intergenerational mobility possible.
7. Changes will take place if they are functional and if they replace dysfunctional relationships.

ECONOMIC ABSORPTION

Today we see that "what started after World War II in underdeveloped countries indicate[s] the fact that the cities are not able to absorb and integrate the population moving in from the villages."[44] If migrants are absorbed into traditional occupations or are self-employed in the marginal services, they establish only symbiotic relationships with the urban environment; the organizational level of these economic relationships does not induce or facilitate changes to non-kin-based relationships. Those with traditional occupations, artisans, do not perform roles through a network of interactions; they only sell their products. Only those with modern employment have a multiplicity of roles. Through interaction with the new environment, they are more likely to change to new relationships. Policies should enable migrants to make this change; but currently in Turkey, arts and crafts are introduced and encouraged through credit systems with the belief that by slow change, instability in the system would be avoided.[45] Only through aiding the migrant in his economic absorption and providing security for him in the process of change can the people avoid instability in the system. Furthermore, instead of encouraging the migrants to take up feudal relationships, the community should establish policies which would provide modern productive relationships with security.

HUMAN RESOURCES

Social transformation policies should be aimed at the development of human resources. As Schultz and Sjaastad say, investment in human resources in terms of education and training is important for social transformation and also for economic growth.[46] Eventually, it would be possible to break the vicious cycle of poverty, and the children of the migrants would have social mobility and greater security.

Conclusion

Thus, policy makers should recognize the potential contribution of the migrants to urban and national development and should use the knowledge of social transformation to incorporate the migrants into the new urban environment. They should be absorbed into the urban environment and should be enabled to use their abilities and capacities because migrants are in the cities to stay. If we do not make the necessary policies to integrate them, migration will continue to be a social and economic problem; yet, social science shows that by proper policies and investments, migration can be an asset for development.

Notes

1. Philip M. Hauser, "The Chaotic Society: Product of the Social Morphological Revolution," *American Sociological Review*, **34**, no. 1 (February, 1969), 1–19.

2. Ibid, p. 6.

3. See *Genel Nufus Sayimi: Gecici Sonuclar* (Ankara: Devlet Instatistik Enstitusu, 1975), table 1; *Genel Nufus Sayimi: Gecici Sonuclar* (Ankara: Davlet Instatisitk Enstitusu, 1970), table 1.

4. See *Genel Nufus Sayimi* (1970), table 4.

5. E. Jurkat, *Urbanization Tables* (Ankara: Ministry of Reconstruction, 1968), p. 18.

6. In 1975, 24 cities had populations over 100,000, and 7,776,000 lived in those cities (19.3 percent of the population). The population of Istanbul was 2,535,000 and of Ankara 1,698,000.

7. The 1965 census showed a considerable proportion of migrants going to regional centers rather than to national centers. See *Kalkinma Plani, Birinci Bes Yil 1963–1967* (Ankara: Devlet Planlama Teskilati, 1963), pp. 471–476; *Bes Yillik Kalkinma Plani, 1968–1972* (Ankara: Devlet Planama Teskilati, 1968), pp. 263–272; *Yeni Strateji ve Kalkinma Plani, Ucuncu Bes Yil 1973–1977* (Ankara: Devlet Planama Teskilati, 1973), pp. 843–856.

8. G. M. Foster, *Traditional Cultures, and the Impact of Technological Change* (New York: Harper & Brothers, 1962), pp. 29–39.

9. John Friedman, "Cities in Social Transformation," *Comparative Studies in Society and History,* **4**, no. 1 (October, 1961), 102.

10. A. Feldman and C. Hurn, "The Experience of Modernization," *Sociometry,* **29**, no. 4 (1969), 378.

11. Philip M. Hauser, "The Social, Economic and Technological Problems of Rapid Urbanization," in *Industrialization and Society*, ed. B. F. Hoselitz and W. E. Moore (Paris: Mouton, 1963), p. 209; D. Lerner, *The Passing of Traditional Society* (New York: Free Press, 1958), p. 60.

12. L. Reissman, *The Urban Process: Cities in Industrial Societies* (New York: The Free Press, 1970), p. 154

13. Hauser, "Social, Economic, and Technical Problems," p. 209.

14. L. Wirth, "Urbanism as a Way of Life," *in Urbanism in World Perspective,* S. Fava (New York: Thomas Y. Crowell Company, 1968), pp. 46–62.

15. See L. W. Shannon and M. Shannon "The Assimilation of Migrants to Cities" in *Social Science and the City*, ed. L. F. Schnore (New York: Praeger Publishers, 1968), pp. 48–78; Taner Oc, "Assimilation of Displaced Rural Migrants in Istanbul and in Samsun, and the Role of Mass-Media in this Process," (Ph.D. dissertation, University of Pennsylvania, 1974), pp. 35–39, 182–185.

16. This is a specialized breakdown of ascriptive criteria. It shows the beginning of mobility, differentiated political, cultural, and value systems, and the growth of communication.

17. M. B. Kiray, "Squatter Housing: Fast De-peasantization and Slow Workerization in Underdeveloped Countries," paper read at the Research Committee on Urban Sociology of the World Congress of Sociology, Varna, (Bulgaria) September 14–19, 1970.

18. Ibid, p. 7.

19. F. Frey, "Political Development, Power and Communications in Turkey," in *Communications and Political Development*, ed. L. W. Pye (Princeton, N.J.: Princeton University Press. 1967), p. 307.

20. R. Redfield, "The Folk Society," *American Journal of Sociology*, **52** (January 1947), 293.

21. D. Avcioglu, *Turkiyenin Duzeni*, (Ankara: Bilgi Yayin Evi, 1968), pp. 284–88.

22. Lerner, pp. 29–43.

23. R. D. Robinson, "Tractors in the Villages." *Journal of Farm Economics*, **34** (November 1957), 451–462.

24. J. Hinderinck and M. B. Kiray, *Social Stratification as an Obstacle to Development: A Study of Four Turkish Villages*, (New York: Praeger Publishers, 1970), pp. 15–31.

25. Kiray, p. 6.

26. Taner Oc, "Samsun City-Centre Study," (M. A. Thesis. University of Chicago, 1970), pp. 70-72. For a definition of cash cropping, see Foster, p. 34.

27. Oc, "Displaced Rural Migrants," p. 72.

28. Ibid, p. 78.

29. Ibid, pp. 80–86.

30. Wirth, pp. 56–63.

31. J. Aldous, "Urbanization, The Extended Family, and Kinship Ties in West Africa," in *Urbanism*, p. 303.

32. Hinderinck and Kiray, "Social Stratification," p. 179.

33. Oc, "Displaced Rural Migrants," pp. 184.

34. Ibid, pp. 88–95.

35. Ibid, p. 82.

36. Ibid, p. 85.

37. Ibid, p. 90.

38. Kiray, p. 9.

39. Ibid, p. 1.

40. Ibid, p. 12.

41. Oc, "Displaced Rural Migrants," p. 94.

42. B. Boran, *Toplumsal Yapi Arastirmalari* (Ankara: Dil Tarih Cografya Fakultesi, 1945), pp. 5–20.

43. B. Rosen "Social Change, Migration and Family Interaction in Brazil," *American Sociological Review*, **38**, no. 2 (April 1973), 198.

44. Kiray, p. 3.

45. The election returns of 1973 and 1977 indicate that artisans voted for the conservative religious National Salvation Party.

46. T. W. Schultz, "Reflections on Investment in Men," *The Journal of Political Economy*, **70**, no. 5, part 2 (October 1962), 1; L. A. Sjaastad, "Costs and Returns of Human Migration," *The Journal of Political Economy*, **70**, no. 5, part 2 (October 1962), 90.

Selected Readings

Argyle, M. *Social Interaction*. New York: Atherton Press, 1969.

Cowan, Peter, ed. *Developing Patterns of Urbanization*. Beverly Hills, Cal.: Sage Publications, 1970, Chapters 1–3.

Cronin, Constance. *The Sting of Change: Sicilians in Sicily and Australia*. Chicago: University of Chicago Press, 1970

Eisenstadt, S. N. *The Absorption of Immigrants*. London: Routledge & Kegan Paul, 1954.

Fava, Sylvia F., ed. *Urbanism in World Perspective*. New York: Thomas Y. Crowell Company, 1968. Chapters 4, 6, 7, 11, 22, 24, and 26.

Feldman, Arnold and Hurn, Chris. The experience of modernization, *Sociometry*, **29**, No. 4 (December 1966, pp. 378–395.

Foster, George M. *Traditional Cultures: And the Impact of Technological Change.* New York: Harper & Brothers, 1962.

Friedman, John. Cities in social transformation. *Comparative Studies in Society and History,* **4**, No. 1, (November, 1961), pp. 86–103.

————. The role of cities in national development. *American Behavioral Scientist,* **12**, No. 5, (May/June, 1969), pp. 13–21.

Hagen, Everett, E. *On The Theory of Social Change.* Homewood, Ill.: Dorsey Press, 1963.

Hauser, Philip M. and Schnore, Leo F. *The Study of Urbanization.* Beverly Hills, Cal.: Sage Publications, 1970.

Hinderinck, J. and Kiray, M. B. *Social Stratification as an Obstacle to Development: A Study of Four Turkish Villages.* New York: Praeger Publishers, 1970.

Hoselitz, Bert F. *Sociological Aspects of Economic Development.* Glencoe, Ill.: Free Press, 1960.

————, and Moore, Wilbert E. ed. *Industrialization and Society.* Paris: Mouton, 1963, Chapters 6, 10, 12, 13, and 14.

Inkeles, Alex and Smith, David H. *Becoming Modern.* London: Heinemann Educational Books, 1974.

Kolars, John F. *Tradition, Season and Change in a Turkish Village.* Chicago: University of Chicago Press, 1963.

Laguian, A., ed. *Rural Urban Migrants and Metropolitan Development.* Toronto: International Association for Metropolitan Research and Development, 1971. Chapter 5.

Mangin, W., ed. *Peasants in Cities: Readings in the Anthropology of Urbanization.* Boston: Houghton Mifflin Company, 1970, Chapters 2, 3, and 9.

Morse, C., ed. *Modernization by Design.* Ithaca, N.Y.: Cornell University Press, 1969, Chapter 1.

Oc, Taner, "Assimilation of displaced rural migrants in Istanbul and in Samsun, and the role of mass-media in this process. Ph. D. dissertation, University of Pennsylvania, 1974.

Reissman, Leonard. *The Urban Process: Cities in Industrial Societies.* New York: The Free Press, 1964.

Schnore, Leo F., ed. *Social Science and The City: A Survey of Urban Research.* New York: Praeger Publishers, 1968.

9
The Impact of Arid-Zone Development on Indigenous People: the Case of Australia

Richard Widdows

In Australia, arid-zone development has been tied to two forms of economic activity: extensive pastoral agriculture and mining. This arid-zone development has brought with it many problems which are connected to the life-support system of the pioneering settlers: transportation, food and water supply, communication, and so on. The technical virtuosity of the settlers in dealing with these problems has been inspiring and is worthy of study in its own right. What has been less admirable and consequently less openly discussed is how the settlers have not successfully dealt with a human problem requiring social virtuosity: the problem of the impact of development on the indigenous people of the arid zone.

These pastoral and mining developments are but a recent stage in the history of the human occupation of arid zones. For some 3000 years or more, the arid zones of Australia were the property of the aborigines who evolved their own way of coping with the difficulties of survival in such an inhospitable environment. The gradually unfolding development by the white settlers brought about competition for the aborigines' life-support system, resulting in the disruption of the indigenous people's way of life and the creation of new and pressing problems for those people.

These problems are not unique to Australia. They have been and are being encountered in arid zones throughout the world as the industrial state, with its apparently insatiable demand for food, resources, and energy, spreads its tentacles over territory previously exclusive to nomadic peoples. The aborigines of Australia (see Figure 9-1) face problems no different in kind to those experienced by the North American Indians, the natives of arid Africa, the nomads of the Middle East, and the Eskimos of Canada. The Australian case merits special attention, though, in that it is very much unsettled now. As recently as 1976, legislation was introduced concerning aboriginal land rights in the Northern Territory's legislative assembly, and this legislation is still stirring controversy.[1] It would therefore be unfortunate if those concerned with planning in arid zones missed this chance to acquaint themselves with the human and social ramifications of arid-zone development currently being raised. The Australian case also merits attention since it is being heard by an apparently liberal, democratic form of government where the cooperation of the black and white peoples involved and the participation of multinational operatives concerned with economic development of arid zones could, theoretically, be promoted. This governmental context opens up the possibility of actual

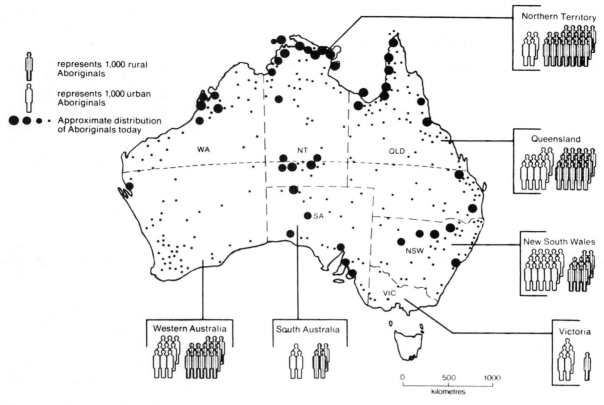

FIG. 9-1. Aboriginal distribution, Australia. From *The Australian Aboriginals* (Canberra: Australian Government Printing Service, 1976), p. 20.

participation by planners of the arid-zone developments in the resolution of the indigenous people's problems.

With this possibility in mind, this chapter will introduce arid-zone planners to the issues arising from the confrontation of recent developments with the aboriginal culture. This will necessitate some descriptive and historical material related specifically to Australia, but it is hoped that this will not detract from the main purpose of this chapter which is the elucidation of grounds for a humane solution to all indigenous people's problems. The essay will proceed as follows: I will first outline how the two forms of arid-zone development have affected the traditional aboriginal way of life; I will detail some policies which have been adopted and are still being adopted to deal with these social and human problems; I will review the current situation; and finally, I will suggest possible solutions and draw the lessons for planners concerned with arid-zone development in general.

Social and Economic Impact of Arid-Zone Development on Aboriginal People

A discussion of arid-zone development and indigenous people cannot proceed without some knowledge of the root causes of the problems faced by both planners and indigenous people where development is actually taking place. C. D. Rowley has claimed that the causes in the Australian case are basically economic and center on two matters: land ownership and labor conditions.[2] A look at the history of development of the Australian arid zones seems to bear him out.

The settler's view of land as an asset to be converted into property and enclosed for mining or cattle grazing runs counter to the traditional aboriginal attitude toward land. Land was, and is, an integral part of aboriginal social organization. Under the clan system, a newborn child automatically becomes a member of the father's clan and therefore partially "owns" that clan's land. This child will remain a member of that clan throughout his or her life and thus will share in the rights and duties toward clan land. The rights involve the unrestricted use of the land for hunting and food-gathering purposes; duties involve religious rites. So strong is the connection between the aborigines and their land that the link is regarded as persisting even after death.

Even where the clan has dispersed and its traditional patterns of life have broken down, the connection with the land continues. Knowledge of where the clan's land begins and ends is passed down from generation to generation in myths and religious teachings. Looking at this inheritance in the Northern Territory, Justice Woodward was led to conclude, "I have no doubt that, even today, the necessary information is available to divide much, if not all, of the Northern Territory into dialect groups or clan regions. If the right people could be taken out to the right places, to demonstrate the position on the ground, I believe there would be little disagreement."[3]

It was against this complex view of landrights that the settlers spread with their British legalistic view of land ownership and their system of money-based landrights. Tension was inevitable with these two views on landrights; and as will be seen later, the competing claims are still being disputed. But this, as Rowley pointed out, is only one of the sources of tension between the indigenous people and the settlers. The introduction of work for wages also created human relations problems in arid zones, for aborigines tend to be paid significantly less than settlers for equivalent work and to share less in nonwage benefits such a housing provisions, medical services, and cost-of-living subsidies. Frank Hardy's report of an interview with the editor of *The Territorian*, a newspaper circulating in the arid zone in the mid-1960s, is telling:

> He paints a vivid description of their [aboriginal stockmen working on cattle ranches] life and conditions. Main diet—salt beef and bread; housing in tin humpies; women molested as a way of life; social service payments paid direct to station managers and to owners . . . . They can neither leave the property nor have visitors without the employers' permission; wages . . . spent on trifles at the company store.[4]

While some of the worst excesses described here have since been ameliorated to some extent through political pressure, job discrimination and abuse still persist. The more recent developments have not totally overcome the bad examples set by earlier settlers. The data in Table 9-1 was compiled by Frank Stevens to show how in 1969 the aboriginal and the settler worker compared at Weipa, a bauxite mining project conducted by Comalco, a development sponsored by Rio Tinto Zinc and Kaiser.

TABLE 9-1. Pay and Benefits Compared at Weipa (Australia) for Settler and Aboriginal Unmarried Plant Laborers (in dollars).

| | BASE | AREA ALLOWANCE | WEEKLY BASE | PER HOUR | WEEKLY (PLUS SHIFT ALLOWANCE) | SIXTY HOUR WEEK | | | WEEKLY REMUNERATION |
						SUBSIDIZED BOARD	SUBSIDIZED AIR FARE SOUTH		
European	42	8	50	1.25	87.50	14.60	1.25		103.35 (100%)
Aboriginal	42	na	42	1.05	73.50	na	na		73.50 (71%)

Data from Stevens, Frank. "Weipa, The Politics of Pauperization." *The Australian Quarterly*, **41**, no. 3 (September, 1969), 13.

In these and many other ways, the pastoral and mining developers in Australia have provided object lessons in how *not* to deal with an indigenous people. Their insensitivity to traditional landrights has been the worst oversight; but discrimination in employment is more shameful in that, in this case, the settlers did have foreknowledge of the basics of the system. To emphasize the point and to introduce the reader more fully to the specifics of the Australian case, three examples of settler-aborigine relations will now be presented.

THE GURINDJI AT WAVE HILL

One of the largest owners of cattle stations in Australia is Britain's Lord Vestey: stations held by Vestey companies cover over 15 million acres. The attitude toward aborigines on Vestey's Northern Territory ranches came to public attention when, following similar action elsewhere, 200 aborigines walked off the Wave Hill ranch in 1966 in protest against low wages. This issue then led the Gurindji people, who traditionally owned Wattie Creek (a part of the Wave Hill station), to reclaim this land as their own and work it themselves. They petitioned the Governor General of Australia for a lease of 500 mi² of the 6158 mi² property. They were unsuccessful; in fact, they were warned against interfering with Vestey's "rights." The cause of the Gurindji was brought to the public's attention by a former member of the Northern Territory welfare office and a well-known Australian author. The Gurindji's action is, perhaps, best explained by Bill Jeffreys, the welfare officer involved (he was subsequently dismissed from his duties for his efforts):

> They [the aborigines concerned] told me a lot . . . . They lived in huts like dog kennels that scorched in Summer and froze in Winter. Amenities, even of the crudest kind, were nonexistent. Medical care was not for the Aborigines, nor were toilets, schooling, decent food or average wages.[5]

Despite official and other opposition, the Gurindji have continued to camp at Wattie Creek, their own way of reacting against development methods practiced by settlers.

THE YIRRKALA AT GOVE

A similar case of aboriginal people reacting against development methods concerns the Gove mining leases. This case is more complicated than that at Wave Hill; what was involved was overseas capital annexing land from a defined aboriginal reserve and from a mission. A French company was first involved in the surveying of reserve land for mineral development at Gove; the Australian government had granted them leases to survey without the consent of the Yirrkala people, the traditional owners. Following a petition from the Yirrkala to parliament and an accompanying public outcry, the French company withdrew. This was in 1963; by 1965, a consortium named Nabalco, with Swiss Aluminium controlling 70 percent, negotiated for leases in the same area. These were granted, again without the Yirrkala's consent. The leases called for the payment of royalties as a concession to the Yirrkala for the loss of some 20,000 hectares of land for the 42 years of the lease.

The Yirrkala community is dissatisfied with the level of royalties which are said to amount to $10 per head for all aborigines in the Northern Territory for the first seven years of the lease. Dealings with the company, however, have been through the government only, an arrangement the company wishes to continue. Responding to this situation, the Australian Land Rights Commission recommended many changes in the Gove contract, including the reversion of the leases to the aboriginal landowners and the payment of rentals for use of land; but at this point it appears unlikely that the recommendations will be followed. The Commission's second report was, furthermore, critical of Nabalco. It closes with the following:

> . . . the Company, apparently as a matter of policy, employs and trains practically no Aborigines. . . . [If] the local community wished to raise questions of training and employment, Nabalco should give them serious consideration. This is so since the letter of understanding dated 23 February 1968 provided "The lessee will employ local residents of the Gove Peninsula so far as is practicable commensurate with skill and training of the personnel. . . . The lessee will endeavour wherever possible to train Aboriginal personnel so as to fit them for employment by the lessee."[6]

These two cases have been described in order to show that development, as it has impinged on the aboriginal people, has been fraught with lack of sensitivity or concern about the ways of life and the beliefs of the aborigines. The cases are not atypical of arid-zone development in general. In Australia, many stories similar to the Wave Hill one have come in from other pastoral leases, and the Gove experience has been repeated on land owned by the Mappoon and Arukun people of Cape York.

THE LARRAKIA AT KULALUK

Of late, the tricky problem of urban arid development has also emerged. For example, some 30 years ago, the Larrakia people, traditional occupants of land within Darwin City and a "saltwater" people, were offered, as compensation, 14 mi² of land 40 mi inland from Darwin. They refused to go so far from the sea and moved instead to an area known as Kulaluk, 1 mi inland. Developers have recently moved into this area, prompting the Larrakia to put in a claim with the government for rights to the land. They have so far been unsuccessful, despite the usual run of demonstrations, petitions, and the like. Relations between the indigenous population and the settlers in this area were, furthermore, not improved by the settlers' treatment of sacred ceremonial ground (named Goondal by the Larrakia) which now lies inside the Larrakeyah Army Barracks. Cheryl Buchanan comments on it:

> The Gwalwa Daraniki Association [Larrakia] decided to write to the Commander to see if they could visit. Why should they need a permit to see this sacred place? . . . It took five months before the army men gave permission. . . . Why do the officers and their wives play golf on ceremonial grounds? Nothing is sacred to such people.[7]

It is one thing to make mistakes in development policy due to ignorance; it is quite another to continue with the mistakes as information comes in concerning them. In the case of Australian arid-zone development, what is even worse is that the settlers, as in the case of the Larrakia, often flaunt the supremacy of their development. They thereby show they are not only conscious that what they are doing is contrary to the wishes of the aborigines, but also that they do not care.

This criticism is not meant to imply that there has been no conscious policy toward the indigenous people and their problems. Indeed, at different times, different policies have been applied, some of which are still extant. It would be useful at this point to examine them before proceeding to a discussion of the present situation and the possibility of a planned future solution to the problem.

Past Policies

To talk of the policy of Australian settlers toward aborigines is not easy, for we are not dealing with one unilateral power which speaks for all settlers within the country at any one time. At the very least, we are dealing with several different governments at different hierarchical levels: the federal government with its bureaucracy; the Department of Aboriginal Affairs; the state parliaments and territorial assemblies; local authorities and city councils. In any period, these bodies may be pursuing different policies reflecting the different ideologies of the parties holding the power within them. But even more, we are in a situation where the welfare of aborigines may be subject to the caprice of an individual station boss or police officer in a region where remoteness is a major factor and where the daily difficulties rising out of racial and cultural tension are played out hundreds of miles from the nearest town. In this kind of situation, to talk of policy is misleading. Perhaps it is more useful to talk of attitudes, because policy may vary; but in general, the way that policy is applied will be guided by the underlying attitude held by settlers toward how aborigines should be dealt with and what is "good for them."

A review of publications on the history of the policy of settlers toward aborigines shows that much of the attitude toward them in arid zones has been colonial in nature. As Rowley puts it:

> . . . in these northern and central [arid] regions the social relationships . . . represent an earlier phase brought about by European settlement and show that there are many aspects remaining in the relations between the races which are typical of industrial colonialism. . . . significant also is the relationship of white settlers to coloured labor; and of white missionary to coloured mission community; and of white public servants engaged in native administration, to those who come under the legislation.[8]

While this colonialism is the dominant ethos of the settler, the way it has been put into practice has varied from time to time and place to place. The colonial stereotype of the native as lazy, indolent, and ineducable has flourished, thrives today and has caused further variation in the way policy has been applied. Nonetheless, the history of the policy does show some regularities which can be summed up in these words—annihilation, segregation, and assimilation. A description of each will help planners understand the legacy they are inheriting.

ANNIHILATION

The following paragraph, which opens a 1976 official paper on Australian aborigines, tells a tale in itself:

> It is generally accepted that about 300,000 Aboriginals speaking about 300 languages were living in Australia when European settlement began in 1788. A marked decline in their numbers followed the advent of the Europeans, but in most areas this was halted by 1950. The present wholly Aboriginal population is about 40,000.[9]

While this decline can be attributed in part to disease and the disrupting effects of the spread of settlements on traditional aboriginal life, there was also a conscious policy of annihilation of indigenous people in operation. In some cases this was a response to the inevitable clashes provoked as the frontier spread into the interior. In others, it was unprovoked. Indeed, it seemed the reaction of settlers and authorities to raids varied from fairly restrained police action to large and violent expeditions which were often directed against the wrong people with resulting loss of life. Records also show that some settlers even resorted to the poisoning of flour, and many massacres of aborigines occurred.

SEGREGATION

Actions such as those just described did not, however, go unchallenged; reform movements have existed since the early nineteenth century. While movements met with resistance, attitudes did slowly change; and gradually a form of separate living came to be tolerated by the settlers. Segregation thus became a policy for living together, the segregated areas taking the forms of missions and reserves (reservations).

A leading nursing journal describes the reservation as "... a form of settlement quite inapposite for a people whose traditional way of life is nomadic," and claims that these settlements also reveal serious health problems.[10] Some other commentators concur. Like the missions, as we will soon see, these institutions can be repressive and to the detriment of the "inmates," whose mental condition has been likened to that of someone accustomed to life in any other closed institution, such as a mental institute. For the aboriginal who finally leaves this environment, extra problems of coping with development outside may, as Rowley argues, exist:

> Often the mission will be introducing the inmates to a world which hardly exists outside church circles. This is why the Aborigines from distant missions tend to have an old-world dignity when they come out of "colonial Australia" into the southern areas.... Their innocence is the direct opposite of what is needed for material success.[11]

It must be conceded that the missions, like the reserves, have played a part in ensuring the survival of aboriginal people. Today, however, they play more of a stopgap role slowing down the drift from arid-zone land to towns. In some cases, as at Gove and Weipa, the mission has acted as a representative of the aborigines in their fight for landrights. It has, nonetheless, been claimed that the representatives of Christian charity may not be the best agents for protecting the indigenous people from the representatives of profit.

Missions and reserves which date from the 1800s have mostly been an arid-zone development. They have survived to the present day and are still an important part of policy toward aboriginals. The thinking behind the reserves can perhaps be derived from the following passage:

> Unlike the governments of Canada, New Zealand and the United States, the Australian Government has never recognized the rights of indigenous people to the land they occupied at the time of European settlements. The British Crown declared Australia's land its own. . . . Aborigines were treated as a rural pest, an obstruction to what is called development. Even when the Aboriginal Reserves were established towards the end of the nineteenth century, they were leased not to Aborigines, but to Government departments or religious missions on the assumption that they could best judge the most appropriate form of development.[12]

The land chosen for reserves did not necessarily bear any relationship to traditional lands; as Justice Woodward points out, the larger reserves consisted of land not then required for settlement.[13] The reserves were in many ways a calculated response to public outrage at the treatment of aborigines, and as such they may be said to have guaranteed the survival of their inmates. Survival, modern-day evidence shows, has not necessarily been survival-with-dignity. If it can be argued that the reserves were a "holding operation" ensuring survival, it could just as easily be argued that the time has long since passed for their removal in favor of a freer system of land ownership. In this respect, the laws governing the Queensland aboriginal reserves are a strong indictment of an apparently democratic regime.

The Queensland Aborigines Act of 1971 has been heavily criticized but persists, allowing iniquitious situations to exist. Examples include occasions when a white manager appointed for the reserve has the right to oversee where and when inmates will work; or where the people have a right to vote for two of the aboriginal councilors, but the director who is white can appoint three councilors of his own choosing. Once away from the reserve the aborigines must have permits to return, and even the right to evict people from the reserve and their homes is implicit in the Act. Permission also has to be sought to use electrical apparatus, such as electric irons or razors. These, and other restrictive conditions imposed on the earning potential and opportunities of inmates, have not prepared the reserve dwellers well to cope with the unfolding development going on around them. In the reserves, the inmates are isolated from the general life of the country. Thus, when released for outside work, the inmates often show difficulty in dealing with the more open society.

ASSIMILATION

Though the reserves and missions persist, they can no longer be regarded as a main thrust of policy towards indigenous people, especially since aborigines (especially young people) have started to vote with their feet and leave the reserves. The segregation policy thus yielded some time ago to another notion, that of assimilation.

Assimilation, which was widely adopted as official policy in the 1950s and 1960s, was defined as follows:

> . . . all Aborigines and part-Aborigines are expected eventually to attain the same manner of living as other Australians and live as members of a single Australian Community, enjoying the same rights and privileges, accepting the same responsibilities, observing the same customs and influenced by the same benefits, hopes and loyalties as other Australians.[14]

The policy in practice, however, devolved into what Rowley describes as a managed transition from the current living style of the aboriginals to the typical settler life style.[15] This was accomplished in steps which, to use housing as an illustration, paralleled a filtering process.

Thus, an aboriginal family may be moved into barely adequate housing quarters and moved again into better quality housing as it shows its ability to live according to its neighbors' standards. As one family filters upward, another will take its place in the vacated premises, and so on, with aboriginal families thus eventually becoming scattered in the neighborhoods of settlers. This policy was applied in the 1960s but has since become less popular; the aborigines themselves have objected to the paternalism and cultural violence concerned in it. As with the segregation policy, remnants of the policy persist and will periodically revive with changes in government.

One policy initiative, that of landrights, remains to be discussed; but, in view of the positive response it has received from the aborigines themselves, it better belongs in the later discussion of future directions. Before looking to the future, however, the present first needs to be more fully described.

Present Problem Defined

We have already dealt with the genesis of a set of problems, showing the root causes of the current tension between settlers and indigenous people in the arid zones of Australia; we have shown how past policies, far from pouring oil on troubled waters, exacerbated the problems, flowing as they did from the colonial attitude of the settlers. Two difficulties will thus be experienced by those formulating plans for the development of arid zones today: first, there will be the question of the development's new effects on indigenous people's current way of life; second, there will be the problem of solving the problems which were created in the past. To model today's development on that of the past would be to condone and continue the anti-human policies just described. New initiatives are needed which place as highest priority the wishes of the indigenous people.

Such initiatives have been forthcoming of late in Australia, and it is this author's opinion that they are generally applicable to the question of arid-zone development and indigenous people internationally. Before they can be considered, however, a little more information than has already been given on the effect of development on the aborigines must be supplied.

We must answer the question, what happens when a traditional nomadic culture is assaulted by a modern industrial one?

"WAYS-OUT" DENIED

As did the North American Indians, the Eskimos, and other indigenous peoples of arid zones, the Australian aborigines lived in harmony with their environment in the past. The system of landrights described previously grew out of this and was essential to it. The industrial development of arid zones is predatorial in its attitude toward land and nature and as such is totally incompatible with the traditional aboriginal system of living. The major effect of development is thus to erode the basis of the indigenous culture. What follows from this is well known, for it has occurred in other countries: alcoholism; ill health mentally, physically, and spiritually; poverty in the midst of plenty; racial tension with violent overtones, and so on. For the aboriginals, the most obvious "way out," a return to the traditional way of life, becomes more and more difficult, partly because much of the land is no longer theirs to use and partly because, in the clash of cultures, they have lost some of the knowledge required to live in harmony with nature. Furthermore, by using the hunting equipment of settlers as a substitute for traditional food-gathering methods, the aborigines have violated the conservation rules of their traditional life so much so that they might have difficulty surviving in nature. Pockets of traditional living, modified by degrees through contact with the settler regime, will, of course, persist (and there is evidence of late of some return to the old ways); but more likely is some scenario actively involving settler developments.

"WAYS-IN" DIFFICULT

We have mentioned the main examples of settler-aborigine relations—the pastoral property, the mining development, the mission, the reserve, the rural township. In each case, the aboriginals have had their land annexed by development and have had to live with the results. This is not to imply complicity; on the contrary, there is currently a vigorous and well-backed campaign to repatriate the aboriginal people, as will be seen shortly. But what happens to those people who, alienated from their land, are refused (or refuse) a part in the industrial development of it and do not go into a reserve or continue with a neotraditional way of life on more marginal land?

The answer seems to be that such people drift either to the towns of arid zones or to the cities of the southeast. The latter trend has accelerated recently. The southeastern cities are not, however, in arid zones, and so the effects of the drift will not be considered here. We might note, however, that tapping off some of the people of the arid zones has eased some of the problems by default. The former trend does need to be considered here since it affects arid-zone development directly.

It is not easy for an aboriginal person, drifting into a town of the arid zone from the "bush," to break in on the urban economy. A typical scenario for such towns is reported by Rowley: "Authority has great difficulty in finding sites for Aboriginal houses, because of resistance from

THE IMPACT OF ARID-ZONE DEVELOPMENT ON INDIGENOUS PEOPLE   193

potential white neighbours. It faces problems in the reluctance of employers to use Aboriginal labour, also, initially in enrolling Aboriginal children in the schools and in the tradition of segregation in the cinema."[16]

It is interesting to note that in Australia, a society geared up to provide facilities for foreign migrants, few institutional arrangements, such as hostels or aid, evolved to deal with this internal migration problem. In the absence of such arrangements, the aborigines have evolved their own— the fringe dwelling, a shanty made up of whatever materials can be found and with minimal amenities.

Needless to say, living conditions are not the best in these fringe dwellings. *The Australian Nurses Journal,* in a previously cited special feature on aboriginal health, described fringe dwellers as "living in unspeakable squallor." On the health problems, they comment at length:

> Being restricted to permanent areas of settlement has not resulted in a changed approach to hygiene, and it seems reasonable to postulate that the majority of gastro-intestinal infections may be directly attributed to a failure to observe the necessary standards of hygiene and sanitation which apply to all settled communities.
>
> This pattern of infection is still further exacerbated by the crowded sleeping arrangements which characterise so many Aboriginal communities. Such diseases, as leprosy . . . syphilis, gonorrhoea, pediculi and ring-worm, all of which are communicated through bodily contact, thrive under these conditions, and it is not surprising to find that Aboriginal communities suffer from a far higher incidence than whites.

Nor is this all. They go on:

> But however appalling the physical aspects of the health problems facing Aboriginals might seem, they are at least equalled by psychological maladies. A significant proportion of Aboriginal people suffer from psycho-neurotic disorders, delinquency and anti-social behaviour.[17]

This kind of situation is particularly hard on infants, and it is a matter of record that death rates among aboriginal infants, particularly in fringe dwellings, are among the highest in the world.

One other unfortunate side effect of life in the fringe developments is that it has reinforced the colonial stereotype of indigenous people as lazy, dirty, and drunken. That women may have to resort to prostitution to support a family whose head is denied access to the local labor market is an inevitable result of such prejudice. That the living conditions are a result of a situation which could have, with planning, been avoided is easily forgotten in a barrage of racial prejudice.

Prospects for Problem Solving

It is by now abundantly clear that arid-zone development can have devastatingly adverse effects on the indigenous people of those regions. It is the claim of the present writer that the foremost goal of those concerned with that development should be what Justice Woodward wrote as the first aim of the Aboriginal Land Rights Commission: "the doing of simple justice to a people who have been deprived of their land without their consent and without compensation."[18]

There is little doubt that the aboriginal people of Australia concur with the commission's emphasis on landrights as a basis for a just settlement of their grievances. Through all the confusion of different claims by the various advocates of the aboriginal cause, one message comes out clearly: the granting of rights over land is the only real basis for future planning which concerns aboriginals. This conclusion is not altered whether one is looking at reserve land, pastoral developments, mining leases, or towns. With rights over their land, the aborigines have a chance to mold the development in their own interests—even to the point of rejecting developments to which they cannot reconcile themselves. Without rights, they have no bargaining power, no opportunity for self-management, and their fall by the wayside is inevitable.

In this crucial section, I would like to discuss the form the granting of landrights could take, referring specifically to recent Australian legislation, and relate this to development in arid zones in general. Implicit in this discussion will be a moral position that questions the right of industrial society and its representatives, the settlers of arid zones, to engage in developments which result in cultural genocide and the kinds of problems just described.

THE ABORIGINAL LAND RIGHTS COMMISSION

The issue of landrights has a long history in Australia. It has reemerged recently as a significant political issue following the Gurindji peoples' actions described earlier. The Labor government newly elected in 1972 took up landrights as a central part of its intended program of aboriginal affairs. Since then, two official reports have been issued on the subject, and the succeeding Liberal-Country Party coalition government has introduced the Aboriginal Land Rights (Northern Territory) 1976 Bill.

By far the fullest planning document on landrights is the Second Report of the Aboriginal Land Rights Commission already cited several times in this chapter. It dealt mainly with the arid zones and in particular with the Northern Territory of Australia. Its main administrative recommendations were that an Aboriginal Land Commission for the Northern Territory be set up to look into claims of landrights and to recommend grants for aborigines to develop their own land. This commission would work through two land councils, consisting of representatives of aborigines in the regions of the Territory. These councils had been set up following the First Report (1973) of the Aboriginal Land Rights Commission and were judged "an unqualified success" by the commission.[19] The report, furthermore, envisaged other kinds of action by these and related bodies (such as the Federal Government Department of Aboriginal Affairs) in the different arenas where settler development was affecting indigenous people. It would be illuminating at this point to look briefly into each arena: the reserves; the pastoral leases; the towns; and the mineral developments.

Reserve land would be handed over by the commission to the aborigines living within, the ownership to be vested in a land trust overseen by the relevant land council. The commission's eighth recommendation states that "legislation should provide for the preservation of all traditional rights over the land concerned and for traditional landowners to be consulted before any leases, licences or permits concerning the land are granted."[20] Aborigines thus would have strong, but not inalienable, rights to the land. As owners, and with the consent of the land council, they could issue leases to various bodies (church, government); with ministerial approval, they could give out mining permits. However, the government—and therefore the settler regime—retains a right of compulsory acquisition of the land; the situations under which that right could be exercised are vague.

Concerning the current operators on reserve land, the report (twentieth recommendation) recommends: "The grant of title to Aboriginal Land Trusts must be subject to the preservation of all existing rights in the land. So far as possible, these rights should be renegotiated so that they are held directly from the Aboriginal landowners on terms acceptable to both parties."[21] The acquisition of landrights thus does not necessarily mean the ability to dispense with developments currently felt to be detrimental to the indigenous people by the indigenous people.

Landrights over reserve land are the most comprehensive rights proposed by the commission, and hence the exact terms of those rights have been discussed here: they are as near to a blueprint for the future as the commission goes. In the remaining arenas, the rights are watered down.

While making some positive recommendations concerning the rights of nomadic movement across pastoral leases and concerning the preservation of sacred sites, the commission does not favor handing over to aborigines the landrights over pastoral leases. The aborigines themselves, through the land council, had recommended that the leases revert to those groups of aborigines claiming traditional ownership of the land concerned, with rentals being paid for the land until the current leases expire. The commission rejected this, on the grounds that resolving questions of traditional ownership might take time and be divisive—a statement that seems to contradict paragraph 65—and on grounds that the cattle industry might suffer in the transition from settler to aboriginal ownership of cattle runs.[22] The recommendations in the report include only having the Aboriginal Land Commission prepare a register of claims to be looked into "in about three years' time." Some purchases of land to allow aboriginal communities "an opportunity for small farming ventures such as pig and poultry rearing" are also recommended, something which may involve buying a whole pastoral lease. In general, however, the tone is one of keeping the major issue, of reversion of *all* leases, at arms length.

The principles of land acquisition for towns state that "Special planning of areas for Aborigines should be an integral part of all town planning in areas where Aboriginal Communities live."[23] This would then mean consultation with aborigines at the planning stage of urban development. The report further suggests that "unless there are very strong arguments to the contrary, and if it is their wish, Aborigines should be provided for in the places where they are used to living. *Even if no traditional rights are involved*, these areas are often important to them from long association."[24]

Provisions beyond these for aborigines might include hostel and camping sites, which would help deal with the migrant problem discussed earlier. In line with this, the report notes that some land acquisition might be necessary "to achieve the aim of satisfactory urban living conditions for Aborigines."[25] In making this recommendation, the commission notes that the fringe-dwellers have suffered the most from the coming of white settlers.

The question of rights over minerals on aboriginal land is the most vexing one addressed by the report. The Aboriginal Land Councils were at the time claiming that full ownership of all minerals should go with the land, while the Australian Mining Industry Council, whose membership includes virtually all mining companies of substance, was claiming that land titles should not carry any mineral rights. The discussion of these conflicting claims in the report interestingly considered the traditional aboriginal relationship to minerals. Two relevant sections can be quoted to illustrate the issues concerned. First, from the aboriginal viewpoint:

> . . . it is clear that Aboriginal ownership was not expressed in terms merely of the land surface. In many of the legends which gave expression to man's spiritual connection with his land, his mythical forebears emerged from the ground and returned to it at different points in their sagas. Their spirit essence still pervades those places and are retained in the soil and rocks.[26]

Next, the miners' viewpoint:

> Before European settlement of Australia, the Aborigines' interest in minerals was restricted to the collection of various stones for cooking, weapon-making and artwork. Traditionally, the minerals and metals of modern civilisation had never been part of Aboriginal life.[27]

The report, in its recommendations, leans toward the Mining Industry Council's view and refuses to grant rights over minerals to aborigines holding land. It compromises, though, by allowing the aboriginal people the right to veto mineral developments. This proposed veto right has, however, been the subject of controversy ever since, particularly since it is by no means clear how strong the right is. The source of confusion and controversy is paragraph 569, which says that while aborigines should decide whether developments are consistent with traditional land rights, " . . . their views could be over-ridden if the government of the day were to resolve that the national interest required it."

The report also laments the bad planning of some past mineral developments and, in further support of the aboriginal people's interest, urges greater government participation in exploration and leasing. The report also recommends the payment of royalties to aborigines of 3 3/4 percent of the returns on mineral investments. Of this, 40 percent would go to the land councils and 60 percent, to the local community (or, if none such existed, to an Aboriginal Benefits Trust Fund).

These, then, are the major recommendations of the report, as they concern development of arid zones. It must be mentioned that the report tried to remain flexible wherever possible—a virtue applauded by some aborigines. Flexibility was seen as necessary following the example of North America where unjust settlements were often made with the Indians which "failed to make provision for changing needs in the future."[28]

The commission's report has been the subject of considerable response from various settler and aboriginal representatives. It, and the step-up of aboriginal aid programs under the Whitlam government, prompted a backlash white rights movement among pastoralists which has inflamed racial tension in the Northern Territory. The Mining Industry Council continued its campaign for sovereignty over mineral deposits, but this time it concentrated on the proposed aboriginal right to veto. Its line, as shown in an advertisement used to support its campaign, was that miners do not oppose giving either land rights or veto power, but feel that, "A decision on whether mining should or should not proceed in the Territory is . . . the proper responsibility of the elected government."[29] It is, considering the industry's position, perhaps no coincidence that the elected government of the Northern Territory is sympathetic to both the pastoralists and the mining industry, as Dr. Letts, its leader, has shown in television and radio broadcasts on the landrights issue.

The commentators defending the aboriginal people's case have not, however, been entirely sympathetic to the report and the Whitlam government. The report has been particularly criticized for the limited horizons within which it worked. For example, Joe Camilieri claims that the report focused too exclusively on the Northern Territory, to the exclusion of other claims and that it could have gone further in granting rights over vacant crown lands. He points out that, having given aborigines the right to veto mineral developments, the report dilutes that right by empowering the government and parliament to override the veto in the "national interest." Camilieri broadens his critique into an indictment of the Whitlam government's approach to aboriginal issues. According to Camilieri, the government showed itself to be prepared to go only so far on landrights and to introduce only a limited degree of "positive discrimination" into its dealings with aborigines.[30] Doug White, in a discussion of the Labor Party's policies toward aborigines, tellingly points out that "none of these policies have been formulated by Aborigines, and in that sense nothing has changed."[31] These criticisms are the more powerful, given that many people saw the Labor era as a "new deal" for aborigines.

THE ABORIGINAL LAND RIGHTS 1976 BILL

Since December 1975, power in Australia has reverted to the settler-oriented Liberal-Country Party regime. It is unfortunate, considering what positive steps *were* taken by the Whitlam government, that, when legislation reflecting the thinking of the Aboriginal Land Rights Commission was introduced in the Northern Territory, it was introduced under the auspices of the Liberal-Country Party coalition. The land rights bill entitled "The Aboriginal Land Rights (Northern Territory) 1976 Bill" departs in a number of ways from the report's recommendations. Perhaps the most significant departure is that claims for land based on traditional grounds are clearly separated from those based on need. The latter, particularly important to fringe-dwellers, will now be heard by a body of the settler-oriented Northern Territory government and not the commission. In a second departure, the land councils, important and trusted advocates of the aborigines, are eventually to be abolished; in the meantime, their powers are substantially reduced. In a third departure, the right to veto mining developments is further diluted by a provision which specifies that, should permission for a lease be withheld by aborigines, the federal minister responsible for aboriginal affairs can call in an arbitrator of his choosing to inquire into the "national interest" (undefined). He will offer new conditions for an agreement; if the land council still objects, the minister can sign in its behalf.[32] Many similar modifications of the report's recommendations are built into the 1976 legislation; by examining them, it becomes clear that the aborigines have not yet regained much from the settler regime.

Legislation, however, even if it were truly liberal, could only be a part of the long-term solution to the question of how to guarantee indigenous people's rights over arid-zone development. We earlier tried to demonstrate that the general way policy is carried out is also important. With this in mind, the acceptance of landrights by most as an ingredient in policy was a breakthrough, but it will need to be supported by complementary actions if indigenous people are to be given the more general right of self-determination. It is in providing such complementary action that planners of arid-zone developments can be of most help. Given landrights, given control over developments on their land, given a priority role in urban development planning, aborigines can work with planners to make sure that future events reflect the indigenous people's wishes and promote their interest in the way they wish. There have been some good examples set in Australia, and it would be setting a hopeful tone for the future if this section were to close with a brief examination of two of them.

GROOTE EYLANDT MINING DEVELOPMENT

Though it started out in 1966 without full consultation with aborigines whose land was affected, Broken Hill Property's manganese mine facilities at Groote Eylandt have included integrated services, a training program for aborigines, and the establishment of aboriginal families in the company town. Good relations between settler and aboriginal communities have been fostered by an attitude in the early days of the project that equal treatment would be conducive to productivity. Nevertheless, commentators warn that, without some rights over the enterprise, future developments there could go against the aborigines' interest if there were a shift in the management's attitude: it is, in other words, dangerous to rely entirely on goodwill for the future. Despite this warning, there is some enthusiasm expressed by commentators at the way management has considered the local aboriginal community as an integral part of its development.[33]

ABORIGINAL HOUSING ASSOCIATION SCHEME

A second, encouraging example of the way planners can work with indigenous people is the Aboriginal Housing Association Scheme. This government grant-sponsored scheme sets out to help groups of aborigines incorporate themselves as associations to build houses for their community. The associations were to be self-managed and were to maximize the employment of aborigines. While there have been some failures—put down mostly to lack of management skills—and some ill-advised restrictions on the associations, there have been some successes, too.[34] Planners can help make the successes more numerous by consulting with such groups and initiating new and imaginative housing schemes based on the aboriginal concept of community association. Where such an approach has been taken, the response from indigenous people has been enthusiastic.

Conclusion

In the name of profit, territory previously the traditional land of nomadic peoples in arid zones has been settled by newcomers from industrial societies. As these settlements have developed, the indigenous people's land has been taken; their way of life has been disrupted; their whole culture has been threatened; and their survival has been jeopardized. Australian arid-zone development has been typical of all such colonial situations; the problems faced by the aborigines are typical of those experienced by other indigenous peoples of arid zones.

It is this writer's view that planners of arid-zone development must acknowledge what has happened and is happening to indigenous peoples and must accept responsibility for what is happening to them. The industrial society will as a result, at worst, experience a slowdown in its rate of growth—something which some would claim is actually in its interest. It is hoped that the indigenous population will, as a result, regain self-management abilities and survive with dignity in the manner of their choosing.

Essential to the indigenous dwellers' future is that they have power over present and future developments. They will then be in a position to advise and consult with planners of developments *they approve of* on how they wish to see those developments unfold. It would seem that the best, if not the only, way of ensuring this is to give them inalienable rights over arid-zone land.

In the long run, a change in attitude of settlers toward indigenous people is required to back up landrights. Attitudes must go from white supremacist ones to those allowing the self-evident truth that all men are created equal. While this is in a large measure beyond the realm of planners, they can contribute to it: for example, by promoting integrated services or by boosting the opportunities for indigenous people to participate in development planning, should they want to. An effort by planners to improve housing in towns and to make an assault on the health and hygiene problems of fringe-dwellers, aimed at removing the horror of fringe dwellings, would remove at the same time the model for the colonial stereotype of native living conditions. By thus eliminating the base on which the settlers' attitudes to a large degree rest today, a possibility for a new set of attitudes would be created. The rest, as G. Myrdal said of white Americans in *An American Dilemma*, would be a matter for the mind and conscience of the settlers.

Notes

1. This legislation, discussed later, is entitled "The Aboriginal Land Rights (Northern Territory) Bill 1976."
2. C. D. Rowley, *The Remote Aborigines* (Baltimore, Md.: Penguin Books, 1972). See Chapter 8.
3. Aboriginal Land Rights Commission, *First Report* (Canberra: Commonwealth of Australia, 1973), para. 65, p. 10.
4. Frank Hardy, *The Unlucky Australians* (Melbourne: Nelson, 1968), p. 14.
5. Quoted in Pete Thomas, *The Beef Rustlers* (Brisbane: Coronation Printery, 1968), p. 15.
6. Aboriginal Land Rights Commission, *Second Report* (Canberra: Commonwealth of Australia, 1974), para. 669, pp. 121–122.

7. Cheryl Buchanan, *We Have Bugger All—The Kulaluk Story,* (Melbourne: Australian Union of Students, 1974), p. 16.
8. Rowley, p. 1.
9. *The Australian Aboriginals* (Canberra: Australian Information Service, 1976), p. 3.
10. Jennifer Richardson, "Aboriginal Health—A Vicious Circle," *Australian Nurses Journal,* **6**, no. 2 (August 1976), 25.
11. Rowley, p. 114.
12. L. Broom and F. L. Jones, *A Blanket a Year* (Canberra: Australian National University, 1973), p. 1.
13. Aboriginal Land Rights Commission, *Second Report,* para. 67.
14. Statements from a 1961 conference of federal and state ministers quoted in A. B. Pittock, *Beyond White Australia* (Surry Hills, New South Wales: Quaker Race Relations Publication, 1975), p. 18.
15. Rowley, pp. 40–41.
16. Ibid, p. 31. Rowley's report is based on the 1960s work of A. Gordon, operating with the South Australian Aboriginal Advancement League.
17. Richardson, p. 25.
18. Aboriginal Land Rights Commission, *Second Report,* para. 3.
19. Ibid, para. 335. Land councils are described in paras. 260–276 of the *First Report*; the Aboriginal Land Commission is described in paras. 709–732 of the *Second Report.*
20. Aboriginal Land Rights Commission, *Second Report,* p. 23.
21. Ibid, p. 24.
22. It is interesting to note that, since this idea's promulgation, the cattle industry of Australia has entered a recessionary phase.
23. Aboriginal Land Rights Commission, *Second Report,* para. 278, p. 51.
24. Ibid, (emphasis mine).
25. Ibid, para. 281.
26. Ibid, para. 543, p. 104.
27. Ibid, para. 559, p. 106.
28. The Commission's views on how indigenous people were dealt with in North America are contained in paras. 27–40 of its *Second Report.*
29. Printed in *The National Times* (Sidney, New South Wales) 4–9 October 1976.
30. J. Camilieri, "Under Labor; Aboriginal Land Rights," *Arena,* **36** (1974), pp. 5-11.
31. Doug White, "Aboriginal Culture; The New Welfare," *Arena,* **36** *(1974),* p. *12.*
32. The relationship between the 1976 bill and the commission reports is fully discussed by G. Eames in *Land Rights or Sell Out?* (Alia Springs, Northern Territory: Central Land Council, 1976).
33. See Rowley, pp. 141–147; Aboriginal Land Rights Commission, *Second Report,* paras. 632–645.
34. The Aboriginal Housing Association Scheme was the subject of a confidential government report (The Hay Report). Some of its general findings are outlined in *The Australian Financial Review,* 26 August 1976. An aboriginal response is contained in a letter published in the 2 September issue.

Recommended Reading

Aboriginal Land Rights Commission. *First Report.* Canberra: Australian Government Publishing Service, 1973.
Aboriginal Land Rights Commission. *Second Report.* Canberra: Australian Government Publishing Service, 1974.
Tatz, Colin. *Black Viewpoints: The Aboriginal Experience.* Sydney: ANZ Book Company, 1975.

10
Economic Problems Facing Small Towns in the Arid Zones of Australia

Rodney Charles Jensen

Economists have, for some time, devoted attention to the problems facing urban areas. Virtually all of this attention has been directed to large urban areas where the economic and social stresses inevitably associated with urban growth have been more conspicuous and are frequently the subject of public debate. The (almost) complete lack of attention devoted to the smaller urban areas is mute testimony both to the inability of the residents of small towns to communicate effectively their claim to professional attention, and the lack of concern by the general public and the professions for the "out-of-sight, out-of-mind" problems.

This chapter introduces the reader to the declining small towns in the arid zones of Australia. No doubt they share features with similarly placed small towns in other countries, and therefore this discussion will strike some familiar chords. This chapter provides a brief introduction to small town social and economic conditions and a more detailed discussion of the basic features of the small town business and of the town itself, then redefines the small town problems, and finally discusses policy alternatives and presents policy suggestions. The discussion necessarily goes beyond a simple economic exposé of small towns, for such an approach would ignore the essential social and economic relationships which, if not unique to small towns, certainly contribute to their claim as urban areas of a special character.

Australian Small Towns

HISTORY

Allen describes the period 1860 to 1900 as one of growth of urban areas in the arid or frontier regions and the period from 1900 to 1960 as one of "doldrums and decline."[1] The period during which the "overlanders" or potential settlers moved with stock into the inland regions began in the 1860s. Their routes, dictated by the location of river courses, laid the pattern of settlements which exists today. Along these routes were established centers ranging from the primitive "grog shanty" to the large river ports which developed as distribution points for essential goods and services. This pattern was modified by the emergence of mining towns and later by the construction of the railway network which established new trade patterns and facilitated the emergence of a permanent urban hierarchy based on function. By 1900, the consolidation of sheep and cattle stations had attracted an increased number of station hands, shearers, and rural service contractors; the future of the frontier town seemed assured.

At the turn of the century, circumstances conspired to halt the growth of these rural industries and their urban service centers. The financial crisis of 1893 imposed severe operating restrictions on both station and business operators. Some areas were heavily infested by rabbit plagues in the last two decades of the century and suffered commensurate decreases in stock carrying capacity. The final blow to many pastoralists was the "Great Drought" which began in 1898. The combined effects of overstocking, the shortage of capital, and the still increasing rabbit population transformed the western area: the expansion had ended—"the new century ushered in a period of disillusionment, decline and, at worst, abandonment."[2]

By the early 1900s most frontier urban centers had experienced a population decline; pastoralism had declined, and this decline was reflected in the disappearance of the economic thresholds for some services. The range of private services contracted, and many wayside stopping places and some towns were abandoned. Out of this process of contraction has emerged a number of relatively small towns whose fortunes vary with the vicissitudes of climate. Since periodic droughts are inevitable, the markets for primary products vary. Both wool and beef prices are determined on an international market and are therefore subject to considerable variation also.[3] Some of these urban centers are virtually "shire" towns, dependent largely on the economic activity of the region's local government. A general picture then emerges of urban decline with a small number of towns relatively constant in size or showing low growth rates.

DEMOGRAPHY

This chapter is not concerned with the urban centers exhibiting behavioral patterns which may be categorized as abnormal in the general context of arid zones. Hence, mining towns are excluded from the discussion, along with towns such as Darwin which grow and function as major administrative and political centers and have no major reliance on the economic activity normally considered as the economic base of the arid zones. Rather, the discussion attempts to isolate the features which typify the small town integrated into the arid-zone economy. We can distinguish between two types of such towns according to size, those with a population from 200 to 1000 and those with a population of more than 1000.[4] Using the state of Queensland as an example, the number of arid-zone towns of each type are shown for 1971 in Table 10-1. Clearly, the urban areas in Australia's arid zones may be described as small by any standards, particularly when it is realized that most have populations of less than 1000 persons. A similar number of urban areas with less than 200 persons could also be identified, down to the hamlet of one general store and one hotel.[5]

Any discussion of the economics of these small towns would be rather sterile if it failed to recognize the essential social character of the population. Indeed, the small town is the compelling example of close interaction between economic and social activity, and there is a paramount need

TABLE 10-1. Small Town Size in Queensland, Australia (1971 Census).

TOWN SIZE (POPULATION)	NUMBER OF TOWNS	AVERAGE SIZE (POPULATION)	RANGE OF SIZES (POPULATION)
200–1000	22	471	203–872
more than 1000	11	2242	1331–3948

to consider the urban area as a social-economic unit rather than simply as an economic entity capable of economic dissection. This issue is developed in considerable detail in later sections, but first I shall call attention to some of the more obvious population characteristics of the arid-zone small town.

During the "overlanding" and early settlement stages, the population of the arid zones was distinctly dominated by males. The ratio of males to females has gradually fallen over the century of settlement until the balance of the sexes in the ST is "normal," as shown by item 1 in Table 10-2. However, the SST still demonstrates a markedly high masculinity, 110 males per 100 females (ST and SST are defined in note 5). The extent to which this imbalance is a reflection of the historically high masculinity levels or a product of existing governmental and private sector employment policies is difficult to assess. The question itself draws our attention to a number of other factors.

First, it is clear from item 2 of Table 10-2 that the age structure of the small town (particularly the SST) is different from that of the state. Families in small towns tend to be larger, and hence the proportion of the population in the 0 to 12 age-group is significantly higher. Some of these children are sent to larger centers for schooling or eventually migrate seeking employment; this leaves a lower proportion of the small town population in the 13 to 20 age-group. On the other hand, the proportion in the 21 to 39 age-group is higher than that for the state as a whole, with significant reductions apparent in older age groups. Some of this dominance by the younger work force is due to the placement of junior staff (particularly males) in small towns by stock and station agents, banks and similar private institutions, and by public authorities including the education, railway, and police departments. These employees can expect to move, particularly from the SST, by the time their families require secondary or tertiary education; hence the size of older working groups is lower. Allen demonstrates that the reduction in elderly population is due largely to the reluctance of elderly women to remain in the "pioneer" regions.[6]

As Allen also establishes, there is a dominance of males throughout most working age groups. This is probably due to a tendency among males not to relocate and take advantage of educational opportunities. Item 3, which suggests a lower level of educational qualifications in these areas, and item 4, which points to a lower level of formal education, seem to confirm this tendency.[7]

Another point worthy of note is revealed by item 5 of Table 10-2. This item indicates the proportion of the population which changed residence between 1966 and 1971 and, further, answers the question: Did they move within the same statistical division, within the same state, or interstate?[8] Contrary to common opinion, the small town populations are considerably

TABLE 10-2. Population and Employment Characteristics of Small Towns in Comparison to State Average in Queensland (1971).[a]

CHARACTERISTIC	TOWNS 200–1000	TOWNS 1000+	STATE AVERAGE
1. Males per 100 females	110.3	101.3	101.8
2. Age Distribution			
0–4 years	12.4	11.7	9.8
5–12 years	20.7	20.3	16.0
13–17 years	7.6	9.5	9.3
18–20 years	4.5	4.6	5.1
21–29 years	14.2	13.3	13.5
30–39 years	12.2	12.0	11.4
40–54 years	15.0	17.0	17.0
55–64 years	7.2	6.9	9.0
65+ years	6.2	6.3	9.1
3. Qualifications Obtained (males only)			
Trade	6.7	8.7	12.6
Technician	1.2	1.9	2.0
Tertiary	2.3	2.7	3.5
4. Level of Schooling (highest level attended)			
Level 1–3	7.5	6.1	4.3
Level 4–7	33.2	31.4	33.9
Level 8–10	16.5	20.5	26.3
5. 1966 Residence			
Moved within same Statistical Div.	21.5	20.4	23.0
Moved within same State	22.8	20.1	11.0
Moved to another State	4.2	3.3	5.9
Never moved	48.1	50.7	53.9
6. Occupation			
Professional or Technical	4.6	6.5	7.3
Administrative or Management	8.5	10.3	7.8
Clerical	5.1	8.2	7.7
Sales	3.6	7.3	6.2
Farming, Lumbering, etc.	15.4	10.9	13.7
Mining, Transportation	16.7	12.9	9.1
Trades, Processing, Laboring	41.5	38.1	42.0
7. Industry of Employed Persons			
Agriculture, Mining	12.7	8.4	13.1
Manufacturing	9.4	3.9	16.5
Construction	15.0	11.6	9.4
Retail and Wholesale Trade	17.7	22.3	20.2
Transportation	9.0	9.8	5.6
Communication	3.3	3.3	2.0
Finance	2.1	4.4	6.2
Public Administration, Defence	7.3	7.8	5.9
Community Services	10.0	12.5	10.5
Services and Others	13.3	15.5	10.6
8. Government and Non-Government Employment			
Federal	4.2	5.3	5.6
State and Local	29.0	28.0	16.0
Non-Government	66.8	65.9	78.4

[a]Since the entries in this table are averages of percentages calculated for each town, errors do occur in rounding. Omissions of less significant items also do occur.

more mobile than the state's population, but only in interregional movement.[9] These data reinforce the suggestion that employment placement is an important factor in the demographic structure of the small town and reveals higher levels of transience.

Items 6, 7 and 8 in Table 10-2 provide pertinent information on small town employment. Occupationally, the SST shows lower proportions of professional, technical, clerical, and sales workers than the state. It also shows higher proportions of farming, mining, and transportation (including railway) workers. This data is consistent with that in item 8 which reveals the heavy dependence of small towns on state and local government employment when compared with the state average. It is also consistent with item 7 which shows the small town's relatively heavy dependence on the construction (road building and maintenance) industry, public administration, services, and transportation and lower dependence than the state on manufacturing. Dependence on employment in retail/wholesale sales is lower than for the state in the SST and higher than for the state in the ST, indicating the functional differences between these centers.

Such a brief discussion cannot do justice as a description of the small town population. It does, however, provide some background against which we can study the small town in detail. Also it provides evidence of some differences in function between the ST and the SST by suggesting that the former functions more as an administrative and service center than the latter.

The Small Town Firm

This section attempts to depict in general terms small town economic activity in its social context. It assembles the essential features of the small town by identifying the characteristics and constraints which determine the behavior of the firm. Although the factors are discussed in general terms, it should be recognized that each firm exists to some extent in a unique framework which may not be adequately described in such terms.

SMALLNESS

Economists remain preoccupied with the "large" and the "giant." Whether the concern be with firms, regions, urban areas, or nations, the economist is more comfortable, more secure, and probably more effective in analyzing largeness and its effects than in devoting attention to the "small." Indeed, economic theory (including the theory of the firm and, therefore, relevant to our discussion) implies a degree of largeness which requires sophisticated management decisions based on detailed knowledge of inputs and outputs.

We are here attempting to understand smallness, despite the fact that smallness does not attract the attention of the professions and is often considered akin to backwardness or stagnation. Yet, apart from the obvious claim that the "small" deserves some attention, we can learn a great deal from small concerns which should help us to understand the more intricate large concerns.

In arid-zone small towns, three aspects of smallness deserve attention. First, firms are small. We can appreciate this smallness by visualizing the typical small town retailing firm. It will normally be operated by an owner and (largely unpaid) family labor. The trading pattern will consist of the import of consumer goods from large urban centers for local resale. The owner is personally involved with all aspects of the firm's operation, from management to sales to cleaning. Nonfamily unskilled labor will be employed only if this is warranted by a high level of sales.

Secondly, operators of the small town firm tend to "think small." In most cases, their business experience has been limited to firms of a similar size and function, and their business training has not gone beyond the self-taught common-sense ground rules. The operator is not aware, except in an intuitive sense, of the larger economic forces which shape his local business environment. His planning horizon is thus limited, and his day-to-day routine is manageable. He is an isolated trader: he learns of changes in operational systems and products by diffusion from agents, salespeople, and travelers and adopts changes slowly, according to his interpretation of the likely response of his largely unchanging market. He has limited economic means, and his family's standard of living will vary with the profits derived from the firm. However, the operation of his firm, with the associated personal independence, provides a satisfying life which engenders personal pride and status in the local community.

Thirdly, the towns are small. Without belaboring the obvious, the combined population of SSTs (10,400) is about half the student population at the University of Queensland and would not constitute a medium-sized urban area. The smallness of the town places special constraints on the firm and facilitates the emergence of social-economic norms which are more clearly defined than in larger urban areas. These are discussed below.

CONSTRAINTS

All firms operate within a series of constraints relating to trading practices, prices of inputs and outputs, and market areas. It is, however, difficult to imagine a more closely constrained environment than that in which the small town firm is required to operate. We should examine these constraints in more detail.

Social Environment.   A major constraint is imposed by the social environment of the small town. Particularly in the SST—and to some extent in the ST—the operator is very much a part of the social as well as the economic order. The operator and his family are closely identified in a personal sense with the firm. His customers often regard their purchasing as quasi-social activities and as extensions of their social relationship with the owner. The relationship between the business operator and his customer, therefore, assumes a social significance which is, in general, not present in larger urban areas. These relationships have led to a code of social behavior to be followed by the operator. If the code is fostered by the operator, he is to some extent assured of customer "support"; if the operator ignores the code of social behavior, his business depends on reluctant customers forced to his firm only by their own convenience.

The standards of social conformity impose economic costs on the operator. For example, the need to extend credit for current purchases and to be tolerant in the exercise of credit conditions is dictated to a large extent by social norms of mutual trust in a small town. Clearly direct economic costs to the operator are involved, particularly in periods of extended drought or low product prices for the commodities produced in the region. Then, the credit accommodations made by the operators of firms present severe burdens on the firms' liquidity. In another context, the operator feels constrained to ensure that the social-economic relationship between the firm and the customer is not damaged by customer dissatisfaction. Since each transaction should, if possible, further cement the relationship, the operator avoids hard-sell techniques and provides personal guarantees beyond those extended by his city counterparts.[10] These social constraints are willingly borne by the business operator, who often responds to them by becoming increasingly active in the community.[11]

Commodities. Clearly, the small town business operator will also feel constraints on the type and range of goods and services he can offer to the local markets. Convention and expedience dictate that each type of business offer a recognized range of commodities; often by agreement among operators, these groupings are strictly observed. Within the appropriate groups, each operator selects those commodities which past experience has indicated are in regular demand, have acceptable rates of turnover, and have acceptable inventory costs.

It is important to note here a difference between the range of goods and services provided by the ST and SST and by larger and more distant urban centers. As expected, following the logic of central place theory, the SST will be concerned primarily with lower-order goods and services; in economic terms, the SST firms will trade largely in goods and services of low (price and income) elasticity of demand. Consumer nondurables, which by their nature require frequent purchase and which do not justify journeys to larger centers, will be purchased locally in the SST, regardless of any reasonable price differences. Firms in the SST will provide these services and only limited ranges of higher-order services. Consequently, the SST will include firms such as a grocery outlet, yardgoods store, newsstand, pharmacy, light engineering or "garage" establishment, bank, hotel, and post office. There will be single firms serving these needs in most cases, with multiple firms in a few instances. As the size of urban areas increases to the ST level, wider ranges of goods and services, including the more elastic, higher-order services, become available.

Traveling habits in arid areas, aided by improved transportation facilities, have resulted in an increasing tendency for the residents of the SST and its hinterlands to travel to the ST or larger urban areas in search of a wider choice, particularly in consumer durables. It is thus possible to isolate a trend towards narrower ranges of goods and services offered by the SST. Another major stimulus to this tendency has been provided by the high inflation rates in recent years. Small businesses, particularly those holding stocks of low-turnover goods have, in a period of rapid inflation, simply been unable to replace stock after sales, in either the quantity or range originally held. Their problems have been compounded by taxation laws which ensured that increases in the value of stocks were treated as taxable income.

Prices. Firms in small towns typically import goods for resale or as inputs into lower-order "manufacturing" processes such as bakeries, vehicle repair, etc. Two aspects of prices thus need to be considered: the prices paid for inputs and the prices received for outputs or commodities sold. As far as the former are concerned, the firm is almost completely constrained. Purchases are almost inevitably made from wholesaling firms located in large urban areas which offer goods at a fixed price (normally excluding transportation costs) on a "take it or leave it" basis. As small volume purchasers, the small town firms have no bargaining power and are conceded no discount privileges; they are "price takers" in the real sense of the term.

Little research and much speculation has been devoted to the methods of price formation for commodity sales in small towns. One study applicable to small towns generally examined price formation processes, considering in the process four alternative price formation procedures.[12] The study concluded that retail price maintenance was the dominant method of price determination, i.e., that legislatively enforced or "suggested" price lists provided the basis for the majority of prices charged by small town firms. The study noted in particular the heavy reliance on the suggested price lists issued by wholesalers or retail organizations, almost as if a certain "righteousness" were associated with the observance of these prices. The operator seems to feel that his firm is not enjoying its "rightful" profits unless prices are at least as high as the suggested prices and that the consumer recognizes the right of his firm to fix prices at these levels to earn a "just" profit. On the other hand, the operator seems to feel that the consumer would consider it "exploitation" if prices charged were in excess of the manufacturers' suggested levels. However, certain items such as meat are normally priced according to a cost-plus formula in the absence of an organized marketing organization and in recognition of the daily fluctuations of livestock prices.

The extent to which the study's results can be generalized and found applicable to arid zones is not known. It is often suggested that the firms in more remote areas, because of their so-called monopoly or near monopoly positions, may rely more heavily on cost-plus or "what the market will bear" methods of pricing. If this is the case, they are then less constrained in price formation than their nonarid counterparts.

One fact relating to price formation is, however, quite clear. The theory of spatial price discrimination is an inappropriate explanation of the pricing behavior of small town firms. Although technically these firms may be spatial monopolists, or nearly so, any suggestion that they act in the manner ascribed to such market situations by conventional price theory is unrealistic. By observation, it appears that prices above suggested levels for goods and services may be justified to some extent by higher transportation costs and to some extent by higher inventory costs associated with lower stock turnover rates; in reality, such prices may be in the interests of local consumers. The higher price may provide sufficient marginal incentive to provide the commodity locally, whereas the normal price would ensure that the commodity was available only at more distant centers with higher consequent local welfare losses. Certainly, both the operator and the local consumer recognize that price levels locally are higher than those prevailing in larger urban centers and accept this as a normal and justified situation. The differences in general price levels represent a negative locational rent associated with relative isolation.

Competition.   In the SSTs, most "sectors" or industries will consist of a single firm. When multiple firms do occasionally exist in the SST (more frequently in the ST), the conventional representation of competition between firms is quite misleading. The previous discussion relating to price formation suggests that active price competition between firms in the same industry in a small town is very weak, and this would appear to be the case. Certainly the suggestion that price competition by individual commodities exists in any form is unrealistic.

Competition in general price levels does become manifest as towns increase in size and provide thresholds for businesses based on higher turnover levels, namely supermarket operations. In addition, firms in some industries, for example grocery retailing and automobile sales and service, are often allied to larger distribution groups. The only local competition in prices is that reflected by the competition at a national level between these groups, reflected by the "price lists" for goods and services issued by the groups. This national competition, transmitted to the small town level, appears to be applied in a manner which does not discriminate between towns; i.e., the nationally competitive price levels apply even if the local member of the retailing group is the sole firm in the local industry.

Nonprice competition does, however, exist in a subtle but nevertheless very real form. An operator's ability to foster the social aspects of transactions, to be understanding when credit problems arise, and to create a friendly atmosphere are significant determinants of his success in competing with similar firms in the same town and with larger firms in larger urban areas. Since local businesses recognize and to some extent resent any tendency for the local population to journey to larger urban areas to make purchases, local retailers must rely on their nonprice attributes to retain local trade and to foster the sentiment that the local residents should feel some obligation to support local industry and strengthen the local community. This loyalty concept has definite economic ramifications. Although the tradition of consumer loyalty appears to be weakening with the passage of time, it illustrates the importance of social relationships in the economic life of the small town. Willingness to provide civic leadership and to become involved in local civic problems appears a greater asset than some marginally lower product prices.

The Amalgam of Attraction. The preceding discussion suggests that total markets will be small, largely independent of local price levels, and dependent on the social as well as the commercial attractions of both the individual firm and the town. This leads to a discussion of the concept of the "amalgam of attraction" as the determinant of the market for the small town firm.[13]

The amalgam of attraction concept was developed in the context of nonarid-zone small towns. It is based on the observation that "consumers both urban and rural, in country areas, develop purchasing patterns based on a subjective evaluation of the towns to which they have reasonable access."[14] Consumers, in other words, appear to evaluate those aspects which contribute to the attractiveness of a small town in terms of the availability and range of the goods and services they require for personal and commercial use, the general level of prices existing in the town, and the general social environment. The amalgam of these three factors, together with access (in terms of distance), determines the degree to which consumers prefer one small town to another and establish habitual patterns of purchasing in individual centers.

Some important consequences or constraints for the individual firm arise from this amalgam of attraction. The collective attraction of all firms in a town is one important determinant of the market (measured in turnover or sales) for each individual firm. Thus, each firm helps determine the market for other firms and for the town as a whole. The number of consumers habitually visiting an individual small town will be determined by the total attractiveness of the town, and this in turn provides an upper limit to the sales which each firm can expect. The implication is that each firm is dependent to a large extent for its market on the operational characteristics of firms in other industries, including even its competitors if such exist. Thus, action by the individual operator to increase his own level of sales by reducing prices will have limited success, and the degree of this success will be determined largely by the extent his actions attract more habitual buyers to the town as a whole. However, in this case, his fellow operators will share the benefits of his actions.

Observation suggests that a hierarchy of importance exists among types of firms in determining the amalgam of attraction. Leading in importance are firms providing immediately required commodities such as groceries, petroleum, health services, etc. Failure of these more important contributors to the amalgam of attraction to provide locally acceptable standards of service will cause a substantial loss of revenue, not only for the offending firm but for other firms in the town as well.[15]

The extent to which the amalgam of attraction affects arid-zone small towns is difficult to assess. Allen's work suggests that it has been the basic feature which has led to the existing urban hierarchy in frontier areas of Queensland.[16] It would, however, be reasonable to expect that the effect of the amalgam of attraction would be less obvious when consumers are faced with fewer and more distant alternative urban centers. Its main effect should surface in the consumer's choice between the SST and the ST, i.e., in the choice between the smaller and larger urban centers. Evidence suggests that the current tendency is for the market area of smaller towns to be decreasing in relation to those in the larger urban areas.

The amalgam of attraction, if considered in the light of changing national markets, helps to explain this tendency. As the demand for some goods and services declines at the national level and that for other goods and services increases, certain types of businesses in small towns have tended to disappear (e.g., the traditional blacksmith) and others to increase in number (e.g., automobile services). Due to the effects of technological change, particularly in transportation, some structural change in industry mix and in the market possibilities of small towns has occurred. For example, as technology in rural industries has improved, an increased demand for access to specialized technical services has tended to place the ST at an advantage over the SST.

Objectives. The close sense of identification between the operator, the family, and the business has already been mentioned. Due to this, it is inevitable that the objectives of this business are closer to personal objectives than to those normally attributed to a business in conventional microeconomic theory. Even a small degree of familiarity with the small town business would convince an observer that such businesses do not attempt to maximize sales or profits or minimize costs except in a general observance of common-sense progress towards these criteria collectively.

Rather the business is seen primarily as a means of support for the family. Survival is the primary objective, particularly if survival is threatened.

Variations in the level of surplus funds from the firm result in corresponding variations in the living standards of the operator and his family. In a declining region (which includes most of Australia's arid zones), the reduced markets of some types of businesses have resulted in reduced living standards for operators. Subsequent ultimate closure of the business is a frequent occurrence, eminently unnoticed outside the local scene. The strong personal attachment of the individual to the business, however, frequently ensures that the declining business remains in operation well beyond the point when the operator could earn higher income in alternative employment; this has been one of the important reasons for the emergence of a low-income group of small business operators in small towns. On the other hand, businesses with increasing markets tend to bestow higher living standards on their operators, and perhaps on their employees. This has led, to some extent, to the emergence of operators of technically based firms as the more influential members of local society.

Small Town as an Economic Entity

In its simplest sense, an urban area is a concentration or collection of individuals, families, organizations, and firms. The sheer complexity of large urban areas defies the neat and ordered categorization and identification of causation which is required for a detailed understanding of economic interaction. The student of the small town has the decided advantage of his subject being less complex in terms of identifying interactions. It is manageable in detailed empirical scale and can be visualized, perceived, and dissected in toto without difficulty. Finally, it has characteristics as a social unit which are identifiable. In arid zones particularly, the individuals in a small town and its reasonably accessible hinterland are inevitably cast by circumstances into constant proximity. The town therefore acts as a center for the distribution of goods and services and for administration, as well as the focal point of personal identification and communication. Economic, social, and administrative aspects of life become intertwined in a way that provides some sense of community, less identifiable and less tangible as we move from the SST to the ST. As we now turn our attention to the identification of the economic characteristics of the small, relatively isolated town and to the degree to which it may be identified as an entity, these lessons should be remembered.

DEPENDENCE AND INDEPENDENCE

Our previous discussion presented some of the constraints that apply to the small town business. These businesses collectively form the commercial and economic structure of the town and share a common market area in most respects. As outlined previously, the town will present an amalgam of attraction which will ensure that the town as a whole increases or decreases in size, vis-à-vis any competing towns. The businesses also collectively share in the vagaries of the market for the commodities purchased by the local base industries. Because of these common constraints, the town as a whole may be seen as incurring increases or decreases in income levels. Businesses thus have a common interest in attracting potential consumers, corporate or individual, to their town.

Although it is tempting to thus visualize the small town as an economic entity and to analyze it as such, the concept breaks down upon a closer inspection of its economic structure. Table 10-2 illustrated a reasonably balanced distribution of employment among industries or sectors; but the mutual interdependence among these sectors, an important part of the economy of larger urban areas, is missing in the small town. A recent input-output study of a small town has demonstrated those links to be very weak and the resulting multipliers to be quite small.[17] This study illustrates that the nature of the simple import-for-resale type of activity in the small town causes each industry to operate largely in economic isolation from others in the town and to experience a low level of interbusiness sales.

In practice these weak linkages have some important effects. When new industries become established in the town, spillover benefits to existing firms are minimal; similarly, with the closure of businesses, negative spillover effects are small. Thus, any growth which occurs in the town is not "locked in" as it tends to be in larger urban areas. The vulnerability shown by arid-zone small towns in recent years clearly demonstrates this tendency.

LONG-TERM STRUCTURAL CHANGES

Evidence and observation suggest that some important long-term structural changes are taking place in arid-zone small towns. Changes in the amalgam of attraction of a town tend to be self-reinforcing. Thus, a reduction in the amalgam of attraction leads to fewer consumers, which in turn reduces the level of services, which in turn further reduces the amalgam of attraction. Furthermore, as mentioned above, the apparent tendency for consumers in the SST to purchase more demand-inelastic goods locally and to travel at least to the ST (and maybe farther to larger urban areas) for consumer durables and many demand-elastic goods appears to be increasing. This has the dual effect of reducing the role of the SSTs as they supply a narrowing range of services, and promoting the growth (or slowing the decline) of the STs as centers producing goods and services higher in the market order.

Two factors cause structural change in the small town industry mix. The first has already been mentioned in our discussion of changes in the markets of the businesses found in small towns. For various reasons, certain types of businesses tend to be disappearing from small towns as their market areas contract. These are often replaced, particularly in the ST, by new businesses in industries where the market areas are expanding. It has been suggested that this will apply particularly in technically oriented industries providing services to cope with the technological advances in primary industries.

A second factor causing structural change is related to economies of scale in some manufacturing industries combined with the effects of decreasing rural population on market areas. The rural to urban shift in population has reduced the market available to small town manufacturing enterprises, such as bakeries. Other factors aside, this tends to lower the sales level of the enterprise, possibly to the point where the firm is forced to close. Supplies will then have to be imported to the small town, often over long distances. Already arid-zone small towns (particularly the SSTs) commonly receive a number of regularly consumed commodities by rail. The businesses threatened with closure in most cases will be operating at low technological levels. In the bakery example, substantial technological improvements in the industry have led to increased concentration, and then bakeries enjoying the benefits of large-scale production in larger urban centers invade the markets of small-scale bakeries in small towns. This effect, a centralization-by-concentration, has also increased the extent to which small towns, particularly the SSTs, act as agency centers for larger scale industries in the ST and, increasingly, in the larger urban areas.

SHORT-TERM CHANGES

Arid zones, by their very nature tend to be monocultural, or at least they tend to produce a very limited range of rural commodities dictated by local climatic conditions. In Australia, these are almost inevitably sheep and beef products, both of which are sold on international markets and are therefore subject to periodic price-level fluctuations. Couple these fluctuations (of considerable size in the past) with the inevitable appearance of drought and exceptionally good seasons, and the economic climate of the small town is often unstable. Although local periodic moods of pessimism and optimism occur, small towns show a remarkable degree of resistance to the vagaries of nature and fluctuations in rural commodity price levels due to three important factors.

First, local business operators accept as normal, or at least manageable, fluctuations in their economic environment of a size which would cause distress to business operators in larger urban areas where a more diversified economy engenders an atmosphere of stability. While not unconcerned, the small town operator has learned to cope personally with a less stable economic environment and is therefore unlikely or unable to take precipitate action in a time of financial crisis. His close personal relationship with his firm and the fact that the firm in most cases represents the major portion of his wealth will encourage him to adapt as fully as possible in times of economic hardship.

Secondly, to some degree the small town (the SST in particular) exhibits a degree of immunity to economic fluctuations in the local economic base. It was observed above that the smaller towns (SSTs) tend to provide the more demand-inelastic goods and services and the STs and larger centers higher proportions of higher elasticity goods and services.

It follows from this observation that reduced local incomes in a period of short-term economic hardship will tend to affect the SST operators less than firms in larger centers. In other words, reductions in expenditure will tend to be directed towards those goods and services where consumer discretion can be exercised most conveniently, and these will tend to be those purchased outside the SST. It follows that the worst effects of local economic recessions may bypass the SST and settle on the ST and larger urban areas, and the beneficial effects of local affluence or growth will have a minimal effect on the smaller urban areas.

Thirdly, experience has indicated that the small town is equipped to weather the storms of short-term economic adversity. The fact that the local operator reacts to the economic problems of his customers by accepting lower earnings from the business for personal use and by extending credit more generously has already been mentioned. However, an obvious limit exists on the ability of the local firm to absorb the temporary financial misfortunes of consumers; at some stage in the local recession, the problem is transferred to the financial institutions which operate in the arid zones. These include the major trading banks, stock and station agencies, and a small number of government-sponsored institutions. All such financial interests want to preserve the long-run stability of rural industries in arid zones, a concern that springs either from a desire to protect the value of loans advanced to primary producers or from specific government policies to alleviate hardship.

The local moods of optimism and pessimism which accompany better or worse climatic conditions or price levels usually last a sufficient number of years for the moods to be cumulative. In affluent years in particular, it appears that optimism creates unwarranted enthusiasm for the establishment of new firms. In small towns, marginal businesses tend to enter the town in industries which do not show sufficient long-run markets or thresholds for permanent survival. Hence, there is some argument that the small town should be viewed as consisting of a number of core businesses and a number of marginal businesses which appear and disappear with changing economic climates. Although it was not possible to test such a hypothesis, it appears that the disappearance of the marginal business in the small towns has been more pronounced in the last decade. There would appear to be no doubt that a wider variety of firms could now be classified as marginal in the SST.

SUMMARY

Both the ST and the SST are highly dependent on servicing local primary producers in fairly unstable industries. Furthermore, each town exists under a series of economic and institutional constraints, dictated to a large extent by the rest of the nation. The town's level of economic activity depends primarily on its collective ability to attract consumers while competing with other centers. This common economic interest through interbusiness dependence is embodied in the amalgam of attraction concept and consists largely of a series of businesses operating with a minimum of economic interaction or cohesion. Both the ST and the SST face unfavorable long-run economic trends with a tendency for the ST to gather trade at the expense of the SST. The SST, however, shows some immunity to the effects of short-term economic instability, apparently at the expense of the ST and larger urban areas.

Small Town Problems

Keeping the economic prospects in mind, we will now attempt to outline the so-called problems of the arid-zone small town, often seen simply in terms of the rural to urban population drift which leads to the decreasing size or stagnation of arid-zone towns. It is more appropriate, however, to define the so-called problem in terms of the long-term structural changes occurring in the Australian economy, changes held in common with other advanced economies. In this context, the relative decline of the rural sector and general centralization of the economy and the population appear to be both appropriate and inevitable.

We must not expect that large structural changes will occur without stresses in both the economic and social fabric of the nation. The small town problem is just one of these stresses. It is necessary to remove from our minds any prospect of the small town's revival to the former glory and activity which it may have enjoyed in the past. Indeed, there are no prospects of existing small towns blooming through even modest growth. Rather, we must accept the inevitability of the present trends, identify individually the most important stress effects, and consider the options available for removal or alleviation of these stresses. The following discussion considers some of these stresses in more detail.

CAPITAL COSTS TO OPERATORS

It has already been established that the market areas of some types of businesses in small towns are declining, frequently decreasing the personal income of the operator and his family to levels which most people would regard as unacceptable. Apart from any social affinity with the town, the operator is to some extent locked in to his business. The business represents a major investment on his part, and the sale of the business if markets are declining would involve significant capital losses; the proceeds from the sale would likely be insufficient to establish a similar type business in a more affluent area. It is no longer appropriate to consider the operator and his family as "pioneers" striving to provide a service to remote areas as an act of heroism. They are simply families seeking to survive in an economic environment which is inevitably decreasing their income, and their departure would involve the sacrifice of the greater part of their present wealth.

CAPITAL COSTS TO RESIDENTS

The residents of the arid-zone small town are locked in by declining housing values in the same way that operators are locked in to their firms. For most residents, a housing purchase will represent their largest single investment, and the disposal of a house in a declining market will involve significant capital sacrifice. Certainly, if residents contemplate migration, the proceeds from the disposal of housing in an arid-zone small town would be insufficient to purchase replacement housing in a larger urban area. The declining value of housing furthermore discourages expenditure on maintenance or improvements.

CAPITAL COSTS TO TOWNS

Declining firms invoke those few cost-reducing methods at their discretion. Apart from the maximum use of family labor, the owner may allow his assets and buildings to deteriorate. In declining towns, particularly the

SSTs, the opportunity value of business assets tied to the location is close to zero. This also applies generally to transportable capital assets which are often in an advanced state of depreciation or obsolete in a world of changing technology.

From the point of view of national economic efficiency, it could well be considered appropriate that capital assets with low or near zero marginal productivity, because of their fixed location, are allowed to depreciate rapidly or fall into disuse. The spatial context of the declining value of capital assets in declining regions is analogous to that of declining industries in a sectoral context, and governments recognize that industries which are declining due to falling demand for their product cannot be supported permanently by public funds.

Although the same conclusion must inevitably apply to declining small towns, two local aspects of capital depreciation should be mentioned. First, since decline has caused rapid capital depreciation, entry of new firms, in particular technically based firms, requires high levels of investment because local capital assets are either obsolete or in a poor condition. Secondly, the low or zero opportunity value of the capital assets ensures that they will remain in use for longer periods because of asset fixity. Thus, if the operator has no opportunity to sell his assets locally, he is encouraged to continue using them while their marginal productivity is still positive.

PERSONAL COSTS

The local population in the small town and its hinterland has minimal access to many of the services regarded as normal by populations in larger urban areas. In remote areas the question of access to services is thus a critical factor in determining the population's welfare. The problem is manifested in several ways.

First, locally provided retail goods and services, notably in the SST, are narrow in range and quality due to the cumulative effects of the amalgam of attraction. The range of choice can now be extended only by travel to larger urban centers. Second, retail price levels, although probably set according to price guidelines, are recognizably higher than those in larger urban areas. Although no definite information is available on income levels in small towns, it would appear that these higher price levels are not matched by higher personal income levels. Indeed, items 6, 7, and 8 of Table 10-2 suggest that a higher proportion of the population is engaged in less skilled occupations than in the more skilled technical or professional categories; this in turn suggests lower income levels for the nonfarm population. Considering all the aspects of the cost of living in remote small towns, it now seems reasonable to conclude that lower standards of living prevail in arid-zone small towns than in nonarid small towns. Third, services which society regards as necessary for the protection of life or for the equalization of opportunity are available in remote areas only to a restricted extent. For example, access to emergency services such as ambulance and fire protection is limited simply by virtue of the distances involved. Medical services are, of course, often limited locally to general practitioners and low-order hospital facilities. Item 4 of Table 10-2 suggests that educational services have also been less effective in small towns.

It is more difficult to comment on the supposed societal disadvantages of living in small towns, particularly in the SST. The higher mobility of small town residents (item 5 of Table 10-2) is almost certainly due, to a large degree, to the transient workers moving temporarily into the town as teachers, bank staff, etc. These workers tend to feel a more limited affinity with the town than the more permanent residents; they are more reluctant residents to some extent and feel at some societal disadvantage. On the other hand, permanent residents of the small town, despite what may be argued on their behalf by sociologists, appear to feel less at a disadvantage and may actually prefer the small town as a social environment.[18] This preference appears in the ST and larger urban areas in country districts as well.[19]

GOVERNMENTAL DEFICIENCIES

Although endowed by legislation with a wide variety of powers and responsibilities, local government, by virtue of intergovernmental fiscal arrangements, has been effectively limited to the exercise of a few rather basic functions in remote areas. The decline of economic activity in remote areas has reduced the local tax base. Coupled with a less than imaginative use of its limited power by local government, the problems of declining urban areas have not been faced positively. The local governmental units are large in area and contain a number of small towns. While this arrangement may be preferable for planning at the regional level, small town communities feel alienated from decision-making at all levels of government and in fact have no formal institutional framework for decisions which are purely local in nature. These deficiencies make problem solving more difficult.

Policy Alternatives

Any policies relating to small towns in arid zones should be an integral part of the general regional governmental policies and must be consistent both with these policies and with the economic and social environment. For example, if the existing unstated policies of Australian state and federal governments encouraging the general centralization movement are continued, there is no point in developing separate, conflicting policies relating to small towns.[20] It is with this assumption that we examine three policy alternatives available to governments in the arid zones.

"HANDS-OFF" POLICY

This approach, from all appearances, is the existing policy of government at all levels in Australia. It suggests either that the attention of government has not been sufficiently drawn to the problems associated with the decline of arid-zone small towns; or if the problems have been recognized, they are seen as generally insoluble or incapable of general alleviation. Apart from occasional measures in response to special problems in remote areas, Australian governments have been content to allow the market to force structural changes in small towns through the appearance and disappearance of firms.

The hands-off policy, however, is more than this. As exercised, it specifically excludes any positive action by governments to shape public expenditure patterns in any way or to undertake any initiatives to influence the pattern of decline. It suggests that governments either believe that their own activities have little influence on the pattern of decline or that they are unwilling to interfere in the existing pattern. It also suggests that government believes the pattern of private sector decline should set the pattern for changes in governmental services.

STIMULATION OF SMALL TOWN ECONOMIC ACTIVITY

Although it is easy to be critical of the current hands-off approach, this policy does at least recognize the inevitability of the economic forces which set the pattern of structural change in the economy. A policy to stimulate economic activity or growth in small towns or, in more general terms, to reduce the rate of decline would amount to ignoring reality. It would either be prohibitively expensive in terms of the national economic resources required to reverse or inhibit national economic structural change, or such a policy would be doomed to failure before conception. If stated effectively, this approach might provide moral support or continue to stimulate the confidence of small town inhabitants in the future affluence of their towns; but in the long run, it would prove ineffective.

PROTECTION OF THE WELFARE OF LOCAL POPULATIONS

A third approach—and one favored by this author—involves planning initiatives to accommodate rural decline and to protect the income and welfare levels of those who choose not to migrate from arid zones. It implies that governments will shape their own expenditures towards this end, both in influencing the location decisions of the private sector and in providing a mix of governmental services suited to arid zones.

Conclusion: A Recommended Policy

The approach advocated here is based on the fact, observed earlier in this chapter, that interdependencies or linkages between industries or sectors in small towns, as reflected in intersectoral multipliers, are very weak and tend to strengthen only as the size of the town increases. Stronger intersectoral linkages would tend to lock in previous urban growth or at least reduce the rate of decline of urban areas. In other words, small towns need to grow in scale terms before they can develop the characteristics of strong linkages which engender growth or restrict decline. At first glance, this does not appear to be a useful conclusion. However, some important implications for arid zones follow from it.

Clearly arid-zone small towns will continue to decline if each continues to exhibit low linkages. The preferred alternative thus selects a limited number of STs and thrusts scale growth upon them by governmental measures in order to capture the benefits of scale growth and to thereby inhibit decline in at least some of the centers providing services to arid zones. This proposal amounts to a collective maximization of any growth or of any forces resistant to decline for arid-zone small towns in the region. Since most small towns cannot be included among the towns selected, their decline could well be accentuated to ensure the scale growth of the selected centers.

Two types of policy measures appear to be necessary to achieve the desired end. Positive or offensive (aggressive) measures aimed at achieving scale growth in selected urban centers should be initiated in order to develop inherent multiplier growth by the strengthening of local linkages—if necessary, at the expense of the SSTs.[21] These offensive measures would rely heavily on positive action at the various levels of government. State governments would need to assemble in the selected centers the various nonessential operations which are scattered among the smaller towns. Similarly, local governments would have to concentrate their administrative and maintenance functions in these same centers, which could also serve as the locations for the Australian government representatives and any designated regional offices. Not all of the existing governmental functions could rationally be centralized at the selected centers; it is however apparent that the economic effect of substantial local centralization would be significant. Certainly, the collective value of the assembled operations would be higher than the sum of their individual values scattered throughout a number of SSTs.

If, in addition, government were to partially decentralize its total activity so that some of the services provided to remote areas from distant urban centers were provided locally, a further significant increase in local economic activity could be expected. In light of inevitable and perhaps accelerated decline of the small towns not selected for positive action, a set of defensive measures should be designed to protect residents from many of the effects of decline. Constant monitoring of the level of availability of essential services would be necessary, and steps would have to be taken to ensure that minimum levels of basic services are available.

To a degree, the offensive and defensive measures appear contradictory in their effect on the unselected towns. The former suggests that any nonessential services located in these centers be moved to the selected centers, further reducing the local economic base and threatening the level of even local essential services. The unselected towns would retain these services at some minimum level. The apparent contradiction highlights the need to distinguish between essential and nonessential services and the need for policy measures to be developed specifically for the arid zones.

At present, no level of government has accepted responsibility for local regional planning in Australia's arid zones. State governments have been more concerned with those parts of the state where population pressures promise to present major planning problems; local governments conventionally have neither the experience nor the funds to consider the problems; federal governments have shown a singular lack of interest. Clearly the implementation of both offensive and defensive measures must involve a concerted and interested approach by the three levels of government.

Local government in the arid zones of Australia is simply a poor reflection of local government in the more densely populated areas. With few exceptions, arid-zone local governments have fallen in with the conventional pattern of supplying household services and road construction and maintenance and have not attempted to tailor their activities to the unique circumstances of their region, or to involve themselves in monitoring and planning the decline of the region.[22] Local government could contribute substantially to the implementation of the suggested policy, particularly in reference to the defensive measures. As the level of government supposedly closest to the local problems, local government could suggest the minimum level of services required in the unselected centers and tailor their budgets accordingly to provide services not available through the private sector. There seems to be a clear need for local government to become welfare-oriented or service-oriented in arid zones, rather than road-oriented or simply survival-oriented as at present. At this stage in the arid zones, local government is not concerned with local welfare or service problems in any real or substantial sense and is either unwilling or unable to become involved. One highly desirable defensive measure would be the establishment of agency-type offices in each small town to conduct local government business and, desirably, the welfare and administrative services of higher levels of government. These offices could provide a mechanism for the distribution of services, thereby taking the local government significantly beyond a monitoring function.

Higher levels of government also could contribute substantially to defensive measures. In other contexts, government loans have been made available to firms in declining industries (notably, the dairy industry) to enable amalgamations of firms to form viable economic units. The extension of this scheme to the small town firm would have highly desirable consequences without undue long-term costs. First, it would enable operators to relinquish their firms without incurring complete capital losses; this would partially remove the locked in restraints under which the firm now operates. Secondly, it would ensure that the service previously provided by the operator would remain available to the small town, although as part of the services provided by a larger firm. Thirdly, the remaining operators would have larger firms and would experience the higher personal incomes and the increased stability associated with larger firms.

Amalgamation would lower the thresholds required for the provision of a service from that required to support the operator and his family to that which, in a marginal sense to a larger operator, simply makes providing the service a commercial asset. In existing circumstances, the disappearance of a firm may result in the absorption of its function by a remaining firm. An amalgamation scheme would reduce the personal hardship involved in the closure of a firm and enable the surviving firms to plan for the combination of the services on a suitably financed basis. An amalgamation scheme for firms in arid-zone SSTs would be of minor proportions. It could therefore be simply administered and monitored by the local government on behalf of the financing state or federal governments.[23] The combined costs of the offensive and defensive measures would not be substantial at any level of government. The proposed policy involves a redirection of current expenditures more than a substantial increase in the volume of those expenditures.

This chapter has presented a description of the arid-zone small towns in Australia and the economic constraints which mold the behavior of the small town firm and dictate the structure of the town as an economic entity. The main conclusions drawn from this discussion were simply that the firms and the town both exist in an environment of structural change that will inevitably lead to a continuation of the decline of small towns and that planning and policy should be made in this context. The chapter briefly examined alternative policy approaches to the small town problem and insisted that policies can be formulated to alleviate the problems by maximizing the resistance of the regions to decline and by protecting the welfare levels of the inhabitants of arid zones. The preferred policy alternative aims at offensive measures to stimulate selected centers to develop stronger intersectoral linkages and defensive measures to ensure the retention of minimum levels of basic services in the very small towns.

Notes

1. A. Allen, "Frontier Towns in Western Queensland; Their Growth and Present Tributary Areas." *The Australian Geographer,***11** (1969), 119–137.
2. Ibid, p. 127.
3. There are a limited number of larger urban centers dependent on major mining ventures.
4. No data is available on Australian towns with populations less than 200.
5. For convenience, throughout the remainder of the chapter the term "small town" will be used with reference to both types. The abbreviation "ST" will be used exclusively for arid-zone urban areas with more than 1000 residents; the abbreviation "SST" to those with less than 1000.
6. A. Allen, "The Stagnation of Settlement in Interior Queensland—Is There No Alternative?" *Capricornia*, **6** (1970–71), 7–27. In this respect, the coastal small towns are quite different from the arid ones.
7. Access to educational opportunities is significantly lower in arid regions than in temperate ones.
8. In 1971, Queensland contained 14 statistical divisions or regions.
9. The higher interregional mobility is even more striking when it is remembered that intraurban residential movement in metropolitan areas is significantly higher than intraurban movement in small towns.
10. The cost of providing such guarantees is often indirectly transferred to the customer. Retailers in the small towns attempt to avoid the cost of handling returned defective goods by offering for sale only medium to high quality merchandise. This of course reduces the range of goods available to consumers by removing cheaper or lower quality products from the market place.
11. In recent years the business operator has been selectively absorbed into the more influential and leadership groups, gradually replacing the larger landowners in this respect.
12. R. C. Jensen and R. Widdows, "Price Formation in Small Country Towns," *Urban Issues*, **4**, no. 2 (1973), 54–65. This study was not directed exclusively at arid-zone small towns. The four procedures were (1) Inflexible Retail Price Maintenance (prices set either by law or coercion); (2) Flexible Retail Price Maintenance (by voluntary observance of price lists); (3) Cost-Plus Pricing; and (4) the pricing of goods at "what the market will bear."
13. See R. C. Jensen and R. Widdows, "The Socio-Economic Environment of Firms and Economic Analysis: A Case Study in a Queensland Town," working paper, Department of Economics, University of Queensland, May 1974, for a full definition of this concept.
14. Ibid, p. 6.
15. In field studies of one small town, it was estimated that a change in ownership of the single grocery store from a conventional small town operator to one who ignored the small town norms of business operation reduced the sales of other retail firms in the town by 15 to 20 percent.

16. Allen, "Frontier Towns," p. 133.

17. G. Dawe, et al., "Intersectoral Flows in a Small Town in Queensland," *Urban Issues,* **4** (1974), 142–155.

18. R. Widdows, "County v. City: A Study of Attitudes to Country and City Living in a Small Town," *Australian Journal of Social Issues,* **9**, no. 3 (1974), 196–208.

19. P. W. Salmon and R. E. Weston, *Human Adjustments in Rural Towns: The Impact of Changes in Agriculture on Quality of Life* (Melbourne: School of Agriculture and Forestry, University of Melbourne, 1974).

20. The author is implying that the existing, stated decentralization policies, acknowledged by serious observers as largely ineffective, are a *de facto* acceptance and encouragement of centralization trends.

21. No data exist which might pinpoint the size of an arid urban area in Australia at which growth tends to become locked in. In temperate rural areas, the required size seems to be as low as 10,000 to 12,000 inhabitants.

22. Some local governments in arid zones have accepted the responsibility for supplying milk and operating movie theatres and other usually private sector businesses for which local economic thresholds have disappeared.

23. Higher levels of government could also extend government services either by assigning new functions to existing local facilities or by expanding mobile services in order to accommodate the physical isolation of the individual in SSTs.

11
Remote Communities in Tropical and Arid Australia

P. W. Newton and T. B. Brealey

The pattern of settlement which characterizes Australia reflects the great influence that the physical setting has had in limiting agricultural land uses and restricting urban development to the periphery of the continent, particularly to the southeastern seaboard. The "dead heart," a descriptive term long associated with the interior of the continent, conveys the qualitative image that most residents in the south and east hold of that part of the country—an isolated, empty landscape coupled with a harsh climate. More quantitative definitions of Australia's tropical and arid regions are available, however. Among the most useful, perhaps, is a measure of heat discomfort, which in addition to temperature, humidity, and air movement, takes account of metabolic heat rate, net radiation, and insulation of clothing.[1] The resultant discomfort map (see Figure 11-1) shows the average number of days per year when physiological stress will occur in a person doing light manual labor at 3 P.M. Since our primary concern is with human settlements in tropical and arid regions, the heat strain index is preferred over other climate or vegetation-based classifications.[2] The similarities with other classifications are understandably high, however: Köppen's tropical (Aw: confined to the northern sections of Western Australia, Northern Territory, and Queensland) and dry (BSh, BWh) climates are located in areas where heat discomfort will be experienced for more than 25 days per year. The southern limit approximates the southern boundary of Australia's pastoral zone (see Figure 11-2).

History of Development

Australia's tropical and arid region can therefore be delineated as the area north of the 25-day heat strain contour, an area which represents almost 90 percent of the country's land surface and which contains less than 7 percent of the nation's population.[3] Prior to the 1960s, the history of development in this area centered upon pastoral activity, with large sheep runs (stocking rates as low as to one sheep per 200 acres) in the southern pastoral zone, giving way to extensive cattle properties in the tropical regions.[4] This emphasis upon pastoral development and crop returns based on acreage rather than yield per acre encouraged sparseness instead of a concentration of settlement. Inland gold booms in the 1850s and 1890s might have brought about major concentrations of population; but without any other industrial base to support the people attracted by gold, dispersal

223

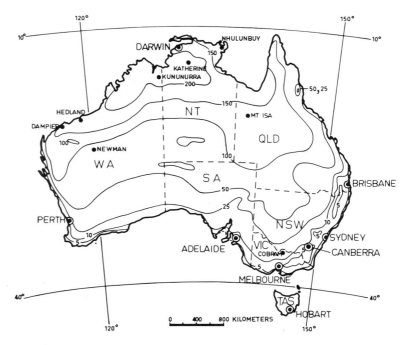

FIG. 11-1. Heat discomfort in Australia (average number of days per year when the relative strain index at 3 P.M. exceeds the critical discomfort level). From Australian Bureau of Statistics, *Official Yearbook of Australia 1975 and 1976* (Canberra: Australian Government Publishing Service, 1976), p. 61.

followed as gold mining declined. Much of this flow was back to the coastal cities.

After a lull of almost half a century, the burst of uranium discovery in the early 1950s helped swing exploration to tropical Australia, for the new fields lay near the northern coast. The deep copper found at Mt. Isa in 1955 quickened the swing to the north; in the same year, the discovery of bauxite deposits suggested that tropical Australia might soon rival Southern Australia in mineral wealth. The mineral boom of the 1960s had iron ore as its principal stimulus. Although the existence of iron ore in Western Australia had been known for some time, embargoes on its export during and after World War II had prevented exploitation of the deposits. The lifting of the embargo in 1960 precipitated an intensive period of exploration, development planning, market research, financial negotiation, viability study, and related activity.[5]

Over the past decade since the start of the intensive development of massive mineral deposits, ensuing earnings have become increasingly important to the national economy. Mining companies have been obliged to bear most of the infrastructure cost involved and have made strenuous efforts to establish new towns and to attract a population to the region. Their operations, however, have been hampered by extremely high levels of turnover in the work force (of the order of 100 percent per year). The reasons underlying this phenomenon are numerous: isolation from major population centers and family and friends, smallness of the communities, company control or intervention in the social structure of the town, lack of variety in many facilities and amenities, an absence of certain services, social imbalance within the town population, and restricted life chances

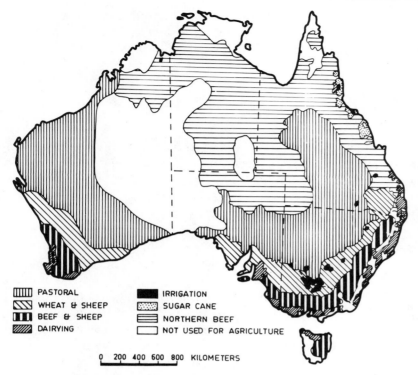

PASTORAL
WHEAT & SHEEP
BEEF & SHEEP
DAIRYING
IRRIGATION
SUGAR CANE
NORTHERN BEEF
NOT USED FOR AGRICULTURE

0 200 400 600 800 KILOMETERS

FIG. 11-2. Australia's farming regions. From Bruce Davidson, "History of the Australian Rural Landscape," in *Man and Landscape in Australia,* ed. George Sedden and Mari Davis (Canberra: Australian Government Printing Service, 1976), p. 64.

for women and adolescents are some of the major influences. Superficially, most of these situations may not seem to have any correlation to the arid or tropical climate. But the harsh climate is the fundamental reason for the region being virtually empty; and this brings along with it the host of problems connected with an attempt to encourage essentially temperate climate urban dwellers to migrate into new, instant townships, expecting them to adapt and enjoy their new home as a permanent residence. Therefore, it is important to consider the social research conducted in several of the new towns in Australia's tropical and arid regions and to direct particular attention to residents' attitudes to life in a remote town and to their prospective mobility intentions.

Town Types, Systems of Administration, and Social Profiles

In studying remote communities in tropical Australia, one will find similar characteristics and resident attitudes on a broad range of issues. But there are a number of fundamental distinctions which result in different attitudes and specific community traits. For instance, one must consider whether the town is on the coast or inland, whether its location is in the arid zone or humid tropics, whether its economic base is associated with mining or agriculture, and whether it is "open" or "closed."[6] Social surveys undertaken by members of the Commonwealth Scientific and Industrial Research Organization (CSIRO) Remote Communities Environment Unit between 1971 and 1976 have attempted to include a broad range of town types (also see Figure 11-1). Table 11-1 lists the towns we will be discussing.

SOCIAL AND DEMOGRAPHIC CHARACTERISTICS OF REMOTE TROPICAL COMMUNITIES

The new mining towns reveal a strong imbalance between the sexes, with the proportion of males ranging from almost 100 percent during the construction phase to a current rate around 70 percent.[7] This imbalance is a direct result of the recruitment policies of mining companies who, until recently, demonstrated an almost total preference for males in the company workforce. This ratio declines for the older mining and nonmining centers to a figure between 50 and 60 percent.

Towns in the tropics also experience a life cycle imbalance with a concentration of individuals in the 20 to 40 years age group (see Table 11-2), although there is a more even distribution in the older centers (Mt. Isa and Katherine). For families, the 20 to 40 years bracket is typically the child-bearing period. This is reflected in the age distribution of the children in the townships (close to 75 percent of all children in households surveyed in Dampier (1975), Hedland, and Nhulunbuy were under the age of 10). Movement to remote communities is less likely for households during the child-rearing phase of the family life cycle, for people are concerned with a child's education and his/her career prospects.[8] To date, the mining companies have avoided the problem of employees' retiring, for the recruitment guidelines for most companies read, "25 to 35 years of age; maximum 45."

In a similar manner, the recruitment policy of mining companies determines the mixture of nationalities within the new resource towns. There is a very high component of migrants from the United Kingdom; this reflects

TABLE 11-1. Australian Remote Towns and Cobram (as a contrast).

Newman—single industry town, mining (iron ore), new, inland, in arid tropics, company administered (1, 2*; 4500**)

Dampier—single industry town, mining port (iron ore), new, coastal, in arid tropics but with frequently occurring high humidities, company administered (1, 2, 4; 3500)

Mt. Isa—based on mining (lead, zinc, silver, copper), established over 25 years, inland, in arid tropics, formerly company administered, but now administered as an open town (1; 25,000)

Hedland—coastal, mining port (iron ore), in arid tropics but with frequently occurring high humidities, open town, first influx of mining company personnel grafted onto existing town of Port Hedland, subsequent growth contained in the new town South Hedland 10 km inland (6; 7000, Port and 5500, South)

Nhulunbuy—single industry town, mining (bauxite), new, coastal, in humid tropics, open town (4, 5; 4500)

Kununurra—based on agriculture and beef production, fairly new, inland, in humid tropics, administered as an open town (1; 1000)

Katherine—based on beef production, old, inland, on the margin of the humid tropics, administered as an open town (1; 2500)

Cobram—long-established, located in the state of Victoria, not classifiable as remote, enjoys a temperate climate (3000)

*1-Investigated in 1971; 2-1972; 3-1973; 4-1974; 5-1975; 6-1976 by Commonwealth Scientific & Industrial Research Organization (CSIRO) Remote Communities Environment Unit
**Population

TABLE 11-2. Age Profile of Surveyed Residents* in Remote Australian Towns and Cobram.

AGE IN YEARS (%)	NEWMAN 1971-72	DAMPIER 1971-72	DAMPIER 1974	MT. ISA 1971	HEDLAND 1976	NHULUNBUY 1974-75	KUNUNURRA 1971	KATHERINE 1971	COBRAM 1972
					TOWN LOCATION OF SURVEYED POPULATION				
<20	0.7	0.0	2.4	2.4	0.0	0.8	2.3	0.0	1.2
20-29	50.0	43.8	40.0	34.1	32.5	35.1	58.1	37.2	18.1
30-39	37.9	37.5	35.4	24.4	47.9	41.5	23.3	32.6	15.7
≥40	11.4	18.8	22.1	39.0	19.8	22.6	16.3	30.2	65.1
Sample Size	140	160	412	82	117	615	43	43	83

*Refers to age of head
Source: Data from unpublished CSIRO remote community surveys, 1971-76

the selective (most companies require that prospective employees speak English) recruitment undertaken overseas and within Australia (see Table 11-3). Income from employment in resource towns is above the Australian average (which stood at $4650 per annum for males in 1971). A comparison of income levels for heads of households surveyed in 1971 reveals that only 21 percent of the Newman sample had a gross annual income less than the Australian average. Figures for other towns include 45 percent at Mt. Isa (like Newman, an inland mining town, but longer established and a regional center with a larger population and a broader economic base), 59 percent at Kununurra, 61 percent at Katherine (a service center for an agricultural region with a high proportion of public servants), and 71 percent at Cobram.

Each of these towns, however, offers a narrow range of employment opportunities. A distinctive feature of many of the remote communities in tropical Australia is the dominance of a particular industry in the economic life of the township—an influence which can be tied either to private industry (for example, the percentage of household heads surveyed who were connected with the mining and quarrying industry ranged from 99 percent in Newman, 96 percent in Dampier, and 80 percent in Nhulunbuy, to 71 percent in Hedland and 67 percent in Mt. Isa), or public service (the Australian government was the chief employer of 54 percent of heads of Katherine households and 19 percent of heads of Nhulunbuy households. Meanwhile the state government employed the heads of more than 50 percent of the households surveyed in Kununurra). The single industry nature of the small (and principally mining) towns presents a narrow range of work opportunities for people who were not specifically recruited for a particular position. The groups most affected in this respect are women and young people completing school. The proportion of women in the work force in most new mining towns is approximately 15 percent.

NATURE OF HOUSING IN REMOTE TROPICAL COMMUNITIES

Major contrasts exist in the type and quality of housing in Australia's tropical towns, particularly in the open towns where there is a mixture of mining company and public and private dwellings. With construction costs approximately 100 percent higher than metropolitan levels, the quality of housing could be expected to be lower in the remote communities—an expectation which is confirmed by the standard costs of both state housing and most private construction.[9] The state housing commissions have constructed a succession of different house types.[10] Each usually occupies a standard-sized suburban allotment (see Figures 11-3 and 11-4). For the most part, they have been timber framed and asbestos cement clad. Their roofs are constructed with corrugated galvanized iron, and their floors are made of timber on low stumps. The houses are designed for natural cross-ventilation; ceiling fans are provided in bedrooms, living room, and kitchen as standard equipment.

In the new towns (Newman, Dampier, Hedland, and Nhulunbuy) linked to mining operations with a life span extending to the end of this century, company detached housing is typically brick or concrete block with pressed metal imitation tile roofs and concrete slab-on-fill floors. With

TABLE 11-3. Nationality Profile of Surveyed Residents* in Remote Australian Towns and Cobram.

NATIONALITY (%)	NEWMAN 1971–72	DAMPIER 1971–72	DAMPIER 1974	MT. ISA 1971	HEDLAND 1976	NHULUNBUY 1974–75	KUNUNURRA 1971	KATHERINE 1971	COBRAM 1972
					TOWN LOCATION OF SURVEYED POPULATION				
Australia	40.7	67.5	63.3	67.1	53.8	59.7	67.4	81.4	78.3
New Zealand	2.1	3.8	2.2	2.4	6.8	3.4	4.7	0.0	0.0
United Kingdom	45.0	18.1	20.9	9.8	23.1	18.0	9.3	11.6	4.8
Southern Europe	0.7	1.9	1.7	2.4	3.4	2.8	2.3	2.3	12.0
Northern Europe	7.9	6.9	7.1	15.9	6.8	12.7	9.3	2.3	3.6
North America	2.1	0.6	1.2	0.0	0.9	0.8	2.3	0.0	1.2
Other	1.4	0.6	3.6	2.4	5.1	2.6	2.3	0.0	0.0
Sample Size	140	160	411	82	117	615	43	43	83

*Refers to nationality of head
Source: Data from unpublished CSIRO remote community surveys, 1971–76

FIG. 11-3. Public detached housing, Hedland.

FIG. 11-4. Public town housing, Hedland.

minor variations such as wide eaves and cyclone screens, the homes are essentially similar in plan, appearance, and quality to the medium to high quality project-built homes found in all southern capitals (see Figure 11-5). A number of mining companies have experimented with high quality medium density accommodations (see Figure 11-6); while not the dwelling type preferred by the majority (as is the case in the southern cities, the detached dwelling is the "ideal"), there are many people whose life-style and life cycle stage are well-suited to this form of housing. Single men's quarters and one and two bedroom flats for married couples complete the housing inventory for most remote centers.

The mining companies offer better housing (compared to that available to other residents) as a major inducement to prospective employees in northern centers. In comparison, state housing provides accommodation for public servants on two-year transfers and for noncompany employees who are normally desperate for any form of permanent accommodation.[11] Hence, there is not the same motivation to provide a higher standard dwelling.

FIG. 11-5. Company detached housing, Hedland.

FIG. 11-6. Company cluster housing, Hedland.

The contrast in housing is one possible cause of the social schism which exists between mining company employees (the *haves*) and government or other noncompany workers (the *have nots*) in the open towns of the humid and arid tropics. In addition to higher incomes, company residents also enjoy a considerable rent advantage (at least 50 percent below public housing rentals). Their homes are fully air conditioned, the cost of electricity consumed in air conditioning is borne by the company, and they do not have to bear the cost of water. This is reflected in the superior condition of their fully landscaped gardens. Company personnel pay none of the charges usually associated with owning or renting a house, such as home insurance or local government and other levies which help pay for roads, storm water drainage, sewerage, garbage collection, and community amenities such as library and recreational facilities. This pampering of mining company employees, when combined with their overtly economic motivation for migrating to the new towns, partly explains their detachment from the local community and their higher propensity for subsequent movement from the town.

As a means of promoting community integration, the concept of social mix has become a cause célèbre among the majority of Australia's state housing authorities. The State Housing Commission of Western Australia is no exception, and South Hedland is one center where an attempt has been made to integrate markedly different population groups within the town's fabric. This commission has been able, through its control of land in South Hedland, to allocate parcels of land among major client groups (see Figure 11-7). There is also evidence of "pepper-potting," a practice of scattering individual aboriginal households throughout a residential block. Despite the contention by some researchers that architectural design or type of land development has no effect on the efficacy of social mix, the difference between state housing and company housing in South Hedland provides one of the greatest contrasts in housing quality and design available within Australia.[12] In metropolitan areas where the contrast between private and public detached housing is not as marked as in tropical Australia, a level of social stigma also has been found associated with occupants of Housing Commission accommodations.[13] Levels of stigma appear higher in South Hedland where a major division is apparent, largely along company-noncompany lines. A major contributing factor is the difference

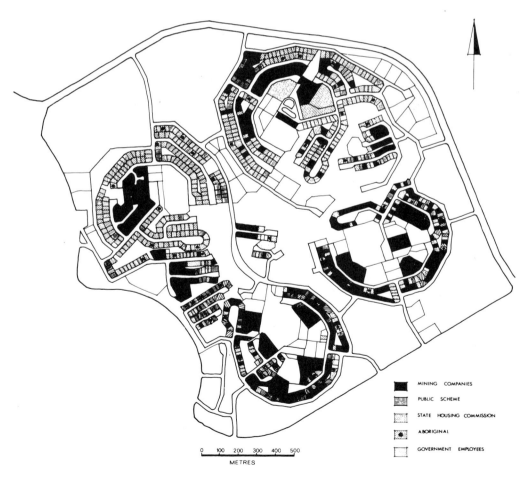

MINING COMPANIES

PUBLIC SCHEME

STATE HOUSING COMMISSION

ABORIGINAL

GOVERNMENT EMPLOYEES

0 100 200 300 400 500
METRES

FIG. 11-7. Pattern of tenure, South Hedland.

in the quality of housing provided for the two groups of residents which reinforces the other advantages of being in company employment (e.g., lower rentals, higher wages, and fringe benefits). For future development within South Hedland and similar open communities, there is an obvious need for a convergence in standards between state and company housing (i.e., an upgrading on the part of the state and a slight downgrading on the part of mining companies). This step should help reduce disparities in the standard of living of residents in mixed communities.

Community Attitudes toward Life in A Remote Town

Since 1971 CSIRO, in a study of Australia's remote tropical towns, has tried to identify community deficiencies and areas of residential dissatisfaction. Given the problems associated with attracting people from Australia's coastal cities in the south and east to the isolated (principally mining) towns, and the high level of turnover which characterizes the population which enters the towns, researchers had to determine ways to enhance the quality of living or social well-being of the residents in these centers and to reduce the level of later out-migration. Questionnaires were used to survey attitudes.

INCOMPLETE STATEMENTS QUESTIONNAIRE

Incomplete statements have been included in all the remote community surveys undertaken to date, so that residents could comment upon those aspects of their community environment considered most important to them and not be constrained by closed questions not always completely relevant to their situation. The virtually free-format type of inquiry and the fact that the term "living conditions" was loosely defined provided an almost unlimited scope for response. Therefore, there was a great range in the nature of the comments recorded.

After the responses were gathered, the examiners had to establish some sort of order out of the collected data. This was achieved by classifying responses according to the set of categories and subcategories shown in Table 11-4. It is important to understand that this was not a preconceived classification. It was formulated during the interpretation of the completed forms and was shaped by the nature of the responses.[14]

PRESENTATION AND INTERPRETATION OF INCOMPLETE STATEMENTS ANALYSES

The categorized data from the Incomplete Statements Questionnaire is summarized graphically for all towns (see Figures 11-8 to 11-16 in conjunction with Table 11-4). The height of each rectangle in the histograms reflects the ratio of the responses of each category to the whole. The position of the rectangle above or below the datum band indicates whether the responses were favorable or unfavorable. Within each rectangle, the lengths of the lines shown are proportional to the number of responses in each of the subcategories. The circle included within each figure provides a convenient representation of the degree of favorability of the total information presented.

TABLE 11-4. Analysis of Incomplete Statements Questionnaire:
Categories and Subcategories Legend.

1.0 *Built environment*	6.0 *Community dynamics*
.1 Buildings	.1 Alcohol and Gambling
.2 Utilities	.2 Social Relationships
.3 Streets	.3 Civic Pride
.4 Town Planning	.4 Children's Future
.5 Pollution	.5 Standard of Living
.6 Other	.6 Work Opportunities and Relationships
	.7 Family Cohesiveness
2.0 *Natural environment*	.8 Other
.1 Climate	
.2 Temperature	7.0 *Economic considerations*
.3 Topography	.1 Cost of Living
.4 Flora and Fauna	.2 Rent, Rates
.5 Dust	.3 Wages, Savings
.6 Other	.4 Land Prices
	.5 Construction Costs
3.0 *Isolation and access*	.6 Other
.1 Undefined Feeling of Isolation	
.2 Communications	8.0 *Miscellaneous*
.3 Transportation	.1 Challenge
.4 Holidays	.2 Length of Stay
.5 Relatives	.3 Native Welfare
.6 Other	.4 Travel
	.5 Local Origin
4.0 *Administrative policy*	.6 Origin
.1 Work Situation	
.2 Town and Citizen Welfare	9.0 *Nonidentifiable*
.3 Other	.1 Various
5.0 *Community facilities*	
.1 Education	
.2 Entertainment and Recreation	
.3 Health	
.4 Shopping, Commercial Services	
.5 Local Transport	
.6 Other	

In all the tropical towns surveyed, the sum of the unfavorable comments exceeds the sum of the favorable. The highest level of negative response was from Kununurra residents (74 percent unfavorable) followed by Hedland and Katherine (each 67 percent), Mt. Isa (63 percent), Newman (62 percent), Dampier (58 percent in 1971; 56 percent in 1974) and Nhulunbuy (53 percent). These data suggest that a milder coastal location is a desirable tropical town site, for it offers a broader range of leisure activities than inland areas.[15] The level of negative response which characterized all centers initially led to the suspicion that it is human nature to prefer to comment on the unfavorable aspects of life. If this were the case, a technique such as the Incomplete Statements Questionnaire may have an inherent bias towards unfavorable comments. However, this suspicion was considerably allayed by the pattern of responses identified during an identical survey conducted for comparative purposes in Cobram in Northern Victoria (see Figure 11-16). Not only did Cobram residents exhibit much different patterns of concern, but they reacted more favorably to their living conditions (56 percent favorable). We will now examine in more detail the variation in comments from different remote communities (see Figures 11-8 to 11-15).

Built Environment. Of the five subcategories of the built environment, the building subcategory accounts for the majority of comments. Company

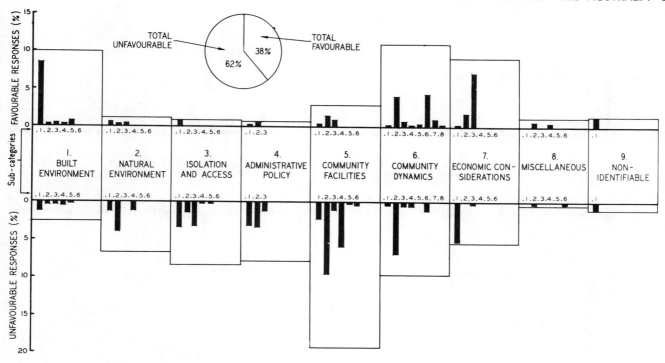

FIG. 11-8. Profile of resident attitudes, Newman, 1971.

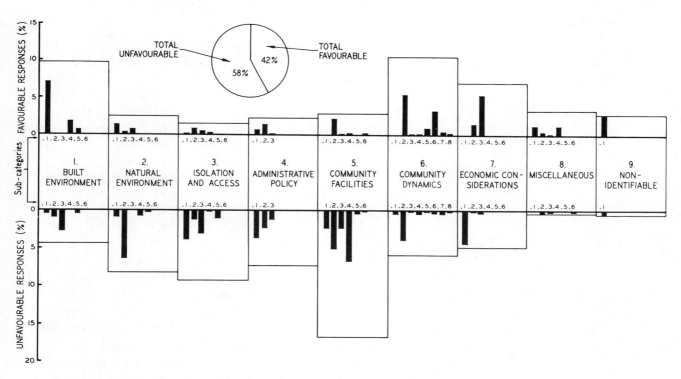

FIG. 11-9. Profile of resident attitudes, Dampier, 1971.

accommodations in Newman, Dampier, and Nhulunbuy consist of relatively new, high quality, air conditioned homes with furniture supplied by the employing company. Rentals for all homes are extremely low, so it is not surprising to find a high level of favorable comments (Newman 8.6; Dampier 7.1 (1971), 7.7 (1974); and Nhulunbuy 4.5 percent). The open

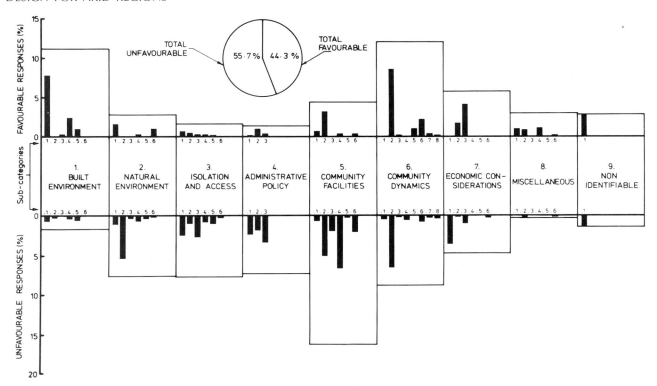

FIG. 11-10. Profile of resident attitudes, Dampier, 1974.

towns of Hedland and Mt. Isa receive a mixed response (4.6 percent favorable versus 2.5 percent unfavorable in Hedland; 3.7 versus 2.0 in Mt. Isa). The different responses at Mt. Isa are due to the mixture of old and new houses; and in Hedland, they are due to the disparity in the quality of housing which exists between company and noncompany sectors.[16] At Kununurra and Katherine, there is a preponderance of reasonably new houses, few of which had air conditioning. Their varied designs are prepared both by government agencies and private builders. The fairly high scores (5.9 percent at Kununurra and 6.8 percent at Katherine) reflecting unfavorable responses to buildings indicate an inability to meet the occupants' expectations.

The only town with a noteworthy score with respect to utilities is Katherine (3.5 percent unfavorable). Here there were complaints of turbidity and the taste of chlorine in the water, and the service reservoirs were of marginal capacity. Because Dampier (1971) had no street lighting, there were unfavorable responses in this subcategory by residents. An interesting commentary on town plans is provided by the different evaluations in the new towns at Nhulunbuy, Dampier, and Hedland by their residents. In South Hedland where an attempt was made to employ Radburn principles in the town layout, thereby providing a radical departure from the more conventional designs in existing tropical towns, resident reaction was clearly unfavorable (3.1 percent).[17] The South Hedland layout omits many of the fundamental elements of the Radburn design, however. Therefore, comments do not represent a condemnation of the Radburn principles, but rather a criticism of areas where modifications were made to the principles. (For example, there was a lack of community

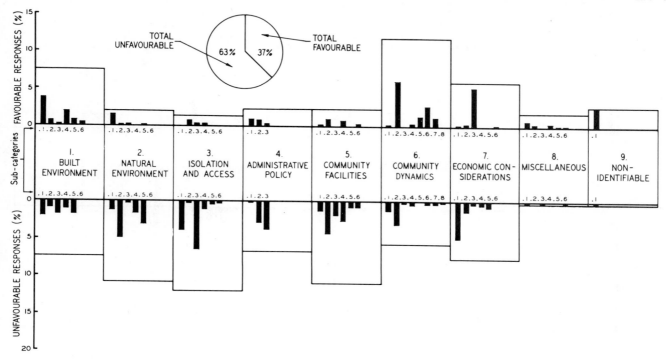

FIG. 11-11. Profile of resident attitudes, Mt. Isa, 1971.

facilities within the superblocks; there was a pathway system with no logical focus; the design of detached housing was not compatible with access from both the walkway and the road; the length of the culs-de-sac was excessive.)[18]

Although climatic aspects of the environment were severe (as described below), they were not the overriding considerations in determining resident attitudes to their towns.

Natural Environment. The temperature component of climate attracted high percentages of unfavorable comment from all locations in either the humid or arid tropics in both wet and dry seasons. Wherever the need for air conditioning or satisfaction at having air conditioning was expressed, an unfavorable response by inference was recorded for temperature. Thus, although temperature is a significant topic in all towns, in Newman, Dampier and sections of Hedland, Nhulunbuy, and Mt. Isa, measures to combat its effects in the interiors of homes and some other buildings have already been taken.[19]

Isolation and Access. Temperature alone does not typify these regions. All towns surveyed scored unfavorably on "undefined feeling of isolation," and the inland centers generated the highest level of response. One important feature to emerge, however, was the drop from a 3.9 percent to a 2.4 percent unfavorable comment among Dampier residents between 1971 and 1974 (see Figures 11-9 and 11-10), a period which saw an increase in the town's population and a decrease in its level of population turnover. Comments relating to the adverse position of remote communities' residents in regard to transportation and communications are a

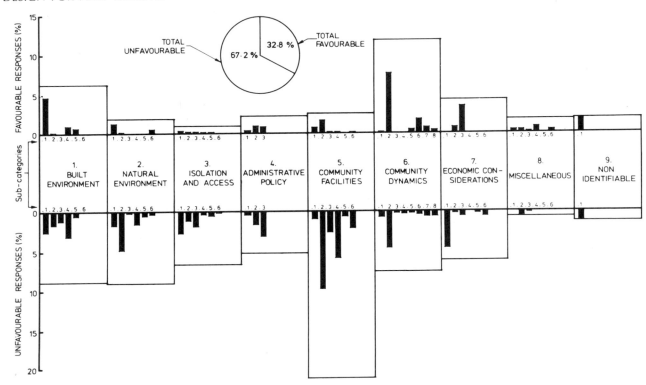

FIG. 11-12. Profile of resident attitudes, Hedland, 1976.

reflection of the area's inaccessibility to the country's total air network and the susceptibility of the road and rail network to disruption during the "wet" season.[20]

Administrative Policy. The only towns which generated a significant unsatisfactory response to their work situations were the two company towns of Newman (3.4 percent) and Dampier (3.0 and 2.3 percent in 1971 and 1974 respectively). The underlying reasons for this type of response are best illustrated by a selection of resident comments from Dampier in 1971:

> "Living here would be fine if it wasn't for company control."
> "There is too much emphasis on company rule and the fact that men are continually on call because they live in a company house in a company town."
> "Although living in Dampier we do enjoy in all respects but there is only one thing, I wish we could feel more secure in a company town than we do."
> "There is too much emphasis on position held at work carried on after completion of working hours."[21]

In contrast, Nhulunbuy will be governed by a town corporation until the local government is instituted in the area; and although there are significant links between the mining company (which constructed the town) and the corporation, the corporation projects a sufficiently independent image to allay accusations by residents that the company is running the town.

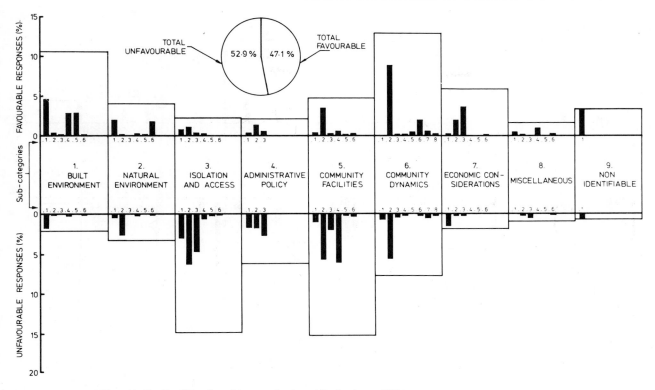

FIG. 11-13. Profile of resident attitudes, Nhulunbuy, 1974.

Community Facilities.   Most towns recorded high levels of adverse comment with respect to educational facilities. The major exceptions were Mt. Isa and Hedland where educational facilities are more extensive than in any of the other towns. All towns produced very high unfavorable scores on the entertainment and recreation subcategory, but closer inspection of Figures 11-9, 11-10, and 11-13 reveals a significantly favorable response for Dampier and Nhulunbuy. The favorable response is due to the range of water-centered activities which are available to residents in these coastal locations. The unfavorable response for all centers is related principally to a lack of organized indoor activities and a lack of facilities for the youth of the town. Mt. Isa residents utilize a nearby lake as a recreational resort, and this combined with the greater size and diversification of the town could explain why the adverse score for entertainment and recreation is somewhat lower (4.3 percent) than the others.

Respondents in all towns expressed notable levels of dissatisfaction with shopping and other commercial facilities; the tenor of the responses indicates that it mainly stems from a lack of variety in shopping opportunities. The company towns of Newman and Dampier had among the highest unfavorable scores (5.9 and 6.7 (1971) and 6.6 (1974) percent respectively). Although most essential needs are catered for in these towns, company policy does not allow the duplication of certain retail outlets. Mt. Isa has fairly comprehensive and diversified shopping facilities, even though they are not comparable to those in a capital city. The level of dissatisfaction expressed (2.6 percent) in that town is probably a fair indication of its essential superiority (which, in turn, is largely a function

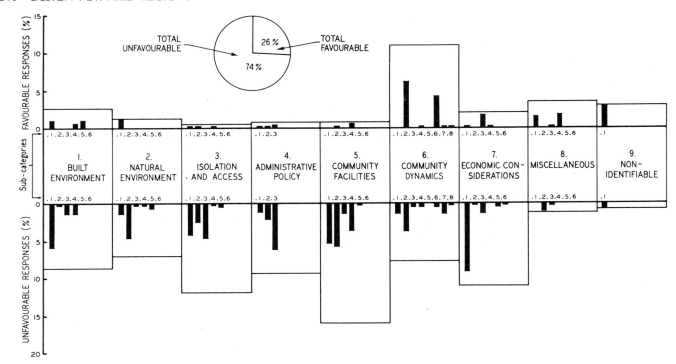

FIG. 11-14. Profile of resident attitudes, Kununurra, 1971.

of town size and absence of a restrictive retailing policy) over the other towns. The high level of unfavorable responses expressed in Hedland (5.9 percent) is boosted by the dissatisfaction felt by residents in the new town of South Hedland over the time taken to provide basic shopping services.

Community Dynamics. Scores for all towns on the topic of social relationships were high with respect to both favorability and unfavorability: Hedland (7.6 percent favorable, 4.6 percent unfavorable); Newman (4.1, 7.0); Dampier 1971 (5.4, 4.1); Dampier 1974 (8.5, 6.5); Nhulunbuy (8.8, 5.6); Katherine (5.9, 4.5); Kununurra (6.1, 4.0); Mt. Isa (5.9, 3.2), respectively. Newman was the only town where there was a dominance of unfavorable responses (relating to high levels of population turnover, excessive emphasis on money-making, boredom, depression, and loneliness—comments characteristic of all towns). Favorable comments normally stressed the relaxed way of life and the friendly atmosphere of the towns.

All settlements produced favorable scores with respect to work opportunities and relationships for the breadwinner. The results emphasized the importance of these aspects in the community, and they also tended to confirm motivation for taking up residence in the tropics.

Economic Considerations There was a high level of adverse comment on the cost of living in all towns.[22] Kununurra probably has the highest cost structure for consumer goods of all the towns visited and, with the possible exception of Katherine, offers fewer opportunities for earning high wages than any of the other towns. However, responses were generally

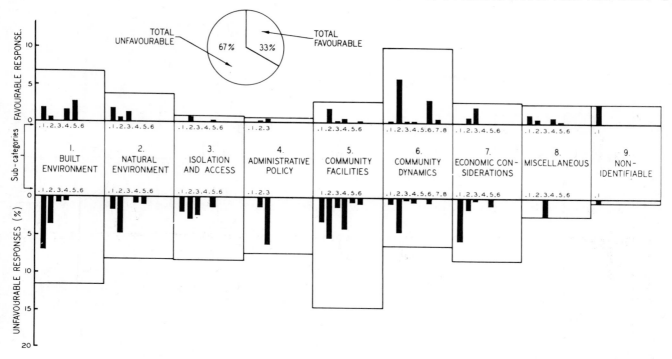

FIG. 11-15. Profile of resident attitudes, Katherine, 1971.

favorable on the subject of wages and savings, and they were especially positive in the mining towns.

These surveys of attitudes show prominent features of living patterns in tropical and arid Australia. Those areas of the total community environment which residents consider to be important can be identified and separated into components which can be manipulated to varying degrees. The built environment is probably the most tractable of these, while others such as the natural environment and the isolation and access components are somewhat more difficult to modify. Nevertheless, some degree of modification is possible for each component, whether it takes the form of economic concessions, reorganization of administrative policies, or the provision of extra facilities.

The summaries of attitudes show varied reactions to aspects of life in remote communities. These aspects, whether favorable or unfavorable, can be ranked in the order of importance assigned to them. Community planners should note that these cover a much broader spectrum than the physical aspects of the environment which, all too often, have been their standard currency in the past. Such rankings should not constitute an inflexible set of priorities for community development because technical, economic, and other considerations may sometimes justifiably override them. Nevertheless, they do provide the basic means through which realistic planning, geared to the wishes of people, can be launched.

The analyses of attitudes have possible practical applications, even at the early stages of project development. For instance, they provide a convenient means for evaluating the public acceptance of an existing community environment. Aspects of the community setting needing im-

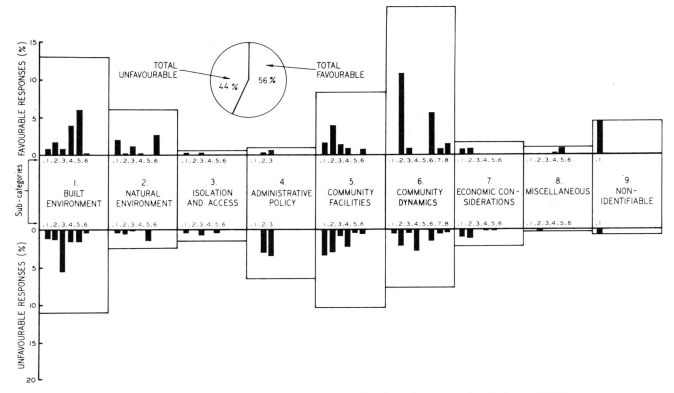

FIG. 11-16. Profile of resident attitudes, Cobram, 1972.

provement and those on which expenditure has been unnecessarily extravagant can be identified. The analyses could also be used for comparing the success, from the viewpoint of residents, of separate towns designed and developed according to different sets of planning concepts. When viewed together and assessed in light of the nature of the towns surveyed, the analyses of residents' comments can provide community developers with an insight into the likely reaction of people to the decisions which will shape the physical, social, economic, and administrative environment of any proposed new town.

Population Mobility

One of the characteristic features associated with the new, remote communities of tropical Australia is the flux in their constituent populations. Census data indicate that many of the towns are growing at rates far in excess of their capital city counterparts. The nature of population flows to these remote (principally mining) communities has been documented elsewhere, and it indicates that most mining company recruitment within Australia occurs in urban interstate and intrastate localities.[23] There are low levels of movement from rural areas. The resulting demographic composition contrasts with that of agriculturally based towns such as Kununurra and Katherine where the resident population is almost equally divided between those with a rural and those with an urban background.

Most striking, perhaps, is the level of population turnover in these townships, particularly in those connected with the mining industry. Annual turnover rates during establishment of mining towns were extremely high, about 200 to 400 percent for most companies concerned. Two years after the start of production, Goldsworthy Mining Ltd. had a work force turnover of 140 percent per annum—an example fairly typical of the experience of other companies.[24] The level of turnover tends to decline over time, however, as townships grow, friendship networks develop, and a greater variety of community services and facilities are established. Moderate to high levels of population turnover continue to characterize many of the remote communities in tropical Australia and are perhaps, in themselves, fairly sensitive indicators of the quality of life attainable in those centers.

MOTIVATION FOR MIGRATION

The factors instrumental in population movement to the new mining towns are financial or employment-based (see Table 11-5).[25] Migrants are responding primarily to positive factors associated with the destination, although certain variations can be detected among the townships. Migrants who go to Newman have almost wholly economic motives. In contrast to Newman, Mt. Isa has many households who have moved to the town for social or kinship reasons. This is a function of the length of time Mt. Isa has been established. Many residents of the coastal sites of Dampier and Nhulunbuy moved to these areas primarily for the enjoyable life-style which could be found there—a feeling which apparently was not shared by migrants to the older town of Port Hedland.[26]

The study undertaken by Stockbridge, et al. in the Pilbara towns of Dampier, Karratha, Wickham, Roeburne, and Port Samson confirms these same principal motivations for migration, although the results are not directly comparable since secondary reasons for moving into the area were included in their tabulations. Principal motivations were related to job and money with 46.9 and 41.6 percent of the settlers expressing the two reasons respectively. Environment and family-related attributes each accounted for a further 24.9 of the responses.[27] In Redding's Kambalda study, contrast is made between the staff and wages employee motivations for migration. He says, "The main difference between the two groups is that staff are oriented to career and intrinsic aspects of the job, whereas wages employees are oriented to security and extrinsic aspects of the job. . . ."[28] This statement suggests that a blanket grouping of company personnel (as in Table 11-4) is likely to conceal important intragroup differences. An additional feature of Redding's study was his separation of the women's responses for coming to the town.

For women, by far the most important reason for coming [to the town] was because their husband came. One-third of the wives of wages employees also stressed material living standards. These findings suggest there is considerable potential for dissatisfaction amongst women, if their husband's expectations are not met. There is also an implication that their own needs (e.g., for employment) should also be met.[29]

TABLE 11-5. Motivation for Migrating to Remote Australian Communities (and Cobram for contrast).

REASON FOR MIGRATION (%)	NEWMAN 1971–72	DAMPIER 1971–72	DAMPIER 1974	MT. ISA 1971	HEDLAND 1976	NHULUNBUY 1974–75	KUNUNURRA 1971	KATHERINE 1971	COBRAM 1972
						TOWN LOCATION OF SURVEYED POPULATION			
Financial	66.4	48.8	40.6	40.2	41.0	33.7	14.0	0.0	1.2
Employment	24.3	33.8	34.2	30.5	41.0	41.3	62.8	65.1	49.4
Climate and health	1.4	4.4	2.9	6.1	2.6	2.9	2.3	0.0	2.4
Standard of living	1.4	0.6	0.0	2.4	1.7	1.3	0.0	2.3	6.0
Style of life	5.7	11.9	17.1	2.4	6.8	16.1	16.3	9.3	4.8
Established ties	0.7	0.6	4.6	17.1	6.0	4.2	2.3	23.3	28.9
Other	0.0	0.0	0.5	1.2	0.9	0.5	2.3	0.0	7.2
Sample Size	140	160	409	82	117	615	43	43	83

Source: Data from unpublished CSIRO remote community surveys, 1971–76

244

Results from the Hedland study suggested that the motivations for migration appeared to influence a household's prospective intentions to move on to a much greater extent than, for instance, in Stockbridge et al.'s study, although in the same direction.[30] That is, those respondents who gave employment or job as a principal reason for migrating were more likely to continue residence in the township than those who were attracted by financial inducements. Motivations relating to life style and family relationships were also associated with a disposition towards stability of residence.

INTER-TOWN COMPARISONS ON MOBILITY ATTRIBUTES

When surveyed residents in Dampier (1974), Nhulunbuy (1974–75), and Hedland (1976) were asked what their intended duration of stay in the township was to have been, no more than 10 percent in any community indicated "permanently." There is therefore a level of turnover already built into such communities which is not so much a function of the characteristics of the communities themselves, but is a function of the predisposition of their incoming populations. It was not suprising, that in the Hedland survey 60 percent of households changed their minds about their intended period of residence and were expecting to extend their stay. (Almost identical percentages were found for Dampier and Nhulunbuy.)

It could follow that a residue of households from each influx into the towns would decide to become long-term stayers and would induce others to remain. Table 11-6 presents data on the duration of residence for a selection of tropical communities. Between 1971 and 1972, the percentage of households residing six years or more in Dampier and Newman—1.9 and zero percent respectively—indicates the recent development of these centers (also see Nhulunbuy); and by 1974, this category of household in Dampier had grown to 15.8 percent. Just how far this process of increased stability among the township population is likely to extend is difficult to say, but an examination of the longer established centers of Mt. Isa and Katherine (and in Victoria, Cobram) suggests that a pattern resembling that in Mt. Isa is not an impossibility for communities that are not company towns.

Information on the future mobility intentions of residents currently living in tropical centers tends to confirm the proposition that small company towns are the least likely of all types of centers in the northern regions of Australia to attract a permanent population (see Table 11-7). Almost 70 percent of Mt. Isa households surveyed indicated that there was a strong likelihood of their remaining in town for the next four years or more; less likely to remain were (in order) households in Katherine, Hedland, Kununurra, Dampier, Nhulunbuy, and Newman.

MOBILITY BEHAVIOR AT HOUSEHOLD LEVEL: THE HEDLAND STUDY

Apart from rather broad factors connected with the administrative status of the town (that is, whether under company management or not), its employment structure (that is, whether or not it is a single industry town), and its location (coastal or inland)—all of which have influenced the population turnover in remote centers—it is also likely that there are additional

TABLE 11-6. Years Residence in Remote Australian Towns and Cobram.

LENGTH OF TIME IN THE TOWN (%)	TOWN LOCATION OF SURVEYED POPULATION										
	NEWMAN 1971–72	DAMPIER 1971–72	DAMPIER 1974	MT. ISA 1971	HEDLAND 1976	NHULUNBUY 1974–75	KUNUNURRA 1971	KATHERINE 1971	COBRAM 1972
Less than three months	12.1	3.8	8.7	3.7	4.3	5.5	7.0	2.3	4.8
Three but less than six months	23.6	6.3	11.4	0.0	5.1	6.5	7.0	9.3	3.6
Six but less than twelve months	32.1	11.3	8.3	6.1	10.3	13.9	20.9	9.3	1.2
One year but less than two years	25.7	21.3	12.6	9.8	18.8	22.7	20.9	16.3	9.6
Two years but less than four years	5.7	40.6	21.1	12.2	20.5	42.6	14.0	11.6	3.6
Four years but less than six years	0.7	15.0	22.1	6.1	22.2	8.4	7.0	7.0	9.6
Six years or more	0.0	1.9	15.8	62.2	18.8	0.5	23.3	44.2	67.5
Sample Size	140	160	412	82	117	618	43	43	83

Source: Data from unpublished CSIRO remote community surveys, 1971–76

TABLE 11-7. Future Mobility Intentions of Australian Households in Remote Towns and Cobram.

LIKELIHOOD OF REMAINING IN TOWN FOR THE NEXT FOUR YEARS OR MORE (%)	TOWN LOCATION OF SURVEYED POPULATION								
	NEWMAN 1971–72	DAMPIER 1971–72	DAMPIER 1974	MT. ISA 1971	HEDLAND 1976	NHULUNBUY 1974–75	KUNUNURRA 1971	KATHERINE 1971	COBRAM 1972
Very unlikely	36.4	18.8	29.7	13.4	15.4	27.3	21.4	14.0	10.8
Unlikely	13.6	5.6	7.1	2.4	13.7	10.6	7.1	11.6	4.8
Likely as not	19.3	19.4	9.2	9.8	6.8	10.9	21.4	9.3	7.2
Likely	12.9	16.9	13.6	4.9	16.2	16.4	9.5	7.0	3.6
Very likely	17.9	39.4	40.4	69.5	47.9	34.9	40.5	58.1	73.5
Sample Size	140	160	411	82	117	616	42	43	83

Source: Data from unpublished CSIRO remote community surveys, 1971–76

variables at the individual or household level (relating to the nature of the dwelling, the social-demographic composition of the household, and the satisfaction its members derive from residing in a particular township) which are connected with a household's residence history and prospective mobility intentions.

An analysis of household data was based on a survey conducted in Hedland in 1976. Several variables were found to have a connection with the "number of years a household had lived in Hedland."[31] Citizens born overseas proved to be longer-term residents than their Australian-born counterparts; however, the most recently arrived migrants were likely to remain in the township for a shorter period than those who had been in Australia for some time. Income of head was marginally associated with length of residence. In fact, there was little difference in duration of residence over most of the income range. Only being in the highest income bracket (over $15,600 per annum) appeared to induce a longer stay.

The future mobility intentions of residents were solicited by a question concerning planned location of residence four years hence. Unlike urban based studies which normally produce a well-identified prospective mobility model,[32] only one variable—the education of the head member of the family—was significantly associated with household future mobility intentions. In the Hedland sample, the groups of households most likely to stay four years or more were those whose head did not complete secondary school. This result may indicate an inability of such individuals to compete successfully in the urban job market.

Another approach to the mobility question seeks to identify the type of household which is likely to extend its stay in a township beyond an initially nominated period. The framework lacks a certain degree of specificity, for no particular temporal span is involved; but given the unstable nature of the resident population in the new mining townships, it is perhaps a realistic approach. Households which would most likely extend their stay were those:

1. Whose head had a primary education only or else did not complete secondary school.
2. Who were from Perth or overseas. (Households unlikely to extend their stays were from Western Australian locations other than Perth, other capital cities, or from other Australian locations.)
3. Who have been living in the township for a longer period of time. (A duration-of-stay effect seems to be in operation whereby the longer an individual or family remains in an area, the longer they are likely to remain.)
4. With no previous experience of living in remote or tropical communities. (It would appear as though those households with prior experience were able to make a more realistic assessment of their expected length of stay; their initial expected period of residence was also found to be significantly longer than those households with no previous experience of life in tropical or remote areas.)

To investigate in more detail the relationship between the household community-related attitudes and household mobility intentions, measures of association were obtained between these two movement-related indices (decision to extend stay, prospective mobility intentions), and a set of household community-related attitudes.[33] Those households who intended to leave Hedland within four years indicated general dissatisfaction with the supply of fresh fruit and vegetables, entertainment and recreation outlets (e.g., restaurants, picnic areas, hobby clubs), and cleanliness of the town. Of greater significance, however, is the relatively large number of references to deficiencies in social relationships among the households who were predisposed towards movement; for example, the residents said:

"It is lonely in this town."
"We have no friends here with whom we could discuss a personal problem."
"Since coming to live here, we miss our near relations very much."
"We rarely go visiting."

A similar set of statements dominates when attention is directed to the question of a household extending its stay (undefined) in the township. People say:

"We don't have many friends in this township."
"Our children find it hard to make friends easily here."
"We know few of the residents in the townships."

Therefore, there is little doubt concerning the importance of interpersonal relationships, friendship linkages, and people-oriented community ties to the residential stability of households in Australia's tropical remote towns.

Mining company management has recognized the importance of high wages, good quality housing, and the provision of community services and facilities in attracting suitable personnel to their towns. From studies already made, we can see that high incomes and good quality, low cost accommodations are not, by themselves, sufficient inducements to retain as many of the workers as companies would wish. A certain proportion of households are likely to extend their length of stay as the town grows and community facilities develop. Many more households would stay if they did not experience the loneliness and isolation which appear more evident in the new towns of Australia's tropical north than they do in the southern and eastern cities.

Conclusion

The magnitude of the resource base in the humid and arid tropics of Australia suggests that the upsurge in the growth of settlement in this region, which has been characteristic of the last decade, will continue and increase into the 1980s and 1990s. Yet there are a number of features which have characterized development which should be avoided in future planning at both the town and regional level. The difficulty is anticipating all the practical, social, and psychological needs of a future population in a town which has yet to be built. However, some significant, imaginative, but often costly measures have already been adopted to overcome environmental difficulties in the tropics. The solutions adopted often take the form of direct confrontations with the environment such as whole-house refrigerated air conditioning systems. Little concern is shown for the consequent high costs of installing and running these systems. Often, opportunities to exploit natural conditions are ignored. Reduction of heat loads through correct orientation, the selection of roof color, and mutual shading in building complexes also have sometimes been ignored. Refrigerated air conditioning systems have been adopted in climates where the much cheaper and quieter evaporative system would have worked admirably. Occasionally, housing has been located where it is subject to dust and pollution by gases and noise from industrial plants. Provision of essential community facilities has been the rule; but after residents have settled, they have expressed a desire for a wider variety of facilities.

Most residents see a considerable need to improve the suitability and quality of noncompany housing in open towns. The extremely favorable response to housing in some mining company towns suggests that reasonable levels of satisfaction may have been achieved at a lower expenditure. In towns such as Port Hedland where both mining company and nonmining company personnel are housed, to keep community harmony, a decrease of mining company housing standards and an increase of nonmining company housing standards could be argued.

Over the past decade, the development of the mineral industry throughout the Australian tropics and in the desert fringes has demonstrated some problems which emerge when there is no firm regional planning policy. Mineral producers argue that there can be no control over the location of ore deposits, and they use this fact as the basis for their insistence on the establishment of closed company towns in close proximity to the mine site. These towns are characterized by the company being the only employer, the town administrator, and the landlord. While the location of some remote ore bodies justifies the existence of a small isolated settlement, there are many instances where separate development was not warranted (For example, in the vicinity of Dampier in the Pilbara there are five separate small settlements within a radius of 30 km).

A number of studies have documented the impact that location in small remote mining towns has on the social, physical, and psychological well-being of the residents.[34] It is our contention that many of these problems are products of town size and company dominance. For instance, the social and demographic profiles of new mining communities reveal a strong imbalance between the sexes, a disproportionate number of single adults, a predominance of married couples in the 20 to 35 years age-groups with preschool or primary school age children, and a narrow range of occupational groups. This situation often leads to a lack of concern for those who are underrepresented numerically, e.g., adolescents, the middle-aged, and the elderly.

The company tends to dominate the whole community. In closed towns, company control is most apparent in the area of housing: generally there is a lack of variety in housing types (in many cases there is an excessive bias towards single-family detached dwellings on suburban-sized allotments); housing tenure is tied to the job (requiring a move from the town upon termination of employment); and housing allocation policies are extremely rigid, removing any element of individual choice and restricting intratown movement—a fact which is further exacerbated by policies which prevent alterations or additions to property. Opportunities for home ownership, if permitted at all, are economically unattractive in a small town with an uncertain life span; and there is the problem of accommodating employees who retire and wish, for reasons of family or satisfaction with the area, to remain in the town. Company influence on community life is more difficult to identify and quantify. Compared with a town in which government or other agencies also share in the ownership and provision of housing and services, a major problem of closed towns involves the permeation of the company hierarchy through the whole social structure of the community.

CSIRO social surveys have also shown that much dissatisfaction with life in small, remote mining communities is attributable to what residents see as a low level of services and amenities. Respondents have complained of a lack of variety in shopping facilities, commercial services, entertainment, and, to a lesser extent, recreation. The single retailer policy which is imposed in most company towns invokes images, albeit ill-based in many cases, of inflated prices and poor customer service.

Health, social, and legal services and educational facilities (particularly secondary and tertiary) are deficient in most remote communities. The result often means dislocation of family life as certain members complete their schooling, undertake tertiary training, or enter hospitals in capital cities or regional centers. Most of the small settlements, at best, support only periodic services: doctors, dentists, veterinarians, lawyers, accountants, and counseling services make circuits on either weekly, fortnightly, or monthly bases.

When we look at the structure of the community as a whole, we see that the single industry nature of small mining towns limits work opportunities for those not specifically recruited for a company position. The groups most affected in this respect are women (principally wives of employees) and young people leaving school. Female employment opportunities are currently under study by a number of mining companies. This effort represents a move away from the more traditional male-dominated policies of the 1960s and early 1970s and indicates a response to several factors:

1. An attempt to economize on recruiting and housing employees.
2. An attempt to retain married couples in the township for as long a period as possible.
3. An anticipation of impending legislation concerning sex discrimination.

Two major obstacles exist, however: the economic efficacy of attracting further industries to a small town and the patriarchal attitude of trade unions.

When attention is turned from economic to social activities, it seems as though the teenage section of the community is less well-catered to than the married women. The teenagers appear to have no meaningful roles in the community, yet they could be among the most important sources of recruitment for future residents. In an attempt to retain the existing (married) work force, some companies offer apprenticeships and create office and laboratory jobs for youth completing school. These opportunities are very limited, however, and represent only a small proportion of annual labor intake. Skilled workers are normally sought from urban and rural centers in southern Australia and overseas. Unskilled workers are often drawn from the ranks of the large group of itinerants (mostly single males) passing through the region.

Centralized towns could be the solution to these problems.[35] Mining town development to date has consisted primarily of separate and unrelated projects. Increased mineral extraction and the expected associated industrial activity (e.g., secondary processing, heavy industry) will, however, require a greater need for government to be involved in the planning, coordination, and financing of a more permanent development.

The development of centralized towns that would service several mining operations (and, where relevant, their rural hinterlands) within a reasonable commuting distance provides an opportunity to aggregate personnel from different companies and to remove the dominance of a single company from the economic and social life of the townships. Aggregation should not be seen as the panacea for all the problems which confront small remote towns, but it would reduce the intensity of the problems outlined above. For instance:

1. Levels of individual choice would increase for residents in a variety of areas: shopping, entertainment, recreation, health, education, professional services, employment, and housing.
2. Company influence would be reduced. Township management would pass from the "benevolent directorship" of mine company management toward autonomous local government.[36] Retailers would be open to free competition as would the employers of labor.
3. Levels of population turnover would decline. A larger town with a broader employment base would instill a greater sense of permanency among the residents; a greater demand for home purchase among employees would also be likely to follow.
4. Infrastructure costs, particularly those concerned with contractors' establishment and with headworks, would be considerably reduced because of economies of scale.

It is apparent, therefore, that future planning research concerning new communities should be directed not only toward the social well-being of the residents, but also toward policy-related questions of whether a regional center, a centralized town, or a nonpermanent community is required.

Notes

1. Colin E. Hounam, "Climate and Air-Conditioning Requirements in Sparsely Occupied Areas of Australia," in *Building Climatology Proceedings*, **109** (1970), pp. 175–184.
2. It has been argued, for example, that the relative heat strain map can be used for planning purposes as a criterion for air conditioning requirements: ". . . 25 days a year might be accepted as the 'climatological' boundary north of which air conditioning is highly desirable" (Hounam, p. 179).

3. Australian Bureau of Statistics, *Official Yearbook of Australia 1975 and 1976* (Canberra: Australian Government Publishing Service, 1977), pp. 133–172.

4. Bruce Davidson, "History of the Australian Rural Landscape," in *Man and Landscape in Australia*, ed. George Seddon and Mari Davis (Canberra: Australian Government Publishing Service, 1976), pp. 63–81.

5. Geoffrey Blainey, *The Rush that Never Ended: A History of Australian Mining*, 2nd ed. (Melbourne: Melbourne University Press, 1969), p. 349

6. Most of the new towns in tropical Australia are company or closed towns. The (mining) company constructs the towns, administers them, owns the houses, and is virtually the sole employer. In a few towns, the population comprises mining company employees and a substantial number of other residents such as government employees who followed in the wake of the mineral boom. These towns are administered by conventional local government authorities. Such communities also have a variety of house tenures and are known as open towns. Agriculturally based towns are open.

7. Terence B. Brealey and Peter W. Newton, "Migration and New Mining Towns," in *Mobility and Community Change in Australia*, Ian Burnley, Robin Pryor, and Don Rowland, eds. (Brisbane: University of Queensland Press, 1980).

8. In the resource towns of Dampier and Nhulunbuy, almost 10 percent of dependent children were living away from their parents. This figure dropped to a little over 1 percent for Hedland, a larger, longer established, broader-based town which possesses an adequate range of primary and secondary (but not tertiary) educational institutions.

9. *The Pilbara Study* (Canberra: Australian Government Publishing Service, 1974), p. 17.

10. This is fully described and illustrated in: Western Australian Government Housing Study Group, *Northern Housing in Western Australia* (Perth: Western Australian Government Printer, 1976), pp. 11–141.

11. For example, the waiting list for state rental housing in Hedland stood at 245 in March 1976 and 280 in February 1977. The stock of public housing at the latter date stood at 4600. Caravan (trailer) accommodations act as temporary housing for most of these households.

12. Australian Housing Research Council, *Social Mix in Public Housing* (Sydney: Department of Social Work, University of New South Wales, 1976), p.1.6.

13. Cecily Gribbin, *Occupying Housing Commission Accommodation as a Source of Social Stigma*, Commonwealth Scientific and Industrial Research Organization, Division of Building Research, Internal Report 77/15, 1977.

14. A detailed explanation of the coding procedures used is contained in Terence B. Brealey, *Living in Remote Communities in Tropical Australia* (Melbourne: Commonwealth Scientific and Industrial Research Organization, Division of Building Research, 1972), pp. 19–28.

15. On this particular point, it is interesting to note the recent decision by one Western Australian sand mining company to locate its work force on the coast (at Leeman, 300 km north of Perth) and transfer personnel by air conditioned bus over 40 km of unsealed road to the inland mine site.

16. A more extensive examination of differences between company and noncompany residents in remote tropical communities is contained in Terence B. Brealey and Peter W. Newton, *Living in Remote Communities in Tropical Australia: The Hedland Study* (Melbourne: Commonwealth Scientific and Industrial Research Organization, Division of Building Research, 1978), pp. 1–88.

17. Radburn planning has as its main aim the separation of pedestrian movement from fast moving vehicular traffic. Its major element is a super block containing residential units and an appropriately sized amenity core consisting of community facilities such as a school and a shopping center. A ring road designed to carry high volumes of fast moving traffic encircles the super block and all internal roads take the form of short culs-de-sac or service courts which limit traffic density and speed. A footpath system linking housing units to community facilities is provided, and this is separate from the vehicular system. One side of the house is approached by foot and the other by vehicle. There should be a minimum number of intersections between footpaths and roadways; where these are unavoidable, ideally, there should be grade separation. Radburn planning requires a reoriented house plan which provides entry suitable for visitors from either the pedestrian footway or vehicular service court side of the allotment. The more conventional town layout of Nhulunbuy is fully described in

J. Agius, "Nhulunbuy: A New Town in the Australian Tropics," in *New Towns in Isolated Settings* (Canberra: Australian Government Publishing Service, 1976), pp. 251–261.

18. A detailed appraisal of the South Hedland town plan is contained in Brealey and Newton, *Living in Remote Communities: The Hedland Study*, pp. 1–88.

19. Subjective observations suggest that a fully air conditioned house (as provided by mining companies) acts as a captive agent for the occupants (principally housewives), thereby reducing the potential for out-of-doors contact. In certain climatic regions (hot, arid), evaporative cooling can provide adequate relief from high ambient temperatures, but this process is not capable of producing the artificially low temperatures generated by refrigerated air conditioning which cause the captive effect.

20. A. J. Holsman, "The Structure of Australian Air Networks," *Australian Geographical Studies,* **15**, no. 1 (1977), 64.

21. Verbatim comments to incomplete statements questionnaire during CSIRO survey in Dampier in 1971.

22. Also see W. D. Woodhead, *Living in Remote Communities in Tropical Australia: Freight Costs and Price Levels* (Melbourne: Commonwealth Scientific and Industrial Organization, Division of Building Research, 1972), pp. 1–17.

23. See Brealey and Newton, "Migration and New Mining Towns."

24. Terence B. Brealey. *Report on Tour of North West Australia and Northern Territory* (Melbourne: Commonwealth Scientific and Industrial Organization, Division of Building Research, 1968) pp. 1–49.

25. Responses to the question concerning the reason for moving to a particular township were allocated to one of six principal categories:
    1. Financial—principally references to salaries and other money matters;
    2. Employment—references to job or business opportunity, gaining experience, transfer, promotion, job security, job conditions;
    3. Climate and Health;
    4. Standards of Living—furthering education or training; obtaining good standard housing;
    5. Style of Life—reference to being "away from city," "change of scene," "facilitates transient life style," "came for a holiday then stayed";
    6. Established Ties—including having family cohesiveness; being born or living part of life in or near the area concerned.

26. Variation in response to the reason for moving question was even more marked among different employee groups residing in the Port Hedland-South Hedland area. Occupants of mining company housing were attracted primarily by financial inducements (high salaries, low cost-high quality accommodation, and a potential for saving) and job vacancies. Most of the government employees (e.g., teachers, police, health officials, etc.) moved to the Hedland area as a result of a job transfer. Occupants of the State Housing Commission accommodations fill many of the service occupations within the township, and their motivations for migration are not polarized to the same extent as those of the previous two groups. See Brealey and Newton, *Living in Remote Communities.*

27. Margaret Stockbridge, et al., *Dominance of Giants, A Shire of Roebourne Study* (Perth: Department of Social Work, University of Western Australia, 1976), p. 63.

28. P. J. R. Redding, "Kambalda Case Studies—3. Living in Kambalda," in *New Towns in Isolated Settings* (Canberra: Australian Government Publishing Service, 1976), pp. 201–214. (For administrative purposes, mining companies divide their work force into two groups which are designated "wages" (or award) workers and "staff." Wages workers are all those whose job is classified below foreman level. They usually outnumber staff workers by the ratio of about five or two to one. Authors' comment.)

29. Ibid, pp. 201–214.

30. See Brealey and Newton, *Living in Remote Communities: The Hedland Study.*

31. Ibid.

32. Peter W. Newton and J. Ross Barnett, *Modelling Residential Mobility. The Mover-Stayer Decision,* Commonwealth Scientific and Industrial Research Organization, Division of Building Research, Internal Report 77/12, 1977.

33. Residents' assessments of the quality of life in Hedland were obtained by asking respondents to evaluate over 80 statements such as: "I think that there are sufficient

meeting places for teenagers," and "My children find it hard to make friends easily here," and "There is insufficient medical staff in this town." Residents placed these statements into any one of seven categories which ranged from "strongly agree" to "strongly disagree." See Brealey and Newton, *Living in Remote Communities: The Hedland Study.*

34. Norman E. P. Pressman, ed. "New Communities in Canada," *Contact,* **8**, no. 3 (1976); *New Towns in Isolated Settings,* Australian and United Nations Educational, Scientific and Cultural Organization Seminar on Man and the Environment (Canberra: Australian Government Publishing Service, 1976).

35. Terence B. Brealey and Peter W. Newton, "Mining Towns—the Case for Centralisation," *Mining Review,* (July, 1977), 7–9.

36. Subsequent to the compilation of this chapter in 1977 one major mining town (Newman) has undergone a "normalization" process in which responsibility for town administration has passed to elected local government. Other company towns are currently preparing for this transition.

Suggested Readings

Blainey, Geoffrey. *The Rush That Never Ended: A History of Australian Mining.* Melbourne: Melbourne University Press, 1969.

Brealey, Terence B.. *Living in Remote Communities in Tropical Australia: Exploratory Study.* Melbourne: Commonwealth Scientific and Industrial Research Organization, Division of Building Research, 1972.

———, and Newton, Peter W. *Living in Remote Communities in Tropical Australia: The Hedland Study.* Melbourne: Commonwealth Scientific and Industrial Research Organization, Division of Building Research, 1978

Davidson, Bruce. *The Northern Myth.* Melbourne: Melbourne University Press, 1966.

New Towns in Isolated Settings. Australian and United Nations Educational, Scientific, and Cultural Organization Seminar on Man and the Environment. Canberra: Australian Government Publishing Service, 1976.

12
Resource Management of Australian Arid Lands

Michael D. Young

Approximately 70 percent of Australia is arid and receives insufficient effective rainfall to allow pasture improvement or cropping without irrigation. Hence, almost all the agricultural production from this area is pastoral in nature and is reliant on the region's natural vegetation.[1] The climate in the north of the arid zone is subtropical and in the south, mediterranean. The land is either unoccupied (26 percent), used for aboriginal reserves (7 percent), for national parks (2 percent), or for pastoral stations (65 percent) (see Table 12-1). Because the area's climate and natural vegetation are not homogeneous, some areas are better suited to cattle and others to sheep (see Figure 12-1). Throughout Australia's arid zone there are also many exploited mineral deposits which have had a major influence on its infrastructure. For instance, Broken Hill, a large mining town in New South Wales, has become the pastoral center for much of the southeastern arid zone (see Table 12-2). Broken Hill's mining population justifies the construction of substantial hospitals, schools, roads, and railways which the pastoral industry alone could not support. The main exception to this rule is a town located in the very center of the arid zone, Alice Springs. This town evolved as the communication center for much of northern and central Australia and now attracts many tourists who came to see the "red center" (see Table 12-2).[2]

In 1973 and 1974, 35 percent of the 64,163 people directly employed in Australia's mining industry were located in the arid zone. They produced $2,732 million of Australia's minerals which is 37 percent of her total

TABLE 12-1. Arid Lands as a Percentage of the Total Area of Each Australian State.

	TOTAL AREA (MILLIONS HA)	ARID LANDS (%)	AREA OF STATE OCCUPIED BY PASTORALISTS (%)
Victoria (Vic.)	23	—	—
Tasmania (Tas.)	7	—	—
Australian Capital Territory (A.C.T.)	0.6	—	—
South Australia (S.A.)	98	84	49
Western Australia (W.A.)	253	85	45
Northern Territory (N.T.)	135	76	46
Queensland (Qld.)	173	55	54
New South Wales (N.S.W.)	80	43	43
AUSTRALIA	768	70	46

Source: Extracted from map in Wilson, A. D. and R. D. Graetz. "Management of the Semi-arid and Arid Rangelands of Australia," In *The Management of Semi-Arid Ecosystems.* B. H. Walker, ed. Amsterdam: Elsevier Scientific Publishing Company, 1979. p. 83.

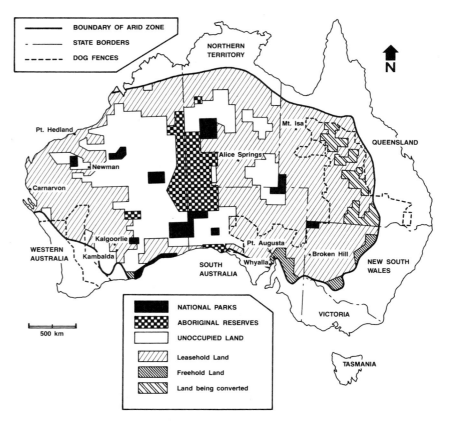

FIG. 12-1. Land appropriation in arid Australia. 1976. Based on Northern Territory of Australia, Pastoral Map (Canberra: Division of National Mapping, Department of National Development, 1953); Map of Western Australia (Perth: Office of the Surveyor General, 1970); Pastoral Map of South Australia (Adelaide: Office of the Surveyor General, 1972); Atlas of Australian Resources Land Use (Canberra: Department of Minerals and Energy, 1973); *Report of the Department of Public Lands for the Year Ended 1961* (Brisbane: Government Printing Office, 1962); *The Reader's Digest Complete Atlas of Australia.* (Sydney: Reader's Digest Association, 1968), pp. 42–47, 70–77; unpublished data supplied by the Division of National Mapping, Department of National Resources, Canberra, in 1977. The boundary of the arid zone is that defined by the Co-ordinating Panel on Pastoral Ecosystems of the Arid Zone in 1974. Small areas of national parks, particularly those in New South Wales, are omitted.

production.[3] The area is also extensively used for less productive uses such as national parks, aboriginal reserves, and large military bases. In 1971 the total population of the area was approximately 234,000 people, that is, one person to every 33 km² or 1.83 percent of Australia's population. Only 95,700 people reside on pastoral stations or in small towns and 138,000 in large towns; 22,000 of the latter are directly employed in the mining industry.[4] Only 65 percent of the land is used for pastoral purposes.

Pastoral System

Australia has a relatively developed economy. Most of the food and fiber produced in the arid zone is exported to people who live in urban Australia and overseas. This is achieved via an efficient transport network

TABLE 12-2. Ten Largest Arid Zone Towns.*

TOWN	POPULATION 1976	% CHANGE OF POPULATION IN LAST 10 YEARS
Whyalla, S.A.	33,382	51%
Broken Hill, N.S.W.	27,647	−8%
Mt. Isa, Qld.	25,377	50%
Kalgoorlie–Boulder, W.A.	19,041	−5%
Alice Springs, N.T.	13,092	25%
Port Augusta, S.A.	14,149	121%
Port Hedland, W.A.	11,144	480%
Carnarvon, W.A.	5,341	73%
Kambalda, W.A.	4,784	New town
Newman, W.A.	4,672	New town

*Mining towns are in italics. Alice Springs is a communication center with a rapidly expanding tourist industry. Port Augusta is on the coast, and almost all traffic from Eastern to Western Australia passes through it. Carnarvon has a good underground water supply and grows fruit and vegetables for Western Australia's capital, Perth.
Source: Bureau of Census and Statistics. *Population and Dwellings in Local Government Areas and Urban Centres. Australia.* Bulletin 6, Part 9, Ref. No. 2.88.9. Canberra: Commonwealth Bureau of Statistics, 1974. pp. 30–47; and unpublished data supplied by the Australian Bureau of Statistics, Canberra, in 1978.

which takes food to distant people. Unfortunately this system also tends to isolate the small number of people in the arid zone; hence, the majority of Australians, particularly politicians, are insensitive to the arid zone's problems.

The pastoral industry is made up of approximately 5000 stations (farms), each with exclusive grazing rights over the area managed. The owner (lessee or pastoralist) usually owns part of the improvements and livestock on the station, while the remainder is owned by creditors who advance money to allow the purchase of livestock, etc. Each station is run as a commercial venture which must make a profit if it is to survive in the long run. If it doesn't, the station will be sold at a loss or will eventually be declared bankrupt. When a station is declared bankrupt, it is sold by liquidators or taken over by the station's creditors. This process is not common; usually owners remain on their stations until reconstruction or sale. The variability of production in the arid zone has been poorly understood, and many optimistic investors have lost huge sums of money speculating on future production which did not occur.[5]

Formerly, stations usually raised either sheep or cattle, but not both. However, recent increases in cattle prices have caused the movement of cattle into what are regarded as sheep areas. The reverse has never occurred because sheep are not suited to the climate of northern Australia. Generally sheep productivity increases as one goes south and inland.[6] The movement of livestock is restricted by fences rather than shepherds and, in the more remote parts of Australia, by the strategic location of watering points. These watering points are 5 to 15 km apart; but since the cattle tend to drink at one watering point, the cost savings of this system outweigh the advantages of fencing. The failure to use fences to control cattle has been criticized by some administrators who believe that the construction of fences plays an essential part in the development of the arid zone.[7] Australia is attempting to eradicate tuberculosis and brucellosis from her cattle herds by 1984 and to encourage this is now providing tax concessions for the construction of fences which assist in disease eradication.

One very successful form of pastoral management in arid Australia which combines the advantages of nomadism with sedentary pastoralism has been the establishment of chains of stations which traverse the arid zone. Each chain consists of several stations located to exploit the climatic differences which exist across the arid zone.[8]

In the past, Australian pastoralists have frequently overestimated the potential of the arid areas. A succession of good years with high wool prices have raised hopes and increased the prices of stations, and for many years there was even a belief that overstocked country would recover to its original state.[9] Droughts are frequent but not regular, and it has been the long periods of excellent rain that have caused the greatest degradation of vegetation in arid Australia. In the past, a run of good seasons has often had a seductive influence on men anxious to settle and even crop arid Australia. The advice of men such as Goyder, who drew a line in South Australia beyond which cropping would fail, was ignored in the 1870s. Today this state still bears the scars of attempts to develop and crop her arid regions.[10]

Vermin Fences

To prevent Australia's wild dog, the dingo (Canis familiaris dingo), from destroying Australia's sheep flocks, fences to exclude dingos, 1.8 m high and 15 cm into the ground have been constructed around the areas which are suitable for sheep production (see Figure 12-1 and Table 12-3). The idea of using fences to control vermin was initiated to prevent the spread of rabbits in the 1880s; however this concept failed, and the fences fell into disrepair. Today they are maintained by pastoralists whose stations adjoin South Australia and Queensland and by a team of government boundary riders in New South Wales. Dingos which break through the fence are controlled by poisoning, and there is a bounty for any dingos shot within these fences (see Table 12-3). There are tremendous problems in maintaining fences which are periodically washed away in flash floods. Although pastoralists in Queensland and South Australia are paid to maintain the fence, they often fail to carry out maintenance promptly. In Queensland attempts to control dingos by aerial baiting with poisoned meat are being investigated; if this system proves successful, it is likely that large sections of the fence will be abandoned. Much of the fence in Western Australia already has been abandoned, and only small sections of the southwestern fence are being maintained by the government to control dingos and also emus (Dromaius novaehollandiae). To replace the abandoned fence, the Western Australian government employs professional trappers to control dingos. Some sections of the Western Australian fence which have been officially abandoned are still maintained by pastoralists.[11]

Land Tenure Systems

There are four main types of land in arid Australia—leased, alienated, reserved, and unoccupied. The majority of Australia's arid lands (62 percent) are leased to pastoralists under one of the 26 forms of pastoral lease used in Australia. In most cases these leases grant rights to graze land but do not grant rights to mine, to cultivate, or to fell trees for commercial pur-

TABLE 12-3. The Dog Fence in Australia.

STATE	FENCE	LENGTH KM	MAINTAINED BY
Queensland	Main dingo barrier fence	5,630	Adjacent landholders
	Millmerran dingo barrier fence	118	Adjacent landholders
	Inglewood dingo barrier fence	64	Adjacent landholders
	Wambo-Jondaryon dingo fence	45	Adjacent landholders
New South Wales	Queensland border	349	Wild Dog Destruction Board boundary riders
	South Australian border	269	Wild Dog Destruction Board boundary riders
South Australia	Dog fence	2,173.	Adjacent landholders
Western Australia	No. 1	1,032†	Adjacent landholders
	No. 2	1,418	Adjacent landholders
	No. 3		
Total		11,098	

†In 1950 the maintenance of approximately 800 km of No. 1 fence was abandoned in W.A.; since then other sections have been abandoned, and only a small portion is still officially maintained.
Sources: "Vermin-Proof Fences." In *Australian Encyclopedia.* Sydney: Grolier, 1942. Vol. IV, pp. 34–36; Condon, R. W. "Wild Dogs." *Agricultural Gazette of New South Wales*, **87**, no. 3 (1976), 50; "Rabbit." In *Australian Encyclopedia.* 2nd ed. Sydney: Grolier, 1958. vol. VII, p. 342; and S.J.O. Whitehouse, personal communication, 1978.

poses. The rights to fell trees and mine minerals are usually granted separately to ensure that these resources are exploited to their full potential. A pastoralist may not prevent a licensed miner or forester from extracting or searching for minerals or timber on his lease but may use the timber on his station to build his own fences and buildings.

Very little arid land in Australia is alienated. The little that is was converted between 1861 and 1878 and is held in fee simple.[12] These areas were mostly small areas of land along water courses, strategically placed to obtain secure tenure over large, inexpensive areas of land. This practice was quickly stopped, and more rational forms of land tenure were developed. In some states, it is possible to alienate arid crown land suitable for urban settlement or irrigation. There are two forms of alienated or freehold land in Australia: freehold land which the owner is relatively free to transfer as he wishes, and conditional freehold land which may only be transferred to persons who hold less than a specified area.[13] This second form of tenure is used to stop the aggregation of land.

Since 1958 Queensland has allowed developed grazing land to be alienated to freehold over a period of 40 years, and at present no other state allows this to occur. Since 1958, 8.8 percent of Queensland's arid zone has been used in this way.[14] There is a growing aboriginal land rights movement in Australia, and it is likely that aboriginal tribes will be given freehold title to large areas of unoccupied Australia.

At present some 9 percent of arid Australia is reserved to the crown (i.e., the government). These reserved lands include aboriginal reserves, defense areas, national parks, and traveling stock routes. The remaining 26 percent is still unoccupied and takes in a number of extremely arid areas in the center of the continent, including the Simpson, Gibson, Great Sandy, and the Victoria deserts. In the Northern Territory, the majority of these lands are now subject to claim or are held by Australian aborigines. These areas are being prospected for minerals and may be partly used in the future. In general, the inadequate rainfall, unsuitable topography, and poor soil and surface condition of these lands have prevented their use, and they are still in pristine condition (see Table 12-4).

EVOLUTION OF A LEASEHOLD SYSTEM

Unlike many countries of the world, Australia's arid zone has only been grazed by domestic animals for approximately 110 years. New South Wales was settled during the 1850s, Queensland and South Australia in the 1860s, and the Northern Territory in the 1800s.[15] The aboriginal inhabitants of Australia were hunters and gatherers and did not domesticate herbivores; in comparison with the white man, their impact on the land has been minimal.

The first white settlers came to Australia in late 1700s; but in an attempt to ensure ordered development, before 1836 settlement of inland Australia was forbidden. However, this did not deter squatters from moving inland and taking over unoccupied land. In 1836 the Government recognized this de facto ownership and legalized squatting by issuing licenses to graze livestock for £10 per annum plus a tax on the number of stock each squatter grazed. Initially, these privileges were limited to grazing; but it was not long before the squatters began to demand more rights, particularly compensation for improvements made by them, security of tenure, and preemptive rights to the purchase of their land.

After a great deal of lobbying, the Waste Lands Occupation Act of 1846 and the Order-in-Council in March 1847 gave squatters the right to lease land for a period of 14 years for a rent in proportion to the number of sheep carried. The next 40 years saw political chaos as agriculture expanded into areas which the pastoralists claimed were theirs. This expansion began when legislation was passed to allow men to select areas of land leased by pastoralists for farming purposes. In opposition to this move, pastoralists selected their best lands and developed many schemes to ensure that their lands stayed under their control. The areas which were selected in this period comprise the majority of freehold lands in arid Australia today. The end result of this awkward period in land administration was the leasehold system of land tenure under which most of arid Australia is leased today. This leasehold system was designed as a temporary method to allow the use of land until it could be farmed.[16] Today, many people see leasehold as the best way to administer Australian arid lands.

TABLE 12-4. Land Tenure in Arid Lands.

| STATE OR TERRITORY | ALIENATED (%) | LEASED OR LICENSED (%) | RESERVED LAND (%) | | UNOCCUPIED LAND (%) |
			ABORIGINAL RESERVES	NATIONAL PARKS	
S.A.	4	58	9	4	25
W.A.	1	48	8	0	43
N.T.	0	60	12	4	24[a]
QLD.	9	88	0	0	3
N.S.W.	1	97	0	2	0
AUSTRALIA	3	62	7	2	26

Source: Based on map in Wilson, A. D., and R. D. Graetz. "Management of the Semiarid and Arid Rangelands of Australia."

[a]Most unoccupied arid land in the Northern Territory is now subject to aboriginal and land claims.

ADMINISTERING THE ARID LAND

With the exception of the Northern Territory, land administration and management have always been the responsibility of the state governments of Australia (see Table 12-5). Each state has established a governmental body to do this. For example, the New South Wales and South Australia governments have established respectively the Western Lands Commission and the South Australian Pastoral Board to deal with their arid lands. The South Australian Pastoral Board was formed late in the 19th century, and its early success eventually led to the formation of a similar Western Lands Board in New South Wales.[17] This board became the Western Lands Commission in 1934. Both organizations answer directly to their Minister for Lands rather than reporting through a series of public servants responsible for all state land. This autonomy ensures that administrators have a closer affinity with the arid zone and a greater comprehension of its unique problems.

The Western Lands Commission is managed under the direction of a single commissioner who acts on the advice of his senior staff assisted in some matters by land boards. Each local land board consists of two local pastoralists and an assistant commissioner. Occasionally in the past, the Western Lands Commission in New South Wales has been frustrated by the pastoralists who form a majority on their local land boards. The South Australian Pastoral Board has three members of whom one must have been actively engaged in the pastoral industry. This composition avoids the problems which arise when pastoralists have vested interests in government land policy. Any two members of the South Australian Pastoral Board form a quorum, and they may hold meetings anywhere in South

TABLE 12-5. Administrative Bodies Responsible for Arid Australia.

STATE	ADMINISTRATIVE BODY	COMPOSITION OF BODY	SIZE OF QUORUM
N.S.W.	Western Lands Commission	Commissioner 1 Asst. Commissioner[a]	Refers some decisions to the local Land Board[b]
N.T.	Land Board of the Northern Territory	Chairman Deputy Chairman 10 members	Chairman or Deputy Chairman and 2 members
Qld.	Land Administration Commission	Chief Commissioner of Lands 2 others	Refers some decisions to a Committee of Review[c]
W.A.	Department of Lands and Survey	Minister for Lands Under Secretary of Lands Surveyor General Other officers appointed from time to time	Refers decisions to Pastoral Board[d]
S.A.	The Pastoral Board	Chairman 2 others Governor may appoint a fourth from time to time	Any 2 members

(a) The Act provides for two assistant commissioners. At present the government feels that only one is necessary.

(b) Local land boards are regional bodies which consist of an assistant commissioner and two local pastoralists.

(c) The Committee of Review consists of a member of the land commission (or his delegate) and two men with pastoral experience in the region under consideration. The Committee only considers matters which relate to grazing selections, i.e., the more intensely settled areas.

(d) The Pastoral Board consists of the Surveyor General, the Director of Agriculture, and three other members. One of these is usually a pastoralist and the other, a member of the Department of Lands and Surveys.

Source: Young, M. D. *Differences between States in Arid Land Administration.* CSIRO Division of land Resources Management, 1979. Series No. 4.

Australia. This enables them to travel in pairs throughout the arid zone and make decisions without having to refer to a higher authority, a unique feature which may be one of the reasons many people believe that South Australia's arid zone's vegetation is the least degraded.

Queensland has a Land Administration Commission which administers all of Queensland. The Northern Territory administers its lands through a land board and Western Australia, through the Department of Lands and Surveys. The Department of Lands and Surveys has a Pastoral Board which advises the department on pastoral leases. An important feature of all these administrative structures is the desire to involve pastoralists or pastoral experience in the administration of the leasehold system of land management.

These systems of land management which have evolved are continually changing.[18] In 1980 and 1981, the South Australian and Northern Territory governments undertook extensive reviews of their arid land tenure, management and administrative systems. Substantial changes are likely in the very near future.

THE LEASEHOLD SYSTEM

A lease is a contract between a pastoralist and the government which grants rights under certain conditions to that individual. It is appropriate in this analysis to consider four factors described by Heathcote as associated with a lease to graze arid land—content, time, size, personnel, and use—and also two other factors which are pertinent to this discussion—rent and security.

The contents of any arid land resource can be divided into seven components: space, landscape, wildlife, timber, forage, soil, and rock.[19] A grazing lease grants a pastoralist the right to graze the forage on a lease but restricts the right to mine the rock, remove the soil, or harvest the timber to other people. Cypress pine *(Callitris columellaris)* in New South Wales and sandalwood *(Santalum spicatum)* in Western Australia are removed by licensed foresters who pay royalties to the government for the timber they take. In New South Wales, to encourage a lessee to husband cypress pine, half the royalty from removing it from a lease is paid to the lessee.[20] In all states lessees are allowed to remove noncommercial timber for building and fencing on their land. Pastoralists are also permitted to control wildlife populations on a lease; and in three of the five arid zone states, aborigines are allowed to hunt wildlife on their land. Similarly, pastoralists must not interfere with any person who has a license to search for or mine minerals. Thus a grazing lease is an inferior one; when a more productive use for the land is found, it may be used for this purpose, often without compensating the pastoralist.

Leases are issued for various time periods. New South Wales and Queensland grant perpetual leases, while the other states only offer term leases for specific periods. Term leases are granted for 40 years in New South Wales; 30 years in Queensland (occasionally up to 50 years); 50 years in the Northern Territory; and 42 or 21 years in South Australia. With the exception of four which expire in 1985, all leases in Western Australia expire in 2015.[21]

It appears to be almost customary in the history of Australian arid zone land tenure to attach new conditions to a lease before it is extended or renewed, and for this reason pastoralists often become apprehensive as the expiration date of their lease approaches. Western Australia is the only state in which all leases expire on a common date. To provide adequate security, in 1963 all western Australian pastoralists were offered the opportunity to extend their leases for a further 30 years to 2015. All but four pastoralists accepted this offer on the understanding that it will be repeated in 1995. The four which did not accept the offer preferred to remain under the old conditions of lease and risk losing their leases at the end of 1985. The old conditions gave a pastoralist much more freedom to determine his stocking rate and the Pastoral Board far fewer discretionary powers.

In the Northern Territory, pastoralists may apply for an extension between 10 and 20 years before their leases expire, and in South Australia pastoralists may apply for a new lease seven years before their current one expires. Similarly, all Queensland pastoralists may apply for a new lease during the last 10 years of the existing lease. To provide extra security, a Queensland pastoralist is also guaranteed receipt of an offer to lease at least one living area, providing he has satisfied the conditions of his previous lease.[22]

Australia has always had a fear that its land will fall into the hands of a few; to prevent this from occurring, all states with the exception of South Australia have placed upper limits on the amount of land which any person may hold (see Table 12-6). In New South Wales and Queensland the size constraints have been very restrictive, and the goal has been to settle individual families on each station. This practice is known as "closer settlement" and is in direct contrast to Western Australia which requires all stations to be able to carry at least 6000 sheep or 1200 cattle.[23] Generally, the size of stations has been regulated by controlling the amount of land which may be transferred and by the withdrawal of land from leases as they are extended or renewed.

Queensland specifically excludes companies from owning grazing selections, and New South Wales has had a policy of trying to establish single-family owned production units. The type of partnerships which may be formed are limited, and companies are restricted to certain areas of land. The Northern Territory, South Australia, and Western Australia place no restrictions on the terms under which a lease is held.

The use of a lease is usually subject to many conditions. For example, a South Australian pastoralist may be required to invest $32 per km² by the end of the 13th year of his lease; a lessee in New South Wales may not be allowed to remove timber from a lease, overstock the lease, or take other

TABLE 12-6. Lease Type with Smallest Maximum Area in Each State.

LEASE TYPE	MAXIMUM AREA
New South Wales—Western Lands Lease	2 Home Maintenance Areas
Northern Territory—Pastoral Lease	1,294,994 ha
Queensland—Grazing Selection	18,500 ha, 24,300 ha if area not greatly in excess of 1 living area
South Australia—Pastoral Lease	No constraints
Western Australia—Pastoral Lease	404,686 ha

Source: Young, M. D. *Differences between States.*

people's livestock on agistment without permission. He may also have to maintain all improvements on a lease and use steel posts for fencing. In some states, permission is required to plow leased land.

A condition of all leases is that an annual rental be paid in advance. The criteria for assessing the amount of rent to be paid vary from state to state. In all states except Queensland, rent is assessed according to a lease's carrying capacity, the inherent capacity of the land for pastoral purposes, its proximity to railway stations, and its improved value. In Queensland rent is paid in proportion to a lease's unimproved value which means that rent is not increased when a lease is developed, and hence it is argued people have a greater incentive to develop their leases. The amount of annual rent due is reassessed every 10 years in Queensland, the Northern Territory, Western Australia, and New South Wales. South Australia used to assess rent every 21 years, but it is moving toward a 7-year reassessment period. In all states it is possible for a pastoralist to request an early reassessment of a lease's rent.[24]

Closer Settlement

Queensland's lease system has been designed to achieve closer settlement.[25] Pastoral development holding leases are granted for large areas of poor quality land in need of development. These leases are usually taken up by companies, and a term in excess of 30 years may be granted if the lease is subject to very extensive developmental conditons involving an abnormally high expenditure. Once developed, a pastoral development holding is subdivided into either grazing selections or preferential pastoral holdings which are subject to a size constraint and may not be held by companies.

New South Wales has achieved closer settlement by constantly changing her land laws in an attempt to force subdivision.[26] Her policies have been remarkably inconsistent and the subject of continuous political debate. Underlying 100 years of debate about closer settlement are two fundamental concepts—New South Wales' "home maintenance area" and Queensland's "living area." Although the size of both areas is similar, by definition a living area is slightly larger than a home maintenance area.[27] At present, a home maintenance area is defined as that area of land which, when used for the purpose for which it is reasonably fitted, would be sufficient for the maintenance in average seasons and circumstances of an average family. Prior to 1949 the word "improved" rather than "fitted" was used in this definition. The actual area for any region is determined by a local land board. The size of a living area in Queensland is that area of land which, allowing for the variability of seasonal conditions, will provide a man with a means of an adequate income and enough savings to enable him to meet adverse seasonal conditions and the cost of developing and maintaining the land at a high rate of production.[28] The differences between a living area and a home maintenance area arise from the fact that average seasons and conditions are rarely experienced in the arid zone; prolonged droughts are far more common.

The use of legislation to establish a population of small arid-zone stations managed by individual pastoralists has been widely rejected by

Australian scientists.[29] Holmes earlier summed up the prevalent biological opinion when he said, "Too small an area calls for ruthless exploitation of vegetational resources and eventual abandonment of the land altogether."[30] Similarly, Payne summed up the opinion of most social scientists when he wrote, "In every aspect of land administration a margin in favour of the settler should be left for eventualities such as dry seasons and a fall in prices.... Two prosperous and contented settlers are far better than three disheartened strugglers."[31]

Closer settlement was originally introduced as a way to "unlock" and hence develop land held by wealthy squatters who did not use the land to its potential.[32] Closer settlement was given a new impetus when it was shown in New South Wales that it could be a means of providing jobs for returned servicemen from both World War I and World War II.[33] When we consider broader objectives of closer settlement and specifically look at the history of the Western Division of New South Wales, we see that closer settlement has been primarily sought by a poorly informed urban, not a rural population. Note the following transactions:

1901 The Royal Commission inquired into the depressed condition of pastoralists in arid New South Wales.

1902 The Western Lands Board was formed; one eighth of the area of all leases was withdrawn for closer settlement despite the depressed state of the pastoralists.

1930 All leases were extended to 1964 with periodic withdrawals of land until either 63 percent of a lessee's land had been withdrawn from his lease or he only had sufficient land to carry 6000 sheep.

1931 All extensions granted in 1930 were canceled.

1934 The Western Lands Board was replaced by a Commission under one man; new extensions were granted to 1959 or in perpetuity with periodic withdrawals until either 50 percent of a lessee's land was withdrawn or only one home maintenance area was left.

1942 Land which was not available for withdrawal until 1948 was made available for withdrawal immediately.

1949 Any land held by a pastoralist in excess of two home maintenance areas was made available for immediate withdrawal.

1953 Any land which was not withdrawn by 1953 was given back to the original lessee.

Throughout this period, no monetary compensation was given to lessees who, via the process of withdrawal of land for closer settlement, lost as much as half the land they thought was theirs. It was felt that an extension of a lease of the remaining land was sufficient compensation.

As a result of closer settlement in the past, today 55 percent of Queensland's sheep properties comprise less than one living area, and 68 percent of New South Wales' pastoralists lease less than one home maintenance area.[34] This has occurred despite the ability of many pastoralists to buy back land withdrawn from them.[35]

These frightening statistics contrast vividly with the attitude of the other states which have resisted pressures to try to achieve closer settlement in the arid zone. For example, the Western Australian Department of Lands and Survey recently reported,

It is probable that currently, a viable station unit in the Gascoyne, Murchison and Goldfield pastoral areas would be one, which, when fully developed, soundly managed, and under average seasonal conditions, is capable of carrying not less than 10,000 sheep and the equivalent in cattle (2,000) on not more than 2/3 of the total area, (thus allowing a 1/3 margin for deferred grazing and unforeseen eventualities).[36]

By law all Western Australian pastoral leases must be capable of carrying at least 6,000 sheep or 1,200 cattle on an area which is larger than a home maintenance area. In Western Australia the upper size limit is 404,686 ha which would carry at least 40,000 sheep. South Australia has made no attempt to regulate the size of its stations. Even without size constraints, none of its stations is too big. Most are of suitable size; for the Australian system of progressive taxation, particularly the probate tax, has subdivided most of the original pastoral empires.

One of the greatest problems of closer settlement is that pastoralists tend to take up stations which are too small to support them. To overcome this problem, Queensland introduced legislation in 1927 which gave a lessee priority over vacant land (called additional lands) adjacent to his station. By 1934, the concept was extended to all lessees in the vicinity of the vacant land. This policy has resulted in the mutilation of much good land.[37] As Payne says, "The granting of priority additional areas to increase the size of holdings of small graziers has been for many years . . . one of the most onerous and vexatious features of land administration. Very few have been satisfied."[38]

Similarly, in 1934, it was becoming apparent that some New South Wales pastoralists owned insufficient land. The government felt responsible for these people and established legislation to grant additional areas of land to people in the most need of it. Unfortunately, the amount of land which is available for such purposes is limited, and a local land board must decide which of the applicants is in the most need of additional land. This procedure has resulted in many court cases in which pastoralists vie to prove greater need than their neighbor's.[39]

Initially, Queensland only granted additional land to pastoralists who leased land which adjoined the additional land. This prevented the creation of many small, uneconomical fragments of land. Unfortunately, political pressure caused Queensland to change to the New South Wales system which grants additional land to successful applicants who live within a reasonable working distance (48 km).[40] This policy selects the arid zone's poorer managers and tries to keep them viable. In many cases, it would be more efficient to auction land and speed up the removal of the small inefficient pastoralist.

Land Management

Arid lands can be managed in three main ways—by persuasion, by manipulation, and by regulation. With persuasion, one informs pastoralists and influences the management strategies that they adopt. This method has been very unsuccessful in Australia, largely because there is little technical information to extend to pastoralists. Manipulation, on the other hand, attempts to influence the resource base and the social and economic environment within which the pastoralist works. The arid zone in Australia, particularly its northern half, has been the scene of a great deal of political controversy. Politicians continually wish to develop it but fail to realize that it has little potential.[41] In attempts to attract investment in the area, a number of tax concessions have been instituted. For example, a special tax deduction known as a zone allowance is available over most of arid Australia. The total cost of this scheme to the Australian taxpayer is approximately $21 million annually.[42] During the period 1937 to 1952, in an effort to encourage people to live in the Northern Territory, the government declared income derived by individuals from cattle raising in the Northern Territory was not subject to income tax.[43] The scheme specifically excluded companies, and a successful appeal to the High Court which argued that companies were residents resulted in its being abolished.

In some areas, the government spends far more money in the arid zone than it collects as rent. This is particularly apparent in the Northern Territory where in 1967 the Australian federal government collected $139,802 in rental from pastoral leases, but spent $859,998 on water supply and road and stock route maintenance, and $499,680 on beef roads—almost ten times the amount it collected.[44] No information is available for other areas of the arid zone.

Both the federal and state governments have developed policies which assist pastoralists during droughts. For example, in New South Wales, the government will pay 50 percent of the cost of transporting breeding livestock from an official drought area; in Western Australia the subsidy is only paid for livestock which are removed from the arid zone for at least 12 months after a drought has ended. All other states subsidize the return of breeding livestock immediately after a drought breaks. Western Australia's policy is designed to allow time for the land resource to recover. In some droughts, pastoralists have been paid to shoot and bury drought stricken livestock. Carry-on loans at concessional interest rates are also provided to pastoralists during these periods.

Similarly, land administrators supply rent concessions and often defer rent during a drought. Pastoralists may now average their incomes for taxation purposes and since 1969 have been able to purchase drought bonds to reduce their taxable income. In a year when a pastoralist receives a high taxable income, he may buy up to $50,000 of drought bonds and reduce his taxable income by that amount. In drought years these bonds may be redeemed. Little, if any, tax is paid when they are cashed because income is usually negative in a drought year.

In 1976 this scheme was extended to cover all income fluctuations. Now, by purchasing Income Equalization Deposits, pastoralists may reduce the average income on which they are taxed. Frequently, the viability of stations has been threatened by very high debt levels, and the government has sought to reconstruct stations considered good long-term prospects.[45] Surprisingly, the majority of those applicants who were rejected as nonviable have remained on their stations.[46]

The state governments—and to a lesser extent the federal government—manipulate arid-zone land use by maintaining the region's infrastructure, especially the thousands of km of stock routes and beef roads which are used to take livestock to market. In the past, livestock were walked along stock routes, with watering points and holding yards every 16 km, to the nearest railhead and then by train to market. Recently, a number of roads in the arid zone have been upgraded to allow livestock to be trucked directly to market. These roads are replacing stock routes, and today most cattle are brought to market by big trucks (road trains) which pull several trailers.[47] A road tax is charged for all livestock which use beef roads, and a permit is required to walk livestock along a stock route. The stock must walk a given distance every day (cattle—16 km, sheep—10 km).

All the states also regulate land use and enforce the wise development of their arid zones by the use of conditions attached to leases. For example, in New South Wales a lessee may be required to carefully preserve all timber, scrub, and vegetative cover on leased land: (a) between the banks of and within strips at least one chain (20.1 m) wide along any watercourse; (b) within strips at least one and a half chains wide of the center line of any depression, the sides of which have slopes in excess of 14°; (c) where the slopes are steeper than 18°; and (d) within strips not less than three chains wide along the tops of any ranges and main ridges.

In other states, permission is required to plow leased land, and all leases contain conditions which prohibit overstocking. In all states, the penalty for breach of these conditions is forfeiture of the lease. Forfeiture of a lease, in other than exceptionally severe breaches of conditions, tends to destroy the confidence of the pastoral industry and to threaten the security of tenure of all other leases. For this reason, very few leases have been forfeited, although the threat of such action has been used successfully to regulate land use.

Land administrators have the power to regulate the intensity of grazing on any area of land, and in 1972 a survey of the Gascoyne River Catchment in Western Australia recommended a 43 percent reduction in the number of sheep in the catchment.[48] Lessees were required to fence certain areas and remove all stock from others. A political storm followed attempts to achieve this reduction, for pastoralists believe they should be involved in making such decisions.[49] Australia has yet to find a truly successful way to prevent overstocking as soon as or before it occurs. One method tried by the South Australian Pastoral Board has been the granting of a reduction in rent "... to a pastoral lessee who was prepared to reduce the number of stock on the area controlled by him, or to one who would leave certain areas unstocked for a stated period."[50] In an attempt to prevent a rapid buildup of stock, permission to agist on a lease is required in all states except Queensland where permission is only required to agist for longer than six months.

Leasehold and Freehold Systems

The land in Australia on which common grazing is allowed is restricted to stock routes and common lands which surround some towns. Most of these areas have been overgrazed, supporting the experience of most arid countries that commonly owned grazing rights lead to overstocking. The Australian leasehold and freehold systems of land appropriation grant exclusive grazing rights to pastoralists, and it is believed by most scientists that these methods of land use encourage conservative management, particularly the conservation of forage resources for future drought periods.

Perhaps the greatest advantage of a leasehold system is that it enables the government to have a different policy for each station. Furthermore, when economic and social conditions change, the government can grant individual as well as collective assistance to pastoralists. Individual assistance is usually granted by waiving a rent payment or by deferring its payment for 12 months.

The main disadvantage of some forms of leasehold tenure is that the pastoralist may not receive a new lease when the term of his lease expires; thus, in some states the continuous occupation of an area of land is not guaranteed. In fact, only two of the five arid zone states of Australia—New South Wales and Queensland—are prepared to guarantee an individual pastoralist the continuous occupation of an area of land. New South Wales achieves this by granting a pastoralist a perpetual lease of up to two home maintenance areas of land, and Queensland grants an individual the right to lease at least one living area. The other states usually inform a lessee of his rights to renewal well before his lease expires. Western Australia usually extends all its leases well before they expire and guarantees to inform lessees if theirs will be extended 18 years before expiration. The Northern Territory allows a lessee to apply for a new lease not less than 10 years or more than 30 years before it expires, and South Australia undertakes to inform a lessee if his lease will be renewed in the seventh year before expiration. Before a term lease is extended or a new lease is granted, a lessee's past performance is evaluated. This process may make a term lessee a better manager than a perpetual lessee whose performance is never formally evaluated.

In Queensland, leasehold tenure is also used to ensure the development of land. Big companies are encouraged to take out long-term leases on undeveloped land with the understanding that they develop this land; at the end of that lease period, most of this land is withdrawn from the company. Queensland believes that it is the role of companies to develop arid land, to facilitate closer settlement. Once the land is developed, individual pastoralists are encouraged to take out secure grazing selection leases; since 1958 they have also been encouraged to convert grazing selection leases to freehold land. This gives maximum security of tenure to pastoralists and removes the ability of the Department of Lands to control land use through leasehold conditions.[51]

Good Land Management

The late Sir William Payne, who probably was Queensland's most experienced land administrator, was commissioned to advise the government on land administration before he retired. He made a number of very valuable points in his final report. They were as follows:

- Land differs in its potential; so do the people needed to manage it. There is room for the big man and the small man.[52]
- Since big wealth can be taxed out, there is no need to legislate it out. Be generous to the developer. His inputs benefit the nation more than they do him.[53]

- "Don't slavishly follow precedent. New precedents are waiting to be born."[54]
- "Whilst we must still be regardful of the future, we must resolve not to spoil the lives of this generation because of a desire to serve the next."[55]
- "... Public opinion is a shockingly poor guide in land administration. Nearly all the mistakes in land administration resulting from undue subdivisions... [have] been brought about by the force of public opinion."[56]
- "Land laws are close to the lives of the people. They should be expressed simply and clearly so that anyone who reads them may understand them."[57]

Conclusion

Australia has learned the hard way that it is essential, above all else, to provide three things: maximum security of tenure, generously adequate living areas, and a sympathetic land administration.[58] In the past under political pressure, the government has often violated leasehold contracts for the supposed benefit of the nation. In retrospect, we have destroyed many people and, worse still, forced them to degrade a great deal of land as they fight to keep above the pressures placed upon them. Australia has learned that if one puts pressure on people, they, in turn, put pressure on the land.

Notes

1. R. A. Perry, "The Evaluation and Exploitation of Semi-Arid Lands: Australian Experience," in *Philosophical Transactions of the Royal Society,* series B, 278 (1977), pp. 493–505.
2. D. N. Parkes, "Urbanism and Aridity—Some Geographical Perspectives from an Urban Viewpoint," in *Arid Shrublands–Proceedings of the Third Workshop of the United States/Australia Rangelands Panel,* ed. D. N. Hyder (Denver, Colorado: Society for Range Management, 1973), pp. 135–143.
3. Bureau of Agricultural Economics, "National Economic Aspects of Arid Zone Use," paper presented to Australian Arid Zone Research Conference, Kalgoorlie, July 1976, pp. 2 (a)–14.
4. Commonwealth Bureau of Statistics, *Population and Dwellings in Local Government Areas and Urban Centres, Australia,* bulletin 6, part 9, ref. No. 2.88.9 (Canberra: Commonwealth Bureau of Statistics, 1974), pp. 19–47. Large towns contain more than 1000 people.
5. N. Cain, "Companies and Squatting in the Western Division of New South Wales, 1896–1905," in *The Simple Fleece: Studies in the Australian Wool Industry,* ed. Alan Barnard (Melbourne: Melbourne University Press, 1962), pp. 435–456.
6. G. B. Brown and O. B. Williams, "Geographical Distribution of Sheep in Australia," *Journal of the Australian Institute of Agricultural Science* **36**, no. 3 (1970), 182–198; F. H. Bauer, "Sheep Raising in Northern Australia: A Historical Review," in *The Simple Fleece,* pp. 57–474.
7. F. G. G. Rose, "The Pastoral Industry in the Northern Territory during the Period of Commonwealth Administration 1911–1953," *Historical Studies in Australia and New Zealand* **6**, no. 22 (1954), 150–172.
8. J. R. Anderson, "Spatial Diversification of High Risk Sheep Farms," in *Systems Analysis*

in Agricultural Management, ed. J. B. Dent and J. R. Anderson (Sidney: John Wiley & Sons, 1971), pp. 242–248.

9. *Report of the Soil Conservation Committee* (Adelaide: Government Printer, 1938), p. 10; *Report of the Royal Commission Appointed to Inquire into and Report on the Financial and Economic Position of the Pastoral Industry in the Leasehold Areas in Western Australia* (Perth: Government Printer, 1940), p. 29.

10. D. W. Meinig, *On the Margins of the Good Earth: The South Australian Wheat Frontier 1869–1884* (Adelaide: Rigby Ltd., 1962), pp. 78–92.

11. R. W. Condon, "Report for the Chairman of the Wild Dog Destruction Board: For the Year Ended 31st December, 1974," in *Annual Report of the Western Lands Commission for the Year Ended 1975* (Sidney: Department of Lands, 1976), pp. 27–30; "Vermin-Proof Fences," in *Australian Encyclopaedia* (Sydney: Grolier, 1958), IV, 34–36; B. V. Fennessy, "Competitors with Sheep: Mammal and Bird Pests of the Sheep Industry," in *The Simple Fleece,* pp. 221–240; S. J. O. Whitehouse, personal communication, 1978.

12. S. H. Roberts, *History of Australian Land Settlement (1788–1920)* (Melbourne: Macmillan, 1924), pp. 223–292. Fee simple is a form of land title which grants its owner and his heirs and successors the right to lawfully use an area of land forever.

13. K. O. Cambell, "Land Policy," in *Agriculture in the Australian Economy,* ed. D.B. Williams (Sydney: Sydney University Press, 1967), pp. 173–175.

14. Queensland, Department of Lands, *Annual Report of the Land Administration Commission 1975–1976),* (Brisbane: Government Printer, 1976), p. 5.

15. A. C. C. Allen, "Pioneer Settlement in the Channel Country of Western Queensland," Ph.D. dissertation, University of New England, Armidale, 1968, pp. 132–169; idem. "Marginal Settlement—A Case Study of the Channel Country of Southwest Queensland," *Australian Geographical Studies* **6**, no. 1 (1968), 1–23; K. R. Bowes, *Land Settlement in South Australia 1857–1890* (Adelaide: Libraries Board of South Australia, 1968), pp. 172–204; Ross Duncan, *The Northern Territory Pastoral Industry 1863–1910* (Melbourne: Melbourne University Press, 1967); and F. H. Bauer, *Historical Geography of White Settlement in Part of Northern Australia: Part 2. The Katherine Darwin Region,* CSIRO Division of Land Research and Regional Survey, report No. 64 (1) (Canberra, 1964), pp. 104–118.

16. Roberts, *History,* pp. 155–292.

17. *Royal Commission to Inquire into the Condition of the Crown Tenants [of the] Western Division of New South Wales* (Sydney: Government Printer, 1901), pp. xxiv–xxv.

18. Jim Vickery, "Guest Editorial," *The Australian Rangeland Journal,* **1**, no. 1 (1976), 5–6.

19. R. L. Heathcote, "Land Tenure Systems: Past and Present," in *Arid Lands of Australia,* ed. R. O. Slatyer and R. A. Perry (Canberra: Australian National University Press, 1969), p. 204.

20. J. A. Sinden and O. T. Kingma, "Land Tenure in the Cypress Pine Areas of North-Western New South Wales," *Australian Journal of Agricultural Economics,* **16**, no. 1 (1972), 16.

21. M. D. Young, *Differences between States in Arid Land Administration,* Land Resources Management Series, no. 4 (Melbourne: CSIRO, 1979).

22. Ibid.

23. Ibid.

24. Ibid.

25. W. L. Payne, *Report on Progressive Land Settlement in Queensland by the Land Settlement Advisory Commission* (Brisbane: Government Printer, 1959), pp. 16–20.

26. C. J. King, *An Outline of Closer Settlement in New South Wales: Part I. The Sequence of the Land Laws* (Sydney: Department of Agriculture, 1957), pp. 163–186.

27. *Royal Commission on Pastoral Lands Settlement (Queensland)* (Brisbane: Government Printer, 1951, p. 25.

28. M. D. Young and A. K. Little, "Summaries of Sections of the Land Acts of New South Wales (Western Division), Northern Territory, South Australia, Queensland and Western Australia," in *Differences between States in Arid Land Administration,* Land Resources Management Series, No. 4, ed. M. D. Young, (Melbourne: CSIRO, 1979).

29. J. N. Lewis, "Is the Concept of the Home Maintenance Area Outmoded?" *Australian Journal of Agricultural Economics,* **7**, no. 2 (1963), 97–106; G. N. Gregory et al, *The Land Market in Rural Recession,* Wool Adjustment Summary Report no. 6 (Armidale:

University of New England, 1975), pp. 12–15, 18–20; Tom Connors, "Closer Settlement Schemes," *The Australian Quarterly*, **42**, no. 1 (1970), 72–85; "Closer Settlement in the 1960's: Report of a Study Group," *Journal of the Australian Institute of Agricultural Science*, **28**, no. 3 (1962), 206–210; B. J. Johnston, "A Simulation Approach to Studying the Economics of Amalgamation in the Arid Pastoral Zone of New South Wales," *University of New England Farm Management Bulletin*, no. 18 (1973), 206–216.

30. M. Holmes, *The Erosion-Pastoral Problem of the Western Division of New South Wales*. University of Sydney Publication in Georgraphy, no. 2 (Sydney, 1938), p. 12.

31. Payne, pp. 48–49.

32. S. H. Roberts, *The Squatting Age in Australia 1835–1847* (Melbourne: Melbourne University Press, 1935), pp. 214–280.

33. Connors, pp. 76–79.

34. W. F. Y. Mawson et al., "Current Land Use," in *Western Arid Region Land Use Study*, *Part I*, Division of Land Utilization, Queensland Department of Primary Industries, technical bulletin no. 12 (Brisbane, 1974), p. 89; R. W. Condon, "Rangeland Science and Land Administration," paper delivered to the Australian Rangeland Society, Broken Hill, July 8, 1977, p. 4.

35. R. L. Heathcote, "Changes in Pastoral Land Tenure and Ownership: An Example from the Western Division of New South Wales," *Australian Geographical Studies*, **3**, no. 1 (1965), 13.

36. "The Legal Position of the Lessee in Respect of His Obligations Under Pastoral Lease," in O. B. Williams et al. *Gascoyne Case Study* (Canberra: Department of Environment, Housing, and Community Development, 1977), appendix 1, p. 5.

37. *Royal Commission on Pastoral Lands Settlement (Queensland)*, p. 17.

38. Payne, p. 61.

39. A. G. Lang, *Crown Land in New South Wales* (Sydney: Butterworths, 1973), pp. 472–474.

40. Payne, p. 61.

41. B. R. Davidson, *The Northern Myth: A Study of the Physical and Economic Limits to Agricultural and Pastoral Development in Tropical Australia*, 2nd ed. (Melbourne: Melbourne University Press, 1966), pp. 1–10.

42. H. C. Coombs, *Review of the Continuing Expenditure Policies of the Previous Government* (Canberra: Australian Government Publishing Service, 1973), p. 69.

43. J. H. Kelly, *Beef in Northern Australia* (Canberra: Australian National University Press, 1971), pp. 43–44.

44. Ibid, p. 43.

45. C. B. Johnson and G. M. White, "Current Adjustment Problems in the Australian Beef Industry," *Quarterly Review of Agricultural Economics*, **30**, no. 1 (1977), 47–60.

46. Bureau of Agricultural Economics, *Report on a Survey of Rejected Debt Reconstruction Applicants* (Canberra: Australian Government Publishing Service, 1975), p. 3.

47. Bureau of Agricultural Economics, *Road Transport of Beef Cattle in Queensland*, Beef Research Report no. 1 (Canberra, 1965), pp. 5–11.

48. D. G. Wilcox and E. A. McKinnon, *A Report on the Condition of the Gascoyne Catchment* (Perth: Western Australian Department of Agriculture, 1972, p. 1.1.

49. O. B. Williams, H. Suijendorp, and D. G. Wilcox, "Gascoyne Case Study," paper presented at the United Nations Conference on Desertification, Nairobi, August 1977, pp. 1–4.

50. *Report of the Soil Conservation Committee* (Adelaide: Government Printer, 1938), p. 13.

51. Lands Committee of the Australian Country Party, *Submission on Land Policy and Administration and Other Relevant Matters in Queensland* (Queensland: Australian Country Party, 1968), pp. 1–4, 73–74.

52. Payne, p. 4.

53. Ibid, p. 5.

54. Ibid, p. 8.

55. Ibid, p. 9.

56. Ibid, p. 19.

57. Ibid, pp. 48–49.

58. Ibid, p. 63.

Suggested Readings

Cambell, K. O. Land policy. In *Agriculture in the Australian Economy.* Ed. D. B. Williams. Sydney: Sydney University Press, 1967.

Davidson, B. R. *The Northern Myth: A Study of the Physical and Economic Limits to Agricultural and Pastoral Development in Tropical Australia.* 2nd ed. Melbourne: Melbourne University Press, 1966.

Heathcote, R. L. Changes in pastoral land tenure and ownership: An example from the Western Division of New South Wales. *Australian Geographical Studies, 3,* no. 1 (1965), 1–16.

————. Land tenure systems: Past and present. In *Arid Lands of Australia.* Ed. R. O. Slatyer and R. A. Perry. Canberra: Australian National University Press, 1969.

————. The evolution of Australian pastoral land tenures: An example of challenge and response in resource development. In *Frontier Settlement.* Ed. R. G. Ironside et al. Edmonton: University of Alberta, 1974.

King, C. J. *An Outline of Closer Settlement in New South Wales: Part 1. The Sequence of the Land Laws.* Sydney: Department of Agriculture, 1957.

Lewis, J. N. Is the concept of the home maintenance area outmoded? *Australian Journal of Agricultural Economics, 7,* no. 2 (1963), 97–106.

Meinig, D. W. *On the Margins of the Good Earth: The South Australian Wheat Frontier 1869–1884.* Adelaide: Rigby Ltd., 1962.

Payne, W. L. *Report on Progressive Land Settlement in Queensland by the Land Settlement Advisory Commission.* Brisbane: Government Printer, 1959.

Royal Commission to Inquire into the Condition of the Crown Tenants of the Western Division of New South Wales. Sydney: Government Printer, 1901.

13
Air Quality Trends and Their Application to Planning in Tucson, Arizona*

William K. Hartmann

In earlier decades, Tucson, Arizona, was known for its unusually clean atmosphere, recommended by doctors to patients with respiratory problems. In the late 1960s, as environmental concerns became widespread, controversy erupted in the Tucson news media about the presence and effects of air pollution. Many people spoke of haze or smog, but there were few quantitative data. The first measures of most Tucson pollutants came from a study by Quentin Mees in 1960, followed by first measurements from the Pima County Air Pollution Control District in 1966.[1] In 1967, University of Arizona meteorologists C. R. Green and L. J. Battan found that increasing haze in Tucson correlated with population growth.[2] By about 1969, this author found a stronger increase in haze from 1957 onward and showed that the haze and the sulfur oxide content in Tucson decreased dramatically during a copper strike in 1967–68 when smelters were shut down.[3] This confirmed that smelter emissions were a component of Tucson pollution and smog.

Controversies Over Pollution

To illustrate the past level of controversy, publication of those results elicited comments from a local meteorologist (including comments in news media) who stated that there was virtually no pollution in Tucson and that it was virtually impossible for smelter pollution to get across the mountains into Tucson. This controversy falsely led some of the public to believe that there was only a local source of the pollution in Tucson. Confusion on this point has persisted due mostly to the wording of press reports. For example, a 13-month study by atmospheric chemist Jarvis

*Major portions of this chapter are based on the author's report issued by the Planetary Science Institute to the City of Tucson Department of Planning as part of an effort to provide updated technical information for the development of a comprehensive plan for eastern Pima County. Figures in this chapter are derived from figures used in that report and are used here with permission of the Planetary Science Institute in addition to other permissions granted to the author. I would like to thank the following for discussions and assistance in preparing this report: members of the Pima County Health Department Air Quality Control office, the Pima County Air Pollution Advisory Council, and especially the following members of these and other institutions: Richard Bloomingdale (PCHD); Roger Caldwell (PCAPAC, UA); Clark Chapman (PSI); Donald Conway (PCHD); Donald Davis (PSI); C. Lee Fox (PCHD); Gayle Hartmann; Harry Hayes (Tucson Clinic); Michael Lebowitz (PCAPAC, UA); Jarvis Moyers (UA); Joanne Prenn (PSI); Michael Price (PSI); Allen Solomon (UA); Harry Thompson (UA); and John Valerius (PCHD) [PSI = Planetary Science Institute; UA = University of Arizona].

Moyers showed that 60 percent by mass of the airborne *particles* (distinct from gaseous pollutants) were composed of local dust and the other 40 percent was composed of auto-related materials, combustion products, and other nonsoil matter.[4] This study was headlined on the *Citizen's* front page (June 9, 1975): AIR POLLUTION: WE DID IT with subheading, DUST GETS BLAME. Of course, the study dealt not with all air pollution, but only with particulates. Such reporting gives the false impression that a single source can be identified as responsible for all bad effects (at all times).

This misconception is especially misleading when relating air pollution to health. One person's sensitivity to auto emissions, for example, might be surpassed by another person's reaction to a certain pollen. Different individual pollutants actually exceed critical Federal standards on different days, as shown by Pima County Health Department data. Thus, it is dangerous for elected officials or the public mistakenly to seek the "single agent" causing air pollution.

These kinds of misperceptions, resulting from lack of scientific data and poor public reporting of data, made it difficult in the late 1960s and in the 1970s to carry out adequate planning to react to deteriorating urban air quality. Nonetheless, air pollution data were reviewed in a 1971 report by the Tucson Advisory Committee on Air Pollution (TACAP) a group appointed by the mayor and city council. Major sources of pollution in Tucson were listed in that report as motor vehicle emissions, dust, and smelter emissions; and it was found that Tucson would have difficulty achieving federal and state health standards for particulates (dust). This report criticized lack of data, news media reports of unverified opinions, and misleading advertising from polluting industry.[5]

My own report in 1972 showed that a surge of visible pollution occurred during rush hour traffic in Tucson and was absent on weekends and holidays.[6] Such evidence demonstrates the close relation of traffic patterns to health and economic effects since the traffic-related pollution may cause local concentrations of hazardous materials and since the visible haze (as well as traffic congestion) is damaging to the tourist industry.

The flurry of public concern about pollution about 1969 to 1972 led to increased efforts to identify and monitor different types of pollutants in different locations. Among such efforts are the work of Moyers' group (University of Arizona) and an abundance of data being collected by the Pima County Health Department at various locations both inside and outside the city.[7]

The major problem then became that, while the data were being routinely gathered, there were inadequate funds and staff for analysis; in addition, the results were not efficiently channeled to governmental decision-making bodies where they should influence policies in order to reduce future pollution. This problem was compounded by the fact that urban growth in the southwestern United States "Sun Belt," and in Tucson in particular, had skyrocketed so that the city spread out of the city limits into the surrounding county. The result was a mixed jurisdiction of city and county governments, both of which dealt with problems of air pollution, water depletion, land use, etc. A further difficulty was the clash between exponents of a traditional, business-oriented progrowth philosophy and exponents of a slow-growth philosophy or a deflected-growth philosophy. which would try to deflect growth from the Tucson urban center to outlying smaller communities.

One step toward solving these problems was the creation of a comprehensive planning process (CPP) which attempted to construct a joint city-county long-term plan for growth, zoning, air quality control, etc. Another step was the reorganization (in summer 1975) of a Pima County Air Pollution Advisory Council, appointed by the board of supervisors. In addition, my preparation of much of the data presented in this chapter while acting as a consultant to the city planning department proved helpful at this point. These data became part of the CCP document dealing with air pollution.

At the end of this chapter, I will return to the fate and present status of these attempts to incorporate air pollution as a criterion in a large scale plan to deal with growth in Tucson.

Pollution and Public Health

In recent decades, in the United States in general and in Tucson in particular, consideration of air pollution conditions in city planning policy has been hampered because "pollution" has been regarded to some degree as a subjective quality. Even when objective measures of small but increasing amounts of smog were available, haze was considered an "aesthetic" problem. Indeed, government boards for legal advice in Tucson stated that aesthetic criteria (e.g., smog) could not legally be factored into planning decisions which were to be based on objective criteria such as sewer installation, water availability, etc.

However, by the mid-1970s, three developments changed this attitude. First, early pollution studies showed conclusive evidence that in certain cities, episodes of catastrophically high air pollution caused major surges in death rate. Second, ongoing research appears to be establishing more and more clearly that low levels of pollutants have less obvious but damaging long-term effects on health. For example, a cover story in *Newsweek* at that time summarized such research with a headline on cancer which claimed it to be a man-made disease and indicated that the rising incidence of cancer correlates with increasing artificial contaminants in air, food, and water. Third, the federal and state governments have recognized these facts by establishing standards above which pollutant concentrations should not rise. These three developments indicate that objective data on air pollution trends should be directly used to support planning policy because air pollution affects community health. In fact, 1979 Environmental Protection Agency (EPA) regulations required such policy.

Therefore, if rising levels of a pollutant are detected in Tucson, planners should consider the costs and benefits of policies that would inhibit the rise or reverse it. Data could be used to establish legal precedent for this assumption since pollutants discussed in the report, such as pollens and SO_2, involve known health hazards.

Of course, a stronger case could be made if we had complete data on the exact effects of the various Tucson pollutants on the population of Tucson. Although studies of that type are under way, data are not yet complete. Dr. Michael Lebowitz at the University of Arizona Medical Center, for example, has compiled data on incidence of various respiratory illnesses in the Tucson population. He has found that the incidence of respiratory diseases in this population is significantly higher than in the national population (by factors of 1.2 to 2 or more for typical symptoms and population subgroups).[8] Dr. Lebowitz has also shown that

> Migration to the area specifically for health reasons explained part of the high prevalence of disease found in the study. But natives still had higher rates of disease than those found generally in the United States, especially for asthma and allergic rhinitis [commonly called hay fever].[9]

More specifically, Dr. Lebowitz has found that of Anglo citizens in Tucson in a 1971-1972 study, 43 percent of adults and 30 percent of children (under 15) reported hay fever or allergy problems. Of the same group, 36 percent of adults and 20 percent of children had chest problems; about 13 percent of males over 45 and 4 percent of females over 45 had emphysema and were under medical care; and about 7 percent of men and women over 45 had asthma and were under medical care.[10] (No data are available for other ethnic groups.) The unusually high incidence of respiratory illness in Tucson emphasizes the need for policies to prevent deterioration of air quality in this city. Yet, as this chapter will show, some types of pollutants are rapidly increasing. No policies to restrict increase of pollutants such as pollen were adopted by 1979.

Many physicians believe that incoming citizens are likely to develop sensitivity to pollutants after arriving in an area where the pollutants are common. There is direct evidence of this in the case of some pollens (see Figure 13-1). This figure shows allergic reactions to ragweed pollens (in students previously unexposed to ragweed) two to three years *after* their arrival in a community with pollen. Dr. Lebowitz's statistics show maximum allergic incidence among people in their 30s and 40s, but his search for firm evidence for onset of allergies after arrival in Tucson is

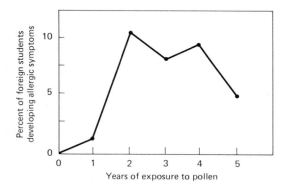

FIG. 13-1. Results of study showing that many foreign students (generally from areas without ragweed pollen) develop allergic reactions to ragweed pollen in the U.S. During the second to fifth pollen seasons, allergies developed in arrivals from other regions ten times as often as among natives; at the end of five years' residence, approximately 1/3 of the foreign students had developed allergies. Redrawn by the author from data in C. J. Maternowski and K. P. Matthews, "The Prevalence of Ragweed Pollinosis in Foreign and Native Students at a Midwestern University and Its Implementations Concerning Methods for Determining the Inheritance of Atopy," *Journal of Allergy and Clinical Immunology* **33** (1962), 130–140.

inconclusive.[11] If evidence of this effect were to be found in Tucson, it could strengthen governmental control for limiting the offending pollutants.

One significant finding published by Dr. Lebowitz is that children exercising in the smelter town of San Manuel showed a more rapid decline in performance than a control group of children in Tucson when exposed to combinations of high pollution and temperature. Lebowitz concluded:

> Exercise alone, in the absence of air pollution and high temperatures did not influence lung function. Exposures to pollutants of either oxidant or reducing type and to high temperatures produced postexercise decreases in forced vital capacity and 1-second forced expiratory volume [measures of lung function] in children and adolescents.[12]

The study is an example of direct damaging effects of pollutants in the Tucson area, although further analyses are needed to clarify the specific roles of specific Tucson pollutants.

Dr. M. D. Lebowitz and Dr. Benjamin Burrows, of the University of Arizona Medical Center, have summarized the available information as follows:

> Recent laboratory investigations indicate that air pollutants are capable of: 1) increasing susceptibility to respiratory infections; 2) inducing the abnormalities of chronic bronchitis; 3) setting the stage for development of pulmonary emphysema; and 4) aggravating the physiological changes of patients with chronic respiratory diseases. Numerous epidemiological studies have confirmed that these adverse effects do occur in the real life situation. Available data suggest that the severity of the effects is related to the level of air pollution. There is, as yet, no conclusive evidence that a safe "threshold level" exists.[13]

In light of all these findings, we can reach some general conclusions. We know there is a negative health effect if pollution levels are great enough, and we suspect that subtle negative effects exist even when levels of certain pollutants are low.

Also it is clear that the planning process should react to reduce pollutants whenever existing health standards are exceeded by pollutants or whenever cumulative annual data show strongly increasing trends in pollutant concentration. Let us now examine each important pollutant further.

POLLENS

Since pollens have familiar health effects but are rarely considered as air pollution, they will be discussed first. Figure 13-2 shows the pollen calendar for Tucson. According to H. C. Thompson, M. D., of the Pima County Health Department, Bermuda grass pollens are the major irritant of this type; and effects suffered by an allergic Tucsonan are related to the proximity of pollen sources to his/her immediate neighborhood (e.g., his/her yard or a neighbor's yard) since the pollens are not uniformly distributed and mixed by the wind. Mulberry pollens are perhaps the second-ranking irritant.[14]

Dr. Allen M. Solomon (Department of Geosciences, U.A.) has kindly provided updated information on pollen statistics in Tucson, permitting a study of trends from 1943 to 1975. Figure 13-3, derived from these data,

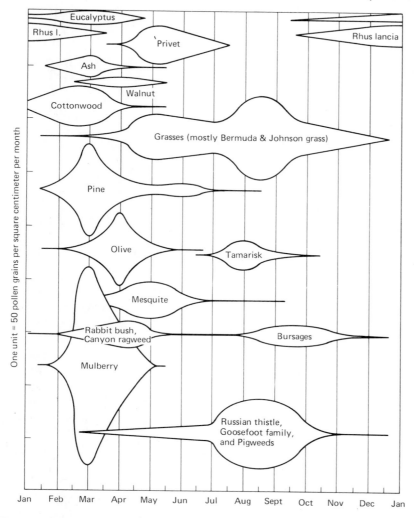

FIG. 13-2. Tucson, Arizona, pollen calendar showing strong bursts of pollen in late March and August. Among worst offenders are non-native plants such as mulberries and Bermuda grass. After chart distributed by the Tucson Clinic.

shows a comparison between imported and native plant pollens. The most striking feature of the graph is that pollens from imported plants have increased by a factor of nearly 100 since the 1940s! The cause is obvious to Tucson residents: due to the strong influx of newcomers in the 1950s desirous of creating nondesert styles of landscaping and due to an abundance of cheap water and time for yard care, nurserymen found a booming business in selling imported shade trees and plants. In addition, due to increased cultivation by increasing numbers of residents, native plant pollens have increased by a factor of two in the same period. Thus, a resident who moved here in the 1950s because of a respiratory sensitivity to certain types of pollen may have had the healthful aspects of his/her Tucson home completely destroyed, depending on his/her location in the city.

Other aspects of Figure 13-3 are of interest. For example, the crossover from local pollen dominance to foreign pollen dominance, occurring in the mid-1950s provides an objective measure of the period when the growing population began to suffer from the significant detrimental en-

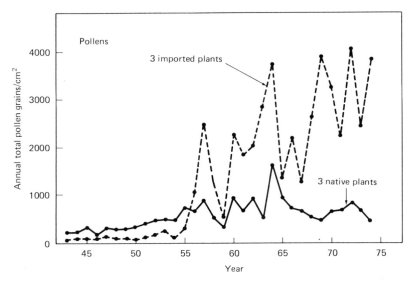

FIG. 13-3. Comparison of native and imported plant pollens as monitored in urban Tucson. "Imported plants" represent the sum of pollens of mulberry, olive, and spring pines; "native plants" represent cottonwood, ash, and mesquite. Derived from original data supplied by Tucson Clinic.

vironmental impact. Figure 13-3 also shows that annual fluctuations of pollen levels are large; some years are bad and some relatively good. (Seasonal variations are also well known; a cottonwood-mulberry, etc., surge comes in March and a Bermuda grass, etc., surge comes in September.)

Figures 13-4 and 13-5 show a technique for future projections, applied to the pollen data. The amounts of pollutants are plotted versus population with the dates for these populations at the top. Past and future projections are based on the CPP document. Figure 13-4 shows the virtual explosion of imported plant pollen at about the time the city's population reached 150,000. Extrapolations into the future involve a range from bad years to good years as shown by the three dashed lines. For example, a good year in the 1990s might be better than a bad year in the 1970s. Figure 13-5 shows a similar pattern.

At present, there are no federal or health standards for pollen pollutants; thus Figures 13-4 and 13-5 cannot be used to demonstrate specific violations of health safety. We can note that the situation is worsening perceptibly every few years.

Efforts to discourage widespread landscaping with pollen-producing non-native plants and grasses would benefit Tucsonans' health and would help to conserve water. This could be done, for example, by establishing areas zoned only for native vegetation or by banning new plantings of offending plants, such as Bermuda grass or mulberry trees. A public awareness campaign sponsored by city government might be in order.

SULFUR PRODUCTS

Sulfur products have a complicated chemistry in the atmosphere. In southern Arizona they are generally related to copper smelter activity, but they can also result from burning of high-sulfur fuel by Tucson Gas and Electric

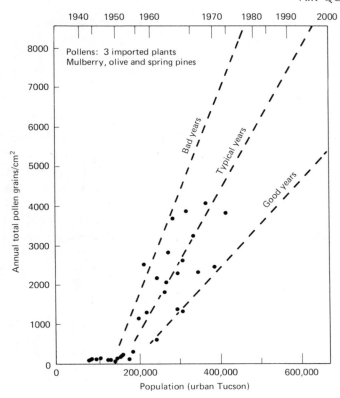

FIG. 13-4. Pollens from non-native plants plotted vs. population levels, showing a strong increase began in the 1950s; there is no decrease in sight. Derived from original data supplied by Tucson Clinic.

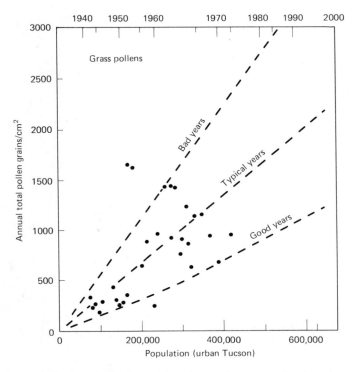

FIG. 13-5. Grass pollens (mostly Bermuda plus native grasses) plotted vs. population. Derived from original data supplied by Tucson Clinic.

(The Tucson utility, later renamed Tucson Electric Power). A major smelter emission product, SO_2, oxidizes to become SO_3. Depending on humidity, much SO_3 may eventually form H_2SO_4 (sulfuric acid) droplets, a possible contributor to visible haze. Different detectors may be sensitive to sulfur in different forms; for example, a detector sensitive to SO_2 only would miss oxidized products.

The monitors placed by the Pima County Health Department throughout the city permit a geographical study of sulfur products. Sulfation rate monitors of the type used are sensitive to various sulfur oxides, with the results converted to, and expressed as, milligrams of SO_3/100 cm² per day. They measure 30-day average concentrations but do not indicate short-term variations.

Figure 13-6 shows a plot of raw sulfation rate data for three sites since 1971. The solid line gives monthly results for downtown Tucson. Several complications are found in using the data in this form. First, a strong geographic effect is present. Measures taken in the area of Redington Pass

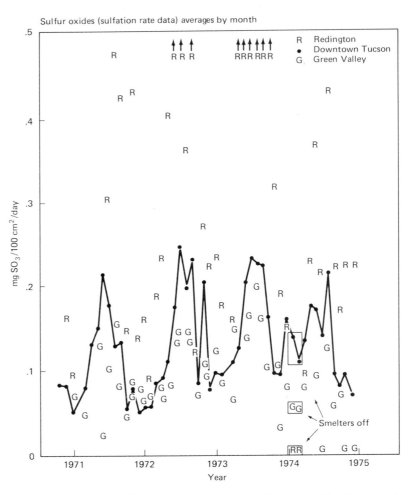

FIG. 13-6. Sulfation rate data showing concentrations of sulfur oxides in three locations. Concentrations in Redington Pass are virtually always highest; Tucson (solid curve) is intermediate; Green Valley is lowest. Boxes bracket 1 month long copper strike, 15 July to 15 August, 1974; smelter off-period equals ½ of each data point in box. Data courtesy Pima County Health Department.

(points marked "R"), where smelter smoke can sometimes be seen drifting into Tucson, have the highest concentrations. Measures in and around Tucson are lower. The lowest concentrations among measured areas were almost always in Green Valley (points marked "G"), the site farthest from a copper smelter. Figure 13-7 shows the geographical effect more clearly: available measures averaged during 1972 show Redington Pass as the most polluted, the village of Catalina (northwest of Catalina Mountains, on Oracle Road) as the second most polluted, sites within urban Tucson as less polluted, and Green Valley as the area least polluted with sulfur emissions. This sequence of sites indicates that pollution generally decreases with distance from smelters. Measurements within smelter communities would be of interest.

A second complication shown in Figure 13-6 is a strong seasonal trend, with the greatest pollution in winter (around December to January). This effect is shown better in Figure 13-8, where averages of all available data from 1971 to 1975 are presented month by month. This provides interesting confirmation of a point made in the 1971 TACAP report by University of Arizona meteorologist L. J. Battan, who notes that inversion layers (bounding the heights within which pollutants are mixed by air circulation) decrease from 10,000 ft in May to 2500 ft in January.[15] In other words, pollutants are compressed to one-fourth their summer volume during the winter, which should increase pollutant density by a factor of four during winter. This is approximately what is seen in Figure 13-8, with Redington Pass sulfur oxides increasing from about 0.15 in summer to 0.60 in winter, and with Tucson increasing from about 0.08 in summer to 0.20 in winter.

It is difficult to relate Figures 13-6 to 13-8 to health standards since standards have concerned only SO_2, but not sulfation rate which measures

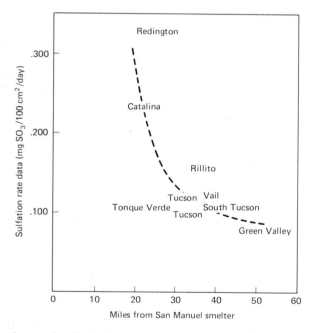

FIG. 13-7. Dependence of sulfur oxide concentration on distance from San Manuel smelter, based on the average of all counts in 1972. Data courtesy of Pima County Health Department.

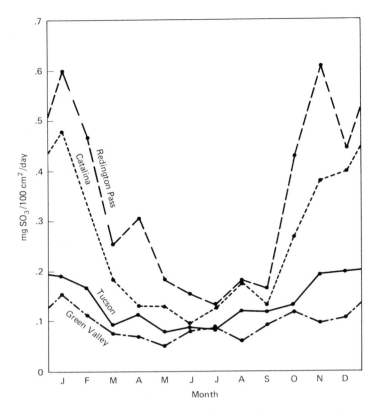

FIG. 13-8. Seasonal incidence of sulfur oxides for four locations near Tucson (1971–75). Conditions are worst during the winter, especially in regions closest to smelters such as the village of Catalina. Data courtesy Pima County Health Department.

the other oxides into which SO_2 transforms. If sulfur pollution is increasing, winter alerts in Catalina, or perhaps even Tucson, could become necessary.

To determine if sulfur oxides are increasing, a long time-scale is needed, and seasonal effects must be removed. This is attempted in Figure 13-9, which combines the recent Pima County Health Department (PCHD) data for downtown Tucson with earlier PCHD data for Tucson gathered in the 1960s. Each point represents a three-month average, and all values have been normalized to the month-by-month data in 1972 so that seasonal fluctuations are removed. In other words, Figure 13-9 shows the levels of sulfur oxides from 1966 to 1975 relative to levels at the same season in 1972.

In Figure 13-9 the three boxed points (1967–68) refer to a nine-month copper strike; when the smelters were turned off all over the state, sulfur oxide levels dropped to near zero. This proves one relation of sulfur oxide data to smelter activity. During a one-month strike in 1974, sulfur levels in downtown Tucson did not drop, although they did drop dramatically in Redington Pass, as shown in Figure 13-6. This might indicate that by that time other sources of sulfur oxides in urban Tucson were present, such as sulfur from power generating plants operating under relaxed emission standards during the recent energy crisis.[16] However, the data in Figure 13-6 are one-month averages straddling the one-month strike, diluting the strike's effect in the graph. Also there is marginal, though surprising,

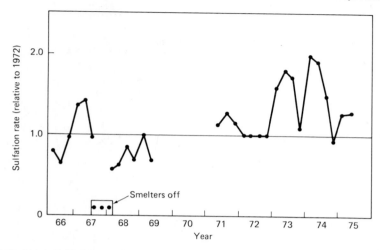

FIG. 13-9. Long-term sulfur oxide trend in downtown Tucson; data have been treated to remove seasonal fluctuations, as explained in the text, by normalizing to 1972. Box contains points during a nine-month copper strike. A marginal long-term increase may be present. Data courtesy Pima County Health Department.

evidence from various strikes that the southern Arizona atmosphere requires several weeks for thorough cleansing after a shutdown occurs; the 1974 strike may have been too short for thorough cleansing.

If we ignore the boxed points, we see that Figure 13–9 indicates increasing sulfur oxides from 1966 to early 1974. After early 1974, there may be a decrease, both in Figure 13-9 and Figure 13-6. Possibly, this may result from smelter control devices going into use in the seventies as a result of environmental legislation. It would be heartening to see a clear reduction of pollution for this reason, for this change would indicate that government and technology can reverse the ominous earlier trend; however, all that can be said now is that Figure 13-9 makes it certain what the future trend of sulfur oxide pollution will be without controls.

An interesting correlation exists with data on the San Manuel smelter activity, provided in an August 25, 1975, letter to the writer from W. L. Parks, executive vice president of Magma Copper Co., San Manuel. The letter shows an increase in processing from 324,000 tons of copper ore concentrates in 1964 to 1966 to 670,710 tons in 1974, which would indicate an increasing trend in sulfur and particulate emissions. However, Mr. Parks points out that the second stack added at San Manuel in 1972 processes discharge gases in order to produce sulfuric acid. This process removes sulfur emissions from the exhaust. According to Mr. Parks' figures, about 107,000 tons of sulfur were liberated each year in the 1964 to 1966 period, but about 106,000 tons would have been liberated in 1974 as well. In summary, one can infer that smelter emissions from San Manuel should have increased from the 1960s to about 1972, but they should have decreased back to the 1960s level by 1974. The future trend is uncertain, depending on production and future controls.

For completeness, Figures 13-10 and 13-11 give data from two other sulfur pollutant monitoring devices. Figure 13-10 shows particulate sulfate particles soluble in water, arising primarily from agricultural fertilizers.[17] The graph plots raw data, as was done in Figure 13-6. Again, the geo-

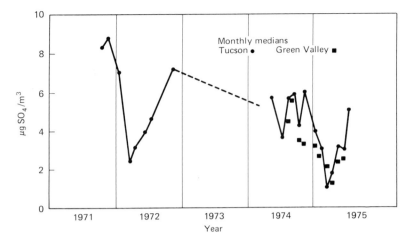

FIG. 13-10. Measurements of sulfate particles in Tucson (solid and dashed line) and in Green Valley (points generally below the solid curve at the right). Data courtesy Pima County Health Department.

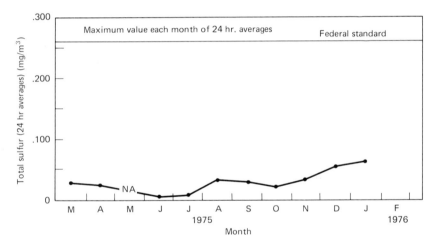

FIG. 13-11. Maximum concentration of sulfur products each month in downtown Tucson. Even maximum concentrations are less than the level set as the federal standard. Data courtesy Pima County Health Department.

graphic and seasonal trends are seen. Green Valley has the least sulfate particle pollution. There is a marginal suggestion of a current decrease in sulfate particle pollution. Figure 13-11 shows data taken within 1976 by PCHD in sulfur products, monitored in 24-hour periods in downtown Tucson; the time period is too short to reveal long-term trends, but the data confirm that, currently, even the highest sulfur levels in downtown Tucson are below the federal standard level.

It should also be noted that catalytic emission control devices on new cars emit sulfates; future trends may be affected by auto emissions as well as by San Manuel and other smelter activities.

At present there appears to be no identifiable health risk from sulfur products in Tucson, though outlying areas such as Catalina or areas near Redington Pass may have hazardous days during winter inversion-layer episodes and adverse health effects have been detected in San Manuel.[18] Long-term trends are uncertain but appear to imply no threat within the next decade. Although no health hazard is obvious in Tucson, the reader should note that sulfur products produce a visible haze of smog in Tucson. This haze implies possible economic hazards in view of Tucson's tourist industry.

AUTO EMISSIONS

Prior to 1975, it was difficult to get air pollution data on specific products of automobile usage in the Tucson basin. However, in 1975 the Pima County Health Department began monitoring levels of carbon monoxide (CO), hydrocarbons, and oxidants. According to estimates for 1975, about 97 percent of the CO and 76 percent of the hydrocarbons are produced by autos. Oxidants are a photochemically combined product of hydrocarbons and nitrogen oxides. Taken together these three pollutants should be indicators of pollution by automobiles. They are plotted as a function of time in Figures 13-12 to 13-14.

Two conclusions stand out from the figures. First, in downtown Tucson, these pollutants occasionally exceed federal standards. For example, the eight-hour average of CO (Figure 13-12) exceeded the federal standard (10 mg/m³) on one day in January 1976; the alert value (23 mg/m³), however, has not been reached. Similarly, the three-hour average for hydrocarbons exceeded the federal standard 21 days in January 1976 and the same standard at least several days each month since August 1975 (through January 1976). No alert level for hydrocarbons is defined, but the maximum reading in January 1976 was more than five times the standard of 160 mg/m³. Finally, oxidants measured at two locations in Tucson (see Figure 13-14) exceeded federal standards on one to three days per month during several months of the data-collecting period.

The second conclusion we can reach from Figures 13-12 to 13-14 is that data are not available for a long enough time period to establish year-to-year trends. The apparent upward trend in figures, such as that shown in Figures 13-12 and 13-13, can be ascribed to seasonal effects; pollution

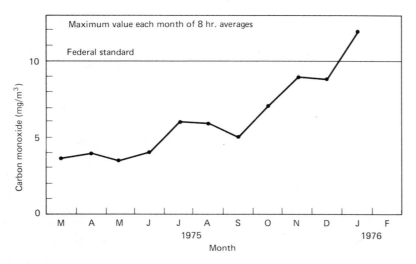

FIG. 13-12. Auto emission pollution: maximum carbon monoxide concentrations recorded each month in downtown Tucson. Concentrations occasionally exceed health standards in winter. A data-taking program began in 1975; the increasing trend is believed to be only seasonal. Data courtesy Pima County Health Department.

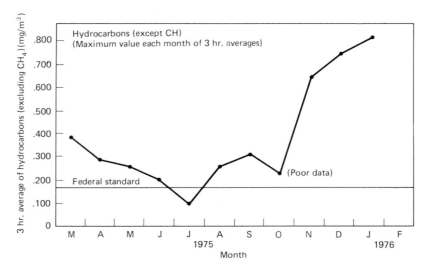

FIG. 13-13. Maximum hydrocarbon concentrations recorded each month in downtown Tucson. Concentrations frequently exceed health standards, for example, on 21 days in January 1976. Data-taking began in 1975; seasonal trends are seen. Data courtesy Pima County Health Department.

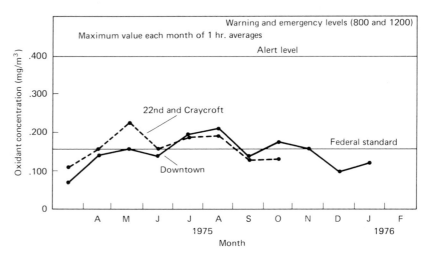

FIG. 13-14. Maximum oxidant concentrations recorded each month in downtown Tucson. Concentrations occasionally exceed health standards. Oxidants are products of photo-chemical reactions, generally between hydrocarbons and nitrogen oxide. Data courtesy Pima County Health Department.

effects generally increase in winter due to Tucson's winter inversion layers. The seasonal profile shown in Figure 13-13 is very similar to that found in Figure 13-8 for sulfur products.

Knowing that auto pollutants exceed standards, the best estimate of future trends comes from considering the trend in total traffic miles driven in Tucson. As can be seen in Figure 13-15, this has been increasing dramatically in recent decades. The increase exceeds even the growth rate of the city. As shown in Figure 13-16, even the number of miles driven per capita in Tucson has been increasing, despite car-pooling and mass transit. This is probably because of the social pattern of the city, rather than technological factors. Professional and merchandising centers have remained in the downtown area, while residential areas have proliferated at

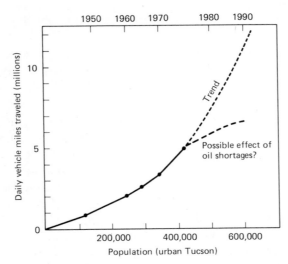

FIG. 13-15. Total traffic miles driven daily in urban Tucson, showing measured increase and approximate projected trends depending on changes such as energy shortages or changes in living patterns. Data from 1975 draft of CPP for Tucson by Planetary Science Institute.

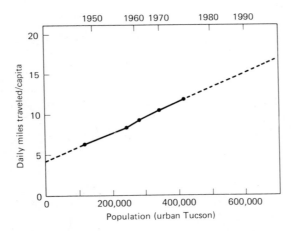

FIG. 13-16. Daily traffic miles driven per capita, showing increase as the city expands, with the approximate projection of the trend (dashed line). Data from 1975 CPP draft for Tucson.

the ends of long arteries (Broadway, Speedway, I–10) many miles away. Thus, as the city grows, the average citizen drives more miles per day in carrying out his/her affairs.

All other factors being equal, the auto pollution will not increase in proportion to the miles driven (see Figure 13-16) because auto emission control devices are coming into play on more and more cars. The combined effects of increasing miles driven and increasing control devices were calculated in the 1971 TACAP report which shows governmental projections. This predicted that "The automotive pollutant emissions in Tucson will reach a maximum in 1970–74, diminish until about 1988, and again increase so that by 1995–2000, we will have the same total pollutant emissions as in 1970."[19]

Because we lack a long enough data-gathering period, we cannot check this prediction using direct measures of auto pollutants. However, as we will see in the next section, there is indirect evidence that this prediction is being confirmed.

The measured pattern of Tucson traffic and the projected pattern of resulting pollution clearly involve future increases in pollution, even beyond the present levels that occasionally exceed health standards. However, these patterns could be affected by changing social patterns. Planning policies for urban growth should encourage people to live closer to where they work and shop (or alternatively encourage businesses to be disseminated into residential areas or adjacent activity centers). A current trend toward inclusion of commercial and professional business areas within planned suburban residential developments may be helpful. Policies favoring mass transit and smaller cars would also be helpful. Zoning and tax policies could be applied to these problems.

Pima County Health Department data show that auto emissions already occasionally exceed federal health standards. Due to emission control devices, we probably have a one- or two-decade reprieve from further increases in these pollutants, but this time must be used to assure that later increases do not occur.

VISIBLE HAZE

Visible haze (smog) is the most directly perceptible form of air pollution but the most difficult to study in terms of cause, for it involves a mixture of effects of all pollutants, some having a more visible effect than others. As the most perceptible form of pollutant, it has the most direct impact on the economy of Tucson through tourism. Its relation to correlated health effects is less direct.

Although haze is caused by a mixture of all pollutants, we must consider it at this point in the report because of an interesting relationship to smelter and auto emissions: smelter emissions were probably a dominant part of Tucson smog in the 1960s, but the smog level has been higher in the 1970s and may be dominated now by auto emissions.

Figure 13-17 shows the incidence of "hazy days," defined as days with visibility less than 60 miles; Figure 13-18 shows "very hazy days," days with visibility less than 50 miles. Several features of these graphs are of

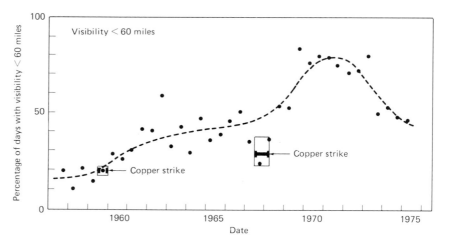

FIG. 13-17. Hazy days in Tucson. Data from weather bureau records.

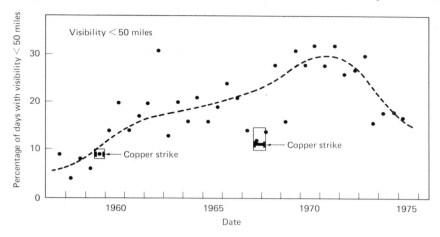

FIG. 13-18. Very hazy days in Tucson. Data from weather bureau records.

interest. First, there has been a long-term increase in visible haze since the late 1950s. Second, when copper smelters were turned off during the major strike of 1967 to 1968, smog dramatically dropped; the atmosphere became nearly as clear as in the late 1950s. This change indicates that smelter emissions (possibly sulfur oxides) were a major source of urban pollution in the 1960s. These two facts taken together suggest that atmospheric haze in Tucson began to exceed its natural level in the late 1950s.

A more extensive relationship between Tucson haze and smelter emissions is shown in Figure 13-19 which compares haze and sulfur oxides behavior in Tucson during the smelter strike of 1967 to 1968. When the smelters were shut off, haze and sulfur oxide concentrations simultaneously dropped in Tucson. This result proves that sulfur emissions from smelters do reach urban Tucson (contrary to some popular opinion) and that they correlate with Tucson visibility, at least during the late 1960s. As noted earlier, the correlation continues into the 1970s, since the sulfur-reducing second stack at San Manuel went into operation in 1972 and caused sulfur emissions to drop to 1965 levels by 1974. Haze shows the same pattern.

There are several lines of evidence that automobile emissions were as important as smelter products in contributing to Tucson's haze by the early 1970s. First, the author demonstrated in 1970 to 1971 a rush-hour surge of haze that did not occur on weekends and holidays.[20] Second, Figures 13-17 and 13-18 confirm the prediction in the 1971 TACAP report which studied growing automobile usage together with effects of pollution control devices. The predicted behavior, a maximum in the early 1970s, is found in the haze curves (see Figures 13–17 and 13–18). This suggests, but does not prove, that the surge in haze around 1970 to 1972 is due to the predicted automobile pollution, which may have surpassed the level of the smelter contribution in the 1960s. The decline in haze around 1974 may thus be due to the combined effects of auto pollution control devices and smelter emission control devices.

Another indication that the haze is due to mixed effects of different pollutants is seen in Figure 13-20 which compares some direct correlation diagrams of haze vs. pollution level for sulfur products (figures A and B)

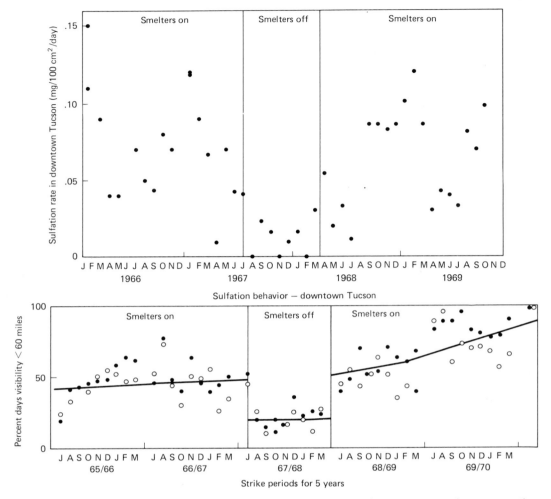

FIG. 13-19. Decrease in sulfur oxides and haze in Tucson during nine-month copper strike, 1967 and 1968. Top: sequence of sulfur oxide measures before, during, and after strike. Bottom: percentage of hazy days at same season as strike for years before, during, and after smelter shutdown. The data indicate that smelter pollutants were an important source of Tucson haze in the 1960s. From Jarvis Moyers, "The Atmospheric Analysis Final Report for Period Oct. 1, 1973 to Dec. 31, 1974 to the Arizona Mining Association" (Tucson: University of Arizona, Department of Chemistry).

and particulates (C). If one source were the only cause of pollution, a strong correlation would exist with low pollutant concentrations corresponding to minimum haze and high pollution to maximum haze. Instead, all three diagrams show a pattern in which no low-haze periods occur if high concentrations of sulfur or dust pollutants occur (i.e., the upper left corners of the diagrams are empty). Hazy days can involve high concentrations of either sulfur products, dust, or perhaps other pollutants. In other words, based on these results plus others, high concentrations of either smelter emissions, auto emissions, or dust (or perhaps other pollutants as well) can independently cause visible haze in Tucson.

Figures 13-21 and 13-22 show the haze data plotted vs. population. The data again suggest a clearing in the early 1970s. The dashed line is a prediction based on the following interpretation. Based on the 1971 TACAP prediction of traffic-related pollution trends, together with the

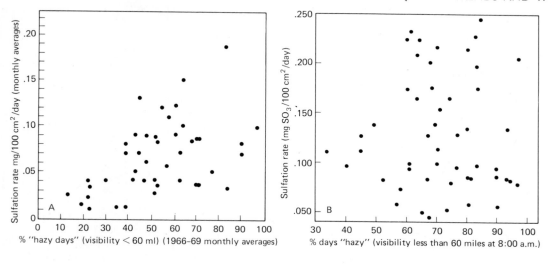

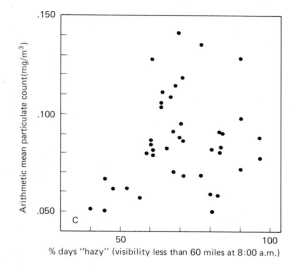

FIG. 13-20. Correlations between specific pollutants and visible haze, Tucson. A: Sulfur concentration vs. incidence of hazy days, 1956 to 1969. B: Same as A, 1971 to 1975. C: Particulate counts vs. incidence of hazy days, 1971 to 1975. The most striking characteristic is the void in the upper left corners which shows that clear days do not occur if concentration of sulfur oxide or dust is high. Redrafted from data in W. K. Hartmann, "Pollution: Patterns of Visibility Reduction in Tucson," *Journal of the Arizona Academy of Science,* **7** (1972).

smelter connection shown above plus general growth trends, the left part of Figures 13-21 and 13-22 can be interpreted as showing increasing pollution due to increasing copper production and increasing auto pollutants. Following the wave of environmental concern around 1969 to 1970 legislation required introduction of more pollution control devices such as smelter scrubbers and auto emission control devices. The apparent decline in haze in the mid-70s is interpreted as due to these technological devices and fits the 1971 TACAP prediction, based on its auto emission projections. However, that prediction showed that we will have only a one-decade reprieve based on those technological devices because of rapid population increase; therefore, an upward trend is shown in the projection dashed line beginning in the 1980s. In other words, Tucson's increasing

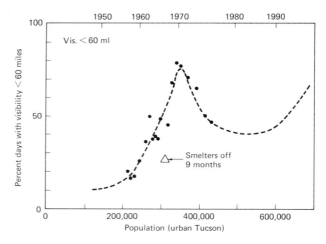

FIG. 13-21. Incidence of hazy days plotted vs. Tucson population, showing the rapid increase in haze as population increased, until about 1971. Decrease after 1971 attributed to growing effectiveness of pollution control devices on autos and perhaps also on smelters. Redrafted from data in Hartmann, "Pollution: Patterns of Visibility Reduction in Tucson."

population is predicted to cause smog increases in the late 1980s unless additional controls come into play. But note that this is a projection of old trends; new energy shortages may reduce auto usage.

An economic impact analysis should be made to determine the effect of increasing visible smog on Tucson's tourist industry. Based on personal discussion with visitors (such as scientists who attend occasional Tucson meetings), I conclude that Tucson already has a reputation as a city with increasing smog. The economic impact study should indicate cost-benefit ratios for various policies, such as instituting mass transit programs, paving dirt streets and parking lots that are now sources of particulate pollution, or permitting new manufacturing industry that might give short-term increase in employment but long-term increase in industrial haze, damaging to the tourist industry.

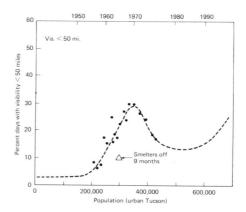

FIG. 13-22. Very hazy days vs. Tucson population. Redrafted from data in Hartmann, "Pollution: Patterns of Visibility Reduction in Tucson."

Particulates

In recent years the Pima County Health Department has operated a series of monitors measuring concentrations of solid particles in the air, mostly microscopic material less than 10 microns in diameter. Generally, this material is related to the so-called dust pollution problem. Figure 13-23 presents raw data, followed by data on geographic distribution and seasonal behavior and then seasonally adjusted material that might reveal long-term trends.

Figure 13-23 plots raw monthly averages of particulate concentration in downtown Tucson and reveals that they are intermittently above the state standard. The dustiest days exceed even the federal standards. For example, one out of 15 samples in August 1975 exceeded the federal secondary standard, and one out of 13 samples in November 1975 exceeded the federal primary standard of .260 mg/m³.

The question is often asked whether the city is cleaner than the natural desert; some people believe that more dust is raised in the dusty desert than in the lawn-covered and pavement-covered city. Figure 13-24 shows that actually the city is far dustier than the desert, for native rock and plant cover accumulate to form a protective layer in the undisturbed desert so that winds pick up little dust. The Tucson basin, on the contrary, can be characterized as a region greatly disturbed by man, but only a fraction of the disturbed soil is covered artificially. Both wind and vehicles kick up loose dirt from unpaved roads and lots. (As shown in Figure 13-24, the most urbanized station in the heart of downtown Tucson actually has slightly less dust than surrounding areas, perhaps due to the nearly total paving of the downtown square mile or two.) The dust concentration 15 miles out of town averages about one-fourth the concentration in Tucson. Even Green Valley appears to be enough of an urbanized area to have consistently more dust than the undisturbed desert.

These results confirm the recent results of Moyers and earlier studies

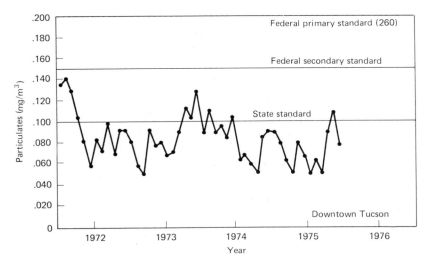

FIG. 13-23. Monthly averages of particulates (dust) concentration in Tucson, showing occasional periods exceeding the state standard and approaching the federal standard. Redrafted from data in Hartmann, "Pollution Patterns of Visibility in Tucson."

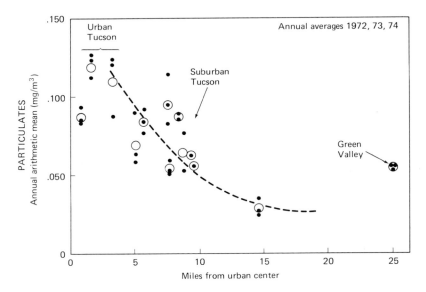

Fig. 13-24. Annual average concentrations of particulates as function of distance from downtown Tucson. Dust concentration in the downtown area is 4 times higher than in most rural measured areas; concentration in Green Valley is lower than in most of Tucson, but it is higher than in the natural desert. Redrafted from data in Hartmann, "Pollution: Patterns of Visibility Reduction in Tucson."

which claim that most particulate pollution in Tucson originates in the city itself. Moyers' chemical analysis of the particulates showed that the majority of the material was fine soil rather than industrial chemicals.[21]

Figure 13-24 indicates a background particulate level of about 25 to 30 μg/m³ (.025 to .030 mg/m³) for the undisturbed desert around Tucson. This is confirmed by 1969 measurements of 30 to 70 μg/m³ in Sahuarita, 30 to 50 in Sells, 20 to 40 on Mt. Lemmon, and 20 to 30 for typical U.S. rural areas.[22] Seasonally, the dust shows the same behavior as other pollutants (compare Figures 13-8 and 13-25). Concentrations are greatest in the winter, and average monthly values exceed state standards in December, evidently due to the winter inversion layers.

An attempt to look for long-term trends in dust pollution is shown in Figure 13-26. Here, the seasonal variations have been removed by dividing each monthly measure by the 1972 to 1975 average for that month. The resulting curve shows only random-looking fluctuations around the average and is insufficient to establish any long-term trend. Dust levels, in other words, seem to be holding about constant from 1972 to 1975.

A second attempt to look for a long-term trend is to compare the 1967 to 1970 averages to the 1972 to 1975 data presented here. The 1967 to 1970 average particulate count was 105 μg/m³ compared to an average near 90 μg/m³ for 1972 to 1975. The low-to-high range in 1967 to 1970 was 42 to 325 μg/m³; the range for 1972 to 1975 was about 50 to 140. These comparisons indicate a near-constant dusty environment, with a possible 15 percent decrease from 1967 to 1972.

Since winter particulate counts already often exceed state standards and have exceeded federal standards in an eight-year period, policies to reduce dust should be given high priority. This suggests an increased priority on paving unpaved streets and parking lots. (The author notes that streets in some residential areas of Tucson are still unpaved. This is ironic in view

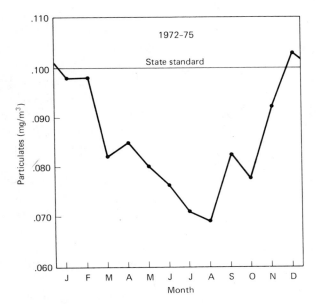

FIG. 13-25. Seasonal behavior of particulates, showing an increase in winter attributed to winter inversion layer formation. Redrafted from data in Hartmann, "Pollution: Patterns of Visibility Reduction in Tucson."

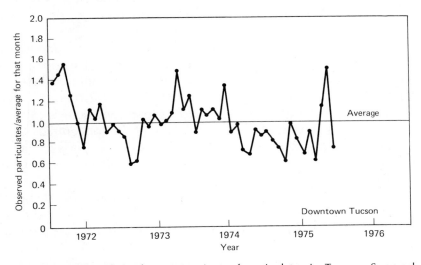

FIG. 13-26. Seasonally adjusted concentrations of particulates in Tucson. Seasonal adjustment permits us to search for long-term trends; none is found for 1972 to 1975, the period for which data are available. Redrafted from data in Hartmann, "Pollution: Patterns of Visibility Reduction in Tucson".

of activity now devoted to modifications of already paved streets. For example, widening of the northsouth artery, Campbell Avenue, has the net effect of disrupting established viable neighborhoods—various houses, including designs by a well-known early Southwest architect were destroyed—to accommodate outlying urban sprawl.)

Planning Strategies

Interesting issues of pollution control planning philosophy emerge from the data in this report. Data on the two pollutants that have been measured since the 1940s or 1950s (see pollens and visual haze, Figures 13-3,

13-17, and 13-18) indicate that Tucson basin air quality began to deteriorate rapidly when the population level reached about 150,000 to 200,000. Probably any artificial pollution in earlier times was less than a natural background level. The deterioration was due in large part to direct population pressures in the Tucson basin, such as cultivation of pollen-bearing plants, increased traffic mileage and auto emissions, increased dust caused by disturbance of desert surface and vegetation, and increased combustion products from power plants, industry, and homes; but it was also due in part to growing peripheral industry not directly related to Tucson's population, such as copper smelters.

To the extent that population pressures caused the pollution, a population of 150,000 to 200,000 could thus be identified as an objective measure (based on Figures 13-3, 13-7, and 13-8) of the population beyond which traditional patterns of social activity begin to degrade the environment in a Tucson-like setting. This figure could therefore be introduced as an objective factor in discussions of "optimum population" for the Tucson community.

Since we are far past that population level now, the question remains concerning what should be done. Planning discussions in response to early drafts of the CPP document centered around three options which might be called the "hands-off option," the "technological option," and the "social option." These options follow directly from the data presented here and have subtle consequences.

The "hands-off option" calls for ignoring the problem under the assumption that it is not a proper concern of government. This option should be rejected for several reasons. If the problem were only aesthetic, as it was portrayed by some a few years ago, the "hands-off option" might be defensible on legal, if not ethical, grounds. However, there is now direct evidence of adverse health effects of air pollution at concentrations above federal standards in American cities (including evidence of such an effect in San Manuel) and growing suspicion that lower levels cause less dramatic health effects.

Therefore, in view of evidence of increases of some pollutants today and projections of increases of others in a decade without changes, government has a responsibility under the mandate of safeguarding the public health and welfare. At least there is responsibility to alert citizens to the current situation of pollen concentration increases and auto emissions occasionally exceeding the federal standards. Furthermore, since southern Arizona is one of the country's fastest growing regions, there is a responsibility to consider how to order (or slow) the growth to protect the health of present and future citizens. Tucson's apparently high incidence of respiratory illness verifies this point. Finally, a "hands-off" policy makes no sense. It is based on the notion that government should not "tamper with" the so-called "unregulated" patterns of growth or residential development. This notion is fallacious because there is no such thing as an unregulated pattern of growth; the way in which the city grows is already regulated by a complex pattern of economic and governmental decisions such as city/county tax structures, zoning plans, and school system quality. There is no philosophical reason why public health effects of air pollution should not be a similar factor in determining the pattern. In short, there is no such thing as a "hands-off option," even though this is the "option" endorsed by many local political figures.

The "technological option" could be supported. Experience with automobile pollutants and possible smelter pollutants shows that government and technology, working together, can identify pollution sources and can begin to bring them under control. Therefore, continued improvement and sophistication of technological devices such as catalytic converters or smelter scrubbers will keep pollution within safe levels without any additional change in social traditions and living patterns. There is thus a strong bias in favor of relying on this solution because it requires the least change in our life styles. However, since Tucson's growth rate is much greater than the national average, it would seem unlikely that the evolution of technological control devices would solve the problem in Tucson. Even if technological controls can be built, there is a question whether this is the best solution because it comes at enormous national cost. Productive natural and human resources are employed merely to clean up our own dirt, and this use increases prices of manufactured goods. This, in turn, increases inflation and causes a drain on society's ability to create new goods, services, and technologies.

With the "social option" we could try to produce incentives for different modes of living that would reduce pollution. Some of these are quite straightforward and belong in the province of planning/zoning decisions. For example, incentives or restrictions to encourage native desert landscaping instead of water-consuming imported vegetation would reduce non-native pollens and water consumption at the same time. Zoning incentives or restrictions to encourage people to establish homes close to where they work (and to encourage dispersal of professional and business centers nearer residential areas) could allow citizens to reduce car use in favor of bicycling or walking. This would decrease auto-related pollution and at the same time would reduce traffic, energy use, and transportation problems. This change would increase public fitness and perhaps contribute to inner-city revitalization and reduction of racial imbalances in city school systems. In other words, if appropriate city-planning measures are feasible, Tucson pollution levels might be reduced in part without gross technological, economic, or human expenditures.

It appears that we have a few years in which to "bend the twig" in the right direction so that the future will see a healthy environment in Tucson. Without corrective changes, several forms of pollution, such as pollens and auto exhausts, will probably continue to increase toward more unhealthy levels within a few decades. Some corrective changes may be imposed by conditions outside city control, such as national energy shortages which are likely because of national dependence on imported oil. However, corrective changes can also be made to reduce air pollution by the way in which we buy our next car, choose the location for our next home, and landscape this new home. These choices can be influenced by tools of city planning. Education and zoning programs are especially important.

Recommendations

In light of the data, I proposed in my consultant study for the city planning department the following recommendations:
  1. Air pollution data should be used by city government on a continu-

ing basis to affect planning decisions since some pollutants already occasionally exceed state and federal standards, raising problems of public health. Inadequate channels now exist to convert pollution monitoring data into effective antipollution planning policies.

2. City planning authorities should maintain contact with local medical authorities, such as Dr. Michael D. Lebowitz at the University of Arizona Medical Center, since these authorities are generating data that may clarify the magnitude of the air pollution-health problem in Tucson.

3. A public awareness program should be conducted to alert citizens that some pollutants exceed standards, that some others are rapidly increasing, and that citizens' individual decisions on auto, home, and landscaping purchases could help rectify the problem with a minimum of governmental intervention.

4. Attempts should be made to discourage widespread landscaping with pollen-producing non-native plants and grasses and to encourage desert landscaping (which tends to be low in pollen), since pollens are increasing so rapidly and respiratory illnesses such as allergies are unusually prevalent in Tucson. Recent city council moves toward desert landscaping of public lands are a step in the right direction. Bermuda grass and mulberry trees especially should be discouraged by public education or by ordinances against new sales, if warranted by medical opinion. Tucson's problem of declining water supply would also be helped by this recommendation.

5. Planning policies for urban growth should encourage people to live close to where they work and should encourage businesses to be dispersed near residential areas, possibly in activity centers. The goal would be to decrease the need for automobiles. Policies should discourage commuting from fringe residential areas into inner-city business areas. These policies might be implemented through planned activity centers, increased fees for city services to outlying residential tracts, or other zoning methods. These policies would have favorable impact not only on auto emission pollution but also on the energy problem, physical fitness, traffic control costs, and possibly racial balance in schools.

6. An economic impact study should be made to determine the effect of increasing smog on the Tucson tourist industry and the similar effect of the perception of Tucson smog by potential visitors from other parts of the country. Trade-offs between the economic advantages of growth (increased smog) and nongrowth or restricted growth (restricted smog increase) should be considered.

7. Since Tucson urbanization is the major source of local dust and since dust already exceeds state standards during winter, paving or stabilizing unpaved Tucson streets should be given high priority. Its present priority, based on traffic flow and aesthetic considerations, should be augmented by health considerations.

Conclusions

The concerns about Tucson pollutants fall in two categories: (1) current state of pollutants and their health effects, and (2) trends. A brief summary of these two categories is given in Table 13-1.

More specific conclusions can also be made. For instance:

TABLE 13-1. Summary of Tucson (Arizona) Pollutants.

POLLUTANT	CURRENT HEALTH EFFECTS	TREND*
Pollen	No standards defined, but Tucson has unusually large number of allergic citizens.	Increasing, out of control.
Sulfur products	Less than federal standard.	Uncertain; roughly constant?
Auto emissions	Exceeding federal standard in winter.	Temporarily decreasing; increase in decade unless auto use changes.
Visible haze	—	Increase through 1971; temporarily decreasing; increase in decade unless changes in controls or social patterns.
Dust	Exceeding state standard in winter.	Near constant, possible slight decrease.

*Trends are difficult to extrapolate beyond 1976 because of probable social changes such as energy shortages.
Source: Hartmann, W. K. "Air Quality: Pollution Forecast and Application to Planning." Tucson, Arizona: Planetary Science Institute, 1976, p. 49 (mimeo).

1. Some pollutants, such as some auto emissions and dust particulates, exceed defined health standards on occasion. In addition, pollen appears important, though no health standards have been set. Although Tucson does not have continual highly excessive levels of pollution, it does have a current, intermittent health problem as defined by air pollution standards.

2. Trends can be considered in two subcategories: current trends as measured in 1976, and extrapolated future trends.

3. Current trends are encouraging in most instances, except that for pollens which appears to be increasing rapidly. Other pollutants—generally the most publicized ones—have been brought under partial control in response to environmental concerns since 1969. The controls are primarily technological and are encouraging: they show that government and technology can make a positive response to the problem. However, the technological solution comes at increased costs for products.

4. Southern Arizona's growth rate is exceptionally high, and it is unlikely that technological controls alone will keep up with the pollution effects of a growing population unless patterns of auto use, landscaping, and other activities change.

5. This is a particularly bad time in which to try to extrapolate present trends into the future because major changes in American life style are likely in the next few decades. Causes include U.S. dependence on foreign oil to maintain current life styles; probable oil (and other energy) shortages (due to embargoes, delays in solar energy technology, etc.); economic effects of food shortages in other countries; increasing costs of luxury items (due to their high environmental costs), etc. Effects of these changes may be negative on traditional economic indicators (depending on how fast they come and how adaptable we are), but may be positive on the air pollution problem.

6. Trends are hard to foresee; but since there are reasonable indications that at least some pollutants' concentrations will grow and will cause adverse health effects, city government has a responsibility to keep in close touch with results from monitoring agencies and medical researchers.

7. Winter brings the most dangerous periods for exceeding health standards because inversion layers hold pollutants in small volumes.

8. Catastrophic pollution episodes such as those found in Donora,

Pennsylvania, or with lesser intensity in New York City, are unlikely to occur in Tucson in the next decade; but more subtle health problems, especially allergies and respiratory illness, are likely to occur in Tucson and probably do occur now.

9. Appropriate planning policies can favorably affect these problems.

10. A legal case could be made for planning policies designed to reduce air pollution because of the increasing data showing the impact of air pollution on public health.

Update

The introduction to this chapter reviewed some of the developments in Tucson leading to the study which became part of the comprehensive planning process (CPP) document for the larger Tucson area. Readers may be interested in the subsequent history of this planning process. In brief, the picture is bleak but mixed in regard to the future environment of Tucson.

In 1978, the Tucson City Council, which had developed a reputation for a slow-growth philosophy, pointed out the rapid lowering of the Tucson water table and instituted a progressive rate structure and lift charges to pay for pumping water uphill to foothill homes in order to accommodate increased water requirements for the projected growth. An opposition group, generally identified with progrowth advocates, seized on this issue, organized a recall election around the single aspect of rolling back water prices, and ousted the "slow-growth" members of the council in 1977. However, water rate increases, mandated by growth, have continued. (See Finkler chapter for full discussion of Tucson water problems.) The massive CPP document referred to above was not endorsed by the new council which appointed a new citizen's board to draft an alternative. An alternative was also submitted by the Tucson Chamber of Commerce.

The final watered down version of the comprehensive plan, proposes policies that "accommodate future population growth and promote the positive aspects of that growth while ensuring that growth is compatible with the region's natural environmental constraints. . ."[23] The "positive aspects" and "environmental constraints" are undefined. Air pollution problems are left to federal regulations.

The fate of the CPP, which would have provided a coordinated rationale for dealing with air pollution, land use, water policy, and other problems of growth is perhaps best summed up by parts of an editorial by Tom Turner in the *Arizona Daily Star:*

> It began in 1975 with tumultuous fanfare that soon became ideological warfare. . .And it hasn't even reached the County Board of Supervisors yet.
> What started out to be 561 pages in eight volumes that took three years, hundreds of hours of hearing and more than $1 million to complete is now a docile document about the size of a child's pamphlet on knitting.
> It is a showcase of the worst possible vagueness that only the push and pull of opposing philosophies can produce, saying little that has not been said a thousand times before. . .[24]

In practice, problems of urban evolution are being met by projecting current population growth trends (as subtly influenced by current zoning, water, and other policies) into the future and then assuming that these trends are the "natural" trends that will continue. Based on the current monitoring of air pollution by the county health department and on projected implementation of EPA regulations, future trends on air pollution are then extrapolated. Ignored are social pressures such as energy crises or effects of different zoning and water policies.

Pollutants that are projected not to exceed federal standards are, in essence, not considered in public policy. In fact, current EPA and state plans to identify "attainment areas" (in which air is acceptable since the standards are not exceeded) explicitly allow for further growth, industrialization, or other land use up to the point where the health standards begin to be exceeded. In the other "non-attainment areas," pollutants exceed health standards; and policies must, by EPA regulation, be adopted to reduce pollutants.

To be specific, projections of auto emissions clearly indicate that the growing numbers of vehicles with emission control devices should decrease this type of pollution in the early 1980s. Population increases may eventually offset this improvement in later decades: but current projections and policies do not attempt to deal with conditions that far in the future, perhaps with good reason. Dust is an example of a pollutant not likely to improve. The plan being adopted to meet EPA regulations on particulates (dust) involves coordination with transportation authorities and is likely to stress paving of unpaved roads in order to reduce dust injection into the air. This plan is qualitatively valid, but development of new unpaved roads in association with new housing and off-road recreation appears to exceed the rate at which old dirt roads are likely to be paved.

Even though the program of EPA regulations and federal implementation of air quality programs appears to have many positive effects on the development of a plan to deal with pollution, the picture is not entirely rosy. As a member of the county air pollution advisory council, I have witnessed the fact that local industries as well as local officials are now confronted by thick documents of legalese, containing new regulations they are expected to meet. The larger companies send their lawyers to hearings; distressed smaller operators appear in person. The costs of trying to understand and meet the emissions regulations are, of course, passed on to customers and represent an underrated part of inflation.

What appears to be happening, at least in southern Arizona, is that we are still encouraging the economic forces that tend to push people into crowded urban areas, even after the benefits begin to diminish for individual residents in terms of air pollution, traffic congestion, and increased per capita costs of services. Yet the metropolitan Tucson area still maintains a tax-supported office to promote "economic growth" at the same time we are imposing extra financial and managerial burdens on ourselves in the form of cumbersome regulations in order to solve these problems.

In summary, problems of air pollution in the urban environment of Tucson have been slowly recognized, and we are just now beginning to deal with them. The pollution problems are not only those common to all cities—automotive and industrial emissions; there also are special problems enhanced by Tucson's arid environment—pollens from imported plants and dust from disturbances of the desert surface. Efforts at solutions at the local level appear to have failed. Current solutions lean more toward pervasive and massive federal regulations with their own negative side effects. Basic patterns of urban concentration and growth, the major causes of air pollution, have not been addressed. Successful planning to deal with these problems will apparently require much better public education about the causes and costs of air pollution, plainer speaking, and probably clearer thinking.

Notes

1. Quentin Mees and Robert Wortman, "Preliminary Report: Air Pollution Surveillance Study," Engineering Experiment Station Bulletin No. 13 (Tucson, Arizona, 1960).
2. C. R. Green and L. J. Battan. "A Study of Visibility vs. Population Growth in Arizona." Journal of the Arizona Academy of Science, 4 (1967), 226.
3. W. K. Hartmann, "Pollution: Patterns of Visibility Reduction in Tucson," Journal of the Arizona Academy of Science 7 (1972), 101; also see Air Pollution in Tucson, ed. R. L. Caldwell (Tucson: Tucson Advisory Committee on Air Pollution, 1971).
4. Jarvis Moyers, "The Atmospheric Analysis Laboratory Final Report for Period Oct. 1, 1973 to Dec. 31, 1974 to Arizona Mining Association" (Tucson: University of Arizona, Department of Chemistry).
5. Air Pollution in Tucson.
6. Hartmann, "Pollution: Patterns of Visibility Reduction in Tucson."
7. Moyers, op. cit.; Pima County Health Department.
8. M. D. Lebowitz, R. J. Kneedson, and B. Burrows. "Tucson Epidemiologic Study of Obstructive Lung Diseases, I," American Journal of Epidemiology, 102 (1975), 137.
9. M. D. Lebowitz and B. Burrows, "Tucson Epidemiologic Study of Obstructive Lung Diseases, II, Effects of In-Migration Factors on the Prevalence of Obstructive Lung Disease," American Journal of Epidemiology, 102 (1975), 153.
10. Lebowitz to Hartmann; (conversation), August 1975.
11. Lebowitz, Kneedson, and Burrows, "Tucson Epidemiologic Study."
12. M. D. Lebowitz et al., "The Effect of Air Pollution and Weather on Lung Function in Exercising Children and Adolescents." American Review of Respiratory Disease 109 (1974), 262.
13. M. D. Lebowitz and B. Burrows, "Air Pollution and Respiratory Illness," Arizona Medicine, (1973).
14. Thompson to Hartmann, 12 February 1976.
15. L. J. Battan in Air Pollution in Tucson.
16. C. Lee Fox, Chief Air Quality Control Officer Pima County Health Department, to Hartmann (conversation).
17. Moyers, op. cit.
18. M. D. Lebowitz, et al. "The Effect of Air Pollution and Weather."
19. Air Pollution in Tucson.
20. Hartmann, "Pollution Patterns."
21. Moyers, op. cit.; also see Quentin Mees and Robert Wortman, in Air Pollution in Tucson.
22. Air Pollution in Tucson.
23. City of Tucson Planning Department and Pima County (Arizona) Planning Department, Comprehensive Planning Process document, 1978.
24. Tom Turner, (Tucson) Arizona Daily Star, 3 December 1978.

14
The Urban Politics of Water and Growth in Tucson, Arizona*

Earl Finkler

As one approaches Tucson, Arizona, there is very little evidence of surface water. Those coming by air might spot a good number of backyard swimming pools, but the rivers and washes which run through the metropolitan area are bone dry at the surface most of the year. For nearly 12,000 years, surface water from springs and streams was the source of irrigation and drinking water for the inhabitants. Yet, following the turn of the century, the water table started a decline which has been generally increasing in recent years due to demands from agriculture, mining, and booming population growth. Today this region is one of the largest metropolitan areas in the United States and is totally dependent on groundwater.

Growth and Water Scarcity

The Tucson region has been growing faster than both the nation as a whole and other metropolitan areas. In 1970, the Tucson Standard Metropolitan Statistical Area (SMSA) ranked 95th out of all SMSA's in terms of absolute size. By 1974, it had jumped to 83rd place. The 1975 population of Pima County was about 448,000 most of which was either in the city of Tucson or scattered within 10 or 20 miles of the city limits. Pima County has grown from some 142,000 in 1950 to 351,000 in 1970, and then by almost another 100,000 in five years to its 1975 population. The city of Tucson had only some 45,000 people in 1950. By 1975, it had some 300,000, a gain of over 500 percent, some of which resulted from annexations.

Tucson is growing primarily by in-migration, as are most of the rapidly growing Sun Belt communities. Between 1970 and 1975, some 18,500 people were added to the population by net natural increase, while four times as many, 74,000 were added by net migration. The new arrivals to Tucson often come with a thirst for trees, shrubs, and vegetation not characteristic of a desert environment. They grow extensive lawns and try to recapture the green atmosphere of their old homesite back East. Per capita water consumption in the Tucson area averages 200 gallons per day, well over the 1970 national average of 166 gallons per day. An article in a local newspaper noting the change in water consumption patterns says:

> Ironically, back in the 1920's and '30's when Tucson's population was small, water was rationed every summer. Verdant lawns and midwestern-type trees

*The author would like to acknowledge the preliminary editing of his essay by his wife, Bonnie.

were uncommon. Then came the war and the impetus of growth-for-the-sake-of-growth took over. Grass and imported vegetation were actively promoted to attract new residents from other parts of the nation.[1]

In Tucson's desert environment, precipitation averages about 11 inches per year. If all this water were actually available, the area would not have a serious water problem. However, more than 95 percent of the rainfall either evaporates or is directly used by plants. That which penetrates the surface down into the aquifer is called natural recharge. The average recharge is 100,000 acre-feet (a-ft) per year.[2] However, the consumptive use (that portion of pumped water which does not eventually return to the water table), runs three to four times greater than the annual natural recharge and is far out of balance with the annual supply.

This means that the Tucson area and other areas of Arizona are in an age of water scarcity. As geologist W. Wesley Peirce notes:

> Water is a so-called renewable resource. This is true only insofar as it is not used faster than it is resupplied. In this context, Arizona's present water supply is a *nonrenewing* resource. Arizona is out of ecological balance in this essential aspect.[3]

The problem of water scarcity is not confined to Tucson or Arizona, as Lester Brown and other researchers at the Worldwatch Institute in Washington, D.C. have noted:

> Examples of population growth exerting pressure on water supplies are legion. From Manila—where population may double in 15 years—to the grazing range of the Ethiopian Plateau, the limited availability of fresh water is undermining health, restricting food supplies, and diminishing hopes of economic development. Population pressure on water supplies is most evident in agriculture, with irrigation needs representing one principal source of future world demand.

To further complicate matters, "Per capita daily water use in the United States has increased more than 75 percent in the last twenty-five years. World water use is expected to triple by the early twenty-first century if projected population and per capita consumption trends materialize."[4]

The cities are not the sole cause of the water crisis in Arizona. Agriculture and mining are also major consumptive users of water both in Pima County and the state as a whole. In Pima County, conservative estimates of consumptive use of water (that water which is not eventually returned to the water table) show that agriculture consumes about 71 percent, urban and recreational uses about 22 percent, and mining and miscellaneous industries about 7 percent. However, the mines and agricultural areas generally have their own wells and are also protected by antiquated state legislation. The major statutes dealing with the appropriation of groundwater in Arizona were passed in 1948 and are very inadequate. Ownership of groundwater generally goes with ownership of the land.[5]

The city of Tucson has purchased and retired nearly 11,000 acres (a) of irrigated farmland in the nearby Avra Valley, but the amount of water used for irrigated agriculture has actually increased in recent years. This is due to the introduction of double-crop farming on the remaining land. Clearly, new state water legislation is needed, but it will be difficult to obtain in a state legislature dominated by rural interests. Thus, Arizona has not come to grips with the water component of its future. The question remains whether it will remain an agricultural and mining state or an area which encourages rapid and sprawling urbanization.

Since the water problem in Tucson is significant, it is important to consider that portion which relates to the area's proposed comprehensive plan and which falls more directly under local control and the local political process. Ultimately, the broader water problems in Arizona will have to be resolved by the state and even the federal government. These include the Central Arizona Project which is designed to augment the water supply of Tucson and other communities starting in the mid-1980s via an aqueduct which will carry water diverted from the Colorado River. Final allocations of water from the project will be made by the Secretary of the Interior. However, litigation initiated by Arizona Indian tribes disputing their preliminary allocation may further delay the process. In any event, imported water such as that from the project will be at least twice as expensive to pump as that from local well fields, and there are serious questions whether there will be enough water left in the Colorado River for the project, given existing allocations to other western states and Mexico.

Historically, man in Arizona and elsewhere has responded to water and other natural resource shortages by leaving a problem area for one of more abundance. That option is diminishing as populations grow and frontiers shrink or disappear. However, the lessons from Tucson do not involve out-migration. Hordes of people are flocking to Tucson and other Sun Belt areas in search of a warmer climate, newer communities, less crime, less racial tension, and other economic or life style advantages.

Therefore, the battle for the turf of Tucson and the water beneath it has reached a fever pitch in the past few years, and water has become a political issue. Evidence of the political importance of water policies is a successful recall election, largely financed by business and progrowth interests. The four-member majority of the Tucson City Council abruptly changed in early 1977.

Politics and Water Scarcity

BACKGROUND FOR THE 1977 RECALL ELECTION

The recall was first organized in August 1976 after the council decided to restructure the water rate system with a number of new or higher charges, including an overall goal of increasing water revenues by 22 percent. The council acted after a consultant study showed that the local water crisis was growing progressively more serious, the existing wells were being rapidly drained, and power costs for pumping were rising significantly. The consultant noted that it would take $60 million in capital improvements in the next six years to continue importing water from one neighboring valley. Also, increased rates were viewed as necessary to finance demands on the system posed by anticipated future growth.

The revised water rate system included some features which should have pleased political conservatives and others which should have pleased political liberals. It did not mandate rationing or any enforced conservation of water; but in a true conservative tradition, it left the solution more in the free market through pricing mechanisms. There was a progressive rate structure so that, above a certain base level, higher water usage resulted in higher rates. There were increased charges for areas at higher elevations, such as the surrounding mountain foothills which required higher pumping costs. The rates also included a $725 connection fee for new residential hookups in order to have new water users pay more of the costs they helped to create.

However, the four-member majority of the August 1976 council had all won election as representatives of a new political liberal movement which was at least skeptical about the benefits of continued rapid growth and was generally proplanning. Although a separate policy report was not released when the new rates were considered or when they went into effect in July, 1976, opponents soon charged that the higher rates were designed primarily to start implementing the draft comprehensive plan. A comprehensive planning process (CPP) had been started in 1972 at both the city and county levels and had likely helped to elect some of the liberal council members. By 1976, the plan was still in draft form and the subject of considerable controversy, especially between the progrowth and antigrowth interests. A revised version of the plan was to be considered for final adoption by the governing bodies by mid-1978.

Given the need for additional water revenues, the council chose a rate structure which among other things could supplement strong land use plans to reduce future urban sprawl. A more detailed analysis of council motivations on the CPP and the water rates will be presented later. However, the facts facing the council were that many people who used a lot of water lived in the urban fringe areas with larger lawns and more landscaping. In addition, the facts showed that single-family houses, on the average, used about three times the water used by mobile home or apartment units. The strongest thrust in the new water rate structure was clearly fiscal. Past councils had failed to deal with staff and departmental requests for additional water revenues, and the problem had grown more serious. The council majority publicly stated that it raised the rates to generate enough money to expand the system and keep up with antici- pated growth. Some of the demands from growth were already present, especially in response to the rapid rise in energy costs. Over 50 percent of the city of Tucson's electrical consumption is devoted to pumping water. The peak in water demand and the peak in electrical demand in Tucson both come in the extremely hot and dry summer months, when both air conditioners and sprinklers are used heavily. Before the rates were in- creased, energy costs for pumping water alone rose by $880,000 over the previous year. Additional bonds would have to be sold to expand and upgrade the lines and other parts of the system, and these bonds would have to be repaid from water revenues.

This fiscal planning approach would seem to appeal to conservatives. It is a "pay as you go" or a "pay a little bit ahead" approach which presumably keeps a community on a sound financial footing and does not let it get into financial difficulties by trying to respond after the fact of rapid growth. However, the conservative elements in Tucson, especially the builders, banks, developers, and real estate interests, did not seem to appreciate such an approach toward financed growth. They charged the council majority with being "no-growth" because the higher rates would discourage new residents from moving in.

ORGANIZATION OF THE RECALL

The revised water rates went into effect as of July 1, 1976. Unfortunately, July is the month of peak water use in Tucson. Despite the fact that the overall increase was only a little over 20 percent, selected individuals, such as those in high lift zones, found their bills rising substantially, from perhaps $50 a month to $200 a month. The council knew that many wealthy people lived in the higher elevations, but they apparently overlooked the lower- and middle-income people in other areas who lived at somewhat higher elevations outside of the plush foothill areas and who also received water bills with whopping increases.

Phones of the four-member council majority who voted for the increase were busy, and irate citizens poured into city hall to protest. The four council members attempted to put out press releases, grant interviews, and hold public meetings to explain their position and some of the features of the new rate structure. They tried to show how Tucson's water rates were lower than those of many other western cities (see Table 14-1.) In August 1976, they even voted to rescind the lift charges and to refund collections made to that date. However, by that time, recall petitions were already being circulated by a group headed by John Varga, an electronics instructor at the local community college who received assistance and support from a number of merchants, car dealers, and developers.

Varga later told the *New York Times* that the revised water rate structure was a "socialistic" plot by university economists and planning advocates to force slow growth on Tucsonans who want a free enterprise system. "Government trying to take control of the natural resource as a weapon?" he said of the rate increase. "I thought I lived in a free country."[6]

A number of known political figures in Tucson refused to run against the incumbents in the special recall election held in January 1977. Apparently some of the older politicians were not sure whether the incumbents were going to look like socialists or martyrs. Thus, while a good portion of the progrowth, more conservative elements in Tucson supported the recall of the proplanning incumbents, they let several relatively new and unknown candidates to do the actual running.

RESULTS OF THE RECALL

The results of the special election showed that the conservatives had no reason for concern. One of the incumbents who was recalled had resigned his seat before the actual election. But in the other three races, the incumbents lost by ratios of almost two to one. Each of the recall candidates in these three races got about 55 percent of the vote or better in a contest where there were multiple candidates. The candidates backed by the recall forces thus swept all four seats. It appeared that the public was bent on revenge against those who raised the water rates. Some observers said that almost anyone nominated by the recall forces could have won an election against the incumbents.

Once the new council members took office, however, it again became

TABLE 14-1. Comparison of Single-Family Residential Water Rates in Several Western (U.S.) Cities. (Ccf = 748 GAL)

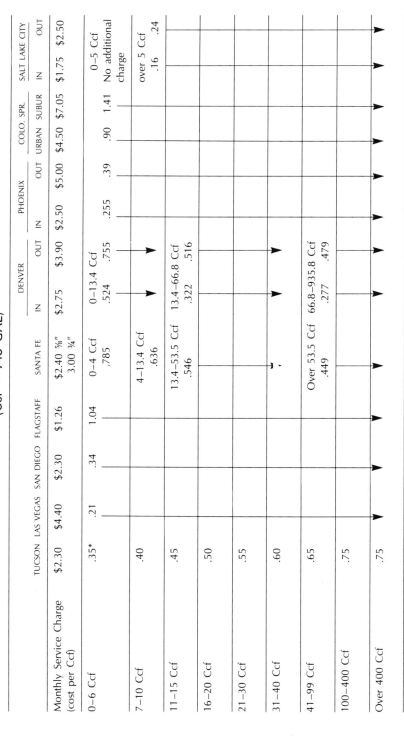

	TUCSON	LAS VEGAS	SAN DIEGO	FLAGSTAFF	SANTA FE	DENVER IN	DENVER OUT	PHOENIX IN	PHOENIX OUT	COLO. SPR. URBAN	COLO. SPR. SUBUR	SALT LAKE CITY IN	SALT LAKE CITY OUT
Monthly Service Charge (cost per Ccf)	$2.30	$4.40	$2.30	$1.26	$2.40 ⅝", 3.00 ¾"	$2.75	$3.90	$2.50	$5.00	$4.50	$7.05	$1.75	$2.50
0–6 Ccf	.35*	.21	.34	1.04	0–4 Ccf .785	0–13.4 Ccf .524	.755	.255	.39	.90	1.41	0–5 Ccf No additional charge	
7–10 Ccf	.40				4–13.4 Ccf .636							over 5 Ccf .16	.24
11–15 Ccf	.45				13.4–53.5 Ccf .546	13.4–66.8 Ccf .322	.516						
16–20 Ccf	.50												
21–30 Ccf	.55												
31–40 Ccf	.60												
41–99 Ccf	.65				Over 53.5 Ccf .449	66.8–935.8 Ccf .277	.479						
100–400 Ccf	.75												
Over 400 Ccf	.75												

*Below rates for zones with zero lifts. Portion of new rate schedule charging 20¢/lift rescinded 8/10/76. Lift charge formerly in addition to basic rate.

Source: Pima County, Town of Oro Valley, City of South Tucson, and City of Tucson. *Comprehensive Plan—Physical Development Guide.* Draft report. August 1976. Section 10, p. 19.

clear that there was much more to city government than merely throwing out some unpopular politicians. The water problem was still there.

Later Political Developments

Toward the end of January, after the recall election, a special 15-member citizens' advisory committee on water rates came to the conclusion that the water system revenues had to be increased to meet capital needs. The members suggested some of the same revenue-raising methods chosen by the old council majority. For instance, they proposed including a progressive rate structure and lift zone charges to absorb the cost of pumping water to higher elevations. They reached their decision after hearing testimony from hydrologists, engineers, and finance officers. However, in essence, their conclusion was the same one reached by the ousted city council majority some seven months earlier.

An editorial in the local newspaper, noting the irony of the situation, had these comments:

- It is an irony that the citizens committee's conclusions could not have been revealed earlier, but the enmity against the former council majority was at such a pitch on Jan. 18 [date of election] that it probably wouldn't have mattered.
- The important thing to remember is that the need for water system improvements and, hence, more expensive water was not recalled.
- It will be impossible for Tucsonans to resume paying the low rates of a year ago and expect the city to be able to accommodate projected growth.
- Rolling back water rates even slightly and keeping them there would surely be a no growth policy.[7]

NEW WATER RATE STRUCTURE

Even though three of the four new council members had made campaign promises to roll back the water rates, they were caught in their own rhetoric when the city manager, the citizens' committee, and various financial experts warned them the city could not sell its water system improvement bonds without some increase in revenues. Thus, they approved new rates intended to increase water revenues by 13 percent in February 1977. This was lower than the 22 percent increase voted by the old council, but it was in the opposite direction from the public's expectations.

In addition, the new rate structure put much more of the financial burden on the lower-income residents of the area. In effect, this new structure would subsidize wealthier residents and new growth. The system development charge of $725 for new residential connections, enacted by the old council majority to recover capital costs to provide water capacity for new customers, was dropped.

An analysis of the new rate structure by the City Planning Department showed that an inner-city customer using 30 Ccf (hundred cubic feet) a month (1 Ccf = 748 gallons) would have had the following water bill at these stages of the water rate controversy:

1. Pre-July 1976 (before any rates were increased)—$11.94
2. July 1976 (under rate structure instituted by old council majority)— $16.25
3. April 1977 (under rate structure of post-recall election council)— $17.90 (winter) and $21.20 (summer)

In contrast, a wealthy resident in the foothills section of the community would have paid the following monthly bills for the same periods for the monthly consumption of 30 Ccf's:

1. Pre-July 1976—$21.82
2. July 1976—$40.25
3. April 1977—$17.90 (winter) and $21.20 (summer)[8]

LATE 1977 ELECTION RESULTS

The majority of the Tucson residents were not impressed with the antics of the new council majority. In the next regular primary and general election held in September and November 1977, they overwhelmingly threw out two of the winners in the recall election. The other two recall winners were not reelected when their terms expired in 1979.

According to one local newspaper article published right after the November 1977 election, the water controversy in Tucson had left voters fatigued and candidates very cautious. It said:

- The public as a whole seemed tired of elections; potential candidates also were either worn out or fearful of the heat that had burned the council incumbents out of office in the January recall.
- Even after the candidates were found, however, the contest lacked many hotly debated issues.
- The races centered on transportation and water, with the overriding concern being governmental efficiency—an issue no one can argue against.
- . . . Water, meanwhile, never developed the importance it held in the recall races.
- The slate of candidates elected in January—with the exception of Lininger—had promised to lower rates, but instead voted in February to increase them. That vote was labeled crucial to Hooton's over-whelming loss in the September primary election.
- This time around, however, the candidates seemed to agree that nothing can forestall further rate increases at some point in the future.[9]

Both of the council members mentioned in the quote—Lininger and Hooton—were persons elected as part of the recall slate in January 1977. Both lost their seats in the fall elections of 1977. Subsequent elections in 1979 and 1981 featured a lack of outstanding candidates and relatively little discussion of water and other vital public issues.

Tucson now appears to be headed back toward a more liberal or at least moderate political leadership, but the prime political characteristic toward the end of 1977 and early 1978 seemed to be instability. No overall comprehensive plan had yet been approved, and the water situation seemed to be puzzling. It would be extremely difficult for civil servants and professionals to gain a clear policy direction in their work, based on the events of the year. The voters had specified that they didn't like certain politicians or maybe politicians in general, but they gave little indication concerning the way the political and planning process should deal with the future development of the city and with the water scarcity problem. In addition, the recall made many local political leaders "gun-shy" on controversial matters.

Lessons in the Tucson Water Controversy

There are some unique aspects to the Tucson water controversy, but there are also lessons which could be helpful to citizens, planners, and decision makers in other arid areas.

USE OF THE FACTS

The facts of the Tucson water crisis had long been analyzed by local experts from various disciplines, including a number of researchers from the University of Arizona in Tucson. However, there was little real communication among the various fields such as hydrology, engineering, and finance. Some engineers, for example, contended that there was ample water in the basin, but they failed to consider questions of water quality and rapidly increasing pumping and energy costs. Also the various specialists did not adequately synthesize their findings into a form which could be understood by politicians and the general public. Assorted facts and interpretations of facts were hurled into the controversy at many points. At one early public meeting, a recall leader blurted out the notion that there was no shortage of water since the oceans covered so much of the earth's surface.

The general reporting of water facts by the local media seemed stronger before and especially after the first council decision to raise the rates than during the previous months when this action was under active consideration. It almost seemed that the water problem by itself was not enough to grab the media's and the public's attention. After the new rates were implemented, the political controversy itself became a headline item. Indeed, there was a rush to interview anyone who knew anything about water.

After the initial water rate increase, the council incumbents held a good number of public meetings to explain their action. However, many of the meetings resulted in loud and lengthy shouting matches between leaders or supporters of the recall effort and the council members. A local environmental group held water workshops just before the recall election, but these workshops seemed to be attended primarily by those who were already the most educated or aware of the water problem.

The four council members who were recalled did not make full use of the various experts at their disposal. Rather, they seemed to want to personally appear in public and in the media and to take the brunt of the attack on themselves. Perhaps this was due to the confused state of the data and the great fragmentation of expertise. No one today in the Tucson area knows for sure what the actual, usable, affordable supply of water is. Both the city of Tucson and the United States Geological Survey have been actively studying the local recoverable groundwater supply, but estimates still vary widely—between 34 million a-ft and 86 million a-ft down to a depth of 1200 ft. However, the city planning department staff has noted that it would be unreasonable to assume that all this water could ever be withdrawn. They note concerns and problems over subsidence, land ownership patterns, individual water rights, water quality, and financial constraints.

Given such complexity and confusion, it is little wonder that the politicians who were recalled chose to run on their own integrity and personal image rather than on the basis of hard water facts or with the open assistance of local water experts. Following the recall election, there was an attempt to synthesize the facts for public consumption through the use of the citizens' committee. However, the new council majority became too caught in its own preelection rhetoric about lowered rates and the facts of scarce financial resources to deal with the problem of water supply. The council raised the rates somewhat, especially for the lower income groups; but in the end, this change apparently didn't please anybody. The post-November 1977 election mood seemed to be one of fatigue rather than a desire for facts. Thus, major questions about water supply and cost still exist in the Tucson area, and few people seem to have the energy to answer them.

INFLUENCES ON POLITICAL ACTION

Even though the facts were somewhat inadequate and confused, there still was enough in the way of at least short-term evidence to indicate that something had to be done about water. For example, there was the 1976 consultant's report which predicted that the local water utility would be in debt by over $82 million by 1982 unless rates were raised substantially. The consultant recommended increases in rates which were considerably higher than those ultimately adopted by the council.[10]

The four-member majority of the council which ultimately voted for the increased rates in 1976 had come into office with a liberal background and a general predisposition toward the environmental movement and the conservation ethic. However, the actual rate increase decision involved a pricing strategy rather than a mandatory conservation or rationing program.

The four council members had been very cautious about working as a majority group to push forth their agenda of programs and goals. Some of the older, more conservative members of the community and the council, such as the mayor, were quick to accuse this majority of "steamrolling" radical programs through the legislative process at the first sign of cooperative effort. The four almost seemed to meet more with old opponents such as real estate persons and bankers, then with their supporters. The water issue was the first major policy item for which they worked collectively and which they actually implemented.

Why did they pick this issue, when they had previously failed to act together or decisively on issues such as the comprehensive plan, a flood plain ordinance, or the city's Community Development Act application? They apparently felt that the consultant's report showed the urgency of the situation. Water is obviously the most important factor in the future growth and viability of Tucson. It is not as abstract as a comprehensive plan, and it does not have the social welfare aspects of a community development application. In addition, the council majority apparently felt that its more conservative pricing strategy would appeal to the conservative interests in the community.

It is not clear whether the four council members had a definite goal of using water to implement the yet unapproved comprehensive plan. Before the vote on the water rates, at least one member said privately that the new rate structure would help the plan to be achieved. However, this was in a conversation with some supporters who were criticizing the council member for not accomplishing more to date. The four had varying degrees of awareness of the tie between the water issue and the comprehensive plan, but they did not meet and conspire to push ahead on water as the first step in a strategy of implementing the proposed plan. Politicians do not often work that way, even liberal politicians who state the need for good planning. Planning is generally viewed as an abstraction when compared to the great number of specific problems and immediate decisions facing a politician.

At first glance, it seems obvious that people themselves constitute a big part of the Tucson water problem. The more people, the more the underground water supply will be drained. Since the major influence on population growth is in-migration, it would seem as though a water shortage, no matter how inadequately described and communicated, would result in a community push to restrict in-migration. In addition, a reversal in the existing sprawling, lower density development pattern would also be anticipated as a way of reducing water demand. As noted earlier, higher density housing uses a lot less water than sprawling, single-family developments with lawns and much more vegetation.

However, the lesson from Tucson is that the water problem has not and is not likely to be used as a political reason for controlling either the rate or the distribution of growth. Contrarily, the progrowth business interests initially charged that there was no real water crisis, but that the council majority had manufactured one to sneak through its real agenda for stopping all future growth. It appears to be very difficult for any politician to confront a controversial growth control scheme as a solution. People usually are not ready to admit that they or their customers are part of the problem.

Much of the controversy about the comprehensive plan had revolved around the growth, no-growth issue for years in Tucson before the council's initial action to change the water rates. The community has been fairly polarized on the growth issue; although those who most directly profit from growth—the newspapers, car dealers, real estate persons, developers, and others—seem to have the time and the resources to keep antigrowth forces out of the public eye or on the defensive. In addition, many people in Tucson might really like to limit population growth but feel there is no legal way to do it. Others who might agree that limiting growth would be a good idea rebel when they learn that it could take more governmental controls to implement such a strategy.

The combination of Tucson's two most controversial problems—growth and water—would appear logical to professionals, especially to those planning or developing in arid lands. However, the lesson from Tucson is that such a combination was just too much for the community to handle. The recall effort which followed the initial revision in water rates used the "no-growth" and "socialistic planners" charges to the fullest possible extent.

Following the recall election, it was apparent that some local political careers had been seriously damaged, if not ended. In addition, there was heavy pressure to fire the planning director and some of his staff who were viewed as radical members who advocated a no-growth policy. Budget cuts were made in the planning department, and reorganization plans were put forth by the conservative mayor and others to dismantle the department. The November 1977 turnabout in the council makeup may have forestalled attempts at emasculation of the antigrowth and proplanning efforts, but the planning director and a number of his top staff have already left Tucson for other jobs.

By the winter of 1981, the planning department had lost a number of positions in a general city cutback, but it was otherwise intact. The growth issue was receiving little professional or public discussion despite continuing reports of uncertainties about the future supply and quality of local water resources.

Conclusion

Many arid areas now face or will soon face the kind of water and planning problems experienced by Tucson, Arizona. There is a decided population shift to the Sun Belt regions of the United States, which means that people are moving from some of the more water rich areas of the country to the water poor areas. Thus many communities will continue to face the inevitable balancing act between people and scarce water resources, between the life styles of the in-migrants from back East and the constraints of many water starved areas of the West.

The Tucson controversy is far from over, but the lessons already noted can be valuable to other communities. The following recommendations are made to help other areas handle planning, growth, and water scarcity problems with less trauma and more meaningful action than has taken place in Tucson to date.

ANALYSIS OF FACTS

There are three vital participants in a natural resource crisis such as the Tucson water situation—the technical experts, the political leaders, and the general public. These participants should be brought together to face the problem, and the first step is to help them base their analysis and actions on the same general kinds of facts. This means that those in power have to strongly encourage the experts to synthesize their perceptions. If the local experts are unable or unwilling to do this on their own initiative, it might be necessary to bring in some outside expertise of a slightly more general nature. The outside consultant or consultants could help encourage such synthesis or, as a last resort, do it themselves. The public and the politicians should then interact with the experts and their facts through a number of steps. Meanwhile, they should never lose touch with the drift of more recent revelations concerning the facts of the matter.

POLITICAL CONSIDERATIONS

The electorate should keep in close touch with its political leaders during the resolution of a scarcity problem like that of the water in Tucson. Campaign promises, personal values, and general political leanings do not seem as important to politicians as their fear of offending the more conservative or more vocal interests. Broader political alternatives, such as pricing versus enforced conservation, are rarely spelled out in advance of a major political decision such as raising water rates. Special interests seem to pick up on possible political drifts or the parameters of such drifts long before the general public. They can then quietly pressure the politicians and in effect veto certain directions behind the scenes.

Once again, local experts should be brought into the picture at an early stage before the final proposal is presented for adoption. These experts should be encouraged to spell out a full range of alternative solutions and should not be restricted to one or two which will be more acceptable to the establishment or the more powerful interests.

Newspapers and the media can be very helpful to the public in explaining a full range of alternative solutions; but as noted earlier, they are not inclined to cover a topic extensively or in depth before it becomes controversial. In addition, newspapers tend to be progrowth and might reject coverage or advocacy of alternatives which reduce or control the growth of population or demand for services.

Formal and informal surveys should be used frequently in the resolution of a resource scarcity problem. There is a great need to move ahead with the public and to be responsive to people's particular concerns.

GROWTH MANAGEMENT AND NATURAL RESOURCES

Communities in arid zones should try to develop general planning policies and basic growth management strategies before they encounter specific problems with a shortage of natural resources such as water. An explicit natural resource scarcity can generate so much controversy and polarization on its own that it becomes almost impossible to add growth control and overall comprehensive planning to the package of solutions.

If a community in an arid zone finds it impossible to get through the planning and growth questions before the water or other scarcity becomes an acute problem, it will likely be necessary to develop some pragmatic solution to the scarcity problem and to have it implemented for the short run. Then it might be possible to get back to the broader growth and planning issues. Legally, however, a clear scarcity problem such as that with water can make an excellent case for developing a growth management scheme which will survive challenges in the courts.

Notes

1. Tom Turner, "Tucson's Water Supply Draining Fast," *Arizona Daily Star,* 19 October 1975, sect. I, p. 1.
2. Pima County, Town of Oro Valley, City of South Tucson, and City of Tucson, *The Comprehensive Plan, Findings and Policies,* report prepared by the planning departments of above jurisdictions, January 1977, p. 8.
3. H. Wesley Peirce, "Arizona's Water Supply—Some Reflections," in *Field Notes,* University of Arizona, Bureau of Mines, **6**, no. 2 (1976), 1.
4. Lester R. Brown, Patricia L. McGrath, and Bruce Stokes, "The Population Problem in 22 Dimensions," *The Futurist,* **7** (October 1976), 243.
5. *The Comprehensive Plan,* p. 12.
6. "Tucson, Dependent on Wells, Finds Itself in a Hole of Water." *New York Times,* 30 January 1977, sect. I, p. 22.
7. "Tardy Endorsement," editorial in the *Arizona Daily Star,* 29 January 1977, sect. A, p. 10.
8. The information was prepared for the author by William Vasko and Kendall Bert of the city of Tucson Planning Department, October, 1977.
9. Diane Johnsen, "Lininger, Castro Beaten," *Arizona Daily Star,* 9 November 1977, sect. A, p. 2.
10. John Carollo Engineers, *Preliminary Report on the Tucson Water Utility,* (Tucson: Department of Water and Sewers, 1976), p. 20.

15
Directions for Arid-Zone Urban Planning in North America

Garrett Eckbo

Arid zones may be defined as those which receive an average of less than 10 inches of annual precipitation. I shall discuss hot, arid zones only. In North America, northwestern Mexico (including all of Baja, California), southeastern California, Nevada, western Utah, southern Arizona and New Mexico, and the western tip of Texas are all arid.

Like all of nature, weather does not respect precise boundaries. Thus, the arid zones merge imperceptibly with the semiarid zones around them where there may be 20 inches of precipitation annually. The western half of North America, extending from the Great Plains to the Sierra and Cascade Mountains, is predominantly semiarid.

Both these arid deserts and semiarid steppes can be further subdivided as either low latitude, continuously hot, or continental, featuring warm summers and cold winters. From a human environmental point of view, these are quite different areas; for as Table 15-1's data reveal, low latitude zones have their most extreme problems in the summer, whereas the continental zones have them in the winter. The North American continent's arid and semiarid stretches, classified as either low latitude or continental, are mapped in Figure 15-1.

The new and growing "Sun Belt" crosses the low latitude zones. Running from subtropical, moist east Texas to subtropical, dry southern California, this belt offers quite variable living conditions. The area is, however, unified by high expectations of escape from the cold north and the sense of participation in the last frontier. With this growth, the Sun Belt may be the stage for a definite battle between ecology and technology, a battle which will not be resolved until everyone realizes that ecology and technology are interdependent.

Arid Living in the Pretechnological Past

From the records of many centuries of desert living without the benefit of technology, from the precise weather data themselves, and from directly or indirectly related experience, we have a fairly clear picture of the assets and liabilities of desert living. Averaging out the differences between high and low, hotter and cooler, we can paint the following picture.

Deserts in the American Southwest are very hot for three to five months of the year, warm to cool for the rest. Summer is the difficult season; at that time the nights are for living and the days for hibernating. These de-

TABLE 15-1. Climatic Data for Low Latitude (South) and Continental (North) North American Arid Regions.

Average annual temperature	40–50	(north)
	50–70	(south)
Average January temperature	20–40	(north)
	40–50	(south)
Average July temperature	60–70	(north)
	70–90	(south)
Average annual maximum temperature	80–100	(north)
	90–110	(south)
Average annual minimum temperature	−10–30	(north)
	10–30	(south)
Highest temperature ever observed	100–110	(north)
	110–125	(south)
Lowest temperature ever observed	−10–60	(north)
	0–20	(south)
Average annual precipitation	10–20	(north)
	5–10	(south)
Average warm-season precipitation	5–10	(north)
	2–5	(south)
Average winter precipitation	2–6	(north/ south)
Percent of years with less than 20' of precipitation	100	(north/ south)
Average annual snowfall	10–60	(north)
	1–10	(south)
Average relative humidity January—8:00 A.M.	70–80	(north)
	60–75	(south)
Average relative humidity July—8:00 A.M.	50–70	(north)
	30–50	(south)
Average relative humidity January—noon	50–70	(north)
	30–50	(south)
Average relative humidity July—noon	20–40	(north/ south)
Average relative humidity January—8:00 P.M.	50–70	(north)
	35–50	(south)
Average relative humidity July—8:00 P.M.	20–40	(north/ south)
Percentage of possible sunshine—winter	40–70	(north)
	70–80	(south)
Percentage of possible sunshine—summer	70–80	(north)
	80–90	(south)
Average annual number of clear days	120–220	(north)
	220–280	(south)
Average number of cloudy days	80–120	(north)
	20–80	(south)
Average length of frost-free period	100–200	(north)
	200–320	(south)

Source: *Climate and Man.* Yearbook of Agriculture. Washington, D.C.: USDA, 1941.

serts range from dry to very dry around the calendar. Annual precipitation is always less than 10 inches and may be as low as zero. Humidity is always below 50 percent and may dip below 20. These climatic features make the summers even more difficult. Because there is little or no moisture in the air to form clouds, mist, or haze, deserts suffer from maximum exposure to the sun and feature minimum variation in atmospheric conditions. These climatic features lead to the famous expansive view in desert areas and difficulties for people from hazier atmospheres in estimating distances.

Depending on the topography, deserts may be very windy. One of the well-known characteristics of desert land is its capacity to develop a sta-

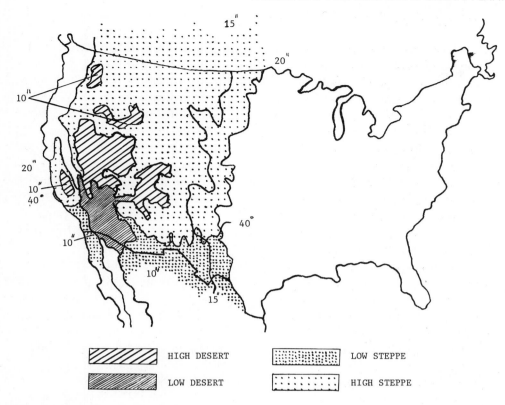

FIG. 15-1. Arid and semiarid regions of North America classified as low latitude or continental (high). Source: *Climate and Man.*

bilizing chemical seal over exposed surfaces, which resists wind erosion. Human activities which break this seal, such as heavy motor traffic, thus help create erosion. When coupled with the lack of vegetative cover, this seal breaking may create substantial movements of dust and sand, even storms. The level of the front lawn may rise six inches in a year. Such wind erosion, however, does produce extraordinary sculptural effects on rock and dune formations. The wind also modulates temperatures to higher or lower extremes.

Vegetation typically ranges from sparse to nonexistent. Therefore, the land is very vulnerable to the erosive forces of water as well as wind. Flying over desert areas, one can see the drainage, erosion, and deposition patterns very clearly. Geological time has compensated for the small amounts of moving water. The desert thus presents the extraordinary contradiction of being heavily eroded by water although virtually waterless.

In such conditions and without the benefits of modern technology, culture supporting life developed over many centuries in the high deserts of central Eurasia and in the low deserts of the Middle East and North Africa. The nomadic peoples of these areas developed survival techniques which gave them special cultural qualities. These preindustrial desert cultures were based on extremely limited resources and the most refined and painstaking disciplines for conserving them. Even in the urban cultures of arid zones this discipline revealed itself in such features as street arcades for shade, narrow winding streets for protection from the wind, and the very limited use of water in gardens and parks.[1]

Arid Living in the Technological Past

What have been the responses of technological society to the special conditions and problems of desert living? One might sum them up as a near total refusal to adjust building forms, land uses, vegetation patterns, or hydrologic systems to desert conditions beyond what is technically necessary—in other words, a determination to have the environment we want regardless of natural conditions or consequences.

The building forms are essentially the same as those used across the more temperate sections of the country. Some care may be taken to reduce or eliminate glass in southern or western walls. But, generally, air-conditioning systems are expected to make the buildings habitable regardless of the weather. Land use generally follows the gridiron patterns and lot sizes of the rest of the country, regardless of how usable the land may be for particular types of buildings.

Technological society relies heavily on irrigation to produce approximations of temperate or subtropical landscapes. Substantial tree growth with its moderating effect on the microclimate is a major dividend. But, when one sees communities using 1 million gallons of water a day to keep an 18 hole golf course green, one may begin to consider the extensive use of vegetation profligate. In some cases substantial "desert landscaping," using cacti, Joshua trees, rocks, gravel, and sand, is turned to both for visual effect and economy. Rarely, however, do these stretches have the sweep and scale of the original desert. A 10 ft² or 4 × 50 ft strip of desert landscape is not very convincing.

Hydrological systems have, of course, stressed large-scale conservation of water through dam building and associated irrigation systems. Once conserved, however, the water is often used frivolously in ways which maximize evaporation and the buildup of salts in the soil. In addition, there are some doubts about the long-term ecological effects of major dam building in desert regions.

Arid Living in the Posttechnological Future

American desert areas have been hit as hard by environmental problems as has the rest of the country. Large generating plants pollute the clear desert air and squander precious water resources. High tension transmission lines march through Indian reservations. Golf courses, parks, and gardens use irrigation water needed by agriculture. Off-the-road vehicles destroy the desert cover that has taken centuries to form.

In light of the predicted shortages of energy and other resources; with the growing environmental consciousness reinforcing the traditional wisdom that nature knows best; and with the increasing flow of people and industry from the north and east to the Houston-to-Los Angeles Sun Belt (an area which includes the desert cities of El Paso, Albuquerque, Tucson, Phoenix, Palm Springs, El Centro, and Las Vegas)—what standards, principles, and guidelines should be applied to planning and design in those desert areas from now on? Questions of landscaping, of land use, of housing design, of appropriate technology, and of the visual quality of the environment must, among others, be considered.

The future ecological approach to desert living will be roughly equivalent to the old natural approach. It will dictate that we do not produce extensive irrigated landscapes with grass, trees, and exotic shrubbery in the desert. Instead we must retain, preserve, or reconstruct the particular kind of desert landscape in which we find ourselves. This may range from sand, gravel, and rock to fairly substantial mesquite and saguaro vegetation. The existing local landscape rather than our imagination and technology must set the limits for landscaping. But there should still be space for small special cultivated gardens of special elegance, using alternative technologies as in the Moorish tradition.

Urban settlement patterns, of course, begin not with landscaping but with land-use planning. Normally the planner subdivides the land into blocks, establishing street gridirons which become corridors for both traffic and utilities. Relations between buildings and open spaces follow from this primary pattern. Many of our most difficult land-use problems nationwide stem from these warped priorities. Results would be much better if we could first design our building-open space relationships and then develop transportation and utility systems to suit those primary complexes.

As for shelter, an ecological conscience may not go so far as to say that we should use only what we find—caves, cliffs, large rocks, mesquite. Even wildlife watchers like to return to the civilized amenities of shower and martini. However, houses and other structures should no doubt be designed in harmony with the desert landscape: no pink stucco cubes with neon signs and no concrete, steel, glass, or plastic cubes. Adobe blocks, as used in Mexico and New Mexico, are more appropriate for desert construction. Plastered walls of the right color over any sort of stable core material will have nearly the same effect.

Complete air conditioning is certainly questionable as is central heating for those chilly low desert winter nights. Thick walls and roofs, double roofs with an air space between, lattice shades over doors and windows, and fireplaces are as much as we may be allowed. Most appropriate of all may be the underground construction which has been developed in the Southwest in recent years.

Our technology has made it possible in the past for us to set very narrow ranges of temperature and humidity for comfort. Yet, for thousands of years, what we call primitive or barbaric cultures survived in diverse climates with little more than a tent and an open fire. It will be necessary to establish new (closer to the old) ranges of physical comfort. For control of too high temperature ranges and the associated wind and sun problems, we will have to turn to the structural forms mentioned above, to solar energy, and perhaps even to irrigated trees and other greenery. The omnipresent sun should make solar energy a major resource throughout North American desert areas. It should control low temperatures in high deserts as well as the reverse. Choices will have, of course, to be made between active solar technology, which uses complex and expensive mechanical elements, and passive technology, which tries to work with natural and structural elements. Inasmuch as desert areas are not limited range, balmy climates like the subtropics, we will have to continue to use completely enclosed buildings from which outside extremes can be excluded. However, the ranges within those buildings need not be as limited as air conditioning makes possible today. We do not need San Francisco in Arizona.

There is an intimate interdependence between indoor and outdoor climate control. The building which is sheltered from the sun by trees will not need as much energy for cooling as one which is not. Green ground cover on the west and south sides of buildings will reduce or eliminate reflected heat from bare ground or paving. Many complex designs will have to be devised to deal with indoor-outdoor climate control, using fixed structural and landscape elements and mechanical systems relying on varying energy sources.

Problems of visual quality will be intimately linked with the choice of ways of controlling the climate. With an appropriate range of climate controlling forms will go an appropriate range of environmentally compatible visual effects. Desert urbanism today, even at its most opulent, makes too few concessions to local landscape qualities. Its choices tend to come from high-style Hollywood visions and plastic architectural concepts which are truly out of this world rather than from a desire to complement the landscape. Whether conceptions such as underground cities or cities built to look like rock mesas, abutments, and cliffs are possible in this cultural climate, however, is a difficult question.

People have always tried to modify climatic extremes in order to live more comfortably. Structures and trees shelter us in varying degrees from rain, snow, sun, wind, and the extremes of cold and heat. Before the advent of industrial technology, buildings were designed to ameliorate local climatic conditions. Industrialization produced mechanical systems for climate control which, with sufficient equipment and energy, worked in any climate. Regional structural variations then became obsolete. The same concrete, steel, glass, or plastic cube could be built anywhere—from desert to tundra, from plains to mountains. The air conditioned cube became the symbol of man's total conquest of nature.

Pollution and the imminent shortages of many major resources have shaken our faith in this conquest. Nature seems to be fighting back or taking revenge. Perhaps she only lured us into the ultimate ambush of ecological suicide. Now, throughout the educated and affluent Western world, the old slogans predicting growth and technological progress have been received with increasing skepticism. Perhaps this has been most true in the older and more sophisticated sections of the northeast and northwest United States. But the West and Southwest are not immune.

Recommended Directions

The central problem for planning and design in our arid—as well as all other—zones is to seek small alternative technological solutions between the extremes of total submission to nature and high technology's ignorance and destruction of nature. The basic environmental elements of earth, rock, water, vegetation, and construction must be used in forms and arrangements derived from the preindustrial environmental wisdom and modified, advanced, and refined by 20th-century sophistication, to provide us with nonenergy-consuming comfort and pleasure.

Environmental quality control combined with resource conservation must begin with a precise inventory and critical analysis of existing structural and natural physical landscape conditions, macro- and microclimatic environments, and technical and cultural resources. Easy, preconceived, habitual procedures for land use planning, high technology utility systems, motor vehicle movement patterns and ranges, the use of standardized structural boxes, and minimum or nonexistent landscape vegetation will have to be reexamined. Core concepts of building-open space relationships sensitively adapted to local conditions will have to be developed. From these concepts, new and more relevant patterns of land use, circulation, and community facilities will emerge. Both new developments and the redevelopment of existing complexes will require this new thinking.

Of the basic elements of the physical environment (rock, water, earth, vegetation, and construction), the first four represent nature which dominated the world totally before people began to settle down on the land and to urbanize some 10,000 years ago. The human construction engendered by settlement and urbanization has since spread so that it now dominates perhaps 10 percent of the earth's surface and has a major impact—pollution or corruption—on the balance. It is now well established in conservation and professional planning circles that environmental quality is dependent upon balanced quantitative and qualitative relations between the four basically natural elements and the construction introduced by people. Such balance has a peculiar urgency—and special requirements and possibilities—in desert regions.

Rock, the basic material of the entire earth, is common on the surface. In scale it ranges from sand and gravel through pebbles and rocks to boulders, stone outcrops, and mountains. Unprotected by vegetation, rock may accentuate the reflected heat and glare of the desert. However, rock can also provide moisture-conserving mulch and shelter for plants. Rock is used in human settlements in a variety of situations ranging from natural landscape arrangements to construction. Stone buildings provide better insulation from weather than do those of thinner or lighter materials. In desert regions, because of the scant vegetation, the form, color, and texture of rock become an important element in the landscape.

Water is the central necessity for biological life. In the desert it is most scarce and most precious. Preindustrial cultures worked out elaborate and disciplined procedures for conserving it. Industrial cultures, however, have squandered it shamelessly. It is to be hoped that postindustrial cultures will retreat to some level between these extremes.

The shortage of water in desert regions gives both the water and the kind of disciplined life required to survive such limitations a peculiarly accentuated value. Modern technology, to the extent that it eliminated the shortage, eliminated also this accentuated value. More sophisticated design processes using alternative technologies can return us to a new and more sensitive mode of desert living vis-à-vis water. Hopefully, we will not again be taken over by the level of intellectual idiocy embodied in recent proposals to cut down all the trees in desert drainage basins in order to reduce loss of water through transpiration.

Earth, seen as land, results from the effects of water and wind erosion upon the original rock and the stabilizing and soil-building impact of vegetation. Vegetation and animal life create the difference between land as a mass of finely ground rock particles and soil as organism composed of those particles, humus derived from decomposed vegetation, microorganisms, the roots of living plants, and subterranean animals. Typically, desert soils are high in chemical nutrients which have neither been taken up by plants or leached to lower levels of drainage basins. On the other hand, they are low in organic content and are alkaline rather than acid.

The amount of vegetation is directly determined by available moisture. In the hottest and driest deserts, there is none; whereas in tropical rain forests, its exuberance defies description. The application of water will make the desert "blossom as the rose"—until increased humidity and salt accumulation begin to spoil the picture. Large-scale agricultural cultivation of the desert through irrigation may be justified by citing national needs if the just noted problems can be solved. The large-scale irrigation of temperate-style parks and golf courses is probably more difficult to justify. Hardy drought-tolerant trees and shrubs, however, can be successfully irrigated underground by deep slow watering, a system much more efficient and effective than the wasteful overhead watering required by large lawn areas. Bare ground shaded by trees and shrubs loses many of its objectionable qualities of heat, glare, reflection, and dust. In desert climates we also need protection from sun and wind. Protection may be provided by structures, or by trees, or by both.

Construction is our ultimate resort for climate control in regions which feature difficult climate extremes. We have a technology of construction, a historical art of architecture, and an emerging art of environmental design through which we are learning how to deal with the ongoing interaction between nature and architecture.

Architecture has been through three basic phases: First, there was architecture *of* this world which featured the grass, wood, brick, adobe, or stone shack growing naturally from the land and site. This is called primitive or indigenous architecture. Historically, it happened everywhere. It may still happen anywhere. Second, there was architecture *over* this world which featured the projection of geometric forms over the landscape. It began in Egypt and grew and expanded through Roman, Moorish, and Renaissance interpretations to its ultimate expression in Versailles and Paris and its academic decline in L'Ecole des Beaux Arts. Third, there is architecture *out of* this world, the ultimate product of modern architecture which features glass, steel, concrete, and plastic structures deliberately unrelated to the land of their sites or the landscapes around them. It is more and more dominant in current architectural production.

The sequence may be seen as expanding in cultivated sophistication, as reaching the ultimate in frivolity, or as expressing the growing conscious alienation of people from nature. However, such rationalization tends to obscure the basic fact that all three types of buildings, regardless of theories held or designs intended, must sit *on* land, *on* a site, and *in* a surrounding landscape of some sort. Interaction between building and surroundings—technical, functional, and visual—must be determined and given form by landscape or environmental design processes.

In the desert the interaction between buildings and surroundings takes on peculiarly special significance. In summer in the low desert and in winter in the high desert, extreme outdoor temperatures force us to seek maximum modification indoors. The essence of the ecological design problem is to achieve this modification with natural or structural elements which are self-sustaining and use little or no energy for operation or maintenance. The most consistent natural desert materials, rock and earth, can be used most effectively as a means of climate modification, as berms for protection from sun and wind, as insulation reducing the loss of heat or moisture, and as the dry and constant temperature enclosure for underground construction.

Construction, the ultimate in complete climate control, can thus be used in unlimited variations in form and in relationship to landscape conditions. The inspirations of the future will derive from the interaction between such structural and environmental concepts, rather than from purely technical and cultural considerations as they have in the recent past.

Note

1. See the dune trilogy by Frank Herbert for a science fiction portrayal of an ultimate desert culture. See *Dune,* Chilton Co. (1965), and *Dune Messiah* (1970) and *Children of Dune* (1976), Berkley Publishing Co.

Index